Studies in the History of Law and Justice

Volume 28

The purpose of this book series is to publish high quality volumes on the history of law and justice. Legal history can be a deeply provocative and influential field, as illustrated by the growth of the European universities and the *Ius Commune* , the French Revolution, the American Revolution, and indeed all the great movements for national liberation through law. The study of history gives scholars and reformers the models and courage to question entrenched injustices, by demonstrating the contingency of law and other social arrangements. Yet legal history today finds itself diminished in the universities and legal academy. Too often scholarship betrays no knowledge of what went before, or why legal institutions took the shape that they did.This series seeks to remedy that deficiency.

Studies in the History of Law and Justice will be theoretical and reflective. Volumes will address the history of law and justice from a critical and comparative viewpoint. The studies in this series will be strong bold narratives of the development of law and justice. Some will be suitable for a very broad readership.

Contributions to this series will come from scholars on every continent and in every legal system. Volumes will promote international comparisons and dialogue. The purpose will be to provide the next generation of lawyers with the models and narratives needed to understand and improve the law and justice of their own era. The series includes monographs focusing on a specific topic, as well as collections of articles covering a theme or collections of article by one author.

José Franco-Chasán

The Reception of Positivism in Spain

Pedro Dorado Montero

Springer

José Franco-Chasán
Law
University Rey Juan Carlos
Madrid, Spain

ISSN 2198-9842 ISSN 2198-9850 (electronic)
Studies in the History of Law and Justice
ISBN 978-3-031-46434-8 ISBN 978-3-031-46435-5 (eBook)
https://doi.org/10.1007/978-3-031-46435-5

This Springer imprint is published by the registered company Springer Nature Switzerland AG
The registered company address is: Gewerbestrasse 11, 6330 Cham, Switzerland

Paper in this product is recyclable.

"The moral and medical foundations of this story are even more relevant today. Medicine is in the midst of a vast re-organisation of fundamental principles. Most of our models of illness are hybrid models; past knowledge is mishmashed with present knowledge.
These hybrid models produce the illusion of a systematic understanding of a disease—but the understanding is, in fact, incomplete. Everything seems to work spectacularly, until one planet begins to move backward on the horizon. We have invented many rules to understand normalcy—but we still lack a deeper, more unified understanding of physiology and pathology".

SIDDHARTHA MUKHERJEE

Acknowledgements

To Professor Aniceto Masferrer for his everlasting guidance and patience. To Professor Phillip Hellwege and his efforts to merge me in the German university.

To Jesús Ballesteros and Encarnación Fernández for their gentle and constant support. To Professor Alfredo Obarrio who transmitted to me the passion for the academic life. To Maricarmen (†), my ubiquitous supporter and traveling companion.

To Cristi (†), mirror of my personality.

Contents

1 Introduction 1
References 3

2 Contextualising Dorado Montero 5
2.1 A Christian Childhood 8
2.2 Relativism vs. Religious Convictions 16
2.3 A Brief Romance with Positivism 22
2.4 Krausism: The Relevance of Instruction and Education 27
2.5 A Socialist in Spirit 29
2.6 The Interspersion of Anarchism 33
2.7 A Struggle to Unify Sociology 36
References 38

3 Historical Background 43
3.1 Spain and the Two Centuries 43
3.2 Scenario for the Reception of Positivism 47
3.3 Development of Positivism: Status Quaestionis 55
3.3.1 The Neoclassical Schools 56
3.3.2 The Positivist Schools 59
3.3.3 The Eclectic Schools 65
References 70

4 Dorado Montero's Foreign Influences 81
4.1 Key authors 83
4.1.1 Immanuel Kant (1724–1804) 83
4.1.2 Karl David August Röder (1806–1879) 88
4.1.3 Georg Heinrich Schneider (1846–1904) 92
4.1.4 Raffaele Garofalo (1851–1934) 94
4.1.5 Enrico Ferri (1856–1929) 98
4.1.6 Vincenzo Lilla (1837–1905) 109
4.1.7 Leo Tolstoy (1828–1910) 110

4.2 Other Influences 117
4.2.1 Karl Christian Friedrich Krause (1781–1832) 117
4.2.2 Antonio Marro (1835–1913) 118
4.2.3 Luigi Lucchini (1847–1929) 119
4.2.4 Giulio Fioretti 120
4.2.5 Ugo Conti (1864–1942) 120
4.2.6 Herbert Spencer (1820–1903) 121
4.2.7 Alexander Herzen (1812–1870) 122
References 122

5 Dorado Montero's Criminal Doctrine: The Protective Law of the Criminals 127
5.1 The Delinquent 129
5.2 The Treatment 130
5.3 Criminal Procedure 131
5.4 Punishment 137
5.5 Imputability 144
5.6 Indeterminate Sentences 149
References 158

6 Locating Dorado Montero in Spanish Doctrine 163
6.1 Labelling the Unclassifiable 164
6.2 The 'Doradian' Contribution 184
6.3 Final Thoughts 190
References 192

7 Conclusions 195

Sources and Bibliography 199
Primary Sources 199
Legal Literature 207
Non-Legal Literature 217
Bibliography 219

Chapter 1
Introduction

This book focuses on the history of legal thought. Some sections also take a chronological approach to the life of Dorado Montero—however, it is not my objective to present a biography, which has already been the subject of outstanding scholarship elsewhere.[1] Instead, I will explore his legal philosophical ideas in relation to each other, in order to present an historical description of his work.

As a work which combines legal history and legal philosophy, no attempt will be made to outline the intellectual phases which Dorado Montero went through, for two reasons. Firstly, as has already been noted, many other biographers, sociologists, pedagogists and criminologists have produced a significant amount of high-quality literature on that matter. Secondly, to assert that he went through particular phases of thinking is simplistic, and certainly something that Dorado Montero himself would have rejected, as he viewed man's nature as ever-changing. I nonetheless describe his personal evolution in 'interrelated' rather than 'independent' blocks, because some broad generalisations are useful in structuring a description of Dorado Montero's thinking. This does not solve the paradox of trying to dissect something that cannot be dissected: human thought. However, it does facilitate a presentation of the ideas of this creative theorist and unconventional author concerning both the penal system and the role it played in the introduction of positivism in Spain.

That being said, a potential risk remains. The objective of this book is not to present an analysis of Dorado Montero's philosophy or jurisprudence. Again, many monographs and PhD theses have already tackled this topic. The goal of this work is

[1]Blanco Rodríguez (1984), pp. 235–242; Blanco Rodríguez (1994), pp. 141–168; Blanco Rodríguez (1979); Blanco Rodríguez (1982); Lima Torrado (2008a), pp. 417–443; Lima Torrado (2008b), pp. 537–550; Lima Torrado (1977); López-Rey (1956), pp. 605–612; Ramos Pascua (1995), pp. 503–546; Rivacoba y Rivacoba (1970), pp. 15–28; Rivacoba y Rivacoba (1971), pp. 1631–1643; Rivacoba y Rivacoba (1962); Rivacoba y Rivacoba (1963); Rodríguez Hernández (1993); Valls (1971).

J. Franco-Chasán, *The Reception of Positivism in Spain*, Studies in the History of Law and Justice 28, https://doi.org/10.1007/978-3-031-46435-5_1

to consider Dorado Montero in relation to a much broader field of study.[2] After my lucky collaboration with a group of academics, to whom I owe a lot, I was able to see the relevance of nineteenth and twentieth century criminal law in Spain (and in the rest of Europe). Detailed studies exist on many technical issues: criminal codes, laws enacted in the different parliaments, ordinances, police regulations, the legal philosophies of great penalist,[3] criminal lawyers and sociologists, etc.[4] At this point in time, it is only logical for me to assert that Spanish doctrine came to accept positivist premises concerning the "mechanisms of the determination of the penalty",[5] but not the "justification"[6] offered by that theory. All in all, Spain was a jurisdiction more suited to eclectic positions,[7] as evidenced by the overwhelming prevalence and development of eclectic schools there: those of Joaquín Francisco Pacheco (the counterpart of Pellegrino Rossi in Italy), Alejandro Groizard y Gómez de la Serna and Luis Silvela y de Le Vielleuze, among others. Dorado Montero was successful in his objective of introducing positivism in Spain via the back door.

The impact of positivism on public law is conspicuous in many European states.[8] However, in Spain, this impact was not mediated via legislation. Under the flag of eclecticism and a purported spirit of moderation, Spain was often viewed as some

---

[2]The most recent and complete work on the reception of positivism within Europe and Latin America can be found in Masferrer (2020a), Issue 17.

[3]In the English-speaking world the term preferred for this is "criminal lawyer". A so-called penalist is a term which is rarely used in Anglo-American literature. Unsurprisingly, whether continental Europe or not, nordic languages tend to match this preference for this expression (criminal lawyer -English-; Straftverteidiger/Anwalt für Strafsachen -German-; Straftrecht advocaat -Dutch-; or kriminell försvarsadvokat -Swedish-). However, it is far more common in the jurisdictions having a romance language (penalista -Spanish-; pénaliste -French-; penalista -Italian-; penalist -Romanian-). Once clarified this issue, I will stick to the term 'penalist' since it better depicts the real meaning that the word holds according to the nationality of Pedro Dorado Montero.

[4]Masferrer (2014, 2017, 2020b).

[5]Set of ideas, generally revolving around legal techniques, addressing how the penalty should be applied. Usually, they are concerned with the iter criminis and its related issues: harder penalties or softer penalties, imposing the punishment on its upper or lower half, having accessory penalties or not, application of mitigating/aggravating circumstances, etc.

[6]The rationale behind this theory of the penalty, i.e. the legal philosophy supporting a given criminal current (positivism, neoclassical theories, eclectical positions, etc.).

[7]The eclectical positions are a group of theories claiming for a middle term between the extremes of the neoclassical schools and positivist schools, as they advocated for a moderate response to criminality. Certain aspects of positivism were good, and the reality and pragmatic character of neoclassical schools should also be considered. In Italy, this trend was named after *Terza Scuola* and its most relevant representatives were Emanuele Carnevale, Bernardino Alimena, Michelangelo Vaccaro, Gabriel Tarde, Ferdinando Puglia, and Giovanni Battista Impallomeni. In Spain, the movement was known as *Eclecticismo* and it was mainly led by the influence of French Doctrinarism, Some of the latter were Constancio Bernaldo de Quirós, Francisco Pacheco, and Alejandro Groizard.

[8]Through the current book, I am using the term "positivism" to refer to the new movement in criminal law which appeared at the end of the nineteenth century, thus, challenging the traditional criminal law (neoclassical schools), and mostly denying human freedom. As a result, people should be convicted not due to their actions but to their propension to commit a crime. It came very close in

sort of 'positivist-free' country, i.e. a jurisdiction in which positivism barely took acceptance. No positivist Codes were enacted, no positivist laws were passed, and no positivist regulations were approved. Yet, I have the impression that positivism did indeed cross our borders and reached our country, remaining dormant until it found the opportunity to spread to a general substratum of national scholars: from penalists to criminologists, from pedagogists to psychologists, from sociologists to politicians.

This was my hypothesis, and to explore how this 'silent' spreading was possible, I focused on doctrine. Theory, manuals, teaching, congresses, and articles are sometimes even more powerful than legislation itself, which is sometimes imposed at any cost by those with authority, and can lack firm foundation. By analogy with the human body, we might think of the different kinds of legislation as different body structures (muscles, blood vessels, organs and viscera). Doctrine, like fascia, is what attaches, stabilises, encloses, separates and connects—simultaneously—the different units between them.

In order to explore this, I decided exclusively to focus on a deep analysis of the ideas of Dorado Montero. However, even a book-length analysis cannot explore every aspect I would have liked to. This work begins what I hope will be a profound and vast exploration extending beyond its pages and into the future.

Once this is clarified, there is little else left to say. Whilst I have sought an intelligible format and orderly arrangement, the style of this text might sometimes appear loose. This is entirely intentional.

References

Blanco Rodríguez JA (1979) El pensamiento político-social de Dorado Montero en el marco de las ideologías sociales de su época: 1880–1917. Universidad de Salamanca, Salamanca

Blanco Rodríguez JA (1982) El pensamiento sociopolítico de Dorado Montero. Centro de Estudios Salmantinos, Salamanca

Blanco Rodríguez JA (1984) El socialismo reformista de Dorado Montero. Revista de Estudios 12: 235–242

Blanco Rodríguez JA (1994) Evolución de un intelectual crítico. Revista de Estudios 34:141–168

Lima Torrado J (1977) La Filosofía Jurídica de Pedro Dorado Montero. Universidad Complutense de Madrid, Madrid

Lima Torrado J (2008a) Las claves de la recepción del pensamiento anarquista en la filosofía política de Pedro Dorado Montero. In: Elósegui Itxaso M (ed) El Pensamiento jurídico: pasado, presente y perspectiva. Libro homenaje al prof. Juan José Gil Cremades, 1st edn. El Justicia de Aragón, Zaragoza, pp 417–443

Lima Torrado J (2008b) Las claves de la recepción del pensamiento socialista en la filosofía política de Pedro Dorado Montero. In: AA.VV. Estudios en homenaje al profesor Gregorio Peces-Barba. Dykinson, Madrid, pp 537–550

time to phrenology. It ought not to be confused with the generally accepted term in law accounting for "codification of criminal law", i.e. *positum* (positive law).

López-Rey M (1956) X. Pedro Dorado Montero (1861-1919). In: Mannheim H (ed) Pioneers in criminology. Stevens and Sons, London, pp 605–612

Masferrer A (ed) (2014) La Codificación española. Una aproximación doctrinal e historiográfica a sus influencias extranjeras, y a la francesa en particular. Thomson Reuters Aranzadi, Cizur Menor

Masferrer A (ed) (2017) La Codificación penal española. Tradición e influencias extranjeras: su contribución al proceso codificador. Parte General. Thomson Reuters Aranzadi, Cizur Menor

Masferrer A (ed) (2020a) GLOSSAE. European Journal of Legal History 17

Masferrer A (ed) (2020b) La Codificación penal española. Tradición e influencias extranjeras: su contribución al proceso codificador. Parte Especial. Thomson Reuters Aranzadi, Cizur Menor

Ramos Pascua JA (1995) El positivismo jurídico en España: D. Pedro Dorado Montero. Anuario de Filosofía del Derecho 12:503–546

Rivacoba y Rivacoba M (1962) El centenario del nacimiento de Dorado Montero. Universidad del Litoral, Santa Fé

Rivacoba y Rivacoba M (1963) Recordación de Dorado Montero. Cenit, Toulouse

Rivacoba y Rivacoba M (1970) Evocación y vigencia de Dorado Montero. Revista de Ciencias Penales 29(1):15–28

Rivacoba y Rivacoba M (1971) Viejas Remembranzas de Dorado Montero. Revista de Estudios Penitenciarios 29:1631–1643

Rodríguez Hernández V (1993) La insumisión en Dorado Montero. El tema iusnaturalista en la encrucijada ideológica de la Restauración. Hespérides, Salamanca

Valls FJ (1971) La filosofía del Derecho de Dorado Montero. Universidad de Salamanca, Salamanca

Chapter 2
Contextualising Dorado Montero

Abstract This chapter analyses the personal evolution of Dorado Montero. Rather than a plain biographical chapter, the main objective is to describe the evolution of his thinking through the different phases of his life. In order to do so, seven major stages are identified. The first one describes the very basics of his thought: the Christian education and a childhood marked by various health handicaps. The second one shows him facing a starter relativism which leads him towards the rejection of moral absolutes. In fact, Dorado Montero remained an atheist his whole life. The third one depicts how his university years and his stay in Italy introduced him to positivism. After that, he only fiercely defended positivism for some more years. From this moment onwards, a particularly critical Dorado Montero would identify the many flaws of the core positivist postulates. Consequently, the 'positivist' vehemence of his early years begins to moderate. The fourth stage illustrates how he explored a very relevant trend in Spain: Krausism. This movement was focusing on the relevance of education, considered by Dorado Montero as the main tool for change. The fifth and sixth stages revolve around socialism and anarchism with truly no relevant order. Even if one cannot assert he was an anarchist, both socialist and anarchist ideas appear to be mixed within this period. Finally, the last period was showing the peak of his intellectual maturity. He held a very open vision and showed himself particularly keen on Sociology and the role it should play in society. For him, the legal norms should be established not based on the 'principles of absolute justice', but on the observance of the social reality. Dorado Montero retired to a lonely countryside house in order to meditate on his last years of life.

Pedro Dorado Montero[1] lived in a time of transition; between the years 1861 and 1919.[2] Thus, his life straddled two centuries. Prominent events such as the loss of the Spanish Empire in 1898, the establishment of the Spanish Protectorate in Northern

[1] His actual name was Pedro Francisco García Dorado Martín Montero, but this is controversial. Vid. Barbero Santos (1996), p. 261. In it, the author offers a very detailed scheme which leads the reader to an almost completely different surname.

[2] Diccionario de catedráticos españoles de derecho (1847–1984) (2009).

J. Franco-Chasán, *The Reception of Positivism in Spain*, Studies in the History of Law and Justice 28, https://doi.org/10.1007/978-3-031-46435-5_2

Morocco in 1912 and its posterior conflict (the Rif War), and the First World War (1914–1918) impacted him. The influence of these events was not just symbolic: they created a period of time where change was both possible and attainable. Dorado Montero knew the prevailing trends of the old century, and the currents of the new, coming one. It was precisely this detailed knowledge of both worlds what would allow him to become one of the greatest masters of 'legal change' in Europe, and particularly in Spain. Whether referred to as 'legal change' or 'legal revolution', the main issue behind this is the ancient concept of transition.

Nowadays, the word "transition" has limited use. The official definition of a 'transition' is "the process or a period of changing from one state or condition to another",[3] but it does not have a neutral connotation. The term is usually used to indicate a 'soft' change allowing us to go from one reality to another: from the past scenario to the one ahead of us. If one wants to lay emphasis on the fact that a certain event constituted a ground-breaking transition, he has to inevitably use "transition" jointly with the adjectives "hard" or "violent". In its broad conception, the noun has been stripped of any revolutionary flavour it once had. In ordinary discourse, a "revolution" is an important change; but a "transition" is a timid, mild, half-hearted word.

Therefore, let us propose Dorado Montero as a transition author. He forced Spanish old-fashioned standards to face the new era of legal dogmatics[4] (which were at their initial stage).[5] Naturally, one could think that the school of eclecticism already did so in a diffuse. However, eclectics sought to elaborate a middle ground: ideas resting somewhere between neoclassicism and positivism.[6] Even neoclassical penalists were not able to defend the purely neoclassical premises of earlier periods, because they were now working in positivist times and, in Spain, under the influence of Dorado Montero. We will return to this point later.

It has been said that Dorado Montero, along with Sales y Ferré "contribute [d] decisively" to the introduction of the positivist mentality in Spanish society.[7] Academics have identified four major stages of his scholarly evolution: (1) Krausoinstitutionalism; (2) Italian Positivism; (3) Sociology (with trends to organicism and evolutionism in its early stages in Spain);[8] and (4) Radical criticism

[3]The Oxford English Dictionary, the Collins Dictionary and the Merriam-Webster Dictionary are unanimous in this respect.

[4]Though it is not a phrase often used in English writing, it is more common to be found in Continental European countries. It accounts for the doctrinal study of the law. Its goal is to interpret and to systematise the law, being its content revolving around discussions and commentaries.

[5]Perhaps, the sole relevant contribution to criminal dogmatics dating back from the Early Modern Age is that of Decianus (1593). Similarly, in the contemporary scenario Mario Sbriccoli also develops such topic. Vid. Pifferi (2011), pp. 480–487.

[6]Iñesta-Pastor (2017), p. 444.

[7]Blanco Rodríguez (1982), p. 11: "La introducción de la mentalidad positiva - fenómeno al que contribuye decisivamente Dorado Montero junto a Sales y Ferré-".

[8]Blanco Rodríguez (1982), p. 35.

and Pesimism.[9] As regards the first stage, the term commonly used was "krausoinstitutionalism".[10] Other possible variations of it as well were krausofröbelism[11] or krausopositivism,[12] which merges two concepts. Curiously enough, Ferrater Mora stressed the difference between krausists and institutionists. However, this chapter follows a different chronology: (1) Christian background; (2) Relativism; (3) Positivism; (4) Krausism; (5) Socialism; (6) Anarchism; and (7) Sociology.

Several authors have also closely studied and described Dorado Montero's personality, including Manuel López-Rey, Juan Andrés Blanco Rodríguez, Constancio Bernaldo de Quirós, Francisco José Valls, Jesús Lima Torrado, Fernando de los Ríos Urruti, and Barbero Santos. The first of these especially described Dorado Montero's genius as "reserved, austere and not very sociable".[13] Indeed, he was said to be Miguel de Unamuno's nemesis: "they contrasted strongly in their characteristics and it is no wonder that what at the beginning was a promising friendship ended in a rather distant and cold academic relationship. The varied activities of Unamuno, with his wit and his philosophy, were probably not the best means to impress Dorado, with his somewhat introverted personality and his devotion to a single question: Criminology".[14] In the same article, López-Rey points out the paradox of Dorado Montero: his rough, difficult past did not align with the humanitarian goals of his "Protective Law of the Criminals".[15] Nonetheless, Unamuno gave credit where it was due. In one of the letters he wrote to Leopoldo Alas Clarín, he noted the following:

> Those of us who know him [Dorado Montero], we have a very different concept of him than those who judge him in the distance. I do not read him, and given that he barely says anything, always limiting himself to just listening, I cannot judge him. He seems to me to be a man that knows his things and when he gets his pen, he does expose them; yet, about the things he knows, one rapidly gets to learn them as regards the substance. He is, on the other

---

[9]As to such structure, *vid.* Blanco Rodríguez (1982).

[10]Francisco Giner de los Ríos, José Canalejas, Gumersindo de Azcárate or Blanco Rodríguez himself.

[11]Ureña (1990), pp. 43–62.

[12]Blanco Rodríguez (1982), p. 18.

[13]López-Rey (1956), p. 606.

[14]Ibid, p. 607.

[15]In Spanish, the "Derecho protector de los criminales". This was the name Dorado Montero gave to his theory of Criminal law. The name is very descriptive per se, since the approach is aimed at protecting the criminal. Dorado Montero considered that criminals were not evil individuals who acted selfishly, but nothing more than a sick persons; an individual who was motivated by a mixture of instincts and social incapacity, and who was so morally degenerate that the single thing one could expect from the State in response was mercy and compassion—specifically, a treatment to raise them out of their "moral inferiority". Although he also gave his most important work the same name (*El Derecho protector de los criminales*), I will refer to the theory generically to indicate the idea itself. When I am referring to the book itself, the corresponding footnote will indicate so.

> hand, a perfect Castilian man; blind as to the nuances, and deaf to the ineffable. In any case, a very useful man and truly serious.[16]

On the one hand, we observe him as a positivist, practical, earth-bound, efficient scholar, with good technique but no broad vision. On the other hand, his "transcendental doubt"[17] made him a far more open-minded individual than Unamuno's words suggest. The accusation of being "blind to nuances" is certainly intended to describe his practical character, rather than his theory and doctrinal position, which were far more elaborate. As much as Dorado Montero may have been "deaf to the ineffable", he was always a quiet listener precisely because he always took into account many points of view, avoiding taking sides and highlighting that human reality is more convoluted and (biologically) not as knowable as we might think. In this respect, though Unamuno was his opposite, and Dorado Montero might not have been an open-minded bohemian, he was a shy, over-reflective and open-minded scholar. One should never commit the mistake of thinking he was a cold, slow-witted positivist.

Dorado Montero, throughout his theory, exemplified the relevance of transition. Just as a silent water drop corrodes and deforms the shape of a rock, the Spaniard quietly introduced new trends and altered the reigning conceptions of Penal law. Neoclassical scholarship would never be the same again after his death. And Spain's Penal law would never look the same after his teachings and his influence on his pupils- especially Jiménez de Asúa and Cuello Calón, who would complete this change in an arguably more notorious, popular manner. Change is transition; transition is change.

2.1 A Christian Childhood

Pedro Dorado Montero was born in 1861 in Navacarros.[18] An official publication puts the sixteenth-century population at Navacarros at 77 inhabitants,[19] but the actual number of citizens would have been much lower, as the calculation was made in aggregate with two other municipalities.[20] By the time Dorado Montero

[16] AA. VV. (1941), pp. 82–83: "Los que le conocemos de cerca y le tratamos, tenemos de él un concepto muy distinto de los que de lejos le juzgan. Yo no le leo, y como hablando apenas dice cosa, limitándose a oír, no puedo juzgarle. Me parece un hombre que sabe sus cosas y cuando coge la pluma las expone: pero de esas cosas que sabe, se entera uno pronto en cuanto a la sustancia. Es, por lo demás, un perfecto castellano, ciego para el matiz y el nimbo, y sordo a lo inefable. Un hombre utilísimo de todos modos y serio de verdad".

[17] This idea will be explained later.

[18] This is a very small municipality within the province of Salamanca which is, in turn, located in the self-governing community of "Castile and León" (Spain).

[19] González (1829), p. 100. The originals may be found at the *Biblioteca de Castilla y León* (in Valladolid) under the signature G 47449.

[20] Namely, *La Casa del Frayle* and *El Palomar.*

was born, the village had grown significantly, reaching 482 inhabitants in 1860: this was probably triggered by a boom in the local textile industry in the judicial district of Béjar.[21] Nowadays, the population is once again small, barely exceeding 100 households.[22] Navacarros, therefore, has always been a small village in one of the inner regions of Spain.

Nineteenth-century Navacarros was barely a hamlet, very close to the city of Béjar.[23] Traditionally, the areas in the interior of the Spain have tended to be very conservative, communitarian, and religious.[24] Consequently, Dorado Montero received a very strict, traditional, Christian education from a young age. This is evident in his ideas of good and evil, which are very clear and rigid. He began to form an idea of what is meant by "justice". His initial perception of legal wrongdoing and unlawful actions was clear and did not vary with context. It was enhanced by a Christian moral universalism which was heavily critical of moral relativism. Tomás y Valiente has described how "sin" and "delict" were thought to be synonymous in this model.[25] However, this idea was recently challenged by Masferrer, who has argued that this is an oversimplification: punishing actions solely on the grounds that they were sinful was not accurate.[26] Thus, the basis for the approach was not theological but philosophical.

This simplistic starting point was Dorado Montero's first attempt to connect what is morally right and legal, on the one hand; and what is morally reprehensible and illegal, on the other. The use of the Christian ideals of "what is good and what is

[21] Figure as provided by the Official Census of Spain at the National Institute of Statistics. The document surveyed all municipal populations within the province of Salamanca in the year 1860. Vid. Instituto Nacional de Estadística (1860).

[22] According to the census of 2019, the population of Navacarros amounts to 112 inhabitants.

[23] Hernández Díaz (1983), p. 218.

[24] Madrid, the capital, is an exception with more varied influences.

[25] Tomás y Valiente (1969), p. 331: "crime and sin were far from just being parallel realities, for they were converging ones".

[26] Masferrer (2017), pp. 693–756. According to Masferrer, even during the Middle Ages, there was a distinction between crime and sin. There was a brief moment of confusion in the Modern Age, but for the most part, there was a common philosophical substratum on morals which allowed scholars to make the differentiation between morality and religion. From the nineteenth century on, such theory was confirmed, and it was held that man was entitled to develop a moral philosophy and moral conclusions completely independent from religion, based on reason and on natural law. See as well Masferrer (2020a), p. 2: "There is no doubt that not all immoral behaviour—or sins—should be criminalized: sins and crimes are not the same, as the moral and legal orders differ. It follows that Human law should never attempt to forbid all vices. The relation between criminal law and morality derives from the relation between politics, law and morality, whose provinces are different. Moral laws and civil laws have different limits and practical purposes. The sphere of moral law is much broader than civil law, which means, for example, civil laws should never concern themselves with the criminal thoughts a person may have inasmuch as they do not go beyond that, i.e. any kind of external act. As to practical purposes, civil laws have their own ethical-practical rationality, which affects not only the reasoning process but also the realm to which it applies". Indeed, in another work, he came to the conclusion that "every 'legally protected interest' has a moral substratum", vid. Masferrer (2020b), p. 289.

wrong" has its roots in his religion. The formation of a "wrong order" is constructed in opposition to the "desirable order", i.e. the punishable order only exists insofar as it can be contrasted with an ideal society. Such a Manichaean conception of morality was very useful in Dorado Montero's particular childhood, because it gave him a sense of constancy and the persistence that would allow him to continue studying despite the terrible conditions in which he lived. His home was very far away from his school, and he travelled every day from Navacarros to Béjar to attend- a distance of nearly 10 km.[27] His challenges were accentuated when, whilst playing in a yard with his friends, a rock holding a parked cart was displaced and the cart ran over Dorado Montero, leaving him lame and with a crippled right arm.[28] His parents were committed Catholics and very methodical. Despite being poor, uneducated farmers, they were dedicated to the objective that their son should keep on studying. However, there is debate as to why. Some authors, such as López-Rey, maintain that it was a common aspiration among Spanish peasants to send their children into the academic world, as conditions were deemed less precarious and salaries were higher.[29] Another interpretation is that, since farming or manual work in the textile industry were the main means of livelihood in the region, "his parents became aware that he had been deprived from the only tool which poor people had to subsist: a healthy body. Therefore, they decided he should devote his life to study".[30] Whatever the reason, this commitment to the idea of his education, and having a clear objective to achieve, was crucial for him to thrive in life.

Unsurprisingly, Christian philosophy was to be central core to Dorado Montero's religious and philosophical intellectual thought.[31] The so-called Philosophia Christi, as the Dutch philosopher Erasmus of Rotterdam named it, has deep roots in the thought of Dorado Montero. Similarly, the influence of the Spanish humanist and philosopher Joan Lluís Vives played an important role too. This latter reproached to Erasmus[32] for having underquoted him: "the appearance of the *Ciceronianus* would give rise to both the protests of those who saw themselves criticised and satirised, and the reproaches of those who were not quoted at all or not quoted enough".[33]

Such Christian thought was also reinforced by Enrique Gil Robles. He is better known as the father of José María Gil-Robles, a Spanish politician who played a definitive role in the period prior to the Spanish Civil War, as well as afterwards. José

[27] As the crow flies, the distance between the two points is 4.31 km, but the route via the current road is 7 km.

[28] López-Rey (1956), p. 606.

[29] López-Rey (1956), p. 606.

[30] Pascual Matellán (2018), p. 112: "sus padres fueron conscientes de que había sido privado de la única herramienta que tenían los pobres para garantizar su subsistencia: un cuerpo sano, y por ello tomaron la decisión de que se dedicara al estudio". Also, vid. Pascual Matellán (2021).

[31] Lima Torrado (2008a).

[32] Von Rotterdam (1528).

[33] Bomartí Sánchez (2006), p. 70: "La aparición del Ciceronianus va a suscitar, aparte de las protestas de quienes se vieron criticados y satirizados los reproches de aquellos que no se vieron citados o de los que se consideran insuficientemente reseñados".

María Gil-Robles was the leader of the CEDA,[34] an extremist right-wing association supporting the dictator Franco and his fascist ideology. Enrique Gil Robles was at that time one of the leading intellectual authorities in Salamanca, and he inspired several religious fundamentalist publications (such as *La Información* diary).[35] His very conservative, strongly religious influence dominated Dorado Montero's early thinking. In time, however, this changed.

Before moving to Bologna, the young Dorado Montero created and managed a political party with tendencies towards "ultramontanism". This clerical-political idea within the Catholic Church strongly emphasises the prerogatives and powers of the Pope. Other Catholic influences can be seen in his early thought, where he made a distinction between natural law and positive law. His secondary education had also involved indirect influence from the doctrine of Nicomedes Martín Mateos.[36] Two of Mateos' pupils (namely, Juan García Nieto and Eloy Bejarano) would end up directing the high school where Dorado Montero had studied. Via their influence, Martín Mateos and Kant had an impact on the developing thought of Dorado Montero: "The Kantian imperative as received by García Nieto and the spiritual sense as infused by Martín Mateos permeate the thought of a Dorado Montero who approaches the University of Salamanca".[37]

As we will see, later in life most of the unexamined Catholic doctrine would disappear from Dorado Montero's thought. However, his political philosophy continued to have a Christian background, which was a part of Dorado Montero's subconscious even when he was less religious. Sometimes, a Christian concept was renamed after a socialist idea he liked. For example: the idea that there should not be people oppressing others (arising in socialist theories) was derived from the Christian ideal of fraternity among all humankind.[38] Another example was the defence of the human race in Christianity, which he somehow felt closely related to the "third dimension of Tolstoy's Christian anarchism".[39] López-Rey concludes that Dorado Montero's description of the philosophy behind his criminal theory is grounded on a special mixture: it goes beyond a plain positivism or a mild correctionalism. It seeks to reconcile Comte's philosophy with the principles of the Old Spanish School aiming at the moral 'enmienda'.[40] This refers not to

---

[34]The acronym stands for Spanish Confederation of Autonomous Rights (*Confederación Española de Derechas Autónomas*).

[35]The newspaper *La información* defended Enrique Gil Robles and his ideals, and so did the diary *El Criterio* and *El Lábaro* with Father Cámara, and the diary *La Democracia* with Dorado Montero. Balcazar y Sabariegos (1935), p. 49.

[36]A Spanish philosopher born in Béjar (1806–1890) concerned primarily with spiritualism and neo-cartesian thought.

[37]Blanco Rodríguez (1982), p. 15: "El imperativo kantiano recibido a través de García Nieto y el sentido espiritualista inculcado por Martí Mateos impregnan el pensamiento del Dorado que se acerca a la universidad salmantina".

[38]Lima Torrado (2008b), p. 540.

[39]Lima Torrado (2008a), p. 431.

[40]Moral amendment in English. López-Rey (1956), p. 608.

'correction', but to a 'moral emendation': all previous mistakes must be completely erased from the criminal's record, and he should be protected against new convictions.[41] The continuing influence of Dorado Montero's faith should be seen no within one denomination, but within a wider Christian spirituality:

> His theory, therefore, is not the expression of a particular faith, but the expression of a Christian spiritualism in which other elements than those strictly orthodox from a Catholic point of view play a rôle.[42]

Dorado was therefore a reformer and a pioneer "firmly rooted in the Christian ideas so prevalent among the Spanish penologists",[43] and the first stage of his academic development was characterised by strong and rigid convictions. But, as he matured, his certainty and conviction tended to evaporate, and he was seized by transcendental doubt. He frequently considered the role that religion should play in regards to the treatment of offenders, as well as the dichotomy of religion and law that can be observed when contrasting the concepts of sin, confession, and penitential sanction, on the one hand; and offence, confession, and criminal punishment, on the other.[44] He did not much care about the impact of the crime, or restitution of the damage caused, as expressed in a religious metaphor: "For whom takes care of souls, the most important thing is not the determination of the acts carried out and their remedies, but rather the status and the tendencies of such souls. What matters is the sinner, *in lieu* of the sin".[45] This Christian idea had a practical manifestation in his design for a new penal system, wherein he shifted the focus away from the action itself to the agent. He asserted that "if in the sphere of penitence, confessions tend to be more habitual and more honest than in the field of state criminal justice, it is because redemption is sought by the sinner himself. In penitence, he sees nothing but benefits while, at the same time, he flees from justice (which he deems a great enemy which is going to inflict pointless suffering on him – unlike penitence, which has regenerating aims for him)". And so, he foresees that "such a difference in treatment shall only last until the criminal justice turns into a psychological treatment, i.e. a soul healing science".[46]

Three long paragraphs of Dorado Montero's core work are of a particular relevance here, as one can clearly identify Christian ideas in them. In the first, he draws a parallel between 'good behaviour' and admission to society, and 'good behaviour' and admission to heaven.

[41] Ibid, p. 608.

[42] López-Rey (1956), p. 608.

[43] Ibid.

[44] This tendency has been observed at the European level and was not solely developed in Spain. *Vid.* Masferrer (2019), pp. 219–238.

[45] Dorado Montero (1915), p. 181: "Para quien cuida de las almas, no es lo principal la determinación de los actos efectuados y el remedio de los mismos; lo es el estado y las inclinaciones de aquéllas [. . .] es el pecador, más que el pecado ya cometido, propiamente, lo que le importa".

[46] Ibid., p. 183: "esta diferencia no puede durar sino el tiempo que tarde en convertirse la justicia penal en un tratamiento psicológico, en una cura de almas".

> The penalty has never been but a mechanism for heaven to gain souls. Though it has been so, mainly, for the 'terrestrial' heaven (referring to the social order). It could even be deemed as a way to send to hell the social detritus, as a last resort [...] This must not be forgotten: both terrestrial heaven (civitas diaboli) as well as celestial heaven (civitas Dei), cannot tolerate rebelliousness in their midst. They only want righteous, not sinners. They must be just on the outside and on the inside.[47]

For him, the aspect of justice that requires intervention and amendment is the internal perspective. Traditional conceptions of justice focused on tackling the external aspect of justice, but "justice needs in the first place to be so at the will". Taking nature as an example, he stated that "out of the internal justice (the tree), external justice will come soon after (the fruits)". Only once we have focused on the tree, might we obtain the fruits, "whose recollection is the only thing that matters". Dorado Montero knows that "the one who controls the will, will count on the whole man; whereas, the man who only controls the body (by means of a criminal threat) will never reassure himself". This did not preclude sometimes acknowledging elements of the old criminal law system as necessary:[48] they all made it materially impossible for the criminals to commit more crimes". However, he pointed out that the old system was somehow a 'failure' and that its mechanism was far too simple to produce the deep, more complex changes that a society needs (because "his will of committing a crime is, simply, hindered").[49] In a second extract, he advocates for changing the penal system in order to 'cure souls':

> And so, Criminal law has either been outlawed or at least radically changed as regards juvenile criminality. It has been outlawed, if by criminal law we mean the retributive and atoning Criminal law which resorts to real penalties and sacrifices. It has been radically changed, whether we also consider the correctionalist function to be Criminal law, which does not use penalties as such, but only educative, will-transforming means [...]. Childhood and juvenile correctionalism have stopped being just sentimentalist and have an added scientific character. [...] Nowadays, institutions of correction are much more than mere charity establishments run by philanthropists and altruistic individuals (friars or nuns, as it was before); they are 'soul hospitals' run by people in the technical position of making that healing possible (i.e. pedagogues, physicians, psychiatrists, psychologists...).[50]

[47]Ibid., pp. 164–165: "La pena no ha sido jamás, me parece á mí, sino un medio de "ganar almas para el cielo", principalmente para el cielo terrestre (si es permitida la unión de ambas palabras), para el paraíso á que damos el nombre de orden social—destinado á nuestra bienandanza—, ó un medio de arrojar al infierno, á la desesperada, á los detritus sociales. sto no debe ser olvidado. El cielo terrestre (la civitas diabolí), lo mismo que el paraíso celestial (civitas Dei), no puede consentir rebeldías en su seno. Sólo quiere justos, no pecadores. Justos por fuera y justos por dentro".

[48]Shackles, prisons and chains are only resorted to because, simply, "one does not know how to use other means of punishment". Dorado Montero (1915), pp. 166–167. 'Necessary' here does not mean "something which is needed", but rather "something that cannot be avoided". In Spanish, the word also possesses a second sense which has a flavour of 'fate' or 'unavoidability'. Given that society was configured in a particular way, undesirable means were sometimes 'necessary', and their usage could not possibly be avoided, because society did not have (or had not yet practically implemented) other alternatives.

[49]Ibid., pp. 166–168.

[50]Ibid., p. 224: "De este modo, el derecho penal ha quedado proscrito ó radicalmente cambiado—como se quiera—con relación á la delincuencia juvenil: proscrito, si sólo se da tal nombre al

In a third extract, he addresses the need to individualise the penalty, especially when the penalty seeks to prevent or preserve against future crimes by changing the criminal. He develops this idea as follows: "it could be said that it consists of a personal, psychological work; no soul can be influenced without penetrating it. No will can be changed, except by investigating its roots and, hence, trying to modify them. Souls, just like any other thing, cannot be known except through observation and concrete analysis. Precedents are of the first importance here. Every individual behaves as what he is, and this can only be found out by observing what he does. The story of one person is the most reliable indication of his future behaviour [. . .]. When people seek the moral regeneration of the convict, they obviously seek his healing. They wish he would change his behaviour and that, if until now he was inclined to evil, he would reverse this path and tend to good. They want to renew his will, or even better, his entire soul by both spiritual and bodily means. And so, they ask for a penalty with a greater educative character, so that the outcome achieves social benefits and not harms (as has been happening)".[51]

Dorado Montero summarises the function which he thinks the penal science should fulfil: "the so-called function of criminal justice administration is a true soul healing".[52] He is close to positivism when arguing that the important fact is not responsibility for a single deed, but rather a disposition to certain kind of actions which makes a soul evil. For a soul can be well-oriented or naturally good, even if the person has committed several unlawful deeds. A truly evil, twisted soul can also

derecho penal retributivo y expiatorio, al que hace uso de verdaderas penas ó castigos; radicalmente cambiado, si también se llama derecho penal á la función correccionalista, donde no tienen lugar alguno las penas, en cuanto tales, y sí tan sólo los medios educadores y trasformadores de la voluntad [. . .] El correccionalismo infantil y juvenil ha dejado de ser meramente sentimentalista, y, sin perder este carácter, ha reunido al mismo el que podemos denominar científico [. . .] Los institutos de corrección son hoy algo más que establecimientos de beneficencia, á cargo de filántropos y de individuos altruistas y compasivos, v. gr., frailes ó hermanas de la caridad, según ha pasado antes; son, juntamente con esto, hospitales de almas para la curación de las mismas—aun mediante el cuerpo—y dirigidos al efecto precisamente por personas que estén en condiciones de realizar tal curación; es decir, por pedagogos, por médicos, por psiquiatras, por psicólogos".

[51]Ibid., pp. 479–480: "Aquí puede decirse que consiste todo en obra psicológica personal. No se puede influir sobre un alma sino penetrando en ella. No se puede cambiar una voluntad sino indagando sus raíces, al intento de poder así modificarlas. Y las almas, al igual de otra cosa cualquiera, no se conocen más que por medio de la observación y el análisis concretos. Los antecedentes tienen aquí una importancia de primer orden. Cada uno se porta según es, y sólo sabemos cómo se porta y cómo es averiguando lo que hace. La historia de un sujeto es el indicio más fiable de su comportamiento futuro [. . .] Cuando las gentes desean que por la pena se busque la regeneración moral del reo, es claro que persiguen una obra curativa de éste. Apetecen que cambie de conducta, y que si hasta ahora se hallaba mal inclinado, deje de estarlo en lo sucesivo y propenda al bien. Quieren renovar su voluntad, ó mejor dicho su alma entera, sea como sea, ya por medios puramente espirituales, ya también por intermedio del cuerpo. Hablan por eso de educación y exigen de día en día con mayor imperio carácter educativo á la pena, para que los resultados obtenidos de su aplicación produzcan beneficios sociales efectivos, y no, como ahora, casi siempre daños".

[52]Dorado Montero (1911a, b), p. 180: "La función llamada administración de justicia penal es una verdadera cura de almas".

undertake good actions with a perverse rationale or malicious intention. Let us remember his most relevant motto: it is the sinner, instead of the sin, that matters.[53] In parallel, the reparation of damage (a constant in civil law) is also mentioned.[54]

Elsewhere, Dorado Montero contrasted the soul with the state itself. He attempted to depict how public law, a man-made structure, is a clear obstacle to morality, because it contradicts the inner simplicity of the soul. The state "is simply the major hindrance for humanity's moral progress; it is an artifice largely relying upon violence, a construction whose object is to avoid man's set of energies and inherent qualities. It is necessary to suppress that, or humankind will be 'condemned' to perpetual slavery".[55] Soon after, he resorted to Rousseau's description of man's natural kindness, not without disapproval of his simplistic misinterpretation, in order to point out the numerous conventions and synthetic bonds that link individuals together.

Religious analogies continue to appear: there are souls which are naturally predisposed to commit sins, and so, there are men naturally predisposed to commit crimes.

> Certain souls are prone to a determined genre of behaviour in such manner that, under the slightest provocation or stimulus, they wreak their sinful power. They are, so to speak, born sinners.[56]

If the main objective of religious confession is that men are 'cured', and so do not commit further sins, judges should similarly seek to turn men into right-acting citizens. Religious thinking is undeniably link to our conception of Criminal law.

Dorado Montero's youth was dominated by these religious influences, but things started to change with his arrival at university. After obtaining his General Certificate of Education (GCE) at around 17 years old, he was awarded a scholarship to study for a further four years. This allowed him to move to Salamanca and to study in a university residence called San Bartolomé.[57] Within the walls of the University of Salamanca, he was a very successful student, just as he had been during his earlier

---

[53] Dorado Montero (1911a, b), pp. 195–216.

[54] Professor Matthew Dyson at the University of Oxford specialises in, inter alia, compensation for harm, the role of injunctions, and negligence. He has shed some light on contemporary thinking on this issue. Dyson and Masferrer (2017), pp. 19–33.

[55] Dorado Montero (1900a), p. 95: "es el estorbo mayor con el que tropieza el progreso moral de la humanidad; es un artificio apoyado en la violencia y hecho para ejercitar la violencia, una construcción cuyo objeto no es otro que impedir el desplegamiento de energías y cualidades nativas de los hombres, y que por lo mismo es necesario suprimir, so pena de hallarse la humanidad condenada a servidumbre perpetua".

[56] Dorado Montero (1915), p. 182: "Ciertas almas están de tal modo propensas á un género determinado de conducta, que á la menor provocación ó al más pequeño estímulo descargan su potencia pecadora. Son, podría decirse, pecadoras natas".

[57] In Spanish a "Colegio Mayor". In this case, the exact name was "Colegio Mayor de San Bartolomé".

education.[58] He studied for a degree in Humanities from 1878 to 1882, and graduated with distinction. In 1882, his academic merits led to his appointment as a Knight of the Order *Isabel la Católica*. One year later, he also obtained his law degree with distinction, specialising in the intersection of Civil and Canon Law. On 7 February 1883, he started teaching in the Faculty of Philosophy and Humanities, having been proposed by the Dean thereof.[59] It was the second scholarship he obtained: the Dean had created a scholarship and Dorado Montero earned it after following a competitive process.[60] Having "concluded the two degrees", he moved to Madrid with the goal of "obtaining his PhD in Jurisprudence",[61] which he did when he defended his thesis before a university tribunal.[62] He obtained the highest award, as usual. A new phase in his life was about to start.

2.2 Relativism vs. Religious Convictions

At the age of 24, the Board of *Colegios de Salamanca* granted Dorado Montero a postdoctoral scholarship with a stipend of 2000 pesetas in order to carry out a research stay at the University of Bologna in Italy. The book he worked on in those two years bore the title: "Organisation and state-of-the-art of the legal studies in Italy in a comparative perspective with Spain".[63]

After his trip to Italy, he was a much more realistic person, and shortly after his return, he became concerned with the 'transcendental problem'.[64] For Dorado Montero, every single topic, every piece of reasoning and lecture was open to further discussion. His own thinking was a building in permanent danger of crumbling, given the extent of the doubts he admitted. Absolute truths had vanished from his

[58] As his academic records demonstrate. GREDOS. Gestión del Repositorio Documental de la Universidad de Salamanca (2009).

[59] The Dean was Mariano Arés y Sanz, a prominent academic with very strong republican and lay ideals. Besides being a remarkable Professor (the Chair of Metaphysics of the University of Salamanca), he encouraged the creation of the special library of Philosophy and Humanities and managed the Board *Colegios Universitarios de Salamanca.*

[60] Valentí i Camp (1922), p. 102: "In the fourth year, through a public contest, he was granted one of the scholarships created on behalf of the initiative of Metaphysics Professor Mr Mariano Arés".

[61] Ibib., p. 102.

[62] The title of his dissertation was "Municipal regime. Subordination of the municipality to the State. The autonomy of the municipality. Administrative Tutelage". Original title: "Régimen municipal. Subordinación del municipio al Estado. La autonomía del municipio. Tutela administrativa". PARES. Portal de Archivos Españoles (2008).

[63] Original title: "*Organización y estado de los estudios jurídicos en Italia, comparativamente á España*". Diccionario de catedráticos españoles de derecho (1847–1984).

[64] Dorado Montero (1905), p. 11: "What guarantee do we have that our thought effectively matches how things really are, that our representations of the world reach an indisputable accuracy? The world, with the many beings and relationships it consists of, will be as it wants to be. We do not know how it is. What we do know, each one of us, is how we conceive it and imagine it".

mind, and he started to perceive reality in a much more complex way.[65] He acknowledged the imperfection of human nature, and was already acquainted with Tolstoy's views on the fallibility of man, reinforcing his stance. Tolstoy's influence on Dorado Montero's Christian Humanism was clear: he adopted Tolstoy's conception of the essence of individuals, i.e. that the only trustworthy and truly meaningful core of religion was based on love. He understood love to mean a state of benevolence for all men, such as is found in children and their tender, deeply honest wish to love everyone.[66] Therefore, divine perfection could be opposed to a very weak human nature: "Real love is an ideal of perfection which is complete, infinite, and divine. Divine perfection is the asymptote of man's life; he tends to it in a relentless manner; he gets closer to it every time, but he can never reach it entirely".[67]

Transcendental doubt was to be a constant in Dorado Montero's scholarly life, even as he engaged with new ideas.[68] Sometimes, while lecturing at the university, he could be explaining one aspect of the criminal code and then turn on his own thought, ending in questioning the very basic concept of liberty. Such was the extent of his broad-mindedness. However, this doubt was not easy to explicitly identify in his doctrine: it was not something that specifically worried him, nor an issue he identified by name. Instead, the concept appeared in abstractly formulations, and was never directly addressed.

This change in his approach led him to face many administrative and religious struggles, beginning on 20 May 1887. From Bologna, he wrote to ask to the Board of *Colegios Universitarios de Salamanca* to defray his doctor title and to reimburse the promised 2000 pesetas for having presented the required book—as had already been formally granted. However, there was a controversy, which would only be resolved after several subsequent events. Firstly, on 3 June 1887, the Dean of the Faculty of Philosophy and Humanities, Santiago Martínez, asked for the temporary suspension of a vote of the Board in favour of Dorado Montero. The evaluation board had produced a favourable report already, but he alleged that a further substantial analysis on the memo which had been presented was necessary. The goal was to evaluate the scientific nature of the work, but also to ensure its Catholicity, as this had been one of the conditions stated in the call for applications.

---

[65] Dorado Montero (1905), p. 22: "Let us change a man's condition and we will witness how he changes his opinions: let us think of him as rich, instead of poor; Catholic, instead of Muslim; producer, instead of consumer; manufacturer; employer, instead of worker; Republican, instead of Royalist; French, instead of Spaniard; trader, instead of peasant or philosopher, and we will be astonished how much his criterion vary, sometimes with the speed and the ease with which an actor changes his roles, his clothes and his physiognomy".

[66] Eltzbacher (1900), p. 202.

[67] Tolstoi (1894), pp. 139–140: "Die wahre Liebe ist "ein Ideal völliger, unendlicher, göttlicher Vollkommenheit. Die göttliche Vollkommenheit ist die Asymptote des menschlichen Lebens, zu der es beständig hinstrebt, der es sich immer mehr nähert, die aber nur in der Unendlichkeit erreicht werden kann".

[68] Barbero Santos (1970), p. 357 and Barbero Santos (1966), pp. 270 ff.

> *Colegios de Salamanca* has a double nature. It possesses both a scientific and a Catholic character. Therefore, they must require scientific performance of their pupils, on the one hand. On the other, they must ensure that the science which they develop is in consonance with the Catholic principles.[69]

After some struggle, on 16 July 1887, the Board of *Colegios Universitarios de Salamanca* referred the question via a query to the state. The Ministry resolved the matter: it asserted that there were no grounds to deny Dorado Montero's petition by simply alleging that the work should be Catholic in addition to 'scientific'. On 27 July 1887, the controversy was conclusively resolved:

> Mr Pedro García Dorado Montero has a perfect right to be paid out his title's sum as a Doctor in Civil and Canon law. Payment of the reimbursement of the two thousand pesetas can no longer be withheld or cancelled, not even on the ground that one needs to wait for the result of his work. This latter criterion was neither previously established nor stated as a prerequisite to the merit or quality of the work, the scholarship only requiring its execution and presentation.[70]

Finally, on 24 August 1887, Dorado Montero was reimbursed. It was not the first setback he would have to face in his life, nor the last.

Relativism was an idea taking over his thinking, as he slowly became aware of the fact that no earthly creature was entitled to know everything (or to even come close).[71] This human reality became a central aspect of his renewed scepticism: "human history, as well as Nature, is very similar to Penelope's weaving, or the eternal and useless work of Sisyphus. What is done today, will come undone again tomorrow".[72] The same idea may be found in Kant's *The Contest of Faculties*.[73] Dorado Montero was, therefore, becoming progressively less dogmatic.

In this respect, he was clearly influenced by Gumplowicz, whose *Philosophisches Staatsrecht* was translated into Spanish by Dorado Montero in 1892. Gumplowicz's starting point, which Dorado Montero based his later theory on, was that:

> The world is infinite and, consequently, it will never be comprehensible by the human spirit as a whole.[74]

Dorado inherited this basic concept, that the human spirit is incapable of understanding the whole world because one can only know fragments thereof. In his

---

[69] Diccionario de catedráticos españoles de derecho (1847–1984) (2009).

[70] Diccionario de catedráticos españoles de derecho (1847–1984) (2009).

[71] "It is all about stressing out the transitional and provisional nature of our judgements, our representations and our constructions [. . .]", Dorado Montero (1915), p. 518.

[72] Dorado Montero (1915), p. 517: "La historia humana, como también, por su parte, de un modo análogo, la de la Naturaleza, se parece mucho á la consabida tela de Penélope, cuando no al eterno y eternamente inútil trabajo de Sísifo. Lo que hoy se hace, se deshace mañana".

[73] Kant (1798): "An absurd dynamism by means of which the good keeps on alternating with the evil through an advance and setback game; therefore, this seesaw movement of our own specied with itself should be considered as nothing but a carnival farce".

[74] Gumplowicz (1877), p. 11: "*Die Welt [ist] Unendliches und daher vom menschlichen Geiste als Ganzes nie faßbar ist*".

scholarship from then on, he rejected the idea of a comprehensive, definitive, philosophical system of knowledge. Not only that, but in the Spanish edition of Gumplowicz's work, Dorado Montero introduced a personal remark in a revealing footnote.[75] In it, Dorado Montero draws attention to the fact that Gumplowicz was writing in 1877: at that time, the influence of eclectic postulates[76] meant that the theory of a so-called absolute, invariable natural law was prominent in Spanish thinking. This theory essentially stated that law was something outside time and place and had an immutable validity. This relates, refers, of course, to the neoclassical conception of law and Kant's approach. Yet, between when Gumplowicz originally wrote the text in 1877 to when Dorado Montero translated it in 1898, an opposite trend had gathered momentum. As a result, Dorado Montero declared this natural law theory a fantasy, an idealisation of the existing legal institutions in at the time of writing. By the end of the nineteenth century, nobody subscribed to this absolute, invariable natural law anymore. However, views in the intellectual panorama were not yet purely positivistic, and most of the old ideas remained. Idealist (neoclassical) trends envisioned the reality of norms a priori, whereas positivism requires scientific observation and checks.

Hence, Dorado Montero's ideas regarding the nature of punishment and Criminal law widened and opened up. He considered the possibility that neither law nor the human mind can understand and control everything. According to this point of view, the traditional approach to law was arrogant, with a legal science which tried to rule, define, and delimit everything. He was outraged that the model of liberal penal law consisted of a mixture of senseless aims: the defence of society, and/or utilitarian ends. Even though the ideas in the sphere of penal scholarship in which Dorado Montero was immersed had some merit, older penal thinking was not positivistic in the traditional sense, because it aimed at the criminal's recovery (Protective Law of the Criminals). Liberal criminal law failed to convince him for two reasons. The first one has already been mentioned: a disagreement as to the goals punishment seeks to achieve. The second is that liberal criminal law completely disregarded the dogmatic part of the law (where all the abstract positions, theoretical developments, and conceptual constructs were considered). Dorado Montero urged the development of a dogmatic of Criminal law, though this would only begin to be a reality a couple of decades later.[77]

In any case, Dorado Montero's academic writing was still sometimes confused into an indirect identification of God with freedom. It is from this points that the Dorado Montero we know began to work: his denial of the existence of freedom led him to doubt everything. This state of permanent doubt might be thought

[75]Gumplowicz (1892), p. 84.

[76]Mainly, thanks to Joaquín Francisco Pacheco.

[77]There is a consensus among legal historians and penalists that the initial development of criminal dogmatics took place at the beginning of the twentieth century, mainly introduced by Dorado Montero's pupil: Luis Jiménez de Asúa.

counterproductive, but it was needed in a time when: (1) societal change was necessary and (2) the dogmatics of penal law were not yet developed.

The situation of the University of Salamanca was also far from perfect, and this continued to present problems despite the efforts to modernise:

> Unamuno, Maldonado and others [tried] to endow the University of Salamanca of the appearance of a great cultural centre, yet this is far from being the reality, as those of us who have visited it have checked.[78]

Paradoxically, the more relativism Dorado Montero accepted and integrated into his doctrine, the less relativism he had in his day-to-day life. Step by step he became more entrenched at the University, and the job uncertainty that characterises the academic world was reduced for him: on 25 August 1887 he took office in his first stable job. He had succeeded in a public tender as auxiliary at the Faculty of Law at the University of Salamanca. Although he had achieved much more than most in a short period of time, in the next two years, Dorado Montero would undergo a very challenging process to become a Full Professor. This is evidenced by the several petitions which the Dean processed in that time: applications in relation to a public tender at the University of Granada for the chair in Elements of Political and Administrative Spanish Law (12 March 1890), public tender at the University of Santiago for the Chair in Institutions of Roman Law (22 May 1890), public tender for an auxiliary vacancy at the *Universidad Central* in Madrid (29 September 1890), public tender at the University of Barcelona for the Chair in Political and Administrative Law (9 January 1891), public tender at the University of La Habana to teach Natural Law (2 June 1891) and public tender at the University of Santiago for the Chair in Natural Law (15 January 1892).[79]

In the middle of this race for a position, he secured his means of living when a position became vacant.[80] On 11 June 1891, he was awarded two thirds of the salary for his work at the Chair of Civil Law, and on 6 May 1892, he became fully in charge of the Chair of Civil Law (first course). Finally, on 3 July 1892, he was appointed as Full Professor in the Chair of Political and Administrative Law at the University of Granada, with an annual wage of 3500 pesetas. However, after less than three months, he switched places with Jerónimo Vida: Dorado Montero stood at the University of Salamanca, while Vida occupied his position at the University of Granada. Thus, he now held the Chair of Criminal Law, initiating an unprecedent scholarly career in Salamanca, beginning to teach in the term 1892–1893.[81] Four years later, he participated in another chair-changing tender and won it, moving to the Chair of Criminal Law at the University of Valencia. However, less than one

[78] Ibid., p. 103: “Unamuno, Maldonado y otros [. . .] para dar a la Universidad de Salamanca apariencias de gran centro cultural, que está muy lejos de ser una realidad, como hemos podido advertir cuantos la hemos visitado”.

[79] Diccionario de catedráticos españoles de derecho (1847–1984) (2009).

[80] Produced by the death of its owner: Mr Hilario Beato.

[81] In this period, a very significant piece of work was published: Dorado Montero (1893).

month later, on 6 March 1896, Dorado Montero filed a waiver application, due to unforeseen circumstances.

After these events, the passing of his Catholic phase is evident:

> Scholarly life was intense. At the University, Mr Enrique Gil Robles (Chair of Political Law) and Pedro Dorado Montero (Chair of Criminal Law) were shining as two first order stars. The former was a fundamentalist; the latter was a republican, and around them revolved most part of professors, though Father Cámara (Bishop of the diocese) did not get on well with any of them.[82]

With Nicasio Sánchez Mata, Full Professor and the Chair of Natural Law, there were the ultramontans.[83] Dorado Montero had supported their ideals in his youth, when creating the political ultramontanist party. Ultramontans held that the Pope should always have a superior power: the term was mostly used in a moment of tension between the powers of the king and the prerrogatives of the Pope. However, his position now brought him into conflict with not the ultramontans, but also with the Bishop: Father Cámara. The latter did not like fundamentalists nor progressives. Dorado Montero suffered constant, serious criticism from Cámara,[84] who was aware that Dorado Montero had experienced a loss of religious feeling and had had a personal crisis over the existence of God.[85] However, Juan Andrés Blanco Rodríguez, Professor of History at the University of Salamanca, viewed this criticism after Dorado Montero's trip to Bologna as 'light'. Besides, Christian influences continued to affect Dorado Montero's thinking throughout his complex intellectual evolution, and constituted a key part of his inner landscape.[86] His Christian education was not erased after his term in Italy: this deep inner struggle continued for the rest of his life.

Relativism in his religious convictions was, however, a consequence of internalising Auguste Comte's philosophical scheme.[87] This has been described as a major influence on him: "[his extreme *correccionalismo*] was influenced by the philosophical system of Comte, rather than by the ideas and principles of Lombroso, Ferri, and Garofalo".[88] However, I have not been able to find any longer, fully-evidenced explanation of this assertion.

---

[82] Balcazar y Sabariegos (1935), p. 12: "Hacíase intensa la vida escolar. En la Universidad lucían como astros de primera magnitud D. Enrique Gil Robles de derecho político, y D. Pedro Dorado Montero, de derecho penal; el primero, integrista; el segundo, republicano y, alrededor de ellos, giraban la mayoría de los profesores, aunque los amigos del Padre Cámara, Obispo de la Diócesis, no se llevaban bien ni con unos ni con otros".

[83] Ibid.

[84] Berdugo Gómez de la Torre and Hernández Montes (1894), p. 85.

[85] López-Rey (1956), p. 607: "At a certain moment, –when he was in Italy and was about twenty-five years old– after a deep spiritual struggle he decided to abandon Catholicism".

[86] Blanco Rodríguez (1982), p. 15.

[87] One of Comte's aphorisms upon which Dorado Montero will heavily rely on is the following one: "Here is the only absolute maxim: There is no absolute maxim!".

[88] López-Rey (1956), p. 607.

2.3 A Brief Romance with Positivism

Dorado Montero was first acquainted with positivism—via the ideas of Lombroso, Ferri, and Garofalo, after his scholarship trip to Bologna.

It has been said that Italians have reinvented Criminal law four times. The first time was during the Roman Empire, with the first great legal work; the second version was Beccaria's command to comply with the law; the third was Lombroso, Ferri, and Garofalo's focus on the study of man; and the fourth reinvention brought together the previous schools in the *Terza Scuola* of criminal law.[89] Dorado Montero is usually placed between the third and the fourth stages, and is often catalogued as a member of the group of eclectics from the *Terza Scuola*.[90]

The legal theory of Dorado Montero has been intensively studied,[91] and positivism clearly played a major role.[92] Lombroso's doctrine, asserting that criminals could be identified by observing this physique, was gradually introduced in European legal thinking, producing legislation in the interwar period between WWI and WWII.

During Dorado Montero's stay in Italy, his perspective changed significantly. He became a great proponent of the work of Italian positivists Roberto Ardigò and Pedro Siciliani. Their influence enabled him to develop an idea of Spanish society which was pre-eminently neoclassical, iusnaturalist, and Catholic. Although Lombroso's *L'Uomo* delinquente[93] was already ten years old, and the main works of Ferri and Garofalo had been in circulation for more than seven years, in Spain, positivism remained largely unstudied.[94] Dorado Montero was captivated by the experimental method, and refreshing ideas developed in a system so different from Catholic scholasticism, but he criticised several of Lombroso's key points, pointing out incoherencies. When Lombroso published *Los últimos progresos de la Antropología criminal*, Dorado Montero also published his *Problemas de Derecho penal* (both in 1895). Among other things, he never accepted the classification of criminals in Lombroso's work.[95] Whenever he had to explain Lombroso's theories

---

[89] Rodríguez Manzanera (1981), pp. 245–246.

[90] I have reservations about the latter, but this is not the appropriate place to develop this idea.

[91] Bernaldo de Quirós (1927), p. 49; Bernaldo de Quirós (1919); Ríos Urruti (1919); Valls (1971); Lima Torrado (1976); and Rodríguez Hernández (1993). There are many other authors whose written contributions must be highlighted, such as Sánchez-Granjel, Cuello Calón, Bernaldo de Quirós, Rivacoba or Jiménez de Asúa.

[92] Ramos Pascua (1995), pp. 503–546.

[93] Lombroso (1884). Also, some of his outstanding works are: Lombroso (1890a, b, 1894, 1895a, b, 1902, 1904, 1910, 1911).

[94] Masferrer (2020c), p. 345: "Until that moment, the positivist school had not constituted 'a compact and definite nucleus'. It never did. As we have seen, not many jurists carried out rigorous studies defending the Italian positivist school".

[95] Dorado Montero (1915), p. 71: "Trends, inclinations, instincts or appetites are known, like everything else, by their effects, and not otherwise. Tendencies are simply powers, potentialities or properties, and no power or property can ever be known or ascertained except by their actions or manifestations".

in his lectures, Dorado Montero would highlight his many objections towards the idea of the born criminal. Ferri offered a much kinder approach to criminals; and one much closer to modern thinking, as he considered factors influencing the crime, instead of simply adopting the idea that criminality is inherent.[96] Ferri's most popular theory was based on anthropological (race, sex, physical constitution, psyche, age, etc.), physical (temperature, climate, etc.), and social factors (religion, education, family circle, etc.). Grispigni supported this approach, adding further differentiation between biological and ideological causes affecting the 'anthropological factors'. Garofalo,[97] however, continued to defend four types of born criminals: the murderer, the violent criminal, the thief, and the lascivious criminal.[98]

Positivism considers a person committing a crime as abnormal. There is a biological anomaly, inasmuch as the person is considered exclusively as a material or biological creature, not as a moral subject as in classical theory. Penalties, therefore, address biological and not moral issues. The individual, according to the most orthodox branch of positivism, will never stop being a delinquent, based on evidence such as phrenology and probabilistic sciences. One of the main obstacles for this theory was—and still is—the idea of a non-moral responsibility. Neoclassical penal law had relied upon a moral conception of crime: when the moral responsibility of the perpetrator was exhausted, he would be free of further penal consequences and be released from the State's restrictive measures (whatever they were; fine, imprisonment, death penalty, etc.). However, the new approach had no moral conception of crime, only a social one. Unlike moral responsibility, social responsibility is inexhaustible. Thus, the control of the State over the citizen,[99] which was relatively easy to ground in neoclassical theory, becomes a legal nightmare and almost impossible to justify.[100] Such control might end up lasting forever, giving rise to the risk of totalitarian legal systems.

Although Dorado Montero's lifetime was chronologically close to the rise of Nazism and fascism in the early twentieth century, ideologically those developments remained some way off. He was not, therefore, as concerned as some about the obvious risks that such a morality-free system entailed. Other contemporary authors

[96] Ferri (1887, 1892, 1893, 1899, 1900a, b, c, 1907, 1925, 1928, 1934, 1982, 1991).

[97] Garofalo (1880, 1886, 1890a, 1895, 1900, 2002).

[98] Iter criminis (2000).

[99] As regarded the limitless power of the State, Professor Masferrer identified the origin of this problem. Masferrer (2012), pp. 292–293: "Whereas the main stream of the natural law theory (Francisco Suárez, Hugo Grotius, Samuel Pufendorf, Christian Thomasius, etc.) defended that the law was based upon a reason, a - relatively new- line of thought, influenced by 'nominalism' and 'voluntarism'- adopted by, and disseminated among Protestants-, maintained that the law was based upon will. Authors like John Austin, Hegel and Rousseau, among others, shared this view, regarding the law as a 'command' (of the State)". For a complete opposite approach on the same issue, vid. Martín Martín (2017), pp. 259–273.

[100] Cartuyvels and Masferrer (2020), pp. 1–21: "The liberal constitutional state or 'Police State' is in a crisis, incapable of responding effectively to the real inequalities, which the abstract principles of individual responsibility and formal equality of the liberal constitutional state do little to conceal".

like Jiménez de Asúa were very more aware of the danger in such an approach but even Asúa did not realise until a very late stage the significance of the Nazi regime in Germany, or the fascist regime in Italy.

> If Primo de Rivera's dictatorship made him realise the relevance of maintaining the legality principle and, consequently, the liberal criminal law, WWII did nothing but affirm this idea.[101]

Dorado Montero was not able to foresee this; rather, he postponed his proposals for a new criminal law because he thought that society was not yet evolved enough for it to be properly applied. Even socialism had not yet emerged as a major political idea. Dorado Montero carried out a comparison of legal systems, which he found differed depending across time. In the early stages of the development of legal science, law was conceived as a subjective application of a theory of justice imposed by force, usually controlled by the chief of a tribe, a king, the strongest man in a group, or a primitive judge (usually, the latter corresponded to religious institutions). While this mode of legal thought lacks procedural elements,[102] it links to a widely held idea that man is a transcendental being, rather than just flesh. However, sometime after the French Revolution, ideas about law changed focus. Legal protections and the number and extent of basic legal principles[103] increased with the aim of protecting individuals from the uncertainty perceived in past systems. Law became more rigid, and lost vitality, as the focus shifted to its formal and procedural aspects: this was form over content. While acknowledging that the first model of law was frequently characterised by injustice, Dorado Montero preferred that to this latter option, and he defended a focus on 'content-over-form' in law. History moved like a pendulum as Dorado Montero returned to consider the first stage, and this is what he attempted to reflect in his *Protective law of the criminals*, despite the risk inherent in its proximity to emerging fascist and Nazi conceptions of law.

Dorado's main criticism of the new school can be summed up in a few lines. Positivists, after all, insist on seeking the reasons for action, as well as trying to elaborate a catalogue of degrees of responsibility. This is contradictory, as it implies that individuals control their actions.

> Should we take for granted that the existence of mitigating circumstances, or the system of relative freewill were admissible, it would be necessary to establish infinite grades of criminal capacity. Since the strength of such circumstances can be infinitely diverse depending on the situation, it would be extremely unfair to equate and to treat the same way the very different influences and situations in which subjects find themselves when committing a crime.[104]

---

[101] Roldán Cañizares (2018), p. 270: "Si la dictadura de Primo de Rivera le hizo ver que era fundamental mantener el principio de legalidad, y en consecuencia, el derecho penal liberal, la II Guerra Mundial terminó de confirmar esta idea".

[102] Legal guarantees were virtually inexistent in primitive times.

[103] Namely, legality principle, actus reus, and softening of penalties.

[104] Dorado Montero (1915), p. 429: "Dando por supuesto que la existencia de las circunstancias atenuantes, ó ei sistema del libre albedrío relativo, fuera admisible, sería preciso establecer grados infinitos de imputabilidad; puesto caso que la fuerza de tales circunstancias puede ser infinitamente

Further, Dorado Montero thought positivists were committing the same mistakes as the Classical (or Neoclassical) School had: responsibility—even if mitigated—had no place in the new system. But then, what is the point in punishment? If a criminal does not control their actions, they are not masters of their own destiny. He also criticised Garofalo for talking about 'natural crimes': this was absolutist and more suited to the postulates of the Classical School and its religious, deductive concepts.

It is tempting to describe Pedro Dorado Montero as a positivist, but he was not really a part of that school (or, at least, he was not a *Lombrosian* positivist) at all. Positivism clearly influenced him, but Dorado Montero departed from its premises and vehemently criticised Italian positivism many times. On the other hand, attempting to diminish the positivism in his thinking in favour of an eclectic position is also inaccurate. From Italy, he wrote *El positivismo en la ciencia jurídica y social italiana*: the product of his baptism of fire in the new trend.[105] In that text, he opposed mild, indeterminate concepts like 'eclecticism' (as has already been mentioned): he generally rejected any position which he saw as incoherent. He reflected that some were unable to adapt to changes in the world, and that as they "sway[ed] in uncertainty" they chose sides "depending on the circumstances".[106] He included "Pessina, Gabba, Del Giudice, Filomusi-Guelfi, Miraglia and even, to a certain extent, Carle himself" in this category.[107] He saw these scholars as "paying tribute to idealism" especially Hegelian thinking, whilst at the same time acknowledging the need for Legal Philosophy to "have regard to the developments" in the "so-called experimental sciences". He concluded, poignantly: "Actually, they do not belong to the critical direction which we are examining [...], neither can they be exactly included within the purely idealist direction".[108]

Leaving aside the purely technical legal aspects, Dorado Montero concluded by reasserting that the grounds of both positions were united: "Hence, the harmonisation between the two opposed schools (idealist and positivist) far from being impossible, as it might look like prima facie, is required by the inner exigency which they both represent: the theory of the social contract, reduced to its just limits, purged of exaggerations as regards liberty, restricted to its own circle of action (that of the 'rational liberty'), unites itself in a loving consortium, and forms one single

varia, según las ocasiones, y sería grandemente injusto «equiparar, cual sucede al presente, y tratar de la misma manera, las diferentísimas situaciones en que los sujetos se hubieren encontrado al cometer los delitos bajo el influjo de circunstancias limitadoras de su libre albedrío".

[105]His first work had been published a year before in 1890.

[106]Dorado Montero (1891), p. 249.

[107]Dorado Montero(1891), p. 249.

[108]Dorado Montero (1891), p. 249: "En realidad no pertenecen á la dirección critica que examinamos, entendida del modo que queda dicho, pero tampoco pueden incluirse exactamente en la dirección puramente idealista".

[theory] along with the theory of determinism, its mistakes corrected in turn, especially that of mechanistic determinism".[109]

Notwithstanding this, many things remained incomprehensible, especially regarding human nature. For instance, if a criminal is born that way and cannot help his tendencies and criminal acts, how could someone like Lombroso treat him with such hatred and contempt? In this sense, Dorado Montero bit the intellectual hand that fed him, and as a result endured discrimination from both sides. Neoclassicals and eclectics showed rejected his arguments absolutely. Positivists could never understand why he rejected their basic principles, or why he questioned the originality of their movement:

> Let us determine the extent to which the claim of the 'novelty' of the anthropological school can be considered legitimate, and so also, to which extent the accusation of the 'destruction' and 'dissolving' of the social order made by many of his detractors is accurate.[110]

Even if Dorado Montero praised certain aspects as the outstanding contribution of positivism,[111] he acknowledged that "its approach in general was far inferior than that of the former schools, particularly the correctionalist school".[112]

His approach and adherence to positivism led to a number of setbacks, which he overcame, although not without suffering. A political struggle began on 5 February 1897, when Salamanca's Bishop, Father Cámara, raised a concern in the aftermath of a collective complaint from certain pupils concerning "the explanations of Professor Dr Pedro Dorado Montero". These had been deemed "as contrary to Catholic truth and grounded on the reprobate systems of positivism, materialism, and determinism".[113] The Bishop asked the Chancellor of the University of Salamanca to exempt students from attending Dorado Montero's lessons, and to replace him with another professor. Two days later, the Chancellor argued before the Directorate-General of Public Instruction that the law did not enable him to appoint another professor who would approach Criminal law from a Catholic perspective. On 19 February, the Dean of the Law Faculty, Teodoro Peña Fernández, filed an appeal against the decision of the Chancellor re-establishing Dorado Montero's duties. After some

[109] Dorado Montero (1891), p. 248: "Por donde se ve cómo la armonía entre las dos escuelas contrarias, idealista y positivista, lejos de ser, como á primera vista aparece, imposible, es una necesidad reclamada por la interna exigencia que ambas representan: la teoría del contrato social, reducida á sus justos límites, purgada de sus exageraciones en orden á la libertad, y contraída al círculo propio de su acción, el de la libertad racional, se une en amoroso consorcio y forma, por así decirlo, una misma con la teoría del determinismo, corregida, á su vez, de sus yerros, sobre todo del determinismo mecánico".

[110] Garofalo (1890b), p. 8: "indiquemos siquiera dentro de qué límites puede considerarse como legítima la pretensión de novedad que caracteriza á la escuela penal antropológica, y dentro de qué límites, por tanto, es exacta la acusación de disolvente y destructora del orden social que lanzan contra ella muchos de sus contradictores".

[111] Namely, the "study of the criminal (criminal anthropology) and the analysis of some external -mostly social- causes of the crime (criminal sociology)". Garofalo (1890b), p. 30.

[112] Garofalo (1890b), p. 30.

[113] Diccionario de catedráticos españoles de derecho (1847–1984) (2009).

months, the Chancellor wrote a report on the student complaints and the performance of the Dean. According to this report, the action taken by the Dean against Dorado Montero was blatantly illegal, since the appeal lodged did not fall under the Regulation. Besides, he quoted a section of the University Council (16 June 1897) in which a third party to the dispute, the Dean of Sciences, considered that the actions taken against Dorado Montero had been ultra vires. As a result, the Dean of Law changed his tactics. He switched the focus to the fact that both the Faculty of Sciences and the Faculty of Medicine had been recently created, attempting to undermine the weight of their opinions. However, he did not succeed. On 23 June 1897, the Chancellor's decision was reached and communicated to the State: the suspension was void. Dorado Montero had won the battle.

2.4 Krausism: The Relevance of Instruction and Education

Krausism differed enormously from the postulates defended in the first stages of Dorado Montero's intellectual activity. He changed his ideas about education and religion to their very opposites, going from one extreme to another, but without ever being deemed a radical.[114]

The German philosopher Friedrich Krause was fiercely opposed to dogmatic models of teaching and advocated for, inter alia, academic freedom, laicism,[115] and freedom of conscience.[116] His Spanish counterpart was Julián Sanz del Río, a great Castilian jurist responsible for introducing the movement in Spain. His pupil, who was better known than his teacher, was Francisco Giner de los Ríos, who created the *Institución Libre de Enseñanza* in 1876. The latter was a private Krausist centre, conceived as an alternative to official education, and known for its lay spirit. In practice, this was intended to prompt reform of the Spanish education system,[117] often through a debate framed as a dichotomy between religion and science.

Marcelino Menéndez Pelayo, meanwhile, openly rejected evolutionist trends, and confronted both liberalism and laicism. The tension is illustrated by the reception of the Spanish naturalist Marcelino Sanz de Sautuola y Pedrueca, who discovered the prehistoric paintings of Altamira[118]—a finding which clashed with prevailing ideas.

It was during Dorado Montero's time in Madrid conducting his PhD studies that he got to know Francisco Giner de los Ríos. From that moment onwards, his theories would always relate law and pedagogy.[119] It is possible that Dorado Montero was

[114] Sánchez Rojas (1919); Blanco Rodríguez (1994), pp. 141–168; Ledesma (1919).

[115] Krause (1871), p. 33. In the "Preliminary Ideas" of his *Urbild der Menschheit*, he nonetheless insisted that man "must live in religion united with God and subordinated to Him".

[116] Krause (1803).

[117] Giner de los Ríos (1933).

[118] The paintings were discovered by Modesto Cubillas, a farmer from Asturias.

[119] Gil Cremades (1969), p. 273; Hernández Díaz (1983), pp. 217–228.

also part of a masonic lodge at this time; his most outstanding pupil, Jiménez de Asúa, was reported to be in one.[120] Masonic lodges were not understood by reference to a formal membership, but in a way akin to J. G. Fichte's conception. For him, lodges were nothing but a way of completing the fragmentary education of one individual. Such an education is a product of 'big societies': being born in a certain country, in a certain social estate, and with a certain partial education.[121] Though personally not very sociable,[122] Dorado Montero believed in the organisational aim in philanthropic, reformist societies. He borrowed directly from Krause when he insisted that masonic associations had no hidden political aim, but were brotherhoods with educational purposes:

> The art of educating human beings as human beings, and to humanity as humanity, purely and universally, is waking them up from their lives.[123]

Krause would not be his sole influence here: Fröbel would play a role as well. However, the latter was less relevant for legal history, since in practice, Krausism refers to Krausefröbelism in an inclusive way: "Krausefröbelism attempted to unify the philosophical impulse of the Krausist circle with the pedagogic power or the Fröbelian circle".[124]

As time passed, Dorado Montero, one of Spain's most international scholars, felt the call to conduct research abroad again. This time, he selected France, having applied on 15 May 1909 to the Board of Extension of Studies for an allowance to enable him to develop certain topics.[125] One option was "proceeding for teaching Law at the French, German, English, Swiss or American Universities". Failing that, the other option was "the study in France, Belgium, Germany, Switzerland and Austria of the exercise of criminal justice and of penitentiary administration". The latter proposal depended on his command of French, German, English, and Italian. However, he remained in Paris for only four months, as a neurasthenia he had been suffering from for many years prevented him from working properly. This did not, however, prevent him from publishing prolifically.[126]

---

[120] Roldán Cañizares (2019), p. 35.

[121] Ureña (1990), p. 47.

[122] Ríos Urruti (1919), p. 93.

[123] Krause (1820), p. 17: "Sie ist also die Kunst, den Menschen als Menschen, und die Menschheit als Menschheit, rein und allseitig zu erziehen, das ist, ihr Leben zu wekken".

[124] Ureña (1990), p. 61: "El krausofröbelismo pretendió unir el impulso filosófico del círculo krausista con el impulso pedagógico del círculo fröbeliano".

[125] Diccionario de catedráticos españoles de derecho (1847–1984) (2009).

[126] Dorado Montero (1909–1911, 1911a, b).

2.5 A Socialist in Spirit

Dorado Montero was never a member of the Spanish Socialist Party (he was a member of the Republican Party of Salamanca), but socialism had a role in his life, and he had respect and sympathy for it. It is no surprise that, although he was a devoted full-time scholar, "he had assumed civil responsibilities of public nature as well".[127] The most relevant of these was as town councillor at the City Hall of Salamanca. Although this was the lowest administrative level of Spanish politics, his dedication was noted. The day of his funeral, not only did the City Council honour his memory, but Miguel de Unamuno addressed a moving and very emotional speech in the professor's remembrance:

> The municipal session of that day was cancelled on the occasion of the death of Dorado Montero. The Corporation appointed a Commission to represent the City Hall during the burial. Clairac and Riesco voted against, based their decision on their religious beliefs. His burial was a civic event. During the march, the University clock's bells rang. There were many representatives from the University, the Municipal Council, workers, and political parties. It was raining and people crowded around the mud on the narrow streets. Students and workers carried the coffin. [...] The corpse was surrounded by twenty flags from workers' unions [...] Around five-hundred people assisted at the civil cemetery. Unamuno addressed the bishop's refusal to allow the corpse in the Catholic cemetery: '... we bury in this sacred and blessed land, blessed by those who rest here, under the same heaven which shelters everyone, under its light, whose shine equally illuminates us all'.[128]

Interestingly enough, the civic, socialist, and republican spirit which predominated at his burial and commemoration was not the only tone. His very good friend, Mariano Arés y Sanz,[129] also made an address at Dorado Montero's burial which referred to his progressist spirit:

---

[127] Hernández Díaz (1983), p. 218: "también asume responsabilidades ciudadanas públicas".

[128] Málaga Guerrero (2018), p. 598: "Se suspendió la sesión municipal por la muerte de Pedro Dorado Montero que fue concejal del Ayuntamiento. Se nombró una comisión para que representase a la Corporación en el entierro. Clairac y Riesco votaron en contra amparándose en sus sentimientos religiosos. El sepelio de Dorado Montero fue un acontecimiento ciudadano. Durante el recorrido, las campanas del reloj de la Universidad no dejaron de doblar. Asistieron representaciones de la Universidad, del Concejo, obreros y partidos políticos. Llovía y la gente se agolpaba pese al barro en las calles de las inmediaciones. Estudiantes y trabajadores cargaron el féretro. Abrieron la marcha del cortejo fúnebre los maceros de la Universidad con sus mazas enlutadas. Rodeaban el cadáver las veinte banderas de las sociedades obreras. Al pasar el entierro por la plaza Mayor dobló la campana del Consistorio. Con el féretro a hombros, dieron la vuelta al ágora. Asistieron 500 personas al cementerio civil. Unamuno dijo refiriéndose a la negativa del obispo a dejar enterrar el cadáver en el cementerio católico: '...enterramos en esta tierra sagrada y bendita, tierra bendecida y sagrada por los que aquí reposan, bajo el mismo cielo que a todos cobija, bajo su luz, que a todos ilumina por igual".

[129] Dorado Montero had dedicated his 1901 work to him. Dorado Montero (1901a, b, c), p. 5: "Profesor que fué de la Universidad de Salamanca, a quien tanto debe esta Escuela, y cuya falta se advierte en la misma de manera bien ostensible".

> His burial was a resounding event due to the civil character represented by Arés himself, and aroused controversy and disapproving reactions in the conservative University of Salamanca and the City of Salamanca.[130]

Dorado Montero was deeply concerned with social questions, and this did not go unnoticed in academia or the intellectual circles of his time. Issues such as inequality, advances in labour law and relations, variations in poverty and illiteracy figures, changes within Spanish society, empowerment of the working class, reform of the education system or the eruption of anarchism were constant topics among scholars. As documented,[131] socialism had a definitive impact on him, in two particular ways. There were two important consequences: firstly, new disciplines would originate and develop. Secondly, most of the social sciences would adopt a scientific method. From this confluence of events it followed that:

(1) Some misunderstandings and illogical incoherencies arose;
(2) many sciences declined, related to other areas, or even converged: sociology, criminology, psychology, pedagogy, penal law or anthropology;[132]
(3) a vast reorganisation of disciplines and their roles took place.

There were inherent risks within this multiaxial, comparative and often interdependent scholarly environment. Many theories or trends would lack a clear, technical response to the problems they aimed to solve. The combination of approaches from the old and new disciplines generated the appearance of fullness and completion of work, where in reality most of the proposed ideas did not address certain issues. Especially in the *cuestión social*,[133] responses were often too generic, vague, and usually relied on pseudoscientific knowledge and unproven ideas.[134] In this period, these reserved and poorly grounded proposals were the most common way in which authors dealt with such issues. People with a basic knowledge of anthropology or with vague notions of sociology would then write many reviews, flyers, and pamphlets, and middle-class intellectuals would discuss those topics at an amateur level.

[130]Hernández Díaz (2002), p. 256: "Su entierro fue sonado por el carácter civil que dispuso el propio Arés y suscitó viva polémica y reacciones de denuncia en la conservadora Universidad y ciudad de Salamanca".

[131]Blanco Rodríguez (1982), p. 133; Blanco Rodríguez (1979), pp. 252–278; Blanco Rodríguez (1984), pp. 235–242; Lima Torrado (2008a).

[132]In practice, it led to a great confusion between those related disciplines. Masferrer (2020a), p. 4: "it is easy to set out the boundaries between the new theories, such as, for example, between correctionalism and the positivist school (or Criminal Anthropology), as Bernaldo de Quirós acknowledged". Also, Fernández Ruiz-Gálvez (1992), pp. 407–427.

[133]López Castellano (2018), p. 63.

[134]The so-called *cuestión social* referred to a hotspot topic back in the nineteenth century. It depicted all sort of concerns over several problems that emerged after the industrial revolution, mostly revolving around poor quality of life of the working class and riots arising as a negative response to it.

Dorado Montero's theory, however, did not suffer from these flaws. It must not be forgotten that he was a penalist: his Protective Law of the Criminals relied heavily on legal knowledge (even if he dared to engage with wider disciplines). Thus, his assertions were properly considered and specific. Consequently, many core developments in penal dogma took place many years after his death, in the works of his disciples. By neutralising existing cultural and economic inequalities, Dorado Montero attempted to transform the ethical and mental structures of individuals. Materialism was, therefore, a key element in Dorado Montero's ius-philosophical thought, as is demonstrated in a brief article he published in *La Lucha de Clases*.[135] A superficial reading of the article, might suggest that Dorado Montero was against materialism, but he was not. He did, however, agree with the critics of materialism that economic decision making is not what triggers human conduct.[136] Instead, he thought hunger and love did so. When Dorado Montero said: "Isn't it possible that the animal existence is the economic element, i.e. the indispensable physical basis of everything else?",[137] he pointed out that the engine that directs human action is driven by his nutrition *and* reproductive needs, not only the former.

The exploration of the *cuestión* social[138] did not take place exclusively in academic circles. There were plenty of social reforms and changes within the Spanish State between the nineteenth and twentieth centuries, with certain organs such as the *Comisión de Reformas Sociales* (Social Reforms Commission)[139] and the *Instituto de Reformas Sociales* (Institute of Social Reforms) created ad hoc.[140] Salamanca, however, was slow to change:

> In 1898, the relations between the State and the Church were very close. The public powers had to authorise some religious services, among which were those referring to the undeclared war. The Ministry of Justice and Grace agreed to the celebration of a Te-Deum asking for peace in the Philippines at the Cathedral.[141]

The city and its surroundings lacked hygienic infrastructure, and *El Adelanto* still prominently advertised medicines for malaria, a disease which was then endemic in Spain. The terrible economic circumstances also led to illicit trades. Such activities, where they involved food, lacked quality control:

---

135 Dorado Montero (1900a).

136 Dorado Montero (1900b), p. 2: "The observation is exact, but not appropriate, in my opinion".

137 Dorado Montero (1900b), p. 3: "¿No será la existencia animal, el elemento económico de la base física indispensable de todo lo demás?".

138 Dorado Montero (1901a, b, c).

139 Álvarez Junco (1986), pp. 147–154; Pérez Ledesma (1986), pp. 155–166.

140 These constitute the same organ. The Commission started work in 1883 and turned into the Institute in 1903. It worked until 1924. Biblioteca Nacional de España (1711) BNE, Madrid. http://datos.bne.es/.

141 Málaga Guerrero (2018), p. 33: "En 1898 las relaciones Iglesia-Estado eran muy estrechas. Los poderes públicos tenían que autorizar algunos cultos, entre ellos aquellos que se referían a la guerra no declarada. Desde el Ministerio de Gracia y Justicia dieron su visto bueno a la celebración de un Te-Deum en la Catedral pidiendo la pacificación de Filipinas".

> the consumption of untreated milk produced endemic diseases, tuberculosis, and brucellosis, this latter known as the Malta Fever.[142]

Miguel de Unamuno, former friend and intellectual nemesis of Dorado Montero, appeared in public to speak about the issues related to the *cuestión social*: "*El Adelanto* placed a great typographic boast of Unamuno's speech made on 25 August 1904 in Gijón on its front page" and "the endeavours of Unamuno for the cities and towns of Spain were acknowledged and followed by the people of Salamanca. The newspapers were in charge of elaborating reports on his interventions".[143] Similarly, the pitted and open dispute with the Father Cámara and the conservative Government had partially originated in their fear of socialism. There were other threats to Dorado Montero, too: the conservative Government wanted to remove him from the academic world. This was particularly painful, as he had a reputation all over the region:

> Dorado Montero acquired fame at the end of the last century, reaching the wider public, after having lived in the dark for many years after the excommunication that Father Cámara (Bishop of Salamanca) had sentenced the distinguished professor to. The conservative Government was very close to enacting an arbitrary measure similar to that of Mr Manuel Orovio, which separated Salmerón, Giner, and other relevant full professors from their positions. However, Cánovas did not dare do so with Dorado Montero, who firmly maintained his position defending academic freedom.[144]

A careful study of the documents at the Foundation Pablo Iglesias, demonstrates that the Spanish professor was not an anarchist: the evidence links him to socialism, including in his relationship with the PSOE.[145]

> He contacted anarchist reviews and collaborated with them, but from 1894 he appears linked to the PSOE, as well as to its organ of expression; *El Socialista*, where he collaborated without interruption for the whole of his life.[146]

---

[142] Málaga Guerrero (2018), p. 35: "El consumo de leche no tratada producía enfermedades endémicas, tuberculosis y brucelosis, esta última conocida como fiebre de Malta".

[143] Ibid., p. 217: "*El Adelanto* se hizo eco en primera, con gran alarde tipográfico, del discurso de Unamuno pronunciado el 25 de agosto de 1904 en Gijón [...]. Las andanzas de Unamuno por las ciudades y pueblos de España eran conocidas y seguidas por los salmantinos. Los periódicos se encargaban de hacer largas crónicas sobre sus intervenciones".

[144] Valentí i Camp (1922), p. 104: "Dorado Montero adquirió cierta notoriedad a fines de la centuria pasada, llegando al gran público, después de haber vivido obscurecido durante muchos años, con motivo de la excomunión que el P. Cámara, a la sazón obispo de Salamanca, lanzó contra el insigne profesor. Entonces, el Gobierno conservador estuvo muy cerca de dictar una medida arbitraria semejante a la de don Manuel Orovio, cuando separó del profesorado a Salmerón, Giner y otros eminentes catedráticos. Pero Cánovas no se atrevió con Dorado Montero que sostuvo en aquella ocasión, con bravura, su punto de vista, defendiendo la libertad de cátedra".

[145] The acronym stands for "Spanish Socialist Worker Party" in Spanish.

[146] Fundación Pablo Iglesias (1926): "Tuvo contacto y colaboró en revistas anarquistas, pero desde 1894 aparece ligado al PSOE y a su órgano de expresión *El Socialista*, donde no dejó de colaborar a lo largo de su vida".

However, even if he was more socialist than anarchist, his socialism was not orthodox: it was full of Marxist connotations, and "Dorado Montero's socialism, similarly to that of other intellectuals in his time like Unamuno and Álvarez Buylla, shows many ambiguities, and his ideology, which constantly changed, mixed certain Marxist ideals with other trends emerging in social thought. He partially knew the work of Marx, but through Italian intellectuals, especially Aquiles Loria, from whom he obtained a great part of his vision".[147] A supporter of this mixture of socialism and anarchism was Manuel de Rivacoba y Rivacoba,[148] who in some sense equated this thinking to Bertrand Russell's thought.

2.6 The Interspersion of Anarchism

One of the works by means of which Dorado Montero did analyse and spread anarchist ideals was Paul Eltzbacher's work *Der Anarchismus*,[149] which the former translated into Spanish.[150] When translating the chapter devoted to Leo Tolstoy, the most important aspect for him was the defence of the law of love (Christ's most supreme law) as the principle to rule the existing order. Even so, Dorado Montero described himself as an atheist, and the whole of his thinking was purely existentialist. The influence of anarchism in his life is undeniable,[151] but he was far from being an early anarchist. When he is described as such, it is because of the role of anarchist doctrines in his legal thought, the degree to which he received libertarian doctrine, or his affinity (variously described as either major or minor) with certain varieties of anarchism. As might the latter case be the familiarisation[152] with the so-called *Freirechtsbewegung*.[153] The aforementioned movement was a current of legal and cultural thought which took place mainly in Germany between the end of the nineteenth century and the beginning of the twentieth century. It held that every legal system has sources other than norms arising from a legislative source, i.e. extra-legal norms. Regarding those, the judge could act more freely whenever the legislative text proved not to match the concrete needs of the case. Therefore, the jurist had both

[147] Blanco Rodríguez (1994), p. 165: "El 'socialismo' de Dorado, al igual que el de otros intelectuales de su época como Unamuno y Álvarez Buylla, presenta numerosas ambigüedades, y en su ideología, en constante evolución, conviven algunas ideas marxistas con otras procedentes de diversas corrientes de pensamiento social. Conoce parcialmente la obra de Marx pero básicamente a través intelectuales italianos, particularmente Aquiles Loria, de quien procederá buena parre de su ideario económico y social cercano al socialismo".

[148] Rivacoba y Rivacoba (1970), pp. 15–28; Rivacoba y Rivacoba (1971), pp. 1631–1643; Rivacoba y Rivacoba (1962); Rivacoba y Rivacoba (1963).

[149] Eltzbacher (1900).

[150] Eltzbacher (1901).

[151] Lima Torrado (2008a), pp. 417–443.

[152] As pointed out by Blanco Rodríguez on many occasions.

[153] Riebschläger (1968).

the duty and the power to seek the law. To do so, he could consider facts (social relations) as well as other non-normative sources. It presented an undeniable advantage: effectively filling the gaps in positive law. Unsurprisingly, it inspired certain elements for Nazism and other totalitarian movements such as the case of Russia under the rule of Stalin. The main point is that, although the main representatives of this current were Ehrlich, Fuchs and Schmitt, Dorado Montero drank directly from Kantorowicz and his vision of it.

Dorado Montero published in socialist,[154] as opposed to anarchist,[155] reviews, more often, but Jesús Lima Torrado argues that, at the time it was common for authors not professing the ideology of a particular publication to contribute to them. Lima Torrado gives six reasons why Dorado Montero wished to publish in these journals, including:[156] (a) he considered them an instrument for regeneration, and as a way to fight the decadence of Spanish society in the nineteenth and twentieth centuries in accessible language; (b) they reflected his preference for exploring social problems over the 'official' problems of legal and bureaucratic issues, instead allowing him to advocate for addressing abuses of power, poverty, and lack of education; (c) he maintained countless bonds of friendship with anarchist personalities (like Federico Urales)[157] as well as with intellectuals collaborating with the anarchist press (Miguel de Unamuno and Franciso Giner de los Ríos); (d) as a simple matter of strategy. The 1896 Act against Anarchist Propaganda made anarchist only reviews impossible, so reviews which accepted anarchists' contributions (such as work from Anselmo Lorenzo, Tarrida del Mármol, Ricardo Mella, Malatesta, or Malato) mixed them with contributions from known intellectuals (like Francisco Giner, Manuel Cossío, Gumersindo de Azcárate, González Serran, Unamuno, or Dorado himself). A further reason, e) was that it allowed Dorado Montero to address a nineteenth century problem: the legitimacy of law and dominant social powers.

It is important to note that in Krause's home country of Germany, Krausism did not have much impact,[158] but he had a powerful influence in Portugal and in

[154] Lima Torrado is very clear about this: *La Revista Socialista*, *La España Moderna*, *Sozialistische Monatshefte*, *La Lectura*, *Estudio* and the *BILE* (*Boletín de la Institución Libre de Enseñanza*). He also pointed out some newspapers, such as *La Lucha de Clases* or *El Socialista*. Furthermore, it is worth highlighting that when Blanco Rodríguez analysed the works in Dorado Montero's personal library, he found the quantity of socialist works vastly exceeded those addressing anarchism in number. *Vid.*, Blanco Rodríguez (1982), p. 133. In the latter, the author attempts a non-exhaustive list of all his socialist influences.

[155] As regards the anarchist publications, there were two main reviews he contributed to. First: Dorado Montero (1899b), pp. 471–474; and Dorado Montero (1899a), pp. 141–144. In the second place, Dorado Montero (1898), pp. 225–233.

[156] Lima Torrado (2008a), pp. 420–422.

[157] His real name was Juan Montseny Carret (in Spanish) or Joan Montseny i Carret (in Catalan). Back then, it was a common practice for anarchists to use a pseudonym to protect themselves.

[158] Dierksmeier (2002), p. 4: "Rechtsphilosophen Karl Christian Friedrich Krause (1781–1832), dessen Philosophie sich in Spanien, Portugal und Lateinamerika seit 150 Jahren großer Aufmerksamkeit erfreut". Also vid. Dierksmeier (1999), pp. 75–94. Besides, in the three-year period I have been employed at *Universität Augsburg*, every German scholar I have met or talked

Spain.[159] Antón Oneca acknowledged this when he said that the "*Besserungstheorie* did not have any adepts in his country" where it seemed "forgotten or hardly mentioned in the works dealing with penal theories".[160] This is why it is necessary to mention that Krausism was inextricably connected with anarchism: it acted as a catalyst which allowed certain anarchist ideals to penetrate the old Iberia. Those postulates, even if they were disliked or opposed, were certainly not unknown in the rest of Europe. When Lima Torrado identified the key aspects of Krausism,[161] he indirectly defined the degree of Spanish acceptance of anarchist ideals:

(a) The rejection of Law as a coercive, exterior order and, consequently, the rejection of the official State's law;
(b) a trend towards the spiritualisation of law: the idea that the future will consist of an ethical, internally accepted, non-repressive State;
(c) a sense of humanity and solidarity;
(d) education as a means transforming both man and society; and
(e) a non-superstructural mode of social organisation.

Oneca also outlined five dominant points of intersection[162] which are particularly helpful in outlining Dorado Montero's influences: the sociological thesis of Alfred Fouillée, the evolutionist thesis of Herbert Spencer, the Kantorowicz conception, Max Stirner's thought (he translated his main work),[163] and certain contemporary influences like Wargha. I remain, however, slightly sceptical when it comes to the comparison of his thought with the critical positivism of Vaccaro's *Terza Scuola*. In Dorado's work,[164] he refused to call the *Terza Scuola* "eclectical", and was very clear that he thought the school was conciliatory, rather than eclectic:

> There are those who, still sticking to the old ideas, seek to maintain them along with the new ones, thus uniting them in an impossible connubium, which we do not even dare to name eclecticism, as we cannot betray the etymology of such a word.[165]

This was not to mention the "many positivists who, as shown before, are determined to correct positivism", and who could be included "within the fledgling positivists

to about my research topic was very surprised to hear of Krause, who is considered a figure with virtually no relevance there. Also, in formal discussions (such as the *Doktorand Seminars*) and informal conversations, no colleague was aware of the relevance of Krause in Spain.

159 Giner de los Ríos (1916).

160 Antón Oneca (1960), p. 1016.

161 Ibid., pp. 427–428.

162 Ibid., p. 429.

163 Stirner (1843).

164 Dorado Montero (1891), p. 249: "no es ecléctica, sino crítica y conciliadora, y que tiene, por consiguiente, un entero valor científico que no tienen las teorías eclécticas; que abraza y funde en un solo término los dos que eran antitéticos, tomando como base las doctrinas naturalistas y levantándose sobre ellas á la concepción del ideal".

165 Dorado Montero (1891), p. 249: "aquellos que, apegados todavía á las ideas antiguas, pretenden mantenerlas al lado de las nuevas, uniéndolas en imposible connubio, que ni eclecticismo nos atrevemos á llamar, siquiera por no hacer traición á la etimología de la palabra".

(the so-called critical positivists)".[166] Dorado Montero identified and listed them: mainly "Puglia, Cogliolo, and Vanni", but he also specifically mentions three other authors who accepted the contractual organism of Fouillée, namely Gustavo Bonelli (with "certain differences"), Colajanni ("revindicating its priority with regards to De Greef"), and Icilio Vanni ("but with certain reservations in the *Programma critico di Sociologia*").[167]

2.7 A Struggle to Unify Sociology

In later life, Dorado Montero retired to a lonely countryside house in order to meditate. He thought the most important part of law was the substance, not the form. This open-mindedness was usually associated with a more abstract approach trying to see beyond observation and empirical reasoning, and even beyond rationalism. He therefore inclined to sociology and to criminal dogmatics—in the latter he would prepare a primitive terrain for later development.

Dorado Montero's late efforts were focused on the sociological aspect of his theory, anticipating the unification of the sciences under the field of sociology. This topic was already being addressed in Spanish doctrine, by virtue of which:

> The initiators of Sociology in Spain were very concerned with determining the relationship of the new science [to other fields], especially the Philosophy of History. Giner and Azcárate attributed different objectives to the two, but Dorado would include the Philosophy of History within Sociology.[168]

During his Italian studies, Dorado Montero became acquainted with many authorities in that field, but he relied in particular on two Italian authors: Vaccaro and Colajanni.

Vaccaro[169] spoke to the empiricist spirit in Dorado Montero. Though utilitarianism was not a central part of his theory, it was empirically based. In this, he agreed with his Italian counterpart that: "a great number of objections have been made

[166]Dorado Montero (1891), p. 249: "Sin hablar de muchos positivistas que, como hemos mostrado, se proponen corregir el positivismo y que muy bien podrían incluirse en el grupo de los positivistas de nuevo cuño, esto es de los positivistas críticos".

[167]Dorado Montero (1891), p. 249.

[168]Blanco Rodríguez (1982), p. 30: "A los iniciadores de la Sociología en España les preocupa extraordinariamente determinar las relaciones de la nueva ciencia, principalmente con la Filosofía de la Historia. Giner y Azcárate le reconocen objetivos distintos. Dorado, sin embargo, englobará el campo de la Filosofía de la Historia dentro del espacio propio de la Sociología". At the footnote of the page, the author clarifies the differences between the two sciences; Philosophy of History focused on 'the laws by means of which History developed itself', whereas Sociology focused on 'everything relating to the essence, nature and structure, in sum, to the comprehensive total of the social organism'.

[169]Vaccaro (1898, 1903, 1908).

against the utilitarian school of Bentham, which I do not respect, since they look unfounded and unfair".[170]

Colajanni[171] was the other key influence. Dorado Montero did not agree with the sphere of exception in the work of the former:

> As much as we want to restrict the bond of liberty, it certainly remains uncontested [the fact that] we can infuse a certain direction to our mind.[172]

Within a deterministic theory, it is tacitly accepted that there is little room for free will. Dorado Montero was actively opposed to such an admission. He deeply criticised the supporters of the so-called eclectic Criminal law school: when there was any free will theory which contained a glimpse of determinism, the whole crumbled and fell apart. His dislike for inconsistencies was not unique and was reminiscent of Spinoza's 'Empire within another Empire'. According to Spinoza, Europe's Judaeo-Christian background meant a common argument for free will was as follows: we can admit that God rules everything and, hence, nothing escapes his control, but we humans are endowed with a small parcel of free will or capacity to decide. For him, this was to make the same mistake as above: we do not know what determines our conscience and, consequently, we think that it flows from ourselves. Spinoza rejected such a possibility: the nature of man cannot be like a state within another state.

In any case, Dorado Montero was particularly enthusiastic about the new role that sociology was to play in society, and he strove to highlight its relevance and assert that "legal norms should be established not on the basis of the 'principles of absolute justice', but on observation of social reality".[173] And so, he came to his famous conclusion, later expressed by one of his most respected pupils: "In a distant future, Criminology will end up swallowing Criminal law".[174]

Dorado Montero died in 1919 after a long and painful illness with intestinal cancer. The cancer made the last three years of his life extremely challenging.[175]

> I am ill. Soon, it will be one year that I have been unable to carry out work of any kind. I have not been able to leave home (not even the bed), for this nor have I been able to give lectures this term. Besides, [there are] other diseases, worries and disorders in the house.[176]

---

[170]Vaccaro (1891), p. 23: "Contro la scuola utilitaria del Bentham sono state fatte un gran numero di obiezioni, che non ripeto, perchè la maggior parti di esse mi sembrano infondate e ingiuste".

[171]Colajanni (1884, 1885). There are more works, yet we decided not to mention them since they are not that related to the topic.

[172]Colajanni (1899), p. 25: "Per quanto si vogliano restringere i vincoli, della libertà, rimane però indubitato, che noi possiamo imprimere una certa direzione alla nostra mente".

[173]Blanco Rodríguez (1982), p. 31: "Observa que las normas jurídicas han de establecerse no a partir de los 'principios de justicia absoluta' sino a partir de la observación de la realidad social".

[174]Jiménez de Asúa (1944), p. 13: "En el remoto mañana la Criminología se tragaría al Derecho penal".

[175]Rus Rufino, Zamora Bonilla (1999), p. 246. VV.AA (1998).

[176]Draft of a letter dated 16 August 1918. Bodero (2006), p. 40: "Estoy enfermo, pronto va a ser un año, imposibilitado para todo trabajo. No he podido salir de la casa (de la cama, apenas), ni por lo mismo, ir a clase este curso. Otras enfermedades, preocupaciones y trastornos en la casa, además".

His ideas would, however, survive.[177] Immediately after Dorado Montero's death, Jiménez de Asúa, showing his devotion to his mentor, vindicated his faith in Criminology and in a future where the ideas of Dorado Montero and socialism would be the guiding norms. This was especially meritorious, as coming despite the fall of the Second Spanish Republic: this had ruined—or at least paralysed—the transition towards the Protective Law of the Criminals.[178]

References

AA. VV. (1941) Epistolario a Clarín. Editora Nacional, Madrid

Álvarez Junco J (1986) La Comisión de Reformas Sociales: intentos y realizaciones. In: Consejo General de Colegios Oficiales de Diplomados en Trabajo Social y Asistentes (eds) De la beneficencia al bienestar social: cuatro siglos de acción social. CGCODTSA, Madrid, pp 147–154

Antón Oneca J (1960) La teoría de la pena en los correccionalistas españoles. In: Estudios Jurídico-Sociales, Homenaje al Profesor Legaz y Lacambra. Universidad de Santiago de Compostela, Santiago

Balcazar y Sabariegos J (1935) Memorias de un estudiante de Salamanca. Librería de Enrique Prieto, Madrid

Barbero Santos M (1966) Pedro Dorado Montero, aportación a su biografía. Revista de Estudios Penitenciarios 22:270-ff

Barbero Santos M (1970) Remembranzas del profesor salmantino Pedro García Dorado Montero en el 50 aniversario de su muerte. In: VV.AA. (eds) Problemas actuales de las ciencias penales y de la Filosofía del Derecho Homenaje al profesor Luis Jiménez de Asúa. Ediciones Pannedille, Buenos Aires

Barbero Santos M (1996) Pedro Dorado Montero, aportación a su biografía. Revista de Estudios Penitenciarios 22:257–317

Berdugo Gómez de la Torre I, Hernández Montes B (1894) Enfrentamiento del Padre Cámara con Dorado Montero. Diputación Provincial, Salamanca

Bernaldo de Quirós C (1919) Dorado Montero y sus libros. Revista de Derecho Privado 67:97–102

Bernaldo de Quirós C (1927) Prólogo. In: Dorado Montero P (ed) Naturaleza y función del Derecho. Reus, Madrid

Biblioteca Nacional de España (1711) BNE, Madrid. http://datos.bne.es/

Blanco Rodríguez JA (1979) El pensamiento político-social de Dorado Montero en el marco de las ideologías sociales de su época (1880–1917). Universidad de Salamanca, Salamanca

Blanco Rodríguez JA (1982) El pensamiento sociopolítico de Dorado Montero. Centro de Estudios Salmantinos, Salamanca

Blanco Rodríguez JA (1984) El socialismo reformista de Dorado Montero. Revista de Estudios 11–12:235–242

Blanco Rodríguez JA (1994) Evolución de un intelectual crítico. Revista de Estudios 33–34:141–168

Bodero ER (2006) Pedro Dorado Montero, el desmitificador de Salamanca. Revista Jurídica Online:21–42

[177] Indeed, his most famous works were written in the last period of his life. A posthumous work worth mention has also been discovered: Dorado Montero (1927).

[178] Roldán Cañizares (2018), p. 330.

Bomartí Sánchez V (2006) Humanistas europeos (siglos XIV y XVI). Editorial Complutense, Madrid
Cartuyvels Y, Masferrer A (2020) An introduction to the birth of criminal positivism in Europe and Latin America at the end of the 19th century: rise and resistance. GLOSSAE. Eur J Leg Hist 17: 1–21
Colajanni N (1884) Il Socialismo. Filippo Tropea Editore, Catania
Colajanni N (1885) La delinquenza della Sicilia e le sue cause. Tipografia del Giornale di Sicilia, Palermo
Colajanni N (1899) La Sociologia criminale. Filippo Tropea Editore, Catania
Decianus T (1593) Tractatus Criminalis. Eredi Niccolò Bevilacqua, Torino
Diccionario de catedráticos españoles de derecho (1847–1984) (2009) Universidad Carlos III de Madrid e Instituto Figuerola de Historia y Ciencias Sociales, Madrid. https://www.uc3m.es/diccionariodecatedraticos
Dierksmeier C (1999) Karl Christian Friedrich Krause und das 'gute' Recht. Archiv für Rechts- und Sozialphilosophie (ARSP) 85(1):75–94
Dierksmeier C (2002) Die Geschichtlichkeit des Rechts in der Methodologie der Rechtsphilosophie K.C.F. Krauses. Forum historiae iuris 1:1–29
Dorado Montero (1891) El positivismo en la ciencia jurídica y social italiana. Imprenta de la Revista de Legislación, Madrid
Dorado Montero (1893) Problemas jurídicos contemporáneos. La España Moderna, Madrid
Dorado Montero P (1898) "La Patria", Ciencia Social, No. 8, Barcelona, pp 225–233
Dorado Montero P (1899a) "¿Quién vigila a los vigilantes?", La Revista Blanca, No. 30, Madrid, pp 141–144
Dorado Montero P (1899b) "Patria", La Revista Blanca, No. 17, vol I, Madrid, pp 471–474
Dorado Montero P (1900a) Concepciones sociales y penales de Tolstoy, según su última novela, Resurrección. La España Moderna 144:94–119
Dorado Montero P (1900b) Sobre el materialismo histórico. La Lucha de Clases 290:1–4
Dorado Montero P (1901a) Contribución al estudio de la historia primitiva de España. El Derecho penal en Iberia. Imprenta de la Revista de Legislación, Madrid
Dorado Montero P (1901b) Del problema obrero
Dorado Montero P (1901c) Estudios de Derecho penal preventivo
Dorado Montero P (1905) Nuevos derroteros penales. Imprenta de Heinrich & Comp., Barcelona
Dorado Montero P (1909–1911) El Derecho y sus sacerdotes: volumen 1. Imprenta de la Revista de Legislación, Madrid
Dorado Montero P (1911a) El Derecho y sus sacerdotes: volumen 2. Imprenta de la Revista de Legislación, Madrid
Dorado Montero P (1911b) La psicología criminal en nuestro Derecho legislado. Hijos de Reus, Madrid
Dorado Montero P (1915) El Derecho protector de los criminales. Ed. Jiménez Gil, Madrid
Dorado Montero P (1927) Naturaleza y función del Derecho. Reus, Madrid
Dyson M, Masferrer A (2017) The lawyers' reality: wrongdoing in Spain in the era of codification. In: Samuel Llano S, Sinclair A (eds) Writing wrongdoing: Spain 1800-1936. Tamesis, London, pp 19–33
Eltzbacher P (1900) Der Anarchismus: Eine ideengeschichtliche Darstellung seiner klassischen Strömungen. J. Guttentag, Berlin
Eltzbacher P (1901) El Anarquismo según sus más ilustres representantes: Godwin, Proudhon, Stirner, Bakunin, Kropotkin, Tucker, Tolstoy, etc. La España Moderna, Madrid
Fernández Ruiz-Gálvez E (1992) Ciencia del Derecho, Ciencias Jurídicas, Sociología del Derecho, Filosofía del Derecho. In: De Lucas Martín FJ (1992) Introducción a la teoría del derecho. Tirant lo Blanch, Valencia, pp 407–427
Ferri E (1887) Los nuevos horizontes del derecho y del procedimiento penal, 2nd edn. Centro Editorial de Góngora, Madrid
Ferri E (1892) Estudios de antropología criminal. La España Moderna, Madrid

Ferri E (1893) Nuevos estudios de antropología criminal. La España Moderna, Madrid
Ferri E (1899) Los Delincuentes en el arte. Librería de Victoriano Suárez, Madrid
Ferri E (1900a) Ciencia positiva. Atlante, Barcelona
Ferri E (1900b) Los hombres y las cárceles. Centro Editorial Presa, Barcelona
Ferri E (1900c) La justicia penal: su evolución, sus defectos, su porvenir. B. Rodríguez Serra, Madrid
Ferri E (1907) Sociología criminal. Centro Editorial de Góngora, Madrid
Ferri E (1925) Proyecto preliminar de código penal para Italia. Centro Editorial de Góngora, Madrid
Ferri E (1928) Principii di diritto criminale : delinquente e delitto. Unione Tipografico-Editrice Torinese, Torino
Ferri E (1934) Homicidio-suicidio. Reus, Madrid
Ferri E (1982) Il magistrato: dal reclutamento alla formazione professionale: esperienze in Italia e nel mondo. Arti Grafiche Jasillo, Roma
Ferri E (1991) Defensas penales, 6th edn. Temis, Santa Fe de Bogotá
Fundación Pablo Iglesias (1926) Fundación P.I., Madrid. https://www.fpabloiglesias.es/archivo-y-biblioteca/diccionario-biografico/biografias/4883_dorado-montero-pedro
Garofalo R (1880) Criterio positivo de la penalidad. Napoles
Garofalo R (1886) Polémica en defensa de la Escuela Criminal Positiva (en colaboración con Cesare Lombroso, Enrico Ferri y Giulio Fioretti). Bolonia
Garofalo R (1890a) La criminología: estudio sobre el delito y sobre la teoría de la represión. La España Moderna, Madrid
Garofalo R (1890b) Indemnización á las víctimas del delito. La España Moderna, Madrid
Garofalo R (1895) La superstition socialiste. Félix Alcan, Paris
Garofalo R (1900) Justicia y civilización. La España Moderna, Madrid
Garofalo R (2002) Indemnización a las víctimas del delito. Analecta, Pamplona
Gil Cremades JJ (1969) El reformismo español. Ariel, Barcelona
Giner de los Ríos F (1916) Principios de Derecho natural. Espasa-Calpe, Madrid
Giner de los Ríos F (1933) Educación y enseñanza. Espasa-Calpe, Madrid
González T (1829) Censo de Población de las provincias y partidos de la Corona de Castilla en el siglo XVI. Imprenta Real, Madrid
GREDOS. Gestión del Repositorio Documental de la Universidad de Salamanca (2009) Universidad de Salamanca, Salamanca. https://gredos.usal.es/handle/10366/19333. Find in the Section "Expediente personal de Pedro García Dorado Montero", within the Collection "AUSA. Expedientes personales de profesores de la USAL"
Gumplowicz L (1877) Philosophisches Staatsrecht. Manz, Wien. Spanish edition: Gumplowicz L (1892) Derecho político filosófico. La España Moderna, Madrid
Hernández Díaz JM (1983) Pedro Dorado Montero y la educación. Historia de la educación: Revista interuniversitaria 2:217–228
Hernández Díaz JM (2002) Del Decreto Pidal al primer Rectorado de Unamuno, 1845-1900. In: Rodríguez San Pedro Bezares LE (ed) Historia de la Universidad de Salamanca. Ediciones Universidad de Salamanca, Salamanca, pp 239–262
Iñesta-Pastor E (2017) Influencias extranjeras en la configuración de la pena en los códigos penales españoles decimonónicos. In: Masferrer A (ed) La codificación española. Tradición e influencias extranjeras: su contribución al proceso codificador (Parte general). Thomson Reuters Aranzadi, Pamplona, pp 401–499
Instituto Nacional de Estadística (1860) Madrid. https://www.ine.es/inebaseweb/treeNavigation.do?tn=192209&tns=192478#192478
Iter criminis (2000) Raffaele Garofalo. http://itercriminis.com/raffaele-garofalo-creador-del-termino-criminologia/
Jiménez de Asúa L (1944) "El derecho penal del futuro"; José Mora Guarnido (dir.), El mundo de la posguerra
Kant I (1798) Der Streit der Fakultäten. Friedrich Nicolovius, Königsberg. Spanish edition: Kant I (2003) El conflicto de las facultades (trans: Rodríguez Aramayo R). Alianza, Madrid

Krause KCF (1803) Grundlage des Naturrechtes. Göpfert, Leipzig
Krause KCF (1820) Die drei ältesten Kunsturkunden der Freimaurer Brüderschaft, 2nd edn. Arnoldischer Buchhandlung, Dresden
Krause KCF (1811) Urbild der Menschheit. Arnoldische Buchhandlung, Dresden. Spanish edition: Krause KCF (1871) Ideal de la humanidad, 2nd edn (trans: Sanz del Río J). Imprenta de F. Martínez García, Madrid
Ledesma Á (1919) El maestro Dorado Montero. BILE 43
Lima Torrado J (1976) La Filosofía Jurídica de Pedro Dorado Montero. Universidad Complutense de Madrid, Madrid
Lima Torrado J (2008a) Las claves de la recepción del pensamiento anarquista en la filosofía política de Pedro Dorado Montero. In: Elósegui Itxaso M (ed) El Pensamiento jurídico: pasado, presente y perspectiva. Libro homenaje al prof. Juan José Gil Cremades, 1st edn. El Justicia de Aragón, Zaragoza, pp 417–443
Lima Torrado J (2008b) Las claves de la recepción del pensamiento socialista en la filosofía política de Pedro Dorado Montero. In: AA.VV. Estudios en homenaje al profesor Gregorio Peces-Barba, Dykinson, Madrid, pp 537–550
Lombroso C (1884) L'uomo delinquente, 3rd edn. Fratelli Bocca, Torino
Lombroso C (1890a) Medicina legal. La España Moderna, Madrid
Lombroso C (1890b) El hipnotismo. La España Moderna, Madrid
Lombroso C (1894) Los anarquistas. Tip. Sucesores de Rivadeneyra, Madrid
Lombroso C (1895a) Los últimos progresos de la antropología criminal. La España Moderna, Madrid
Lombroso C (1895b) Grafologia. Ulrico Hoepli, Milano
Lombroso C (1902) El delito: sus causas y remedios. Librería General de Victoriano Suárez, Madrid
Lombroso C (1904) El antisemitismo. Viuda de Rodríguez Serra, Madrid
Lombroso C (1910) Los fenómenos de hipnotismo y espiritismo. M. Aguilar, Madrid
Lombroso C (1911) Los criminales. Atlante, Barcelona
López Castellano F (2018) Pauperismo y cuestión obrera en la españa del siglo XIX: entre la 'economía de la Salvación' y el riesgo de fractura social. Iberian J Hist Econ Thought 5(1): 57–70
López-Rey M (1956) X. Pedro Dorado Montero (1861-1919). In: Mannheim H (ed) Pioneers in criminology. Stevens and Sons, London, pp 605–612
Málaga Guerrero J (2018) La vida cotidiana en la Salamanca del siglo XX: 1898-1923. Fundación Salamanca Ciudad de Cultura y Saberes, Salamanca
Martín Martín S (2017) Estado punitivo y derechos constitucionales: pasado y presente. Ayer. Revista de Historia Contemporánea 105:259–273
Masferrer A (2012) Spanish legal traditions, 2nd edn. Dykinson, Madrid
Masferrer A (2017) La distinción entre delito y pecado en la tradición penal bajomedieval y moderna. Una propuesta revisionista de la historiografía española, europea y anglosajona. Anuario de Historia del Derecho Español 87:693–756
Masferrer A (2019) Der Beitrag der Theologie und der kanonistischen Wissenschaft zum modernen europäischen Strafrecht. Zeitschrift für die gesamte Strafrechtswissenschaft 131(1):219–238. https://doi.org/10.1515/zstw-2019-0008
Masferrer A (2020a) Criminal law and morality revisited: interdisciplinary perspectives. In: Masferrer A (ed) Criminal law and morality in the age of consent. Springer, Cham, pp 1–26
Masferrer A (ed) (2020b) De la honestidad a la integridad sexual. La formación del Derecho penal sexual español en el marco de la cultura occidental. Thomson Reuters Aranzadi, Cizur Menor
Masferrer A (2020c) The Reception of the Positivist School in the Spanish Criminal Doctrine (1885-1899). GLOSSAE. Eur J Legl Hist 17:303–352
PARES. Portal de Archivos Españoles (2008) Ministerio de Educación, Cultura y Deporte, Madrid. http://pares.mcu.es/ParesBusquedas20/catalogo/description/1492637?nm
Pascual Matellán L (2018) Pedro Dorado Montero. Un pensador heterodoxo. Azafea. Revista de Filosofía 20:111–128

Pascual Matellán L (2021) Pedro Dorado Montero y el correccionalismo español. El difícil desafío de humanizar el Derecho Penal. Tirant Lo Blanch, Valencia
Pérez Ledesma M (1986) La Comisión de Reformas Sociales y la cuestión social durante la Restauración. In: Consejo General de Colegios Oficiales de Diplomados en Trabajo Social y Asistentes (eds) De la beneficencia al bienestar social: cuatro siglos de acción social. CGCODTSA, Madrid, pp 155–166
Pifferi M (2011) A proposito di Storia del diritto penale e della giustizia. Scritti editi e inediti (1972-2007), di Mario Sbriccoli. Rivista di storia del diritto italiano 84:480–487
Ramos Pascua J (1995) El positivismo jurídico en España: Don Pedro Dorado Montero. Anuario de Filosofía del Derecho 12:503–546
Riebschläger K (1968) Die Freirechtsbewegung Zur Entwicklung einer soziologischen Rechtsschule. Duncker and Humblot, Berlin
Ríos Urruti F (1919) Don Pedro Dorado Montero, Filósofo del Derecho. Boletín de la Institución Libre de Enseñanza 43:93–95
Rivacoba y Rivacoba M (1962) El centenario del nacimiento de Dorado Montero. Universidad del Litoral, Santa Fé
Rivacoba y Rivacoba M (1963) Recordación de Dorado Montero. Cenit, Toulouse
Rivacoba y Rivacoba M (1970) Evocación y vigencia de Dorado Montero. Revista de Ciencias Penales 29(1):15–28
Rivacoba y Rivacoba M (1971) Viejas Remembranzas de Dorado Montero. Revista de Estudios Penitenciarios 29:1631–1643
Rodríguez Hernández V (1993) La insumisión en Dorado Montero. El tema iusnaturalista en la encrucijada ideológica de la Restauración. Hespérides, Salamanca
Rodríguez Manzanera L (1981) Criminología. Porrúa, Ciudad de México
Roldán Cañizares E (2018) Luis Jiménez de Asúa: un jurista en el exilio. Universidad de Sevilla, Sevilla
Roldán Cañizares E (2019) Luis Jiménez de Asúa. Derecho penal, república, exilio. Dykinson, Madrid
Sánchez Rojas J (1919) Pedro Dorado Montero. Boletín de la Institución Libre de Enseñanza 43
Stirner M (1843) Der Einzige und sein Eigentum. Verlag von Otto Wigand, Leipzig
Tolstoi L (1894) Das Reich Gottes ist in Euch. Löwenfeld, Stultgart,-Leipzig-Berlin-Wien
Tomás y Valiente F (1969) El Derecho penal de la monarquía absoluta. Siglos XVI, XVII y XVIII. Tecnos, Madrid
Ureña EM (1990) Orígenes del Krausofröbelismo y masonería. Historia de la educación: Revista interuniversitaria 9:43–62
Vaccaro MA (1891) L'utilità nel Diritto penale classico. V. Vecchi, Trani
Vaccaro MA (1898) Les bases sociologiques du droit et de l'état. Giard & E. Brière, Paris
Vaccaro MA (1903) Saggi critici di sociologia e di criminología. Fratelli Bocca, Torino
Vaccaro MA (1908) Genesi e funzione delle leggi penali. Fratelli Bocca, Torino
Valentí i Camp S (1922) Ideólogos, videntes y teorizantes. Minerva, Barcelona
Valls FJ (1971) La filosofía del Derecho de Dorado Montero. Universidad de Salamanca, Salamanca
Von Rotterdam E (1528) Ciceronianus. Spanish edition: De Rotterdam E (2011) El Ciceroniano o Del mejor estilo de oratoria (trans: Romo Feito F). Cátedra, Madrid
VV.AA. (1998) Una polémica y una generación, razón histórica del 1898. Actas del Congreso 1898, Pensamiento Político, Jurídico y Filosófico: balance de un Centenario. León, 10-13 de noviembre

Chapter 3
Historical Background

Abstract This chapter briefly summarises the historical context that shaped the intellectual, scientific and scholarly environment in Dorado Montero's timeline. After the definitive fall of the Spanish Empire, the movement known as 'regenerationism' emerged. It was the opportunity that was to correct the defects Spain had traditionally suffered from and to focus on inner aspects that Spain had neglected. Soon, the Spanish Silver Age started, and the focus shifted from America to Europe. Spain was far more open to the European influences than before. This allowed for the importation of certain doctrines, and a major criticism regarding scientific or scholarly postulates. Liberalism, the influence of France, Doctrinarism, Eclecticism and their influence in the way in which the State was built were very important. Among others, it influenced the way legislation was passed and in which Criminal policy was designed. Furthermore, the main traits of neoclassical, positivist and eclectic schools were outlined to provide with the ius-philosophical background of this chapter.

3.1 Spain and the Two Centuries

Positivism in nineteenth century Spain cannot be understood without the framework of its context. This turbulent century was characterised by a series of events which are vital in understanding how the country dealt with the new trends in penal thought.

One event was particularly impactful: the 1898 Spanish Disaster.[1] This event, straddling the nineteenth and twentieth centuries had its origins in the traumatic process of procuring independence for some Spanish American colonies around 1820.[2] Spain had still ruled over the Philippines, Puerto Rico and Cuba afterwards,

---

[1] Formally known as the Spanish-American War or *Guerra hispano-estadounidense*.

[2] Unlike the British colonies, the Spanish colonies did not obtain their independence on one clear, single date. Where the USA celebrates its independence in 1776, Latin America has no symbolic date for its liberation as a whole. The process focused on each state, with minor variations according to the degree of self-government and stability achieved within their borders: Paraguay, 1811;

J. Franco-Chasán, *The Reception of Positivism in Spain*, Studies in the History of Law and Justice 28, https://doi.org/10.1007/978-3-031-46435-5_3

but this changed after the Spanish-American war,[3] in which those possessions were lost and the Spanish Empire definitively came to an end. This was not just a military conflict, but a multifaceted crisis.

Firstly, the economy was seriously affected. The war took many lives,[4] and caused colossal material losses.[5] The debt incurred by the Spanish Monarchy was unmanageable, and led to a drastic raising of taxes:

> After the loss of the last colonies, Villaverde's stabilisation plan sought to balance the budget for the State based on both a tax increase and a rationalisation of public expenditure.[6]

However, the economic impact of the Disaster was much more limited in Spain compared to the former Caribbean colonies.[7] Spain had learned from their previous experiences in America: its non-recognition of the de facto long-independent states of the Americas "had led to drastic slumps in its trading activity" and threatened to "paralyse its entire trading system".[8] The case of Mexico was illustrative, since even if they intended to sign "trading treaties for no longer than ten years", those arrangements "were premature".[9] Yet, fifteen years after Mexico's political independence, both parties were still searching for a common economic agreement: "The Parties agree on reaching and concluding a trade and navigation agreement grounded on the principles of reciprocal advantages for each country".[10] *Rebus sic stantibus*, this time it was different. The war drove "a great deal of Spanish capital out of Cuba", but many "peninsulars" [Spaniards living on the island] were forced to remain. Despite the "scarce and confusing statistics" of the time, there was a documented "flight of Spanish capital from 1895 onwards", which "reached its peak in 1899". But as early as 1900, a "return thereof" took place and the "Spanish capital that flowed back into Cuba" substantially exceeded "that which fled because of the war".[11] Leaving aside the resumption of legal certainty, a decisive factor was the "North American intervention" which curbed the "descent towards economic

Venezuela, 1815; Argentina, 1816; Chile, 1818; Uruguay, 1820; Colombia, 1819; Peru and Mexico, 1821; Ecuador, 1822; United Provinces of Central America, 1823–1838; Bolivia, 1825; Cuba and Puerto Rico, 1898.

[3]From 25 April 1898 to 12 August 1898.

[4]A quick calculus from previous years to the conflict (1895) to one year after the end of the war (1899) show a total of 32,247 dead soldiers. Maluquer de Motes i Bernet (1999).

[5]For a careful study on dead soldiers and Spaniards returned to the island vid. Moreno Fraginals (1995), p. 296.

[6]Tejada Bergado (2007), p. 117.

[7]Vid. Anes y Álvarez de Castrillón (2009).

[8]Bernecker (2010a), p. 51.

[9]Bosch García (1947), p. 735.

[10]*Tratado definitivo de paz y amistad entre la República de México y su Majestad Católica* (1836), art. 4: "Las Altas Partes contratantes se convienen asimismo en proceder con la brevedad posible a ajustar y concluir un tratado de comercio y navegación fundado sobre principios de recíprocas ventajas para uno y otro país".

[11]Moreno Fraginals (1995), p. 292.

collapse".[12] In the labour force, the period was characterised by three developments: the beginning of syndicalism (1830–1869), the diffusion of internationalism (1870) and emergence of anarchism and socialism (1871–1900).[13] Spain underwent a moment of change and the transformation of its economic fabric. Significant events included the fire at the Bonaplata factory (1835), the creation of the first trade union "Sociedad de Tejedores de Barcelona" (1840), the first general strike in Spain (1855), the arrival of the Working People's Association (1868), the foundation of the Spanish Regional WPA Federation (1870), the passing of the first labour laws (1878), the creation of the anarchist-like Worker's Federation of the WPA Regional Spanish Federation (1881), and the foundation of the UGT (1888).

Politics was also in a period of upheaval.[14] Until that point, the state had adopted up to six different constitutions in less than seventy years (leaving aside the new constitution of 1931).[15] Even in the years prior to the Disaster, the tumultuous political path Spain walked had numerous ups and downs: María Cristina's Regency (1833–1840),[16] Espartero's Regency, O'Donell's uprising and the bombing of Barcelona (1841–1842), the Reign of Isabel II (1843–1868), the Provisional Government (1868–1870), Amadeo de Saboya's rule (1871–1872) and the First Spanish Republic (1873–1874).[17] There was also some regional conflict, like the Carlist wars: institutional normality was far from the general rule in nineteenth century Spain. However, the system laid down by the Bourbon Restoration (1875–1931)[18] managed the political instability well: "the constitutional basis of the Restoration system was the Constitution of 1876, which remained in force until 1933".[19] Surprisingly enough, the technique known as the 'dynastic turn' continued to work. By means of this system, the two dynastic parties (conservatives and liberals) alternated in power. In 1907, an Act was passed in order to eradicate despotism (referred as to *caciquismo*[20] in Spain),[21] but the problem continued for a long time.

---

[12] Moreno Fraginals (1995), p. 297.

[13] Aróstegui Sánchez (2011), p. 172.

[14] Ortega y Gasset (1909).

[15] Namely the Constitution of 1812, the Royal Statute of 1834, the Constitution of 1837, the Constitution of 1845, the Constitution of 1869 and the Constitution of 1876.

[16] Dorado Montero (1906a, b), pp. 141–184. Also, on this period see Pacheco (1841).

[17] Vid. the scheme depicted by Aróstegui Sánchez (2011), p. 82.

[18] Bernaldo de Quirós pointed out a relevant "study by Dorado on *Criminality in Spain during the period of Regency (1885-1902)* which was inserted later on in his *Criminology and Penology*". Vid. Bernaldo de Quirós (1898a, b, c), p. 102. Also, see Dorado Montero (1906a, b), pp. 141–184.

[19] Bernecker WL (2010b), p. 34: "Konstitutionelle Grundlage des Restaurationssystems war die Verfassung von 1876, die bis 1931 in Kraft blieb".

[20] The Spanish Royal Academy of Language (R.A.E.) defines it as follows: "Political system based on the domination or influence of the CHIEF". Diccionario RAE (2014) Real Academia de la Lengua Española, Madrid. https://dle.rae.es/?w=caciquismo. Accessed 5 May 2019.

[21] Commonly referred to as 'Ley Maura', in homage to its creator.

Furthermore, Spain lost prestige because of the Disaster, and this created the conditions for the rise of sub-state nationalist movements, offering a feasible alternative for fatally wounded Spanish pride. Their roots have been said to be in both "the dissatisfaction of small landowners" and the "emergence of a middle and lower-middle class in many countries, whose representatives almost always happened to be intellectuals".[22] Catalonia was in the middle of the *Renaixença*: the "cultural movement of linguistic and literary recovery carried out in Catalonia, Valencia and the Balearic Islands from the second half of the 19th century".[23] This was not a trend solely focused on cultural or literary features, and it acquired a strong political character in the form of Valentí Almirall, one of the ideologists of political Catalanism. This movement solidified with the so-called *Bases de Manresa*; essentially a project for a regional Catalan constitution (often regarded as the birth of political Catalanism).[24] Valencia was also boosted by this movement, whose classical icons are Teodor Llorente and Constantí Llombart. In the twentieth century, Valencianism evolved into a political movement embodied in the creation of *València Nova*.[25]

The Basque Country walked a different path to Catalanism. Where the latter was grounded on a pactist and autonomist tradition, nationalism emerged in the Basque Country as a radical reaction against the suppression of the foral[26] regime.[27] In 1876, the Spanish Government had unilaterally applied the Law of Confirmation of Fueros in the Basque Country. This subordinated the *fueros* of the three Basque provinces and Navarre to the Spanish Constitution of 1837.[28] Juan Iturralde y Suit, Serafín Olave and Hermilio de Oloriz were, among others, the highest representatives of the reactionary movement. They created the Basque Association in 1878.[29] In 1895, the Basque Nationalist Party (PNV) was founded and is nowadays regarded as the main nationalist movement in the region. Galician regionalism was almost reduced to folklore, but just after the so-called *Rexurdimento* in the twentieth century, it managed to cautiously acquire a political character.

---

[22]Hobsbawn (1971), p. 241: "*el descontento de los pequeños terratenientes y campesinos y la aparición en muchos países de una clase media y hasta de una baja clase media nacional, cuyos portavoces eran casi siempre los intelectuales*".

[23]Diccionari Normatiu Valencià (2014) Acadèmia Valenciana de la Llengua (AVL). https://www.avl.gva.es/lexicval/.

[24]De la Granja et al. (2001), p. 71.

[25]This was a movement split from the *Lo Rat-Penat* which struggled to maintain the Valencianist trend headed by Constantí Llombart. It encouraged all political parties to create a Valencianist project.

[26]Further development of the topic.

[27]Masferrer (2012), p. 260.

[28]Some legal historians believe it was unnecessary for Navarre, given that the region had already accepted their subordination in 1841 thanks to the *Ley Paccionada*.

[29]Popularly known as *Euskal Elkargoa*.

Thirdly, the Spanish-American war had an acute impact on the national psyche. The conflict led to the definitive loss of the Spanish Empire,[30] and with it, national pride: "the rapid collapse of Spanish forces in just 112 days, jointly with the loss of Cuba, Puerto Rico and the Philippines, was a long-open wound to national honour".[31] Spain lost virtually all its weight in international politics. There was just no way "to adjust to reality" those "patriotic and jingoistic sentiments" which were streaming from Spain; the conflict was not just a military engagement, but had a dimension engaging national pride and honour. The "ideological discourse" ended up supplanting any "political rationality"—even "generating another rationality".[32] The international press depicted Spain as a decadent nation with an unskilled, old-fashioned army grounded on a wholly corrupt political system.[33]

> Whereas newspapers, political meetings, and hundreds of broadsheets with popular patriotic poetry were increasingly elevating the historical greatness of an invincible Spain, in the theatre of events the American landing in eastern Cuba was taking place [. . .]. Disastrous news was coming from the Philippines. The great voices in Spain that pointed out the reality of the situation were drowned out. On 12 August, Spain and the United States signed the armistice, while Manila was still resisting.[34]

Frustration did not just affect the political ruling class: disappointment and dissatisfaction were widespread feelings across Spanish society.

3.2 Scenario for the Reception of Positivism

After Spain's military hegemony had crumbled,[35] an interesting new scene emerged. Traditionally, Spain had devoted all its resources to the governance, economic exploitation, and military protection of its colonies.[36] This had entailed an unavoidable neglect of some aspects of domestic politics. Fields such as education, science,

---

[30] After the signing of the Treaty of Paris in 1898, Spain not only undertook to leave Cuba, but also two other Spanish territories: Puerto Rico and the Philippines. The United States established a protectorate there. Spain attempted to rebuild its Empire in Africa, but after some years of African colonialism, Spain officially decolonised in 1975. Vid. Griffin (1937).

[31] Moreno Fraginals (1995), p. 295.

[32] Moreno Fraginals (1995), p. 294.

[33] Aróstegui Sánchez (2011), p. 214.

[34] Moreno Fraginals (1995), pp. 286–287: "Mientras los diarios, las reuniones políticas, y centenares de hojas sueltas con poesías populares patrioteras elevaban cada vez más el tono de la grandeza histórica de la España invencible, en el teatro de los hechos se producía el desembarco norteamericano en el oriente de Cuba [. . .]. De Filipinas se recibían noticias desastrosas. Las grandes voces que en España señalaban la realidad eran ahogadas. El 12 de agosto España y Estados Unidos firmaban el armisticio, cuando todavía Manila resistía".

[35] In a previous Cuban war, Cánovas del Castillo (President of the Spanish Government) had stated that they would defend Cuba "to the last man and the last peseta". This reflected Spain's desperation to defend the remnants of its dying empire.

[36] Buisson (1984), p. 249.

and literature, as well as the traditional backbone infrastructure of any thriving modern country (railways, transportation, and general communications) fell far behind average European and American standards. Spain therefore turned to focus on commerce, literacy, and technology. Thus, at least theoretically, there was a favourable context for the reception of positivism: according to the spirit of regeneration, old theories and ius-philosophical postulates gave way to new ones, and positivist theories should have had an easier reception than in the preceding decades. The new climate of openness and criticism allowed positivism to permeate and influence Spanish doctrine (although not necessarily legislation). This included some of the developments set out below.

Firstly, an ideology known as "Regenarationism" emerged.[37] This was an "ideological movement which started in Spain at the end of the 19th century, a product of the decadent feeling that led to a complete regeneration of Spanish life".[38] Scholars defended this position as a unique, single opportunity to correct the defects Spain had traditionally suffered from. According to them, a golden chance had been lost when the Glorious Revolution of 1868 did not succeed (Sexenio Democrático).[39] It was now time for real change. Every cultural proposal included a sharp criticism of mainstream Spanish culture. Costa held that "the Cid's sepulchre should be locked out forever",[40] referring to the need to avoid any attitude based on self-indulgence. Former national glories should be buried forever. Costa's second most famous aphorism, "school and larder",[41] contained the spirit of the new era. The new politics should focus on the well-being of the population: on science, education, and culture.

Then, Krausism—the system of thought conceived by the German philosopher Friedrich Krause and discussed in Chap. 1—came to Spain. Reformist policy, however, did not have much impact on real life: there was a single, shy set of reforms, but these did not manage to tackle structural problems. Instead, the Restoration system from 1898 continued into the first third of the twentieth century. Dorado Montero himself had virtually no faith in this process of renewal. After the loss of the colonies, he commented that:

> Once we concluded our last colonial wars and after the Treaty of Paris was signed; when we Spaniards had to convince ourselves [. . .] that blusters are useless and that strength is not improvised in a day, but must be created painstakingly and gradually. When we felt that spirit of regeneration and after it seemed we were all actually very decided to undertake it, I

[37] Andrés-Gallego (1971).

[38] Diccionario RAE (2014): "Movimiento ideológico iniciado en España a fines del siglo XIX que, motivado principalmente por el sentimiento de decadencia, propugna una regeneración completa de la vida española".

[39] Such period lasted from 1868 until 1874, and it attempted to establish a democratic regime (Amadeo de Saboya's Parliamentary Monarchy) and the First Spanish Republic.

[40] Costa (1914).

[41] Costa (1902), pp. 65 ff.

> showed scepticism and asserted that such an 'awakening' was nothing but an appearance, and after the momentum was gone, everything would be left as before, just as it happened.[42]

Cultural reform was, however, more noticeable. It led to the formation of a very consistent group of intellectuals, writers, and thinkers, commonly referred to as the "98 Generation". Ramiro de Maetzu, Azorín, Valle-Inclán, Machado, Unamuno, Pío Baroja and Marañón were prolific writers who devoted all their energies to thinking about the nature of Spain (or the "*Ser de España*"). Despite being a modern intellectual movement, they strongly rejected European culture and their mission of cultural renewal nonetheless defended Spanish traditions. This cultural change could also be seen in the sciences:

> An unprecedented renewal of Spanish science took place with the introduction of positivism and with new discoveries in medicine, the experimental sciences and sociology.[43]

The development of the new Criminal law and its related sciences in nineteenth century Spain was tentative. Santiago Ramón y Cajal, Gregorio Marañón and other great scientists dominated the cultural scene known as the "Spanish Silver Age". In 1914, the "14 Generation" replaced the aforementioned movement. This cultural and literary trend was characterised, unlike the 98 Generation, by openness to European cultures and a disposition to absorb new ideals known to the rest of the continent. Ayala, Eugeni d'Ors (the main representative of the *Noucentisme*),[44] Gasset (and his *Revista de Occidente*), de la Serna, Miró and others established themselves as the main personalities. The period witnessed how a rise in literacy among the Spanish population, and an expansion of the new media.[45] However, notwithstanding that "schooling became compulsory in Spain in 1857", child labour "continued to be a very widespread reality".[46]

Meanwhile, a new anti-military social conscience had developed. Criticism took place more openly, and several trenchant anti-establishment works saw the light, among which *Oligarquía y caciquismo sobre la forma actual de gobierno en España* was particularly noteworthy.[47] The military was aware of the crisis, and, looking for someone to blame, they turned to the government that controlled them. Given that the 98 Disaster and other significant problems had a common origin in political

---

[42]Costa (1902), p. 361: "Al concluir nuestras últimas guerras coloniales y firmarse el tratado de París; cuando los españoles tuvimos que convencernos, luego de tener la cabeza rota, de que no sirve echar bravatas y de que la fortaleza no se improvisa en nada, sino que hay que irla creando trabajosa y paulatinamente; cuando nos entró aquella calentura de regeneración, pareciendo que todos estábamos decididos de verdad á emprenderla, yo me manifesté desde el primer momento incrédulo y afirmé que aquel 'despertamiento', según lo llamaban algunos, de las energías latentes era todo espuma, simple apariencia, y que pasado el instante de la fiebre volvería todo á quedar lo mismo que antes, como en efecto ha quedado".

[43]Aróstegui Sánchez (2011), p. 215.

[44]The Catalan equivalent to Spanish *Novecentismo*.

[45]Tiana Ferrer (2006), p. 653.

[46]Tiana Ferrer (2006), p. 653.

[47]Costa (1902).

corruption and inefficient leaders, the gap between politicians and military leaders grew. Anti-military positions doubted the role of the military in society, and in turn, the military advocated a hard authoritarianism to suffocate political corruption. The chasm among the two positions widened, until finally, a point of no-return was reached: tensions translated into violence, military outbreaks, and revolts, as well as undesirable outcomes of all sorts like the Primo de Rivera's takeover in 1923 or Franco's coup d'état some years later. The escalating degeneration of army ideals eventually led the Old Continent to the First World War, the rise of fascism, the consolidation of Nazism, and the Second World War.

The influence of positivist theories on European legal orders grew steadily. One of the first manifestations was the draft of the Swiss Penal Code. Its main author, Carl Stooss,[48] proposed a methodical structure for several measures to deal with dangerous individuals (those with learning disabilities, who were non-chargeable or were minors).[49] Nevertheless, this was not officially implemented in criminal legislation, and consolidation waited in most European countries until the end of the inter-war period (between WWI and WWII).[50]

Some countries were pioneers in their reception of positivism (like the Italy of Lombroso or Switzerland), others were latecomers. Two main waves of positivism should be distinguished: early positivism (also referred to as "Social Defence") and social defence (*Défense Sociale Nouvelle—DSN*).[51] What at first glance seemed to be a savage, inconceivable doctrine for many European States (early positivism), was progressively accepted as it was made more palatable by the *DSN*. This brought to an end the controversy on security measures, as their conception was relaxed: "it will go from a penal intervention previous to the commission of the crime, to a conception of the security measure as subsidiary to the penalty".[52] This second framing, which developed in the twentieth century, was the one in force in the majority of democratic criminal codes in Europe.

Spain, like other European states, accepted positivism—but with a nuance. Spanish doctrine embraced positivist ideas on the determination of the penalty. However, the rationale (*i.e.* the justification) of the penalty encountered critical opposition. Even if this rationale was accepted in neighbouring countries (Italy,

[48] For an outline of Stooss' doctrinal criminal environment, vid. Germann (2020), pp. 259–276.

[49] Stooss (1892), p. 215: "Denn die Strafbarkeit des Versuches beruht auf seiner Gefährlichkeit, und diese nimmt zu, je mehr sich der Versuch der Vollendung nähert, sie nimmt ab, je mehr er sieh davon entfernt".

[50] Masferrer (2020a), p. 312: "Although it [the International Union of Criminal Law] was dissolved after the First World War – to be re-founded as the current International Association of Criminal Law (A.I.D.P.) in Paris on 14 March 1924–, it was an institution that also served as a means of reception or understanding of the New School in Europe in general and in Spain in particular".

[51] De la Rasilla (2020), p. 5: "We know nowadays that the doctrine of social defence by Marc Ancel developed into different schools of thought. That being said, a common trait with the school of Saldaña was the pursue of "tailoring the penalty to the personal characteristics of the criminal so as to facilitate his reintegration and to better protect society".

[52] Sierra López (1997), p. 66.

for instance), it did not convince Spanish scholars.[53] The reception of this idea was therefore limited to its technical value, leaving the legal philosophy and positivist rationale in second place.[54] The material conditions for its acceptance (and even for its introduction) were lacking, with known problems in Spanish academia: "the effort of scholars back then at the end of the 19th century had to be titanic: with unskilled professors, a lack of languages teaching at medium and superior level, and poorly equipped libraries".[55]

Liberalism also struggled to gain a foothold in Spain.[56] This ideology was somewhat familiar to intellectual elites and in literary circles in the eighteenth century, but its usefulness in practical terms was not considered until the nineteenth century.[57] The year 1812 brought one of the most popular demonstrations of liberalism: the Constitution of 1812. Popularly known as "La Pepa", it was the clearest example of how liberalism was not something exclusively British.[58] When the king was kidnapped, leaving the government leaderless, the people and leading classes organised themselves and developed a working legal system. The latter, of course, had all sorts of deficiencies, but it had a deep impact on the democratic history of Spain. To modernise the state, to revitalise its legal culture and to offer institutional resistance (not just *guerrillas*) were no small achievements. This heralded the beginning of Spain's "legal age". The Kingdom of Spain reached maturity. Afterwards, the authoritarian and absolutist reaction of the "desired one"[59] entailed an enormous setback, forestalling modern legal culture and liberalism. Both briefly resurged for a short period (the Liberal Triennium: 1820–1823), but were again repressed.[60] The state entered a period of conservatism which established the conditions for a political trend known as "Doctrinarism".

Doctrinarism was a political doctrine which hybridised monarchy with the ideals of the French Revolution.[61] It defended a centrism that advocated for rule by the middle class ("mesocracy"). Its natural tendency was towards a discreet moderatism,

---

[53] Not only the neoclassicals, but also all the eclectics were against it.

[54] This ought not to be confused with a parallel idea: the impact of positivism was translated into doctrine and scholarly influence, rather than laws and codes.

[55] Antón Oneca (1951), p. 7.

[56] Fontana i Lázaro (2007), pp. 9–10.

[57] Masferrer (2012), p. 268: "a period in which both the liberalism and the bourgeois revolution were consummated, with the exception of two periods that witnessed a return to absolute monarchy (1814–1820 and 1823–1833)".

[58] Varela Suanzes (1997), pp. 97–124.

[59] A popular expression of affection used to refer Fernando VII. Ironically, this devotion to the king did not benefit the general populace.

[60] For a general overview of Spanish Legal History, vid. Escudero Antonio (1985).

[61] The Spanish Royal Academy of Language highlights the French influence on this idea: "during the Restoration, it combined both liberal and conservative ideas, and subordinated them to a set of doctrines". Diccionario RAE (2014).

and it was named after "conservatism" in Britain.[62] Doctrinarism was particularly important in both Spain and France, which witnessed a strengthening of their relationship during the eighteenth and nineteenth centuries. This trend avoided extreme positions by bringing together many ideas that had been thought opposed, such as liberty and authority, elite government and popular power, revolution and conservatism, and an inflexible *autoritas* limited by institutions, autonomy, and order. Specifically, in Spain a mixture of a hereditary system (arising from monarchy) and representative government structures (like the *juntas*) was proposed.

This enabled positivist thinking to gain prominence in a way that would not have been possible otherwise. Some countries underwent a radical transformation from the Classical School to pure positivism (like Italy). However, in Spain, cultural and philosophical trends prevented that: either positivism entered Spanish thinking as a part of eclecticism, or it would not enter at all. The role of nature and of natural law in Spain was stressed in the criminal doctrine of the nineteenth century. There was supposedly a common basis, i.e. a shared philosophical culture for all human beings. When Pufendorf revisited and criticised Grotius and Hobbes, he concluded that a common culture can be defended without need of God (and, therefore, without the need for natural law).[63] Doctrinarism facilitated the reception of positivism because it led to moderation in politics and eclecticism in criminal law.[64] Some of the most well-known doctrinaire figures were Joaquín Francisco Pacheco,[65] Cánovas del Castillo,[66] and Donoso Cortés.[67] The latter claimed that "Doctrinarism and Eclecticism are often considered political synonyms".[68]

---

[62]Britannica (1768): "The 19th century was in many ways antithetical to conservatism, both as a political philosophy and as a program of particular parties identified with conservative interests. The Enlightenment had engendered widespread belief in the possibility of improving the human condition—a belief, that is, in the idea of progress—and a rationalist disposition to tamper with or discard existing institutions or practices in pursuit of that goal. The French Revolution gave powerful expression to this belief, and the early Industrial Revolution and advances in science reinforced it. The resulting rationalist politics embraced a broad segment of the political spectrum, including liberal reformism, trade- union socialism (or social democracy), and ultimately Marxism. In the face of this constant rationalist innovation, conservatives often found themselves forced to adopt a merely defensive role, so that the political initiative lay always in the other camp".

[63]Masferrer (2020b), pp. 2–3: "Moral law—or natural law—is the light of the intellect, or practical reason—that directs the acts of everyone in accordance with the purpose—or telos—of human life, namely, happiness. Moral laws are supposed to distinguish good from evil and provide the principles that enlighten human behaviour and lead humans to their perfection and to a life of virtue. Moral laws or natural laws affects the whole moral order, as far as it is naturally knowable to unaided human reason. Natural law is simply moral law as far as it is knowable by natural human reason and it refers to all moral virtues, regulating their rational structure, and also forbids all vices".

[64]Ramos Vázquez (2013), pp. 261–273.

[65]Pacheco (1881).

[66]Cánovas del Castillo (1800, 1892, 1910).

[67]Donoso Cortés (1851).

[68]Donoso Cortés (1984), pp. 8 ff.

The legal character of nineteenth century Spain was therefore one of penal eclecticism, and eclecticism occupied the place that positivism had in other countries.[69] Once it was accepted that Spain was better suited to eclectic approaches, the success of both eclecticism and the new 'positivist' trends was natural. Criminal eclecticism gained momentum in Spain between the years 1844 and 1855 (the "Moderate Decade"). This laid the conditions for the reception of positivism, and predetermined the degree to which Lombroso's theories of would be accepted thirty years later. Positivism did not, however, have a great reception in Spain, and its influence could be considered both anecdotal and isolated.[70] Most of the law manuals indicate this: Spain had few authors writing in this sphere. The legislative trends of the also clearly demonstrate that Lombroso's doctrine was not influential. The Criminal Code of 1822 contained some eclectic elements, and provided a hint as to how a future criminal code would look.[71] Masferrer and Iñesta have discussed a lack of foothold in Spanish doctrine here.[72] It was doubtful that such a code could be effectively applied at the time,[73] but the Criminal Code of 1848 was more important.[74] The latter combined Rossi's eclectic spirit with an older utilitarianism.[75] The main representative of this idea was Joaquín Francisco Pacheco, but virtually all the members of the Codifying Commission were influenced by Rossi. Tomás María de Vizmanos and Cirilo Álvarez depicted the Code as a golden mean:

> we will stumble with both individualism and socialism at the same time; with utility (if not considered as a principle, as a duty to the legislature); with duty as a measure against crime; with the individual's freedom as a general rule; with exculpation based on the limits of intelligence; with the encumbered personality; with proclaimed equality and with the ruins of the former State.[76]

The predominantly eclectic character of the Code was evidenced as well: "Teruel Carralero sees in the 1848 Code the influence of the criminal reform of Beccaria, the penitentiary advances of Howard as well as French encyclopaedism, all adapted to Spanish circumstances thanks to Pacheco".[77] It was not until 1903 that eclecticism was strongly challenged by Silvela. This was partially because the 1848 Code was still predominantly retributive. One of its main features was that it tried to determine

---

[69] Iñesta-Pastor (2013), pp. 65–103.

[70] Masferrer (2020a), p. 337.

[71] Casabó Ruiz (1968).

[72] Masferrer (2020a), p. 337. Also Iñesta-Pastor (2003), pp. 493–521; Iñesta-Pastor (2010a), pp. 151–160; Iñesta-Pastor (2010b); Iñesta-Pastor (2011).

[73] Alonso y Alonso (1946), p. 15.

[74] It would establish the structure that all future criminal codes followed.

[75] Cañizares Navarro (2013), p. 133.

[76] De Vizmanos and Álvarez (1848).

[77] Iñesta-Pastor (2011), p. 277.

the penalty in a very systematic way (almost mathematically),[78] so it reflected the nature of the crime and was proportionate. The principle of "material accumulation" was maintained: "you do the crime; you do the time". This resembled the approach of the *Lex Talionis*,[79] which was important in early Iberian criminal law, as Dorado Montero noted.[80] Mitigating circumstances did not exist,[81] and the code provided for perpetual and long-term penalties as well as afflictive ones. This Code also used penalties aimed at corrective behaviour, but most were focused on retribution. For certain crimes, *e.g.,* Article 238, which concerned false testimony, imposed the same penalty on the plaintiff and defendant if it was proved that experts had rendered false testimony. Intimidation was a guiding principle of this Code. Doctrinarism described a hierarchy of goals in punishment: retribution (expiation), intimidation, making harm impossible, and reforming the criminal.

> Among all of them, the legislature could not disregard the first two, especially retribution since it grounds the legitimacy of the punishment and it is the fundamental one around which other accessory, accidental and variable goals settle themselves.[82]

The predominant role of retribution was clear. Intimidation was also conspicuously present: the death penalty, being chained to a post for public humiliation, degrading punishments, severe penalties for political crimes, public order disturbance crimes, etc. Several kinds of conduct were not considered punishable, on the basis of the principle of lack of amendment. The latter concerned prevailing ideas about reinsertion into society and re-education, the modern ideas concerning which were unimaginable then. Reforming a criminal was difficult, since prison sentences tended to be very long. Cadalso acknowledged the harshness of such penalties, and their incompatibility with the goal of reform.[83] Nevertheless, he defended this Code, asserting it would set a precedent and be the basis upon which the amendment principle developed in future. That principle was indeed improved in later codes, but not until the twentieth century. The Code of 1848 in fact entailed an enormous setback: it was a temporary annihilation of the idea of special prevention.

---

[78] Even such basic rights as association were restricted. According to Isabel Ramos Vázquez, Article 8, of the Criminal Code of 1848 formally acknowledged the right of association, but afterwards new laws restricted it again. Vid. Ramos Vázquez (2020), pp. 393–439.

[79] For the relationship between Criminal law and the Lex Talionis, vid. May (2019), pp. 150–168. For the specific changes in Criminal law depending on the weight of such principle, vid. Van Den Haag (1992).

[80] Dorado Montero (1901), pp. 20–37.

[81] They developed soon after, and their origin can be traced back to the Middle Ages. Vid., Masferrer (2012), pp. 353–354: "The circumstances of the criminal act, which in the codification period were known as aggravating, mitigating or exculpatory and nowadays are still valid, were discussed in earlier normative and doctrinal sources prior to the nineteenth century. Specifically, medieval and modern legal doctrines had pointed to the important role of some circumstances".

[82] Iñesta-Pastor (2016), p. 218.

[83] Núñez (2013), p. 105 and p. 151.

As a last remark on pre-positivist Spain, let us briefly mention the Criminal Code of 1870. Its greatest exponent was Alejandro Groizard.[84] The Code was still anchored in eclecticism, but with some minor modifications carried out by Ortolan and Tissot.[85]

The technique used did not involve any great advance, but it brought certain topics to the attention of the public. Public liberties, suppression of opposition, conspiracy as a punishable crime, crimes of worship and in printing were incorporated into the Code.[86] Unfortunately, it did not change much more, and the core of this Code was still retribution and intimidation.[87]

Finally, Dorado Montero got to see the Proyecto Montilla (1902), elaborated by Bernaldo de Quirós, which "would accept the anthropological and social trends of the time", but he would die before the Proyecto Pinilla (1922) was passed.[88]

3.3 Development of Positivism: Status Quaestionis

The history of ideas is like the movement of a pendulum. From Ancient Greece and Rome to the Middle Ages; from the Middle Ages to the Renaissance; from the Renaissance to Absolutism; from Absolutism to the Enlightenment; from the Enlightenment to Romanticism, etc. The pendulum moves relentlessly from one extreme to another. This process was identified by Emmanuel Kant in *Der Streit der Fakultäten*. Probably under the influence of Christoph Wieland,[89] Kant believed that the progress of history and humanity were not linear, but involved a dynamic set of ups and downs. He powerfully criticised what he called "human foolishness": whenever man decided to take the right path, he would, at some point, invert the direction and ruin everything.[90] Then, he would rebuild and tear everything down once again. Kant compared humankind with Sisyphus' struggle to push a rock to the top of a hill (*e.g.*, achieving a goal, social peace, a fair political system, or whatever other purpose), only to let the rock roll down (demolish everything, contribute to decadence or, simply, allowing it to go), and start again from the beginning. This eternal and, in Kant's depiction "absurd dynamism" meant that "good keeps alternating with evil, by means of advance and setback, so that this game where our species swings back and forth should be considered nothing more than a carnival

[84]Groizard (1870).

[85]They were the main representatives of the Classical School in France, just as they were Romagnosi, Carrara or Carmignani in Italy; Binding, Feuerbach or Berner in Germany; and Francisco Pacheco in Spain.

[86]Iñesta-Pastor (2016), p. 226.

[87]Masferrer (2003).

[88]Castejón (1933).

[89]A German philosopher who dealt with this topic. Vid. Wieland (1774).

[90]It is not our intention to address abderitism here.

masquerade. It does not have even the major value found in other species playing the same game. They [animals] practice it with lower costs and without the waste of knowledge".[91] Criminal law was affected by this reality.

Two trends , and two groups of schools, clashed: the Neoclassical and the Positivist. With minor variations and logical evolutions, the structure of modern criminal law in Europe remained more or less uniform from its birth in the second half of the eighteenth century until the nineteenth century[92] under the influence of dominant Neoclassical Schools. However, at the end of the nineteenth century and beginning of the twentieth, they faced a new competitor: the so-called Positivist Schools[93] which challenged their hegemony.

3.3.1 The Neoclassical Schools

Legal literature often interchangeably refers to this group of schools as "Classical" or "Neoclassical", and both descriptions are valid. However, the latter related to liberal Criminal law more. The most prominent representative of this movement was Cesare Beccaria and his well-known work *Dei delitti e delle pene*,[94] published in 1764. Other authors[95] could also be mentioned: John Howard,[96] the Count of Mirabeau,[97]Jean-Paul Marat,[98] Karl Ludwig Wilhelm von Grolman,[99] Muyart de Vouglans,[100] Scipion Bexon,[101] Giovanni Carmignani,[102] Montesquieu,[103] Gaetano

[91]Kant (2003), p. 156: "un absurdo dinamismo merced al cual el bien va alternándose con el mal mediante avance y retroceso, de suerte que todo este juego de vaivén de nuestra especie consigo misma sobre este globo terráqueo habría de ser considerado como una farsa carnavalesca, lo cual no puede proporcionarle ante los ojos de la razón un valor mayor al ostentado por otras especies animales que practican ese juego con menos gastos y sin el derroche del entendimiento".

[92]The most complete work covering the evolution of Criminal law in this period is Sainz Guerra (2004).

[93]This chapter analyses three principal positions, opting for describing them in plural: Neoclassical Schools, Positivist Schools and Eclectic Schools. This is intended to emphasise the enormous degree of difference even among branches of the same school.

[94]Beccaria (1762, 1804, 2014).

[95]For a longer, detailed catalogue of authors within the neoclassical school vid. Sánchez González (2004).

[96]Howard (1777).

[97]Mirabeau (1775, 1782, 1788).

[98]Marat (1773, 1774, 1780).

[99]Grolman (1810, 1825, 1826).

[100]Muyart de Vouglans (1757, 1762, 1780).

[101]Bexon (1802, 1807).

[102]Carmignani (1831, 1832, 1833, 1837, 1851).

[103]Montesquieu (1750).

Filangieri,[104] Gian Domenico Romagnosi,[105] Jeremy Bentham,[106] Ludwig Andreas Feuerbach,[107] Immanuel Kant,[108] Georg Wilhelm Friedrich Hegel,[109] Voltaire,[110] Manuel de Lardizábal y Uribe,[111] or Marcos Gutiérrez.[112] In turn, some authors mentioned here are doctrinally considered 'eclecticals', which ought not be surprising given the challenge in categorising ius-philosophical thought. Dorado Montero himself acknowledged that during his lifetime "there [were] are many penalists who, despite remaining within the Classical School, admitted the need to make their rigid frameworks more elastic".[113] He was referring to Louis Proal[114] and his work *Le crime et la peine*.[115] The method was to "pay attention to the outcomes of modern scientific research, and even criminal anthropology and criminal sociology".[116]

The key event which led this wide school to decisively depart from mediaeval systems of thought was the French Revolution. Doctrine became well-known for its absolute respect for the legality principle, the elimination of arbitrary justice, commitment to free will and the retribution principle. Some of this arose from a reaction to the rigid precepts of scholasticism and Early Middle Age supporters of ius-naturalism; others originated in opposition to injustices in the mediaeval system. This latter included illegitimate ways of obtaining evidence (torture, physical and psychological coercion or blackmailing, among others), discriminatory treatment depending on the estate one belonged to, etc.

The schools used the deductive method, i.e. an *a priori* method. This methodology was solidly grounded in the thriving rationalism of the age, according to which one might infer something arising from a general norm. The main objective of the law was perceived to be the re-establishment of legal order. Crime affected everybody the same way, and they believed everybody had the same degree of responsibility. Individual liability was grounded on two principles: moral responsibility and freewill.

Notwithstanding this, utilitarian thinking also appeared inside this school, although its precepts seemed to be divided between the Neoclassical and Positivist Schools. Utilitarianism emerged at the very end of the Neoclassical School. It

---

[104] Filangieri (1870).

[105] Romagnosi (1791).

[106] Bentham (1780, 1782, 1830).

[107] Feuerbach (1841).

[108] Kant (1764, 1783, 1784, 1787, 1788, 1797, 1981, 1989a, b, c, 1994, 1999a, b).

[109] Hegel (1807, 1817, 1821, 1968).

[110] Voltaire (1764).

[111] Lardizábal y Uribe (1782).

[112] Marcos Gutiérrez (1826).

[113] Garofalo (1890), p. 23.

[114] Proal (1890a), p. 27; Proal (1890b); Proal (1892); Proal (1900), p. 683; Proal (1890c), p. 52; Proal (1912), pp. 422–443.

[115] Proal (1892).

[116] Garofalo (1890), p. 23.

contained some problematic elements, such as the commercialisation of justice and Criminal law arising from the core postulate of utility and efficiency-oriented positions. More positive aspects involved, remarkably, considering that the penalty should be useful. The idea was that punishment should pursue a higher ideal (rehabilitation), instead of forcing one person to serve a penalty (often a disproportionate and overly long one). Criminal and penitentiary studies have repeatedly shown that, serving a penalty destroys the personality of the condemned, and sometimes prison did nothing but worsen the convict. At the end of the eighteenth century, mainstream ideas about punishment changed, progressively evolving and improving the penitentiary system[117] using ideals introduced by John Howard. At the end of the nineteenth century, positivist ideas had been adopted even by pure Neoclassicists, who also unconsciously implemented positivist elements.

In short, a criminal was not conceived as a "criminal" but rather as a "person that has committed a crime". This individual was "cured" when he served his penalty, and thus, extinguished his moral responsibility. Regrettably, according to Dorado Montero, this was not always the case in reality:

> Not all the individuals carrying out acts considered as criminal, either by laws, writers or people belonging to a certain social circle, are criminals.[118]

That was why crime had a moral aspect: the perspective was not an exclusivist, biological one. Rehabilitating the criminal was not one of the objectives of such schools. Their goal was classical retributionism; although some sub-branches might consider 'rehabilitiation' a remote and accessory objective.[119]

Absolutist theories were usually predominant in the Neoclassical Schools. For them, punishment developed a mere retributive function: an eye for an eye, a tooth for a tooth. The *Lex Talionis* was a forerunner of these absolute theories. Being 'absolute' meant they were not conditioned to anything and the retribution was a *conditio sine qua non* to bring justice. Nowadays, we do not take this attitude, but some scholars have proposed that, according to Hesiod's *Theogony*, revenge as a type of justice was not necessarily irrational:

> The duty of revenge emerges in that a universal principle (*Θεμις*) has been breached – it has been disrespected (*Αlδὼς*)-. Therefore, in revenge the man rises [. . .] because he demands from the other man -he who performed the crime- the retroactive admission of his responsibility.[120]

[117] Ramos Vázquez (2013), pp. 190–208.

[118] Dorado Montero (1902), p. 37: "No todos los individuos que realizan actos de los que se consideran como delitos, ya por las leyes, ya por los escritores, ya por las personas pertenecientes en general á un círculo social determinado, son delincuentes".

[119] Moreu (2006), pp. 755–785.

[120] Ibarra Becerra (2016), p. 295: "*La obligación de venganza aparece por cuanto un principio universal (*Θεμις*) ha sido quebrantado –se le ha faltado al respeto (*Αlδὼς*)–. En la venganza el hombre se eleva, por lo tanto, a su consideración genérica, porque exige retrospectivamente del otro hombre, del que ha perpetrado el crimen –que en este contexto no puede ser otro que el asesinato– la admisión de su responsabilidad*".

Dorado Montero often complained that the 'purportedly' eclectic authors of his time were actually 'stuck' in the neoclassical criminal law framework, with ideas about free will which reverted to traditional views: "what idea do they have other than the penalty is evil and a punishment?".[121] It was precisely this theoretical incoherence, as we shall see later on, that caused them countless "troubles".[122]

3.3.2 *The Positivist Schools*

The Positivist Schools originated in a reaction against the Neoclassical Schools. Their main representatives were Cesare Lombroso,[123] Enrico Ferri[124] and Raffaele Garofalo.[125] Their Spanish counterparts were Quintiliano Saldaña,[126] Concepción Arenal,[127] Rafael Salillas[128] (to whom Dorado Montero devoted an article, later integrated into one of his books)[129] and Federico Castejón y Martínez de Arizala.[130] Contemporary scholars often have discrepancies in how they classify them, and it is important to note the sub-schools within this movement: the technical-legal school (von Beling[131] and Arturo Rocco[132]), critical positivism (Adolphe Prins,[133] Anton Gerard van Hamel[134] and Franz von Liszt,[135] who created the International Union of Penal Law), and the so-called *Terza Scuola* (Emanuele Carnevale[136] and Bernardino Alimena[137]). Unsurprisingly, it was said that "Italians invented Criminal law four times: the first time in the Roman Empire and all its legal work; the second time with Beccaria who commanded men to 'Go and accomplish the Law'; the third with Lombroso, Ferri and Garofalo and their command 'Go and study the man'; and finally, the fourth when trying to reunite and harmonise previous concepts in order to

[121] Dorado Montero (1915a, b), pp. 429–431.

[122] Dorado Montero (1915a, b), pp. 429–431.

[123] Lombroso (1884, 1890a, b, 1895a, b, 1902, 1910, 1911, 1927).

[124] Ferri (1907, 1925, 1928).

[125] Garofalo (1880a, b, 1884, 1885, 1889, 1890, 1914).

[126] Saldaña (1920, 1923, 1929a, b, 1935).

[127] Arenal (1877); Arenal (1883), pp. 468–475.

[128] Salillas (1888); Salillas (1896); Salillas (1899), pp. 117–142.

[129] Dorado Montero (1915a, b).

[130] Castejón (1914, 1926, 1934, 1936, 1944, 1947, 1952).

[131] Beling (1894, 1906, 1928, 1936, 1943, 1968, 1971, 1992, 2002, 2009).

[132] Rocco (1932, 2001, 2003, 2009).

[133] Prins (1875, 1886, 1888, 1899, 1910).

[134] Van Hamel (1889).

[135] Von Liszt (1896, 1898, 1906, 1927, 1970, 1984).

[136] Carnevale (1932).

[137] Alimena (1887, 1894, 1906, 1913, 1915, 1975).

set up the *Terza Scuola* of Criminal law".[138] Further, there was a humanist school (Vicente Lanza[139]), neopositivism (Filippo Grispigni,[140] Ferdinando Puglia[141] and Eugenio Florián[142]), and correctionalism. Correctionalism, in its turn, may be divided into pure correctionalism (Karl David August Röder),[143] judicial protection (Francisco Giner de los Ríos),[144] and the *Derecho Protector de los Criminales* (Pedro Dorado Montero). In the latter, one should include Dorado Montero's most famous supporters: Constancio Bernaldo de Quirós[145] and Jiménez de Asúa.[146]

In his *Problemas jurídicos contemporáneos*, Dorado Montero briefly outlined the main changes the transition from neoclassical to positivist postulates had generated in criminal law, especially the fact that the principle "nullem crimen sine lege" was substituted for the discretion of the judiciary; the abstract principle of equality before the law was replaced by the individualisation of punishments; establishing the amount of time to be served in prison at the outset lost terrain in favour of indeterminate sentences; and the conception of criminal penalties as a punishment evolved into the idea of punishment as a treatment.[147]

At that time, the boundaries between the different manifestations of the Positivist Schools were blurred. This is without even considering those sciences 'less directly related' to law such as social economy,[148] social philosophy or political economy. That being said, the core disciplines (criminal law, sociology and criminal anthropology) were deeply intertwined and often confused. Even for the most talented scholars, there was practical difficulty: "sometimes it is not easy to set out the boundaries between the new theories, such as, for example, between correctionalism and the positivist school (or Criminal Anthropology), as Bernaldo de Quirós acknowledged when dealing with this issue".[149] Notwithstanding this struggle, Dorado Montero pointed out the need to establish a clear delimitation:

[138] Rodríguez Manzanera (1981), pp. 245 y 246. Original text: "*se dice que los italianos han inventado cuatro veces el Derecho Penal: La primera con el imperio de Roma, al realizar la gran obra jurídica; la segunda con Beccaria, al decir al hombre: "Ve y cumple el Derecho"; la tercera con Lombroso, Ferri y Garófalo, al decir al Derecho: "Ve y estudia al hombre"; y la cuarta al tratar de reunir y conciliar los conceptos anteriores para fundar la "Tercera Escuela" de Derecho Penal*".

[139] Lanza (1906). Of the same author, vid. Lanza (1924).

[140] Grispigni (1928, 1945, 1952, 2009).

[141] Puglia (1883). Of the same author, vid. Puglia (1902).

[142] Florián (1925, 1934, 1995).

[143] Röder (1875).

[144] Giner de los Ríos (1875, 1876, 1889, 1898).

[145] Bernaldo de Quirós (1898a, b, c, 1904, 1931, 1940).

[146] Jiménez de Asúa (1913, 1915, 1961, 1963).

[147] Dorado Montero (1893a, b), p. 6.

[148] Dorado Montero (1891), p. 17: "with works like those of Roscher, Hildebrand, Knies, Cliffe, Leslie, Scheel, Roesler, Schäffle, etc.".

[149] Masferrer (2020b), p. 4.

> Criminal law and criminal anthropology are not the same thing, but they are two things which cannot be separated. Criminal sociology and criminal law are not the same thing either, but they are two things intimately related as well, just as the whole and the part are. We believe that the relationship between those sciences is as follows: just as sociology is not the law, but is inside it; law is inside criminal sociology [. . .].[150]

Besides, Dorado Montero explained that "Italian authors writing on positivist legal philosophy and sociology" had never accurately determined "the concept of both disciplines", "their relationship", nor whether "they should retain their independence or should merge into one".[151] Both of them "ought not to be merged", but neither should they be entirely "separated", given that "sociology must wholly assist legal philosophy".[152] Sociology concerned human relationships "with a social character"; and legal philosophy examined the "individual character" of those human relationships.[153] The disciplines were interdependent, and should be complementary.

The main features of the Positivist Schools may be roughly outlined as follows. They used an inductive method, more commonly referred to as the 'scientific method'. The Rationalism that had preceded these schools had allowed some room for the development of a scientific spirit, and for an unprecedented expansion of science, with a renewed faith in the biological sciences, engineering, and mathematics. This system was therefore based in *a posteriori* experience. Conclusions were extracted from observation, study, and the classification of facts. The Positivist Schools aimed to fight criminality, in contrast to the mere distributive principle adopted by the Neoclassical Schools. Positivist Schools held that the phenomenon of criminality did not affect every individual in the same way, such that the consequences of crime, and the degree of punishment, could not be the same for everyone. Positivists based criminal responsibility on social responsibility,[154] displacing older ideas about moral responsibility. Many desirable advances resulted, including the admission of mitigating or exculpatory circumstances in determining the penalty for a crime, security measures, and individualisation of penalties, among others.[155]

If the Neoclassical Schools spoke of penalties, the Positivist Schools would talk of sanctions. The latter had no specific duration, and was linked to the dangerousness of the individual criminal. This entailed a great difference between the two groups: the Neoclassical Schools saw the penalty for a crime as exhaustible, whereas Positivist sanctions were technically not. Positivists also wanted 'penalties' to be useful. They were working during the peak popularity of the utilitarian ideas

[150] Dorado Montero (1915a, b), p. 174.

[151] Dorado Montero (1893a, b), p. 427.

[152] Dorado Montero (1893a, b), p. 429.

[153] Dorado Montero (1893a, b), p. 429.

[154] De Aramburu y Zuloaga (1887), p. 230.

[155] A very detailed study on the subject can be found in Pifferi (2009), pp. 441–459.

developed by Jeremy Bentham,[156] John Stuart Mill,[157] William Godwin,[158] John Austin[159] and Henry Sidgwick.[160] Although utilitarianism was deeply criticised, it had a remarkable impact on the humanisation of penalties. A report conducted by Robert Martinson proved that incarceration penalties (even the most humanitarian, re-educative and reintegrating ones) failed in preventing recidivism:

> For young males as a whole, the degree of success achieved in the regular prison academic education program, as measured by changes in grade achievement levels, made no significant difference in recidivism rates.[161]

Trends like utilitarianism suggested a different approach than that of traditional Criminal law, and encouraged a biological analysis, use of neurology[162] and psychiatry.

The older ideas about penalties were dismissed. Prior to the French Revolution, incarceration penalties had included abuse, torture and arbitrariness, Humanised incarceration had emerged as a concept in the Neoclassical period, but it was the Positivist Schools which caused a major shift: they opted instead for so-called "penal substitutes".[163] This term was coined by Enrico Ferri and referred to a set of measures offering a suitable alternative to penalties involving the deprivation of liberty, which were considered inefficient.[164] The long term impact of incarceration was not the concern here: it was their short term cost to the state, which Adolphe Prins described as "onerous to the Public Treasury", the fact they had "no deterrence effect on toughened [criminals]" and the fact incarceration was "hazardous to individuals who still preserve[d] some feelings of dignity"[165] which led to objections. Ferri's penal substitutes were entirely different to the existing measures in contemporary Criminal law. He defended some initiatives which were not strictly about Criminal law, but had educative, social, civil, and administrative aspects. Others did have a more "penal" approach. A good example was his approach to the current Spanish Criminal Code. It was subject to the Spanish Constitution (CE) and, therefore, should accomplish the resocialisation mandate set out in the first part of Article 25.2 of the CE: "Punishments entailing imprisonment and security measures shall be aimed at re-education and social rehabilitation and may

---

156 Bentham (1830).

157 Mill (1843, 1863, 1865, 1868).

158 Godwin (1946).

159 Austin (1995, 1996).

160 Sidgwick (1884, 1887).

161 Martinson (1974), p. 25: "*For young males as a whole, the degree of success achieved in the regular prison academic education program, as measured by changes in grade achievement levels, made no significant difference in recidivism rates*".

162 Dorado Montero (1906a, b), p. 160.

163 Información de Derecho penal (2013).

164 Ferri (1880).

165 Prins (1899), p. 467.

not involve forced labour".[166] The legislature used this to justify suspension and the substitution of penalties involving the deprivation of liberty. Articles 80–97 of the Spanish Criminal Code ("On substitute forms of execution of sentences depriving of freedom and on probation")[167] demonstrates the scale of change that substitutes underwent.

All things considered, positivism relied heavily on proportionality. Neoclassical Schools defended the equality principle, and generally distrusted the idea of different treatment in different circumstances.[168] Neoclassical Schools favoured formal equality, whereas the Positivist Schools defended a material equality principle. Criminal legislation was not passed exclusively by the legislative power. Positivists saw the legislative power as divided, fractioned and democratised between the legislator and the technical bodies, i.e. criminologists, physicians, sociologists, neurologists, psychiatrists and other professional agents. The Positivists extolled science above all else, but the Neoclassicals argued that science could never possibly foresee the whole of the future; for them, free will should always be respected—and positivists deliberately overlooked that fact. Yves Cartuyvels identified two main elements that explained this phenomenon:

> The absolute trust (if not completely blind faith) in both axiological truth and the neutrality of its own constructions, as well as the drift of a scientific project that used itself for the purpose of achieving certain social goals.[169]

Positivist Schools also established "criminal profiles"; a set of sociological categories providing a sort of catalogue of criminals. Lombroso became the great exponent of Criminal Anthropology, but the evidence showed his theory could no longer be justified, and it has been labelled as 'pseudoscientific'.[170] Many of his concepts, debates and arguments were "rarely based on comprehensive empirical research on crime", but rather drew from "existing law, international comparison, judicial

[166] "Article 25", *La Constitución Española*. For an official version of the Spanish Constitution in English, vid. the Spanish translation by the Spanish Ministry of Justice: https://www.mjusticia.gob.es/es/areas-tematicas/documentacion-publicaciones/publicaciones/traducciones-derecho-espanol.

[167] *Código Penal español*, articles 80–91. For an oficial version in English of the Spanish Criminal Code, vid. the Spanish translation by the Spanish Ministry of Justice: https://www.mjusticia.gob.es/es/areas-tematicas/documentacion-publicaciones/publicaciones/traducciones-derecho-espanol.

[168] One should not oversimplify here: the idea of modifying the penalty according to the circumstances had existed in the Middle Ages. Vid. Masferrer (2012), pp. 353–354.

[169] Cartuyvels (2015), p. 206: "*La confiance absolue sinon aveugle de la science dans la vérité et la neutralité axiologique de ses propres constructions et les dérives d'un projet scientifique qui s'instrumentalise d'entrée lui-même à des fins sociales spécifiques*". Translation is mine.

[170] Little (2019): "What Lombroso was doing was combining phrenology and physiognomy, two types of pseudoscience that purported to explain a person's personality and behavior based on his skull and facial features, respectively". Lombroso was not only criticised by Dorado Montero: much earlier, Pulido Fernández held that "phrenomatic science is a truly doctrinal asylum where each author puts in or out, devises and talks as he wants, and out of whose conflict it is impossible to infer anything permanent". Vid. Pulido Fernández (1883).

arguments, judicial practice and established narratives".[171] However, not all were caught by the Positivist fever. Some "generally sympathised" with the Positivist postulates, but opted for caution, seeking "not to hurry theories" where the facts were not "sufficiently checked". They tried their best "not to fall into a new metaphysics".[172] Dorado Montero included von Liszt, Lacassagne, Tarde, Colajanni and the members of the *Terza Scuola* in this group.[173]

Nevertheless, Lombroso's methodology was very systematic: his atavistic theory was the result of more than four-hundred autopsies of convicted criminals, and of six thousand analyses of living criminals. He declared that the most common physiological criminal traits were head protuberances, prominent cheekbones and slanted eyes.[174] He classified criminals as in general either "accountable" (the famous 'born criminals', those who were habitually criminal, morally foolish, occasionally criminal and professional criminals) or "non-accountable" (the insane, epileptics, etc.).[175] A third criminal category of "passionate" did not fit into either the accountable nor the non-accountable group: it depended upon an exhaustive psychological analysis.

Positivist trends bifurcated into two broad tendencies: a biology-focused determinism (as with Lombroso) and a more social focus (as with Ferri and Garofalo).[176] The specific approach taken varied enormously, depending on the particular author and his particularities. Ferri introduced a far criminal theory which was far more kind than that of Lombroso,[177] and closer to our current ideas. His classification was based upon factors influencing criminal behaviour, as opposed to Lombroso's theory that criminality was both pathogenic and inherent. Ferri's approach particularly[178] considered anthropological factors (race, sex, physical constitution, psyche or age), physical factors (temperature or climate), and social factors (religion, education and family). Grispigni also subscribed to this theory, but added some special remarks. Likewise, Garofalo[179] held that there were four types of born criminal: the assassin, the violent criminal, the thief and the lascivious criminal.

The International Union of Penal Law also played a role within positivism.[180] The IUPL was founded in Vienna in 1889 by three eminent penalists (von Liszt, Prins and Van Hamel) and later crystallised into the International Association of Penal Law.[181] Many laws and codes were influenced by contemporary theories: the Italian Code of 1889, the French Act of 1885 on the deportation of recidivists,

[171] Härter (2020), p. 170.

[172] Garofalo (1890), p. 23.

[173] Garofalo (1890), p. 24.

[174] Vid. an exhaustive study on Lombroso's theory in Musumeci (2012).

[175] Lombroso (1895c).

[176] In Spain, vid. Galera (1991).

[177] Ferri (1887, 1892, 1893, 1900a, b, c, 1928, 1991).

[178] Bonanno (1895), p. 364.

[179] Garofalo (1880a, 1880b, 1885, 1886, 1887).

[180] Vervaele (2020), p. 218.

[181] Officially, that happened in 1924.

penitentiary colonies and criminal mental institutions, and the Spanish Royal Decree of 28 January 1889 creating a penitentiary colony in the Philippines; even draft bills experienced the influence of positivism, such as the Spanish Criminal codes, especially the one promised in 1891 by Villaverde and the French draft Criminal Code.[182]

In conclusion, Positivist theory considered the individual who committed a crime as abnormal. They were considered almost exclusively in their material and biological aspects, rather than with regards to morality, unlike the approach of the older Neoclassical Schools. The issue was widely explored, including through the lens of literature. The Russian writer Fyodor Dostoevsky famously wrote two novels dealing with the complex phenomenon of crime: *Crime and* Punishment[183] and *The Brothers Karamazov*,[184] and they were not the only noteworthy works dealing with such issues.[185] It was argued that the question of the penalty for crime was a biological question, not a moral one. Pseudosciences such as phrenology,[186] probabilistic sciences and a developing discipline of criminology considered the criminal as a product of social factors, with social responsibility. The idea of rehabilitating criminals was a key feature of this approach, but developed at a late stage in its doctrine. Positivist Schools tried to find the causes of crime, and it followed that there were certain scenarios in which the criminal was not sanctioned because they lacked the right kind of responsibility for their actions. The purpose of criminal penalties was to prevent crime, both specifically and generally. The first criminal liberal codes (e.g., the 1822 Spanish criminal code) were also heavily influenced by the related doctrines of utilitarianism and liberalism, and their provisions established the coexistence of a retributive and preventative approach.

3.3.3 The Eclectic Schools

Debates in the social sciences should avoid the risk of falling into a simplistic reductionism which hinders research. The Eclectic Schools sought to do this by taking elements from both Neoclassical and Positivist schools and combining them. A good example of this approach was the eclectic school of Pellegrino Rossi[187] and Francesco Carrara,[188] in which Kant's concept of moral retribution (a Neoclassical approach) was combined with Enlightenment utilitarianism (a Positivist approach).

[182] Garofalo (1890), p. 24.

[183] Dostoyevsky (1956). Originally published as a serial in 1866.

[184] Dostoyevsky (1912). Also originally published as a serial in 1879–80.

[185] Beser (1972); Dolin (1999); Kayman (1992); Leps (1992); Maristany (1973); Miller (1988); Peset Reig and Peset Mancebo (1965).

[186] Pulido Fernández (1880).

[187] Rossi (1843). Of the same author, vid. Rossi (1829).

[188] Carrara (1898–1899, 1926, 1978–1989, 1992).

Thus, Eclectic Schools tended to shy away from revolutionary Enlightenment statements in order to combine the law and morality of previous ages.[189]

In Spain, the rise of the Eclectics was mainly attributable to Pellegrino Rossi and his popular work *Traité de Droit pénal,* which advocated hybridisation: intimidation, making harm impossible,[190] was accepted alongside the idea of reforming criminals (although the former played a more prominent role). The idea of retribution as a punishment was still present, and it was only once this criterion was met that the re-establishment of moral and social order was possible.[191]

Joaquín Francisco Pacheco[192] was also a true eclectic: both doctrinally and in personality. He held deep moral convictions, but he was pragmatic, too. In 1836, he founded the Gazette of Jurisprudence and Legislation (*Boletín de Jurisprudencia y Legislación*).[193] The distinctive traits of his doctrine fit the generic eclectic framework: the penalty had a retributive function (in primacy over other purposes), free will was a fundamental idea on which criminal law and punishment were to be based, and the right to punish individuals was grounded in natural law. Pacheco's development of latter idea was a particular contribution: his idea of the right to punish was not solely grouned in moral or natural law, but also in the preservation of society. He believed in the unification of social interests with respect to usages, traditions and previous norms. Pacheco's work is usually taken to outline the requirements that the penalty should fulfil as: (1) a moral aim, to avoid the corruption of the condemned; (2) having a personal character, since penalties were only applied to the criminal as an individual; (3) equality, avoiding privileges and favourable treatment; (4) divisibility, since the penalty could be proportionately increased or increased to reflect mitigating or aggravating circumstances; and (5) having an analogous and proportional character to the crime committed.[194] Pacheco's ideas generated both positive and negative opinions. The latter argued that he had simply plagiarised Rossi's doctrine. However, Calvo Rubio[195] believed that although Pacheco had some points in common with Rossi, there were certain questions that Pacheco dealt with that the Italian author had overlooked. Asúa[196] believed Pacheco's distinctive contribution was the technique he used. He divided the justification for punishment into three groups (*propias*, unimputability and non-culpability). Ironically, the main criticism of Pacheco came from Salamanca

[189] The intellectual and scholarly environment was shaped by the aforementioned Doctrinarism (also, Conservadurism in Great Britain).

[190] Iñesta-Pastor (2016), p. 214.

[191] Ramos Vázquez (2013), pp. 217–236.

[192] Pacheco (1854, 1862, 1870a, b).

[193] This was the first Spanish legal review, founded by Pacheco and Juan Pérez Hernández, Juan Bravo Murillo, Vicente Hernández de la Rua, Pascual Fernández Baeza and José María Huet, among others.

[194] Iñesta-Pastor (2017), pp. 401–500.

[195] Calvo Rubio (1966).

[196] Jiménez de Asúa (1917, 1920, 1929, 1930, 1934, 1947, 1983).

and Pedro Dorado Montero.[197] Another contemporary critic was Francisco Candil Jiménez, who asserted that "Pacheco's contribution to the writing of the 1848 Criminal Code was [. . .] limited in effect".[198]

Pedro Gómez de la Serna,[199] in turn, believed that morality could not be the sole basis of criminal law, and that utilitarian ideas should also be incorporated:

> I did not defend the system of absolute morality as the single grounding for the criminal system. I believe it is necessary to respect the morality system but united to the utilitarian system. No absolute system is good at all. I condemn the system of the spiritualists as much as I condemn the exclusive system of the utilitarians.[200]

This mixture between realism and a moral foundation was a recurrent feature in all eclectic theories. Essentially, it was the same debate as took place among spiritualists and materialists. Even if Dorado Montero was not an eclectic as such, he highlighted the importance of morality in criminal correction.[201] Another great eclectic was Luis Silvela,[202] who belonged to the Spanish correctionalist branch of the school. For him, the penalty was both a necessary punishment and a state control over those who systematically committed crimes in society. He also insinuated a state prevention mechanism through the correction of the criminal.

The period in which the Eclectic Schools emerged had certain features. A contemporary of Dorado Montero named Benito Mariano Andrade[203] devoted a work to describing this historical period,[204] the first edition of which was rapidly followed by a translation into German by Gustav Stezenbach. Following its success a second edition was printed in 1916[205] with a new foreword from the author demonstrating the repercussions of eclecticism in German doctrine:

> The Germans Catholics, who were deeply concerned about the events in Spain, asked my permission to translate [the book] into German, and Gustav Stezenbach produced an ample edition in Konstanz in 1911, under the title *Maura und die Konservative Partei in Spanien.*[206]

---

[197] According to him, their lessons had "little substance" and that little "was borrowed".

[198] Candil Jiménez (1975): "*su verdadera participación en la redacción del Código penal de 1848 [. . .] fue poco eficaz*".

[199] Gómez de la Serna (1845, 1853, 1859, 1869a, b, 1870).

[200] *Diario de Sesiones de las Cortes* (1848): "*Yo no he defendido el sistema de moralidad absoluta como base única del sistema penal. Creo que es necesario respetar el sistema de moralidad pero unido al sistema utilitario. Ningún sistema absoluto creo que es bueno. Yo repruebo el sistema de los espiritualistas, así como repruebo el sistema exclusivo de los utilitarios*".

[201] Dorado Montero (1898), p. 52. Also, vid. Ramos Vázquez's 'moral accountability' concept in Ramos Vázquez (2013), p. 230.

[202] Silvela (1839); Silvela (1874); Silvela (1886); Silvela (1898), pp. 117–148.

[203] Andrade (1896, 1897, 1899, 1907).

[204] Andrade (1916).

[205] Andrade (1911).

[206] Andrade (1916), p. 5: "*Los católicos alemanes, que a la sazón se preocupaban en gran manera de las cosas de España, solicitaron mi permiso para traducirlo al alemán, y Gustav Stezenbach hizo de él una profusa edición en 1911, en Konstanz, con el título de Maura und die Konservative Partei in Spanien*".

Andrade was extremely humble and attributed his success to the comments and adaptation by his translator:

> The comments of Gustav Stezenbach were certainly so sharp and appropriate that, according to my information, this modest handout obtained great popularity in certain spheres of German opinion.[207]

Positivism may be seen as a late variation of the Naturalism that arose after the Romantic era. Naturalism was characterised by a set of objective, deterministic and scientific features. If Romanticism was about "creative freedom, fantasy and feelings",[208] naturalism had a double meaning. Firstly, it was a philosophical doctrine "that consider[ed] nature as a reference of reality and, consequently, tries to explain it without resorting to the supernatural or to the transcendent".[209] Secondly, it was described as a "literary trend of the 19th century" which stressed the "features of realism in the spirit of both the experimental science and human behaviour".[210] Naturalism (represented by Émile Zola) and positivism (represented by Cesare Lombroso) appeared as two different conceptions of reality, and had different degrees of acceptance within Spain. However, Naturalism appears to have had more influence than Lombrosian positivism:

> Even if in Spain there were never more fervently convinced Lombrosians than the Veronese himself [Lombroso], there was nevertheless a group of writers who were more 'zolian' than Zola himself, who were supporters of the 'extreme version' of naturalism [...] Then, radical or doctrinal naturalism took root and developed.[211]

Notwithstanding the role that naturalism played in Spain, they core reason that positivism did not have such a strong influence there as in other European countries was the legal philosophical grounds and the natural law dominating the peninsula.[212] Radical naturalism, however, was better received: "Naturalism in this version inherited most of the aesthetic postulates of the idealist response or reaction, as well as most of the characteristic novel demands of experimentalism (Zola, *Le roman experiméntel*, 1880) and documentalism (e.g., Zola's *Le document humain*)".[213] Certain ideas like observation and demonstration were vital to signal

---

[207] Andrade (1916), p. 5: "Los comentarios de Gustav Stezenbach fueron, sin duda, tan atinados y pertinentes que, según mis noticias, este modesto folleto mío alcanzó en aquella época gran popularidad en ciertas zonas de la opinión alemana".

[208] Diccionario RAE (2014).

[209] Diccionario RAE (2014).

[210] Diccionario RAE (2014).

[211] Calvo González (2003), p. 264: "Si tal vez no hubo en España lombrosianos más ardorosamente convencidos que el propio veronés, existió en ella empero un grupo de escritores más zolescos que el mismo Zola, partidarios de la 'versión extremada' del naturalismo [...]. Dio así en arraigar y desarrollarse lo conocido como naturalismo doctrinario o 'radical'".

[212] Masferrer (2017), pp. 693–756.

[213] Calvo González (2003), p. 264: "El naturalismo en esta versión va a ser heredero de la mayor parte de los postulados estéticos de respuesta o reacción idealista y de las características exigencias novelísticas de experimentalismo (Zola, *Le roman expérimentel*, 1880) y documentalismo (v. gr.: le document humain de Zola)".

the "moral degradation of the social body".[214] Most interestingly, "the initial naturalist, socio-scientific commitment" evolved into a "method of social prophylaxis".[215] Two of its most relevant representatives were Eduardo López Bago and Alejandro Sawa Martínez, who developed a phenomenon of this period: "the socio-medical novel".[216] Unsurprisingly, in the "naturalist quest for experimentation and sociomoral reformism" a set of popular topics revolving around "the crime and the criminal as an organic pathology", as a "social disease" emerged alongside disciplines such as "anthropology (transformism and social environment)" and "criminal psychology (temperamentalism and phrenology)".[217]

Another figure ideologically very close to positivism in Spain was Remigio Vega Armentero.[218] He belonged to the aforementioned radical naturalist movement, and his novels showed "his will to join Zola's literary reform" with the "radical naturalism from López Bago" mixed with a "post-romantic taste".[219] He was placed within a "doctrinal version of naturalism" essentially constituted by the so-called "medico-social writers". Of the latter, Clarín complained about their excess of naturalist canons, and strogly criticised the underlying Italian criminal anthropology.[220] In this period, doctrinal discussions were fully immersed "in the process of legitimising clinical and judicial psychiatry".[221]

Calvo González pointed out the minimal impact that naturalism had in Spain and, thus, the limited reception of positivism. The fate of the "naturalist movement in Spain" was to attract limited adherence: a "quite discouraging" result.[222] Any "support for Lombrosian doctrine" barely exceeded a "shallow and indirect knowledge".[223] Calvo González noted that Pardo Bazán, a very well-known Spanish writer, had limited knowledge of the "Italian positive school" from "certain criminologists such as Rafael Salillas".[224] Another popular writer, Ramón Pérez de Ayala (1880–1962), similarly allowed these doctrines only a limited role.[225] At the time, Lombroso's theories were frequently either diluted or not systematically applied, considerably weakening an already deficient theory. The clearest case was Zola,

---

214 Calvo González (2003), p. 264.
215 Calvo González (2003), p. 264.
216 Calvo González (2003), p. 264.
217 Calvo González (2003), p. 265.
218 Vega Armentero (1890).
219 Diccionario Bibliográfico Electrónico (2009). For a contemporary taste in law and literature, vid. Obarrio Moreno (2022).
220 Calvo González (2003), p. 266.
221 Fernández (1995); quoted in Calvo González (2003), p. 268.
222 Calvo González (2003), p. 260.
223 Calvo González (2003), p. 260.
224 Calvo González (2003), p. 260.
225 Calvo González (2003), p. 261: "El escaso papel jugado por el lombrosianismo en la novelística española de época algo posterior resulta igualmente evidente en Ramón Pérez de Ayala (1880–1962)".

"often referred to as [Lombroso's] most loyal representative", who became acquainted with Lombrosian theories in writing his *La bête humaine*.[226] Zola was criticised by Lombroso himself for "contradict[ing] the statistical table in his studies" and failing to "fit his criminal profiles".[227] Calvo González concluded that the purported spread of Lombroso's ideals in both literature and wider society was only superficial. However, this is not true:

> In the penultimate decade of the Spanish 19th century, a sort of coincidence between Lombrosians and Zolians, between positivists and naturalists was fostered [...] It was a time of literary disenchantment amongst the latter, when it seemed that the former were on the rise. Leaving aside the echo of Lombroso, this was fostered by the inertia following polemics on evolutionism and social Darwinism, as well as by the rise of phrenology and the Social Hygiene Movement: both Ferri and Garofalo were subject to editorial attention and consecutive translations between 1885 and 1889.[228]

The same could be said about the transplant of Lombrosian theories into legislation and legal doctrine: if this occurred it was at a superficial level, but the substance of his ideas was not adopted.

One final remark should be made. A later chapter will return to the idea that it is difficult to argue that Dorado Montero's 'theory' was eclectic. Nonetheless, his thinking was eclectic: "The movement to approximate the two rival schools has already begun and will consolidate over time, as popular science is penetrated by the idea that no theory, as absurd as it may seem, is without some reason for its existence".[229]

References

Alimena B (1887) La premeditazione: in rapporto alla psicologia, al diritto, alla legislazione comparata. Fratelli Bocca, Roma

Alimena B (1894) I limiti e i modificatori dell'imputabilità. Fratelli Bocca, Torino

Alimena B (1906) Studi di procedura penale. Fratelli Bocca, Torino

Alimena B (1913) Notas filosóficas de un criminalista. Hijos de Reus, Madrid

[226] Zola (1893).

[227] Calvo González (2003), p. 261.

[228] Calvo González (2003), pp. 261–262: "En la penúltima década del siglo XIX español se asiste, por tanto, a una especie de coincidencia más adjetiva que sustancial entre lombrosianos y zolescos, entre positivistas y naturalistas, con el curioso añadido de que es al tiempo del desencanto literario de los últimos cuando parece que los primeros comienzan a alcanzar mayor auge. Aparte el eco mantenido de Lombroso, también nutrido en la inercial influencia que antes habían despertado las polémicas sobre evolucionismo y darwinismo social, así como por los comienzos de la frenología y el higienismo, tanto Ferri como Garofalo son entre 1885 y 1889, en efecto, objeto de atención editorial y sucesivas traducciones".

[229] Garofalo (1890), p. 29: "Y el movimiento de aproximación entre las dos escuelas rivales ha comenzado ya á iniciarse y se consolidará con el tiempo, á medida que en la conciencia común penetre la idea de que ninguna teoría, aun la que parezca más absurda, deja de tener algún motivo de existencia".

Alimena B (1915) Principios de derecho penal. Libr. General de Victoriano Suárez, Madrid
Alimena B (1975) Delitos contra la persona. Temis, Santa Fe de Bogotá
Alonso y Alonso JM (1946) De la vigencia y aplicación del Código Penal de 1822. Revista de la Escuela de Estudios Penitenciarios 11:1–21
Andrade BM (1896) La antropología criminal y la novela naturalista. Sucesores de Rivadeneyra, Madrid
Andrade BM (1897) Estudios penales. Sucesores de Rivadeneyra, Madrid
Andrade BM (1899) Estudio de antropología criminal espiritualista. Sucesores de Rivadeneyra, Madrid
Andrade BM (1907) La moral universal. Victoriano Suárez, Madrid
Andrade BM (1911) Maura und die Konservative Partei in Spanien. Aktien- Gesellschaft Pressverein Konstanz, Konstanz
Andrade BM (1916) Maura y el partido conservador. Imprenta de Ramona Velasco, Viuda de P. Pérez, Madrid
Andrés-Gallego J (1971) Regeneracionismo y política confesional en España, 1889-1899. Diputación Provincial de Sevilla, Sevilla
Anes y Álvarez de Castrillón R (2009) La economía española de 1868 a 1898. In: Girón Garrote J (ed) Un cambio de siglo 1898: España, Cuba, Puerto Rico, Filipinas y Estados Unidos. Universidad de Oviedo, Oviedo
Antón Oneca J (1951) La utopía penal de Dorado Montero. Universidad de Salamanca, Salamanca
Arenal C (1877) Estudios penitenciarios. Imprenta de T. Fortanet, Madrid
Arenal C (1883) Lettre à M. Le Directeur General de L'Administration Pénitentiaire D'Espagne. Bulletin de la Société Générale des Prisons, pp 468–475
Aróstegui Sánchez J (2011) Historia de España. Vicens Vives, Barcelona
Austin J (1995) The province of jurisprudence determined. Cambridge University Press, Cambridge
Austin J (1996) Lectures on jurisprudence. Thoemmes Press, Bristol
Beccaria C (1762) Sobre el desorden monetario y su remedio en los estados milaneses
Beccaria C (1804) Elementos de economía pública, 1804 (posthumous)
Beccaria C (2014) De los delitos y las penas. Alianza, Madrid
Beling E (1906) Die Lehre vom Verbrechen. Mohr, Tübingen
Beling E (1928) Deutsches Reichsstrafprozessrecht mit Einschluss des Strafgerichtsverfassungssungsrecht. Walter de Gruyter, Berlin
Beling E (1936) El rector de los tipos de delito. Reus, Madrid
Beling E (1943) Derecho procesal penal. Barcelona
Beling E (1968) Die Beweisverbote als Grenzen der Wahrheitserforschung im Strafprozess, 2nd edn. Wissenschaftliche Buchgesellschaft, Darmstadt
Beling E (1971) Unschuld, Schuld und Schuldstufen: im Vorentwurf zu einem deutschen Strafgesetzbuch. Scientia, Aalen
Beling E (2002) Esquema del Derecho penal: la doctrina del delito-tipo. El Foro, Buenos Aires
Beling E (2009) Las prohibiciones probatorias. Temis, Bogotá
Bentham J (1780) An introduction to the principles of morals and legislation
Bentham J (1782) Of laws in general
Bentham J (1830) The rationale of punishment. R. Heward, London
Bernaldo de Quirós C (1898a) Las nuevas teorías de la criminalidad. Imp. Revista de Legislación, Madrid
Bernaldo de Quirós C (1898b) Las nuevas teorías de la criminalidad. Hijos de Reus, Madrid
Bernaldo de Quirós C (1898c) Lecciones de legislación penal comparada. Montalvo, Santo Domingo
Bernaldo de Quirós C (1904) Alrededor del delito y de la pena. Viuda de Rodríguez Serra, Madrid
Bernaldo de Quirós C (1931) Derecho Penal. Instituto Reus, Madrid
Bernaldo de Quirós C (1940) Cursillo de criminología y Derecho penal. Montalvo, Santo Domingo
Bernecker WL (2010a) Die Unabhängigkeit Lateinamerikas: europäische Interessen und ambivalente Reaktionen. Ibero-Amerikanisches Institut Preußischer Kulturbesitz 1:1–59

Bernecker WL (2010b) Geschichte Spaniens im 20. Jahrhundert. C. H. Beck, München
Beser S (1972) Leopoldo Alas: Teoría y crítica de la novela española. Laila, Barcelona
Bexon S (1802) Développement de la Théorie des Lois Criminelles par la comparaison de plusieurs législations anciennes et modernes, notamment de Rome, de l'Anglaterre et de la France; suivi de l'application de cette théorie, dans un Projet de Code Criminel, Correctionnel et de Police. Garnery, Paris
Bexon S (1807) Application de la théorie de la législation pénale, ou Code de la sureté publique et particulière, fondé sur les règles de la morale universelle, sur le droit des gens ou primitive des sociétés et sur leur droit particulier, dans l'état actuel de la civilisation; rédigé en projet pour les états de sa majesté le Roi de Bavière; dédié à sa Majesté et imprimé avec son autorisation. Courcier, Paris
Bonanno (1895) La classificazione dei delinquenti e il reo per passione. Archivio di psichiatria 16: 355–371
Bosch García C (1947) Preliminares políticos al primer tratado de comercio entre México y España. El trimestre económico 4(13):712–754
Britannica (1768) Conservatism in the 19th century. https://www.britannica.com/topic/conservatism/Conservatism-in-the-19th-century
Buisson I et al (1984) Problemas de la formación del Estado y de la Nación en Hispanoamérica. Böhlau, Köln
Calvo González J (2003) Naturalismo y direcciones criminológicas a finales del siglo XIX en España. Revista de derecho penal y criminología 12:255–270
Calvo Rubio JA (1966) Pacheco, penalista. Revista de Derecho Judicial 26:28–54
Candil Jiménez F (1975) Observaciones sobre la intervención de don Joaquín Francisco Pacheco en la elaboración del Código penal de 1848. Dialnet, Sevilla
Cañizares Navarro JB (2013) El Código penal de 1822: sus fuentes inspiradoras. Balance historiográfico (desde el s. XX). GLOSSAE. Eur J Leg Hist 10:109–136
Cánovas del Castillo A (1800) Problemas contemporáneos. Tello, Madrid
Cánovas del Castillo A (1892) Historia general de España. El Progreso Editorial, Madrid
Cánovas del Castillo A (1910) Historia de la decadencia de España desde el advenimiento de Felipe III al Trono hasta la muerte de Carlos III. Gutenberg, Madrid
Carmignani G (1831) Teoria delle leggi della sicurezza sociale
Carmignani G (1832) Teoria delle leggi della sicurezza sociale. Biblioteca Italiana
Carmignani G (1833) Elementa juris criminalis
Carmignani G (1837) Legislazione - Una lezione accademica sulla pena di norte. Biblioteca Italiana
Carmignani G (1851) Storia delle origini e de' progressi della filosofia del diritto, 1851
Carnevale E (1932) Diritto criminale. Società Editrice del Foro Italiano, Roma
Carrara F (1898–1899) Opúscoli di diritto criminale, 5th edn. Fratelli Cammelli, Firenze
Carrara F (1926) Teoría de la tentativa y de la complicidad o del grado en la fuerza física del delito, 2nd edn. Góngora, Madrid
Carrara F (1978–1989) Programa de derecho criminal, 3rd edn. Temis, Bogotá
Carrara F (1992) Cuestiones sobre la tentativa. Temis, Bogotá
Cartuyvels Y (2015) La biologisation du crime à la fin du XIXe siècle : quelques enjeux et limites. Jurisprudence. Revue critique, numéro spécial
Casabó Ruiz JR (1968) El Código penal de 1822. Universitat de València, Valencia
Castejón F (1914) Legislación penitenciaria española
Castejón F (1926) Tratado de la responsabilidad
Castejón F (1933) El proyecto Pinies de profilaxis social (maleantes) de 1922 y la ley relativa a vagos y maleantes de 4 de agosto de 1933. Revista General de Legislación y Jurisprudencia 163: 214–288
Castejón F (1934) Datos para una reforma penal
Castejón F (1936) Unificación de estadísticas criminales
Castejón F (1944) Anteproyecto de código, penal subjetivo
Castejón F (1947) Unificación legislativa iberoamericana

Castejón F (1952) Memoria sobre proyecto de Código penal Internacional
Clasificación de los delincuentes (1998) Blogspot, Online. http://criminologiaken.blogspot.com.es/2011/04/clasificacion-de-los-delincuentes-segun.html
Código Penal español, arts. 80–91. Spanish Ministry of Justice. https://www.mjusticia.gob.es/es/areas-tematicas/documentacion-publicaciones/publicaciones/traducciones-derecho-espanol
Costa J (1902) Oligarquía y caciquismo como la forma actual de gobierno en España: urgencia y modo de cambiarla. Imprenta de los hijos de M.G. Hernández, Madrid
Costa J (1914) Crisis política de España: doble llave al sepulcro del Cid. Biblioteca Costa, Madrid
de administración. Imprenta Nacional, Madrid
De Aramburu y Zuloaga F (1887) La nueva ciencia penal. Exposición y crítica. Librería de Fernandó Fe, Madrid
De la Granja JL, Beramendi J, Anguera P (2001) La España de los nacionalismos y las autonomías. Síntesis, Madrid
De la Rasilla I (2020) International criminal justice as universal social defence – Quintiliano Saldaña (1878-1938). In: Megret F, Tallgren I (eds) The dawn of a discipline – international criminal justice and its early exponents. Cambridge University Press, Cambridge
De Vizmanos TM, Álvarez C (1848) Comentarios al nuevo Código penal. Est. Tip. de González y Vicente, Madrid
Diario de Sesiones de las Cortes, No. 81 (13.03.1848)
Diccionari Normatiu Valencià (2014) Acadèmia Valenciana de la Llengua (AVL). https://www.avl.gva.es/lexicval/
Diccionario Bibliográfico Electrónico (2009) Real Academia de la Historia, Madrid
Diccionario RAE (2014) Real Academia de la Lengua Española, Madrid. https://dle.rae.es/?w=caciquismo
Dolin K (1999) Fiction and the law. Legal discourse in Victorian and modernist literature. Cambridge University Press, Cambridge
Donoso Cortés J (1851) Ensayo sobre el catolicismo, el liberalismo y el socialismo, considerados en sus principios fundamentales. Rivadeneyra, Barcelona
Donoso Cortés J (1984) Lecciones de Derecho Político. Centro de Estudios Políticos y Constitucionales (M° de la Presidencia), Madrid
Dorado Montero P (1891) El positivismo en la ciencia jurídica y social italiana. Imprenta de la Revista de Legislación, Madrid
Dorado Montero P (1893a) Problemas jurídicos contemporáneos. La España Moderna, Madrid
Dorado Montero P (1893b) Reseña al libro de Anziolotti: 'La Filosofia del Diritto e la Sociologia'. RGLJ 82(41):427–429
Dorado Montero P (1898) El Reformatorio de Elmira. La España Moderna, Madrid
Dorado Montero P (1901) Contribución al estudio de la historia primitiva España. Imprenta de la Revista de Legislación, Madrid, pp 20–37
Dorado Montero P (1902) Bases para un nuevo Derecho penal. Manuel Soler, Barcelona
Dorado Montero P (1906a) De Criminología y Penología. Viuda de Rodríguez Serra, Madrid
Dorado Montero P (1906b) Los peritos médicos y la justicia criminal. Hijos de Reus, Madrid
Dorado Montero P (1915a) El Derecho protector de los criminales. Ed. Jiménez Gil, Madrid
Dorado Montero P (1915b) "Sobre el libro Hampa del Dr. Salillas", Derecho protector de los criminales, Madrid: Lib. de Victoriano Suárez
Dostoyevsky F (1912) The Brothers Karamazov. Heinemann, London (originally published as a serial in 1879-80)
Dostoyevsky F (1956) Crime and punishment. Random House, New York (originally published as a serial in 1866)
Escudero Antonio JA (1985) Curso de Historia del Derecho. Fuentes e instituciones político-administrativas. J. A. Escudero, Madrid
Fernández P (1995) Eduardo López Bago y el naturalismo radical. La novela y el mercado literario en el siglo XIX. Rodopi B. V., Ámsterdam-Atlanta
Ferri E (1880) Dei sostitutivi penali. Roux e Favale, Torino

Ferri E (1887) Los nuevos horizontes del derecho y del procedimiento penal, 2nd edn. Centro Editorial de Góngora, Madrid
Ferri E (1892) Estudios de antropología criminal. La España Moderna, Madrid
Ferri E (1893) Nuevos estudios de antropología criminal. La España Moderna, Madrid
Ferri E (1900a) Ciencia positiva. Atlante, Barcelona
Ferri E (1900b) La justicia penal: su evolución, sus defectos, su porvenir. B. Rodríguez Serra, Madrid
Ferri E (1900c) Los hombres y las cárceles. Centro Editorial Presa, Barcelona
Ferri E (1907) Sociología criminal. Centro Editorial de Góngora, Madrid
Ferri E (1925) Proyecto preliminar de código penal para Italia. Centro Editorial de Góngora, Madrid
Ferri E (1928) Principii di diritto criminale : delinquente e delitto. Unione Tipografico-Editrice Torinese, Torino
Ferri E (1991) Defensas penales, 6th edn. Temis, Santa de Fe de Bogotá
Feuerbach L (1841) Das Wesen des Christentums. Otto Wigand, Leipzig
Filangieri G (1870) La scienza della legislazione. Milano
Florián E (1925) Il metodo positivo nella scienza del diritto penale. L'Università degli Studi, Modena
Florián E (1934) Elementos de derecho procesal penal. Librería Bosch, Barcelona
Florián E (1995) De las pruebas penales. Temis, Santa Fe de Bogotá
Fontana i Lázaro J (2007) La época del liberalismo. In: Fontana i Lázaro J, Villares R (dir) Historia de España, 1st edn. Planeta, Barcelona, pp 9–10
Galera A (1991) Ciencia y delincuencia. El determinismo antropológico en la España del siglo XIX. CSIC, Sevilla
Garofalo R (1880a) Contra la corrente! Pensieri sulla proposta abolizione della pena di morte nel progetto del nuovo codice penale italiano. Ernesto Anfossi, Napoli
Garofalo R (1880b) Criterio positivo de la penalidad. Nápoles
Garofalo R (1884) Alcune osservazioni sul progetto del codice penale con relazione di Zanardelli presentato alla camera dei deputati da Savelli il 26 novembre 1883. Frattelli Bocca, Torino
Garofalo R (1885) Criminologia: studio sul delitto e sulla teoria della repressione. Frattelli Bocca, Torino
Garofalo R (1886) Polémica en defensa de la Escuela Criminal Positiva (en colaboración con Cesare Lombroso, Enrico Ferri y Giulio Fioretti). Bolonia
Garofalo R (1887) Riparazione alle vittime del delitto. Frattelli Bocca, Torino
Garofalo R (1889) Riforma della procedura penale in Italia. Progetto di un nuovo codice. Fratelli Bocca, Torino
Garofalo R (1890) Indemnización á las víctimas del delito. La España Moderna, Madrid
Garofalo R (1914) Commentario del Nuovo codice di procedura penale. F. Vallardi, Milano
Germann U (2020) Toward new horizons: penal positivism and Swiss criminal law reform in the late 19th and early 20th centuries. GLOSSAE. Eur J Leg Hist 17:259–276
Giner de los Ríos F (1875) Estudios jurídicos y políticos
Giner de los Ríos F (1876) Estudios filosóficos y religiosos
Giner de los Ríos F (1889) La persona social. Estudios y fragmentos I (vols. I-II)
Giner de los Ríos F (1898) Resumen de Filosofía del Derecho (vols. I-II)
Godwin W (1946) Enquiry concerning political justice and its influence on morals and happiness, 3rd edn. University of Toronto Press, Toronto
Gómez de la Serna P (1845) Prolegómenos del derecho. Imp. de Vicente de Lalama, Madrid
Gómez de la Serna P (1853) Tratado académico-forense de los procedimientos, 2nd edn. Librería de Sánchez, Madrid
Gómez de la Serna P (1859) Código de comercio concordado y anotado, precedido de una introducción histórico- comparada, y seguido de la ley de Enjuiciamiento sobre los negocios y causas de comercio...repertorio alfabético de la legislación y del procedimiento mercantil, Imprenta de la Revista de Legislación, 3rd edn, Madrid

Gómez de la Serna P (1869a) Código de comercio arreglado a la reforma decretada en 6 de Diciembre de 1868 anotado y concordado, leyes y disposiciones posteriores, leyes especiales de enjuiciamiento y repertorio de la legislación mercantil. Imprenta de la Revista de Legislación, Madrid

Gómez de la Serna P (1869b) Curso histórico-exegético del derecho romano, comparado con el español, 4th edn. Librería de Sánchez, Madrid

Gómez de la Serna P (1870) Elementos del derecho civil y penal de España, precedidos de una reseña histórica de la legislación española, 9th edn. Librería de Sánchez, Madrid

Griffin CC (1937) The United States and the Disruption of the Spanish Empire 1810-1822. A study of the relations of the United States with Spain and the Rebel Spanish Colonies. Columbia University Press, New York

Grispigni F (1928) Introduzione alla sociologia criminale : oggetto e natura della sociologia criminale il metodo, il concetto sociologico della criminalità. Unione Tipografico-Editrice Torinese, Torino

Grispigni F (1945) Diritto processuale penale, con l'indicazio di tutte le modificazioni legislative posteriori all 8-9-1943 fino al 28-2-1945. Edizioni Italiane, Roma

Grispigni F (1952) Diritto penale italiano. Dott. A. Giuffrè, Milano

Grispigni F (2009) La reforma penal nacional-socialista. Ediar, Buenos Aires

Groizard A (1870) El Código penal de 1870, concordado y comentado. Esteban hermanos impresores, Burgos

Grolman KLW (1810) Ausführliches Handbuch über den Code Napoleon : zum Gebrauche wissenschaftlich gebildeter deutschen Geschäftsmänner entworfen. G.F. Heyer, Darmstadt

Grolman KLW (1825) Grundsätze der criminalrechts-wissenschaft. G.F. Heyer, Giessen

Grolman KLW (1826) Theorie des gerichtlichen Verfahrens in bürgerlichen Rechtsstreitigkeiten. Georg Friedrich Heyer, Giessen

Härter K (2020) Zweckgedanke, social defence and transnational criminal law: Franz von Liszt and the network of positivist criminology (1871-1918). GLOSSAE. Eur J Leg Hist 17:150–175

Hegel GWF (1807) Phänomenologie des Geistes. Bamberg

Hegel GWF (1817) Enzyklopaedie der philosophischen Wissenschaften. Heidelberg

Hegel GWF (1821) Grundlinien der Philosophie des Rechts

Hegel GWF (1968) Ciencia de la lógica. Solar / Hachette, Buenos Aires

History (2019) What type of criminal are you? 19th-century doctors claimed to know by your face, Little B. https://www.history.com/news/born-criminal-theory-criminology

Hobsbawn EJ (1971) Las revoluciones burguesas. Guadarrama, Madrid

Howard J (1777) The state of prisons in England and Wales. W. Eyres

Ibarra Becerra V (2016) La condena de la venganza privada tras la justicia punitiva. Contraste y continuidad entre La Orestíada de Esquilo. Ideas y valores 162(65):291–314

Iñesta-Pastor E (2003) La proyección Hispanoamericana del Código penal español de 1848. Actas y Estudios, XIII Congreso del Instituto Internacional de Historia del Derecho Indiano 2:493–521

Iñesta-Pastor E (2010a) Spanish parliament and woman's penal condition during the legislative period of 1847-1849. In: De Cruz Coelho MH, Tavares Ribeiro MM (eds) Parliaments: the law, the practice and the representations. From the middle ages to the present day. Assembleia da República, Lisboa, pp 151–160

Iñesta-Pastor E (2010b) Història del Dret de l'Ibèria primitiva, la Hispània romana i visigoda. Universitat d'Alacant, Alicante

Iñesta-Pastor E (2011) El Código Penal Español de 1848. Tirant Lo Blanch, Valencia

Iñesta-Pastor E (2013) La Comisión General de Codificación (1843-1997): De la codificación moderna a la descodificación contemporánea. Anuario de Historia del Derecho español 83: 65–103

Iñesta-Pastor E (2016) La interpretación del eclecticismo en la doctrina y en la legislación de la España penal del siglo XIX. Ivs Fvgit 19:209–230

Iñesta-Pastor E (2017) Influencias extranjeras en la configuración de la pena en los códigos penales españoles decimonónicos. In: Masferrer A (ed) La codificación penal española. Tradición e

influencias extranjeras: su contribución al proceso codificador (Parte general). Aranzadi-Thompson, Cizur menor, pp 401–500
Información de Derecho penal (2013). https://www.infoderechopenal.es/2013/05/sustitutivos-penales.html
Jiménez de Asúa L (1913) La sentencia indeterminada. El sistema de penas determinadas "a posteriori". Reus, Madrid
Jiménez de Asúa L (1915) La recompensa como prevención general. El derecho premial. Reus, Madrid
Jiménez de Asúa L (1917) El anteproyecto de Código penal sueco de 1916: estudio crítico seguido del texto íntegro de la parte general del anteproyecto, traducido íntegramente del sueco. Hijos de Reus, Madrid
Jiménez de Asúa L (1920) El estado peligroso del delincuente y sus consecuencias ante el derecho penal moderno. Reus, Madrid
Jiménez de Asúa L (1929) Casos de derecho penal para uso de los estudiantes, 2nd edn. Librería General de Victoriano Suárez, Madrid
Jiménez de Asúa L (1930) Al servicio del derecho penal: diatriba del Código gubernativo. Javier Morata, Madrid
Jiménez de Asúa L (1934) Código penal reformado de 27 de Octubre de 1932 y disposiciones penales de la República, 1st edn. Reus, Madrid
Jiménez de Asúa L (1947) Derecho penal soviético. Tipografica editora argentina, Buenos Aires
Jiménez de Asúa L (1961) Estudios de derecho penal y criminología. Tomo I. Omeba, Buenos Aires
Jiménez de Asúa L (1963) Estudios de derecho penal y criminología. Tomo II, Omeba, Buenos Aires
Jiménez de Asúa L (1983) Defensas penales. Antalbe, Barcelona
Kant I (1764) Sobre la nitidez de los principios de la teología natural y de la moral
Kant I (1783) Prolegómenos a toda metafísica futura que pueda presentarse como ciencia
Kant I (1784) Idea para una historia universal en sentido cosmopolita
Kant I (1787) Crítica de la razón pura
Kant I (1788) Sobre el uso de los principios teleológicos en la filosofía
Kant I (1797) Revisión de la pregunta: si el género humano progresa continuamente hacia lo mejor
Kant I (1981) Crítica de la razón práctica, 2nd edn. Espasa-Calpe, Madrid
Kant I (1989a) El único fundamento posible de una demostración de la existencia de Dios. PPU, Barcelona
Kant I (1989b) Metafísica de las costumbres. Tecnos, Madrid
Kant I (1989c) Principios metafísicos de la ciencia de la naturaleza. Alianza, Madrid
Kant I (1994) Fundamentación de la metafísica de las costumbres. Espasa-Calpe, Madrid
Kant I (1999a) Crítica del juicio, 8th edn. Espasa-Calpe, Madrid
Kant I (1999b) El conflicto de las facultades. Trotta, Madrid
Kant E (2003) El conflicto de las Facultades. Alianza, Madrid
Kayman MA (1992) From Bow Street to Baker Street: mystery, detection and narrative. Basingstoke, Macmillan
La Constitución Española, art. 25. Spanish Ministry of Justice. https://www.mjusticia.gob.es/es/areas-tematicas/documentacion-publicaciones/publicaciones/traducciones-derecho-espanol
Lanza V (1906) L'Umanesimo nel Diritto penale. Reber, Catania
Lanza V (1924) Instituzioni di diritto penale. Catania
Lardizábal y Uribe M (1782) Discurso sobre las penas, contrahido á las leyes criminales de España, para facilitar su reforma. J. Ibarra, Madrid
Leps MC (1992) Apprehending the criminal: the production of deviance in nineteenth century discourse. Duke University Press, Durham
Lombroso C (1884) L'uomo delinquente, 3rd edn. Fratelli Bocca, Torino
Lombroso C (1890a) Medicina legal. La España Moderna, Madrid
Lombroso C (1890b) El hipnotismo. La España moderna, Madrid

Lombroso C (1895a) Los últimos progresos de la antropología criminal. La España Moderna, Madrid
Lombroso C (1895b) Grafologia. Ulrico Hoepli, Milamo
Lombroso C (1895c) L'homme criminel, 2nd edn. Felix Alcan, Paris
Lombroso C (1902) El delito: sus causas y remedios. Librería General de Victoriano Suárez, Madrid
Lombroso C (1910) Los fenómenos de hipnotismo y espiritismo. M. Aguilar, Madrid
Lombroso C (1911) Los criminales. Atlante, Barcelona
Lombroso C (1927) La donna delinquente: la prostituta e la donna normale, 5th edn. Fratelli Bocca, Torino
Maluquer de Motes i Bernet J (1999) España en la crisis de 1898: de la gran depresión a la modernización económica del siglo XX. Península, Barcelona
Marat JP (1773) A philosophical essay on man. J. Ridley, London
Marat JP (1774) Les chaînes de l'esclavage
Marat JP (1780) Plan de législation criminelle. Neuchâtel
Marcos Gutiérrez J (1826) Práctica criminal de España. D. Fermín Villalpando, Madrid
Maristany L (1973) El Gabinete del Doctor Lombroso. Delincuencia y fin de siglo en España, Cuadernos Anagrama, Barcelona
Martinson R (1974) What works? Questions and answers about prisons reform. Public Interest 35: 2–43
Masferrer A (2003) Tradición y reformismo en la Codificación penal española. Hacia el ocaso de un mito. Materiales, apuntes y reflexiones para un nuevo enfoque metodológico e historiográfico del movimiento codificador penal europeo. Universidad de Jaén, Jaén
Masferrer A (2012) Spanish legal traditions. Dykinson, Madrid
Masferrer A (2017) La distinción entre delito y pecado en la tradición penal bajomedieval y moderna. Una propuesta revisionista de la historiografía española, europea y anglosajona. Anuario de Historia del Derecho Español 87:693–756
Masferrer A (2020a) Criminal law and morality revisited: interdisciplinary perspectives. In: Masferrer A (ed) Criminal law and morality in the age of consent. Springer, Cham, pp 1–27
Masferrer A (2020b) The reception of the positivist school in the Spanish criminal doctrine (1885-1899). GLOSSAE. Eur J Leg Hist 17:303–352
May L (2019) Ancient legal thought: equity, justice, and humaneness from Hammurabi and the Pharaohs to Justinian and the Talmud. Cambridge University Press, Cambridge, pp 150–168
Mill JS (1843) A system of logic
Mill JS (1863) Utilitarianism
Mill JS (1865) Auguste and positivism
Mill JS (1868) Speech in favor of capital punishment
Miller DA (1988) The novel and the police. University of California Press, Berkeley
Mirabeau HR (1775) Essai sur le despotisme
Mirabeau HR (1782) Cartas Selladas y Cárceles de Estado
Mirabeau HR (1788) De la monarchie prussienne sous Frédéric le Grand
Montesquieu (1750) L'esprit des loix. Barrillot & Fils, Genève
Moreno Fraginals M (1995) Cuba/España. España/Cuba. Crítica, Barcelona
Moreu ÁC (2006) La recepción de las doctrinas correccionalistas en España. Políticas educativas y metodologías psicopedagógicas. Revista de Educación 340:755–785
Musumeci E (2012) Cesare Lombroso e le neuroscienze: un parricidio mancato. Franco Angeli, Milano
Muyart de Vouglans JP (1757) Institutes au droit criminel
Muyart de Vouglans JP (1762) Institutions criminelles selon les lois et ordonnances du royaume
Muyart de Vouglans JP (1780) Les loix criminelles du Royaume : dans leur ordre naturel. Mérigot
Núñez JA (2013) Fernando Cadalso y Manzano: Medio siglo de reforma penitenciaria en España (1859-1939). Universidad de Valladolid, Valladolid
Obarrio Moreno JA (2022) Antígona. Relectura de un mito de la Antigüedad. Dykinson, Madrid
Ortega y Gasset J (1909) La educación política española

Pacheco JF (1841) Historia de la Regencia de la reina Cristina. Imprenta de Fernando Suárez, Madrid
Pacheco JF (1854) Estudios de derecho penal: lecciones pronunciadas en el Ateneo de Madrid en 1839 y 1840, 4th edn. Imp. y Fundición de Manuel Tello, Madrid
Pacheco JF (1862) Comentario histórico, crítico y jurídico a las Leyes de Toro. Imp. de Manuel Tello, Madrid
Pacheco JF (1870a) El Código Penal concordado y comentado, 4th edn. Imp. de Manuel Tello, Madrid
Pacheco JF (1870b) Apéndice a los comentarios del Código Penal de Don Joaquín Francisco Pacheco ó sea el nuevo Código, comentadas las adiciones que contiene. Imp. de Manuel Tello, Madrid
Pacheco JF (1881) El Código penal concordado y comentado. Imprenta y fundición de Manuel Tello, Madrid
Peset Reig JL, Peset Mancebo M (1965) Lombroso y la Escuela positivista italiana. CSIC, Madrid
Pifferi M (2009) Exporting criminology: the individualization of punishment in Europe and America. In: Beck Varela L (Coord) Crossing legal cultures. Martin Meidenbauer, München, pp 441–459
Prins A (1875) De l'appel dans l'organisation judiciaire répressive. Étude historique et critique
Prins A (1886) Criminalité et répression. Essai de science pénale
Prins A (1888) La loi sur la libération conditionnelle et les condamnations conditionnelles
Prins A (1899) Science pénale et droit positif. Brussels
Prins A (1910) La défense sociale et les transformations du droit pénal
Proal L (1890a) La criminalité féminine. Impr. de Soye et fils, Paris
Proal L (1890b) L'anthropologie criminelle. Le Correspondant 158:431–455
Proal L (1890c) Les médecins positivistes et les théories modernes de la criminalité. Impr. de Soye et fils, Paris
Proal L (1892) Le crime et la peine. F. Alcan, Paris
Proal L (1900) Le crime et le suicide passionnels. F. Alcan, Paris
Proal L (1912) L'expertise médico-légale et la question de la responsabilité. Archives de l'anthropologie criminelle 27:481–502
Puglia F (1883) Prolegomini allo Studio del Diritto repressivo. Napoli
Puglia F (1902) Tratatto di Diritto Penale. Napoli
Pulido Fernández A (1880) La frenopatía y el Código penal. RGLJ 58
Pulido Fernández A (1883) Locos delincuentes. Discursos pronunciados en la Sección de Ciencias Naturales del Ateneo científico y literario de Madrid sobre el tema 'Estado actual de la ciencia frenopática y sus relaciones con el Derecho penal'. Imprenta de la Revista de Legislación, Madrid
Ramos Vázquez I (2013) La reforma penitenciaria en la historia contemporánea española. Dykinson, Madrid
Ramos Vázquez I (2020) Los delitos de asociación ilícita, coalición o coligación en Francia y España a lo largo del siglo XIX. In: Masferrer A (ed) Tradición e influencias extranjeras en la codificación penal española: parte especial. Aranzadi Thompson Reuters, Cizur Menor, pp 393–439
Rocco A (1932) Opere giuridiche. Foro italiano, Roma
Rocco A (2001) El objeto del delito y de la tutela jurídica penal: contribución a las teorías generales del delito y de la pena. B de F, Buenos Aires
Rocco A (2003) Cinco estudios de Derecho penal. B de F, Montevideo
Rocco A (2009) El Problema y el método de la ciencia del derecho penal, 3rd edn. Temis, Bogotá
Röder KDA (1875) Estudios sobre Derecho penal y sistemas penitenciarios: fundamento jurídico de la pena correccional. Imprenta de T. Fortanet, Madrid
Rodríguez Manzanera L (1981) Criminología, 2nd edn. Porrúa, Ciudad de México: Porrúa
Romagnosi GD (1791) La genesi del diritto penale

Rossi P (1829) Traité de droit penal. Paris et Genève
Rossi P (1843) Cours d'économie politique, 2nd edn. Joubert G. Thorel, Paris
Sainz Guerra J (2004) La evolución del Derecho penal en España. Universidad de Jaén, Jaén
Saldaña Q (1920) Comentarios científico-prácticos al Código penal de 1870. Editorial Reus, Madrid
Saldaña Q (1923) El futuro código penal: la reforma del código penal. Editorial Reus, Madrid
Saldaña Q (1929a) El momento de España (ensayos de sociología política). Mundo Latino, Madrid
Saldaña Q (1929b) La criminologie nouvelle. Presses universitaires, Paris
Saldaña Q (1935) Die pragmatische Gerechtigkeit. Verlag für Staatswissenschaften und Geschichte, Berlin-Grunewald
Salillas R (1888) La vida penal en España, Madrid: Imprenta de la Revista de la Legislación
Salillas R (1896) El delincuente español. El lenguaje (estudio filológico, psicológico y sociológico) con dos vocabularios jergales, Madrid: Librería de Victoriano Suárez (available at http://www.cervantesvirtual.com/obra/el-delincuente-espanol-el-lenguaje-estudio-filologico-psicologicoy-sociologico-con-dos-vocabularios-jergales%2D%2D0/)
Salillas R (1899) Los locos delincuentes en España. RGLJ, T. LXIV, pp 117–142
Sánchez González MD (2004) La Codificación penal en España. Los Códigos de 1848 y 1850. Centro de Estudios Políticos y Constitucionales, Madrid
Sidgwick H (1884) The methods of ethics, 3rd edn. Macmillan and co., London
Sidgwick H (1887) The principles of political economy, 2nd edn. MacMillan Company, New York
Sierra López MV (1997) Las medidas de seguridad en el nuevo Código penal. Tirant Lo Blanch, Valencia
Silvela F (1839) Colección de proyectos, dictámenes y leyes orgánicas, o estudios prácticos
Silvela F (1874) El Derecho penal estudiado en sus principios y en la legislación vigente en España. Madrid
Silvela F (1886) El Código penal y el sentido común. Madrid
Silvela F (1898) El Derecho Penal y los sistemas fatalistas y deterministas de la Antropología Criminal. La España Moderna, Madrid
Stooss C (1892) Die grundzüge des schweizerischen strafrechts im auftrage des Bundesrathes vergleichend. Verlag von H. Georg, Basel – Genf
Tejada Bergado C (2007) La Banca extranjera en España, 1898-1921. Su incidencia en la consolidación de la banca actual española, Universidad Complutense de Madrid, Madrid
Tiana Ferrer A (2006) The workers' movement and popular education in contemporary Spain (1868-1939). Paedagogica Historica 32:647–684
Tratado definitivo de paz y amistad entre la República de México y su Majestad Católica (1836), art. 4
Van Den Haag E (1992) Commentary: the lex talionis before and after criminal law. Crim Justice Ethics 11(1):2–62. https://doi.org/10.1080/0731129X.1992.9991905
Van Hamel AG (1889) La responsabilité pour la résultat dans le droit penal. J. Guttentag, Berlin
Varela Suanzes J (1997) El debate sobre el sistema británico de gobierno en España durante el primer tercio del Siglo XIX. In: Alvarado J (coord) Poder, Economía y Clientelismo. Marcial Pons, Madrid, pp 97–124
Vega Armentero R (1890) ¿Loco o delincuente? Novela social contemporánea, Madrid: El Porvenir, 1890
Vervaele JAE (2020) Gerhardus Antonius van Hamel (1842-1917) and the new horizons of criminal justice under penal positivism. GLOSSAE. Eur J Leg Hist 17:211–232
Voltaire (1764) Dictionnaire philosophique
Von Liszt F (1896) La legislación penal comparada. Revista de Medicina y Cirugía Prácticas, Madrid
Von Liszt F (1898) Die Deliktsobligationen im System des Bürgerlichen Gesetzbuch. Kristische und dogmatische Randbemerkungen. J. Guttentag, Berlin
Von Liszt F (1906) Strafrechtsfaelle zum akademischen Gebrauch, 8th edn. Gustav Fischer, Jena

Von Liszt F (1927) Le droit international: exposé systématique. Pedone, Paris
Von Liszt F (1970) Strafrechtliche Aufsätze und Vorträge. Walter de Gruyter & Co., Berlin
Von Liszt F (1984) La idea de fin en el derecho penal. Edeval, Valparaíso
Wieland C (1774) Die Geschichte der Abderiten
Zola É (1893) La bête humaine. Bibliothèque-Charpentier, Paris

Chapter 4
Dorado Montero's Foreign Influences

Abstract The influx Dorado Montero received was varied. Essentially, he mixed a strong rationalism arising from Kant, and some other German authors, with the Italian advances in criminal anthropology (criminology) and sociology. Although the most apparent influence could be Italian, very easily seen in Dorado Montero's first years, another significant influence can be traced to the German-speaking world. Paul Eltzbacher, Immanuel Kant, Franz von Liszt, Josef Scheicher, Johann Gottlieb Fichte, Karl David August Röder, Heinrich Albert Zachariä, Friedrich Julius Stahl, Max Stirner, Ludwig Andreas Feuerbach, Fritz Schiff, Karl Christian Friedrich Krause and Georg Heinrich Schneider. The Italian group was, however, far more nurtured: Raffaele Garofalo, Scipio Sighele, Emanuele Carnevale, Francesco Nitti, Roberto Ardigò, Cesare Lombroso, Arturo Rocco, Pellegrino Rossi, Domenico Giuriati, Cesare Beccaria, Paolo Mantegazza, Enrico Morselli, Augusto Tamburini, Antonio Marro, Luigi Luciani, Angelo Mosso, Giuseppe Sergi, Napoleone Colajanni, Giuseppe Seppili, Francesco Carrara, Giovanni Carmignani, Enrico Pessina, Francesco Poletti, Michele Angelo Vaccaro, Luigi Lucchini, Enrico Ferri, Vincenzo Lilla, Ferdinando Puglia, Ugo Conti, Bernardino Alimena and Gian Domenico Romagnosi.

On behalf of the rest of the influences, mainly French and English ones can be found. It cannot be said that Positivism was an exclusively Italian invention: Comte, first, and the English and the Germans afterwards, have been the leaders of this trend, and they still are. That is why the French influence was studied (Alfred Fouillée, Auguste Comte, Alfred Espinas, Gabriel Tarde and Albert Rivière). Also, there are some brief outlines on the Polish, Russian and American influences, with significant less weight. Finally, out of this scheme, a selection of the most representative authors (up to fourteen) in Dorado Montero's though was carried out.

Dorado Montero was a man of his time. In developing his theory, influences from krausism, socialism and anarchism are visible, among others. His most immediate influences dated no earlier than the eighteenth century, but he also considered ideas from earlier times. A striking characteristic of his work is the series of contradictions between concepts arising from Aristotelian and Aquinian philosophy, and their

J. Franco-Chasán, *The Reception of Positivism in Spain*, Studies in the History of Law and Justice 28, https://doi.org/10.1007/978-3-031-46435-5_4

different approaches in the work of the Nominalists[1] and, later, the Empiricists. Overall, Dorado Montero was one of the most well-educated scholars in Europe, and trying to analyse every influence on his thinking is a difficult task which would far exceed the scope of this volume. This chapter attempts only a general outline of fourteen particular doctrinal influences, and the way they affected him. With further research, much of what is said here could be developed further in both quantity and depth.

The influences on Dorado Montero came from various jurisdictions: German, French, Italian, English, Austrian, Polish, Russian, American, and Dutch. Some were more numerous than others, and some involved more varied authors with fewer insights. However, acknowledging all of them is vital to fully comprehend the construction of Dorado Montero's thought.

From Germany, Dorado Montero engaged with Paul Eltzbacher (1868–1928), Immanuel Kant (1724–1804), Franz von Liszt (1851–1919), Josef Scheicher (1842–1924), Johann Gottlieb Fichte (1762–1814), Karl David August Röder (1806–1879), Heinrich Albert Zachariä (1806–1875), Friedrich Julius Stahl (1802–1861), Max Stirner (1806–1856), Ludwig Andreas Feuerbach (1804–1872), Fritz Schiff (1889–1940), Karl Christian Friedrich Krause (1781–1832) and Georg Heinrich Schneider (1846–1904).

He was influenced by fewer French works, with only five authors identified: Alfred Fouillé (1838–1912), Auguste Comte (1798–1857), Alfred Espinas (1844–1922), Gabriel Tarde (1843–1904) and Albert Rivière (1853–1929).

Italian thinking had a much greater impact on him in the form of Raffaele Garofalo (1851–1934), Scipio Sighele (1868–1913), Emanuele Carnevale (1861–1944), Francesco Nitti (1868–1953), Roberto Ardigò (1828–1920), Cesare Lombroso (1835–1909), Arturo Rocco (1876–1942), Pellegrino Rossi (1787–1848), Domenico Giuriati (1829–1904), Cesare Beccaria (1783–1794), Paolo Mantegazza (1831–1910), Enrico Morselli (1852–1929), Augusto Tamburini (1848–1919), Antonio Marro (1835–1913), Luigi Luciani (1842–1919), Angelo Mosso (1846–1910), Giuseppe Sergi (1841–1936), Napoleone Colajanni (1847–1921), Giuseppe Seppili (1851–1939), Francesco Carrara (1805–1888), Giovanni Carmignani (1768–1847), Enrico Pessina (1828–1916), Francesco Poletti (1821–1895), Michele Angelo Vaccaro (1854–1937), Luigi Lucchini (1847–1929), Enrico Ferri (1856–1929), Vincenzo Lilla (1837–1905), Ferdinando Puglia, Ugo Conti (1864–1942), Bernardino Alimena (1861–1915) and Gian Domenico Romagnosi (1761–1835).

There was also some English influence: Herbert Spencer (1820–1903), Jeremy Bentham (1748–1832), David Hume (1711–1776) and John Stuart Mill (1806–1873); and an Austrian influx: Salomon Stricker (1834–1898), Julius Vargha (1841–1909), and Max Nordau (1849–1923).

Finally, there were some Polish points of contact: Ludwig Gumplowicz (1838–1909)-, some Russian ones—Leo Tolstoy (1828–1910), Fyodor Dostoevsky

[1]Carpintero Benítez (2008), p. 109, 117–131, 133–139.

(1821–1881) and Alexander Herzen (1812–1870)—a Dutch one—Jacob Moleschott (1822–1893)—and some Americans—Franklin Henry Giddings (1855–1931), James Mark Baldwin (1861–1934) and William Tallack (1831–1908).

4.1 Key authors

4.1.1 Immanuel Kant (1724–1804)

Positivism was not an exclusively Italian invention: "Comte, first, and the English and Germans afterwards, have been the leaders of this trend, and they still are".[2] Indeed, positivism had a German flavour. The general movement which prevailed in both the late 18th and in the nineteenth century had its origin in one of the best known German philosophers of all time: Immanuel Kant. His influence should not be a surprise when considering any absolute theories of punishment, nor in works defending relative theories. Among the latter, Feuerbach and Dorado Montero stood out, and both saw themselves as influenced from the very beginning by Kant.[3] It is not possible to distinguish Feuerbach from the Kantian approach solely because he held relative, rather than absolute, theories,[4] and Kant's influence on his conception of criminal law theory was tangible.[5] Dorado Montero acknowledged Kant's influence as fundamental from a very early stage, and he quoted Carle to prove it:

> The reason for this is that Kant, even if he had been strongly resisted, was always the giant who dominated and pushed the rest in the rational direction, and exerted his influence over those willing to fight his doctrines, without excluding our Gioberti and Rosmini.[6]

Dorado Montero's work coincided with years of "vibrancy and fighting" between the supporters and detractors of the 'new school', 'positivist school' and 'anthropological school'. He realised that the differences among them were "not that big" and that they all "commune in spirit and truth within a same church, i.e. the classical church".[7]

Kant's influence was clear in both the Neoclassical and the Positivist Schools, and in Dorado Montero's doctrine. Absolute theories of punishment raised serious concerns about teleological theories (*Zweckstrafe*). For them, the penalty for crime did not have to fulfil any utilitarian goal, and a Kantian conception fit within this

[2]Dorado Montero (1889), p. 13.

[3]Naucke (1962), p. 2: "*Kein Zweifel demnach, dass Kants Werke am Anfang von Feuerbachs geistiger Entwicklung eine bestimmende Rolle gespielt haben*".

[4]Naucke (1962), p. 4: "*Was Feuerbach mit dem Denken vor Kant gemeinsam hat, verringert damit die Gefahr einer allzu grossen Vereinfachung, die die Begrenzung des Themas auf Feuerbachs Verhältnis nur zu Kant (und nicht auch zu anderen Denkern) mit sich bringt*".

[5]Seeger (1892), p. 81.

[6]Carle (1880), p. 33.

[7]Dorado Montero (1893a), p. 9.

array of ideas. In the words of Dorado Montero, "idealist philosophy has dominated in Italy for a long time, especially German idealism".[8] Consequently, he also argued that the development of Italian legal science was, essentially, a development of Kantian doctrine. Nevertheless, he thought that only Carlo Cantoni[9] could be described as a true disciple of Kant.[10] However, this claim is not completely fair: Cantoni criticised certain "inner contradictions" in Kant's thought, and strongly believed in the possibility of developing a "realist-spiritualist" theory.[11] Any follower who raises that many concerns arguably ceases to be a true disciple. The number of corrections and amendments Cantoni made to Kant's doctrine was, in fact, so large that he is often described not as a Kantian but as a "critical realist".[12] Besides, in what we might call his 'reinterpretation' of Kant, he adopted a dualist interpretation very far from, for instance, Fichte's idealism: "The Kantianism of Carlo Cantoni is characterised by the annihilation of all the basic principles with which Immanuel Kant affirmed the creative achievements of the mind and human thought [. . .]. It is not necessary to say that the representatives of New Kantianism, to which Cantoni explicitly adhered [...], did not intend to think any more in the direction taken by Johann Gottlieb Fichte".[13]

Even though even contradictory doctrines shared cornerstone aspects of Kant's "idealist" philosophy, the bigger picture should be borne in mind. Kant was equally responsible for the mental frameworks adopted by both absolutist and relativists, but this should not be over-emphasised: Kant's theory was also in some ways incompatible with relativist theories. Without going any further, Dorado Montero pointed out that idealism only considered Kant's concept of 'rational liberty', not his ideas about 'free will'. Idealism was characterised by the "contraposition of two orders, physical and moral" and the idea the "latter should be subjected to human liberty".

---

[8] Dorado Montero (1889), p. 10: "*la filosofía idealista ha dominado en Italia durante mucho tiempo, singularmente la alemana*".

[9] Italian philosopher and professor in Pavia (1840–1906). His most representative works were: Cantoni (1870a); Cantoni (1870b); Kant (1907); Kant (1867).

[10] Dorado Montero (1889), p. 10.

[11] Cantoni C, *La web de las biografías*. http://www.mcnbiografias.com/app-bio/.

[12] Cantoni C, *La web de las biografías*. http://www.mcnbiografias.com/app-bio/.

[13] Gentile (2016), pp. 409–410: "*So zeichnet sich denn der Kantianismus von CARLO CANTONI aus durch die Vernichtung aller Grundprinzipien, mit denen IMMANUEL KANT die schöpferischen Leistungen des Geistes, des Denkens geltend gemacht hat, und was die bedeutsame philosophische Revolutionierung losgetreten und wenn man so will schon vollführt hat, die der althergebrachten Metaphysik ein Ende bereitet. Dass sich die Vertreter des Neu-Kantianismus, zu denen sich Cantoni zum Abschluss des breteffenden Werks selber ausdrücklich gesellt, nicht mit der Absicht getraten haben, den Kantianismus in der von JOHANN GOTTLIEB FICHTE eingeschlagenen Richtung weiterzudenken, das versteht sich von selbst; und so ist durchaus anzunehmen, dass manche Philosophen, die man mit Fug und Recht als Neu-Kantianer bezeichnen kann, den Kantischen Kritizismus, die Erkenntniskritik über die von Kant gezogenen Grenzen hinaus weitergeführt haben; aber dass man einen zu den Vertretern des Kantianismus rechnet, der die Grundlagen des Kritizismus in Bausch und Bogen zurückweist, diese Einordnung zu vertreten, schein nicht besonders vernünftig zu sein*".

But such human liberty was always concerned with "rational liberty, never free will".[14]

What was the cause of this departure? For Kant, moral duty was the expression of an imperative which prevailed over any need or natural inclination. Every such duty was required to pass the test of autonomy and comply with the principle of universality. A person should decide by themselves what was morally good, without external empirical or theological constraints (free will). But for all that, reason should indicate what could be considered good from a universal perspective (rational liberty); and if both were engaged could one speak of a completely autonomous decision. Kant therefore identified two dimensions to human reason: theorical reason (pure reason, i.e. 'knowing'), and practical reason, which determined the will, i.e. individual moral action. Kant described 'pure' reason as free of external influence from anything empirical, traditional or teleological (such as religion)—a reason which acted by itself (rational liberty). 'Practical reason' determined moral duty assuming its universalisation (free will). Kant held that acting with freedom (free will) entailed acting in accordance with the law, i.e. adjusting conduct to what reason demanded (rational freedom), in spite of whether it was pleasant or desirable.[15]

Thus, the difference between 'free will' and 'rational liberty' played a major role. There is a connection between this and Dorado Montero's comments on the work of the Italian philosopher Ariodante Mambelli. He pointed out that Mambelli admitted all the principles of traditional philosophy, namely the "distinction of two orders (natural and supernatural)", the "categorical subordination of certain things to others (things to animals, animals to man, man to God), the "consideration of man as the single being with reflexive conscience", the existence of "two entities (spirit and body)" and the "contrast of two orders (the physical one and the moral one)".[16] Nevertheless, Mambelli stressed that morality should be subjected to human freedom—"but to 'rational freedom', not to 'free will'".[17] It seemed to unavoidably follow from this that "only a rational being has the capacity to act according to a set of rules, i.e. he has a will".[18] This could be interpreted as indicating the existence of a "capacity to act", which, in turn, also indicated a "minimum notion of freedom or autonomy" as opposed to "not plainly to immoral acting" but to "compulsive acting" (where, strictly speaking, the agent does not participate). Therefore, defining "rational liberty" as somehow "independent from the inclination" implied a "capacity to act emanating from reflection on the action's grounds" and not "compulsively", despite of whether they were moral or not.[19]

Ferri also made a differentiation between 'free will' and 'limited moral freedom':

---

[14]Dorado Montero (1891a), p. 114.

[15]I am grateful to Professor Talavera Fernández from the University of Valencia for being particularly helpful in explaining such aspect of Kant's theory.

[16]Dorado Montero (1891a), p. 112–113.

[17]Dorado Montero (1891a), p. 114.

[18]Marey (2011), p. 91.

[19]Marey (2011), p. 91.

> The most recent criminalists, from the Classical School, have also abandoned the old idea of an absolute freewill as the basis and condition for an absolute moral imputability of the man, and have restricted themselves [. . .] to a limited moral freedom, which would correspond to a limited or relative moral imputability.[20]

Leaving aside the purely legal technical aspects, Dorado Montero concluded by reasserting that the grounds of both positions were united:

> Hence, the harmonisation between the two opposed schools (idealist and positivist) far from being impossible (as it might look like prima facie), is required by the inner exigency which they both represent: the theory of the social contract, reduced to its just limits, purged from its exaggerations as regards liberty, restricted to its own circle of action (that of 'rational liberty'), unites itself in a loving consortium, and forms one single [theory] altogether with the theory of determinism, with its mistakes corrected in turn corrected, especially that of mechanical determinism.[21]

This was the reality of new legal philosophy, which was named the "theory of psychic causality" in psychology, and "critical positivism" in general philosophy.[22]

At the time, Alfonso Testa fought the new Italian criminal trends "with the weapons of 'transcendental idealism'". In 1843, he published a very detailed, critical examination of that trend in *Della Critica della raggione pura di Kant,* and he ended up declaring himself a Kantian.[23] Nonetheless, Dorado Montero was confident that "after examining [the works of the Italian scholars]" one came to the conclusion that the rest was, ultimately, "the very same as what Kant exposed".[24]

Therefore, despite being opposed groups, both the idealists and the experimentalists were influenced by Kant. Dorado Montero briefly outlined the two main schools of idealism: the Catholic Philosophers and the Hegelian School. The former followed representatives of Italian philosophy or *italianísima* (as he posed it), who sought to harmonise Christianity with Kant and Hegel (Mamiani, Galluppi, Luis Ferri, Bertini, Bonatelli, Ferrari, Franchi, Gioberti, Rosmini, and Conti).[25] The Hegelian school highlighted other thinkers, like the Spaventa brothers (Bertran and Silvio), Antonio Tari, De Meis, Nicolas Marselli, Barzelotti and Francisco de

[20]Ferri (1884a), p. 53: "I criminalisti più recenti, della scuola classica, hanno abbandonata pure la vecchia idea di un assoluto libero arbitrio, come base e condizione di un 'assoluta imputabilità morale dell'uomo, e si sono ristretti, collo stesso processo di transizione fra il vecchio ed il nuovo, ad una libertà morale limitata, cui corrisponderebbero una limitata o relativa imputabilità morale".

[21]Dorado Montero (1891b), p. 248: "Por donde se ve cómo la armonía entre las dos escuelas contrarias, idealista y positivista, lejos de ser, como á primera vista aparece, imposible, es una necesidad reclamada por la interna exigencia que ambas representan: la teoría del contrato social, reducida á sus justos límites, purgada de sus exageraciones en orden á la libertad, y contraída al círculo propio de su acción, el de la libertad racional, se une en amoroso consorcio y forma, por así decirlo, una misma con la teoría del determinismo, corregida, á su vez, de sus yerros, sobre todo del del determinismo mecánico".

[22]Dorado Montero (1891b), p. 248.

[23]Testa (1843). This author developed this idea further in other works, especially: Testa (1848).

[24]Dorado Montero (1889), p. 10.

[25]Dorado Montero (1889), p. 11.

Santis.[26] Experimentalism was, however, harder to defend. It differed from idealism and, because it was 'new', its main exponents were "few and very obscured by the idealists".[27] Dorado Montero briefly identified two subgroups within experimentalism: the earlier ones[28] and the main ones. Among the former were Galile, Vico, Giordano Bruno, Pedro Pomponazzi, Genovesi, Spedalieri, and Beccaria. Among the main experimentalist thinkers, he only stressed Gioia and Romagnosi, giving the latter particular importance. Finally, Dorado Montero concluded that even if the experimentalists were important in the appearance of positivist thought (and, thus, in his thinking as well), the influence of Kant could never be denied and constituted a constant, i.e. a common ground, for most scholars:

> That is how Italy, under the influence of Locke and Condillac (the latter being the mentor of Gioia and Romagnosi themselves), and Kantian doctrine itself, has been educating and instructing a whole generation little by little in what is today called 'positivism'.[29]

However, for Dorado Montero, it was self-evident that not all positivists liked to be connected with Kant (or especially with his idea of free will). Yet, "as soon as one examines his works, one will realise that, leaving aside some minor considerations, the rest is, in essence, the same as what was exposed by Kant".[30] This idea was developed in later works when criticising the unstraightforward determinism used by positivist and determinist authors alike. Kantian idealism was one theory, Italian positivism was another based on it, and there were middle ground schools in between: a third tendency which developed was far more rational than the two extremes. Dorado Montero noted that Italians were "very fond of balance, and very willing to move the same distance away from both German idealism and English positivism".[31] He described this third school as transitive and superior, and thought it was likely to outlast the others. However, there are some further points to note here.

When reading the two volumes of Dorado Montero's key work, it is possible to misunderstand his ideas. He devoted a great deal of effort to criticising the detractors of free will, who seemed to betray their own ideals: most of them ultimately resorted to an idea of penal liability. When he also criticised the position of the Third School as half-hearted, he was not arguing in favour of extremist positivism: his criticism was in fact directed towards incongruencies in positivist thinking. Rather than attacking positivism itself, he drew attention to the fact that contemporary ideas

---

[26] Dorado Montero (1889), p. 11.

[27] Dorado Montero (1889), p. 12: "eran escasos, y los que había, casi casi estaban oscurecidos por los idealistas".

[28] Those constituted a sort of 'proto-positivist' group.

[29] Dorado Montero (1889), p. 12: "Así es como Italia, bajo el influjo de Locke y de Condillac (este último maestro de los mismos Gioia y Romagnosi), y bajo el influjo asimismo de la propia doctrina kantiana, ha venido formando poco á poco y educando en lo que hoy se llama 'positivismo' á toda una generación".

[30] Dorado Montero (1889), p. 10.

[31] Dorado Montero (1889), p. 13–14.

about punishment were Kantian. Almost every theory in Criminal law was rooted in the same doctrine from almost three centuries ago: Kant's. This mode of thinking naturally led to a kind of eclecticism; indeed, Catholic philosophers "tried to harmonise Christianity with modern philosophy (Kant, Hegel or Binding); even when, on the other hand, they tried to oppose them".[32]

All of this could suggest that Kant's influence on Dorado Montero led him to a mild eclecticism. In 1889, he described the main aspects of the positivist school: "that universal man, the so-called reference-man (the one as held by idealism) is just pure abstraction, because men in real life have their special way of being [...] Crime is a relative thing and there is no act which is criminal per se".[33] At first, this appears to be a simple description of the positivist school. However, in 1915, he connected his particular theory with positivist characteristics: "There is no crime, just as there is no law either, except that which men create [...] If the mental orders created by each individual would place all men on an equal footing, with none of them imposing on others, communal legal life would be impossible. Therefore, crime would also be impossible".[34]

4.1.2 Karl David August Röder (1806–1879)

Röder has often been classified as a correctionalist.[35] However, when outlining the main theories of criminality, he notoriously paused at absolutist theory in order to criticise it. He explained the main features of absolutist theory, then pointed out its main defect: "the uncertainty of this theory, as well as the fragility of its assertions about the 'purported' opposition between morality and law".[36] Many 'absolutists' wanted retribution based on the external result of an action, whereas others thought that retribution ought to reflect only the internal relation between people.[37]

In the foreword of one of the editions of Krause's work,[38] Richard Mucke asserted the following:

> The subsequent treaty contains the pamphlet on the lectures on Natural Law or Legal Philosophy/Philosophy of the State, as Krause re-wrote it for the first lecture in Göttingen in the summer of 1826, and he amended and improved it for the second lecture in the

[32]Dorado Montero (1889), p. 11.

[33]Dorado Montero (1889), p. 24.

[34]Dorado Montero (1915), p. 15.

[35]Quisbert (2008), p. 56.

[36]Röder (1867): "so zeigt sich hier besonders ausfallend das Unhaltbare der Theorie, zugleich aber die Richtigkeit er Behauptung eines Gegensasses zmischen Recht und Sittlichkeit".

[37]Röder (1867), p. 63: "Was nun den Bregiff des Verbrechens, als des zu Vergeltenden, betrifft, den die absolute Theorie gibt –indem Einige nur äuseren Erfolg der That, Andere aber nur das Innere bei der That: das Gewollte, also die böse Willensrichtung oder Schuld im Sinn des Sprachgebrauchs, vergelten mollen".

[38]Krause (1892).

> summer of 1828 and again later on. Yet, according to the handwritten note of the author himself, not everything in it was presented and not all of what was presented was written down in the pamphlet. [...] Both transcriptions were used by Röder as the main basis for the lectures he published in 1874 on the system of Legal Philosophy (Leipzig, Brockhaus).[39]

As we have seen, like Dorado Montero, who adopted many of the same postulates, Röder was directly influenced by the theories of Krause. In order to complement Röder's view on Krause's writings, it would be interesting to consider Mucke's edition, as that version "contains a great number of deep thoughts or, at least, fragments thereof which Röder did not use".[40] Dorado Montero based his reasoning on Röder's approach to the lack of consistency in positivist doctrines. Röder maintained that "it would be an obvious nonsense to make punishment dependent merely on the existence of an external, even if blameless, damage caused by merely natural human forces (e.g., by chance, unsurmountable error, compulsion)."[41] That was to say, that one should not ground punishment *solely* on the external wrong.

Röder was well-known among Spanish scholars to the extent that he translated a work by Giner de los Ríos into German.[42] He also had some ideas with respect to indeterminate sentences. He "showed himself a pioneer", but "gave into the environment of his time" since he "advocated for the cell-isolation regime" but also supported an intermediate stage "in which evidence of the amendment [of the criminal] was proved and ascertained".[43] Nevertheless, Antón Oneca was not enthusiastic about correctionalism, or Röder's particular approach, because of the degree of legal uncertainty it entailed: "It is based on a concept of law, undifferentiated from morality, which by grounding the legality or wrongdoing of conduct exclusively in the inclination of the will, seriously endangers legal certainty".[44] As for the cell-isolation system, the main reason Röder defended it that inmates had to remain

---

[39] Krause (1892), p. 4: "Die nachfolgende Abhandlung enthält das Heft zu den Vorlesungen über Naturrecht oder Philosophie des Rechts und Staates, wie es Krause für den erstmaligen Vortrag in Göttingen im Sommer 1826 neubearbeitete und zu dem zweitmaligen Vortrage im Sommer 1828 und doch noch später ergänzte und verbesserte. Doch wurde nach des Verfassers eigner handschriftlicher Bemerkung nicht alles darin Enthaltene wirklich vorgetragen und nicht alles Vorgetragene im Hefte niedergeschrieben. [...] Beide Niederschriften dienten Röder zur Hauptgrundlage der von ihm 1874 herausgegebenen Vorlesungen über das System der Rechtsphilosophie (Leipzig, Brockhaus)".

[40] Krause (1892), p. 4: "indem eine grosse Anzahl tiefer Gedanken oder wenigstens Gedankensplitter in dem Hefte enthalten sind, die Röder nicht verwerthete".

[41] Röder (1867), p. 64: "Es würde offenbarer Unsinn sein, bloß vom Dasein eines äußeren, wenn auch schuldlos, durch lediglich naturgesesslich mirkende Kräfte des Menschen (z.B. durch Zufall, unüberwindlichen Irrthum, Zwang) angerichteten, Schadens die Strafe abhängig machen".

[42] Giner de los Ríos and Calderón (1907).

[43] Antón Oneca (1960), p. 1016: "Y Röder, que, en la previsión de la sentencia indeterminada, se mostró precursor, en cambio cedió al ambiente de la época al preconizar el régimen de aislamiento celular, si bien fue también partidario de un grado intermedio donde se asegurase y se sujetara a prueba la reforma que hay podido experimentar".

[44] Antón Oneca (1960), p. 1016: "Se parte de un concepto del Derecho, indiferenciado de la moral, que al hacer radicar la juridicidad o antijuridicidad de la conducta exclusivamente en la inclinación de la voluntad, pone en grave peligro a la seguridad jurídica".

"completely and constantly separate from each other".[45] Otherwise, a prison would be nothing but a corruption centre, since there was "a reciprocal instruction and teaching in perversion".[46] In his opinion, the benefits were numerous: "it calms their 'irritated passions', promotes 'self-reflection', their inner 'retreat' and a taste for work, and turns them into 'more compliant' individuals".[47] This was seen in the "fast progress the convicted demonstrate on their instruction".[48] Röder attempted to rebut criticisms of the "cell-isolation system". It was argued, and still is nowadays, that such a system dehumanised individuals, affected their brains and caused a propensity to depression. For Röder, the latter was not as clear:

> Mental illnesses as such (as opposed to the mere transitory hallucinations) are, just as suicide, less common in equal circumstances in cell-isolation prisons than in the old prisons.[49]

If instead of "moving the inmate away from the company of the rest of the criminals", one was to lock the convicted in a cell without work or contact with anybody, that could cause regrettable outcomes: "Such insane mistakes were made in the first tests conducted in North America, with the terrible results that you would expect".[50] However, as time went on, those mistakes were corrected by "essentially reforming the whole organisation and execution of the cell regime—especially in Europe". As a German, Röder was up to date with the legal developments of his country and quoted a "report addressed to the Senate of Bremen"[51] in which several reasons were offered as to why the isolation system was not harmful. In essence, it was argued that the necessary human contact was provided in the Pennsylvania system since the supervisor, employees and personnel of the prison coming and going was enough to make the prisoner forget his isolation. Besides, there were several complementary activities such as outdoor exercise, religious practices and leisure time which the inmate could "devote to useful readings". Thus, for "no man possessing healthy mental faculties can this regime [. . .] produce the slightest disturbance".[52] The possibility of failure that Röder admitted in the cell-isolation system was in a "defect of the treatment/performance of the regime", e.g., disciplinary measures of deprivation of light, nourishment, etc. The report concluded with the following statement:

---

[45] Röder (1876), p. 332.

[46] Röder (1876), p. 332.

[47] Röder (1876), p. 351.

[48] Röder (1876), p. 352.

[49] Röder (1876), p. 353: "Las enfermedades mentales propiamente dichas (á distinción de las meras alucinaciones transitorias) son, así como el suicidio [...] mucho más raras en igualdad de condiciones en las prisiones celulares que en las antiguas".

[50] Röder (1876), p. 354: "Errores tan insanos se cometieron en los primeros ensayos que de este sistema se hicieron en América del Norte, y con el pésimo resultado que era de suponer".

[51] I have not been able to find any other reference to such a report.

[52] Röder (1876), p. 355: "En ningun hombre que tenga sanas sus facultades puede semejante régimen [...] producir la más mínima perturbación".

> The assertion that isolation leads to weakening and to truncating the strength of the spirit is always contrary to the truth [. . .] The opinion that when those convicted gain their liberty back, they are uncapable of socialising with other men is also false.[53]

Recidivism is the last aspect worth mention in respect of Röder. He did not attribute any responsibility for recidivism to the cell-isoltation system and thought that this was infrequent. It happened with those inmates "whose imprisonment was too short" and criminals "very used to the criminal business".[54] His position as to incorrigible criminals was perfectly summarised:

> In this category of prisoners, neither the cell-regime nor any other can work the miracle of bringing them to a better life before long; they themselves are as difficult to convert as the political criminals, because they are used to acting according to their own principles and opinions (i.e. Communists).[55]

What Röder pursued, rather than trying to annihilate inmates' personalities, was neutralising the kind of criminal subculture that could be found in densely populated ordinary prisons, where the constant contact between inmates corrupted otherwise average or corrigible criminals, since the dynamics of power within a penitentiary usually forced 'good' inmates to fall into the practices, morals and values of the 'evil' or 'corrupted' inmates.[56] Röder extensively listed some of the vices found in prisons, arguing that the "intimate treatment and close connection among a great number of demoralized men" was extremely dangerous.[57] Also, "the cohabitation" between the inmates who had "an analogous way of thinking and of feeling" did not only weaken the force of their punishment, but invested the penalty with "a special charm".[58] The exemplariness of the penalty was destroyed, as some criminals were convicted several times and prison came to "feel. . . like home, and, indeed, nothing in their punishment makes them suffer".[59]

In summary, Röder's writing focused on the "separate" or "Pennsylvania system", as opposed to the "classification" or "Ausburn system". The "classification system" essentially consisted of the separation of inmates into groups, and was

[53]Röder (1876), pp. 355–356: "La afirmación de que el aislamiento conduce á debilitar y truncar las fuerzas del espíritu es precisamente contraria á la verdad siempre [...] No menos falsa es la opinión de que, al recobrar su libertad estos reos, son ya incapaces para el trato social con los otros hombres".

[54]Röder (1876), p. 358.

[55]Röder (1876), p. 359: "En esta clase de reos, ni el régimen celular ni ningun otro puede hacer el milagro de traerlos á mejor vida en poco tiempo; siendo en su mayor parte casi tan difíciles de convertir como los delincuentes políticos: porque también ellos están acostumbrados á obrar por principios y opiniones propias (á saber, comunistas)".

[56]"The purportedly beneficial influence of the bests over the rest of the inmates is nothing but an illusion. On the contrary, they [. . .] end up giving in the general perversion". Röder (1876), p. 332.

[57]Röder (1876), p. 333.

[58]Röder (1876), p. 334.

[59]Röder (1876), p. 335.

particularly associated with the work of William Hendrick Suringar.[60] The Ausburn system only separated inmates at night, but in the daytime there was absolute silence.[61] Röder criticised both approaches, as he thought the only way to create true isolation was the Pennsylvania system.[62] The others "both produce a semi-isolation, a misrepresentation which is more figurative than real [...] thus they constitute the origin of new inconveniences".[63]

4.1.3 Georg Heinrich Schneider (1846–1904)

The works of the German psychologist and philosopher Georg Heinrich Schneider also influenced Dorado Montero, including indirectly through Ferri. In his *Nuovi orizzonti*, Ferri quoted two in particular: *Der thierische Wille* and *Der menschliche Wille*.[64] Both texts addressed a topic of key concern to both Dorado Montero and positivism: the question of the existence of free will and determinism.

In *Der thierische Wille*,[65] Schneider pointed out that "when one speaks of a free will, it is always only relatively free" because of the "victory of more functional ideas over less functional ones".[66] There could not be any question of the existence of "an absolutely free will in man".[67] For him, the will depended entirely on both "our bodily and mental constitution, as well as on our relations to our surroundings" so it was not possible to "speak of an absolutely free choice".[68] This is a challenge, as our will has the "greatest appearance of absolute freedom" when our actions take place.[69] Obviously man's 'moral' principles were a part of the equation,[70] but the action taken was always the "most agreeable", and usually, "the most agreeable is identical with that of the greatest utility".[71]

---

[60]Willem Hendrick Suringar was "one of the founders of the Nederlandsch Genootschap tot Zedelijke Verbetering der Gevangenen", a society set up in 1823 to help rehabilitate prisoners. Vid. *Collections of Adam Pierson* (University of Amsterdam). https://archives.uba.uva.nl/agents/people/1742.

[61]Röder (1876), p. 347.

[62]At the time, isolation was considered a positive feature, unlike in modern approaches.

[63]Röder (1876), p. 349.

[64]Ferri (1884a), p. 35.

[65]Schneider (1880).

[66]Schneider (1880), p. 80: "Wenn mann von einem freien Willen spricht, so ist das allemal nur ein relativ freier. Worin besteht nun diese relativ Willensfreiheit? In dem Sieg der zweckmäßigeren Vorstellungen über unzweckmäßigere".

[67]Schneider (1880), p. 79: "Dass von einem absolut freien Willen auch beim Menschen nicht die Rede sein kann".

[68]Schneider (1880), p. 79.

[69]Schneider (1880), pp. 79–80.

[70]Schneider (1880), p. 80.

[71]Schneider (1880), p. 80.

> The principle of utility in nature has generally allowed only those animals to exist [...] as they are unpleasantly touched and deterred by the perceptions or conceptions of just those things which can harm them.[72]

The distinction between "'free' and 'not free' wills" rightly referred "mainly to human changes of will".[73] Paradoxically, animal instincts could sometimes lead to less useful decisions:

> Lively natures, in which the instincts that arise first are of such intensity that they immediately lead to action, often commit inappropriate actions, and therefore generally have a less free will than other people with less strong instincts, who are accustomed to do everything with deliberation and after careful consideration. The uneducated person, who is unable to assess the consequences of his actions, also acts more often inappropriately and less freely than the more educated person, who is fully aware of the value of his actions for the future. However, as is well known, the relative freedom of the will depends in particular on the extent to which the suppression of inappropriate impulses is or is not practised in education.[74]

Within this outline, Schneider distinguished different "degrees" of "passion and self-control" and "free and unfree will".[75] He concluded that absolute free will was not to be found in man, but admitted that a "relative freedom" was found in the "higher animals and in man". However, in the latter it "developed to a higher degree than in the higher animals"—this maintained the traditional anthropocentrist approach.[76]

In *Der menschliche Wille*,[77] after stressing the influence[78] of Kant, Spencer, Hegel and some others,[79] which in turn also influenced Dorado, Schneider stressed that "objective knowledge as such" was incapable of causing any will; it was only

---

[72] Schneider (1880), pp. 80–81: "Das Zweckmäßigkeitsprinzip in der Natur hat im allgemeinen nur diejenigen Thiere bestehen lassen, bei denen es so ist, denen die Wahrnehmung und Vorstellung gerade derjenigen Dinge angenehm find, deren Besitz dem Individuum nützt, und welche durch die Wahrnehmungen oder Vorstellungen gerade derjenigen Dinge unangenehm berührt und abgeschrekt werden, welche ihnen schaden können".

[73] Schneider (1880), p. 81.

[74] Schneider (1880), p. 82: "Lebhafte Naturen, bei denen gleich die zuerst entstehenden Triebe eine solche Intensität haben, dass sie sofort zur Action führen, begehen öster unzweckmässige Handlungen und haben deshalb im Allgemeinen einen weniger freien Willen, als andere Menschen von weniger starkem Triebleben, die gewohnt find alles mir Bedacht und nach reislicher Ueberlegung zu thun. Auch handelt der ungebildete Mensch, der die Folgen seines Thuns nicht abzuschätzen vermag, öster unzweckmässig und weniger frei als der gebildetere, der sich der Werthigkeit seiner Actionen für die Zukunft vollständig bewusst ist. Besonders aber hängt bekänntlich die relative Freiheit des Willens davon ab, wie weit in der Erziehung die Unterdrückung unzweckmässiger Triebe geübt ist oder nicht".

[75] Schneider (1880), p. 84.

[76] Schneider (1880), p. 84.

[77] Schneider (1882).

[78] Schneider (1882), pp. 265–266.

[79] Also Lotze, Bain and Wolff.

because the "knowledge of the good" was connected with the "pleasure of the good" that we strived for it.[80]

After wondering about the relationship between will and cognition, Schneider agreed with Schopenhauer: the will did not emerge from "cognition", but rather the will was the "original"; it existed "before all cognition".[81]

> In recent times, it has been opined that the will is the first condition for the emergence of cognition and feelings, that feelings only express reactions to the needs and urges of the will, the satisfaction (feeling of pleasure) or non-satisfaction (feeling of displeasure) of the same, and that they form the intermediary link by means of which we learn something about our own will, which is in itself unconscious.[82]

Schneider was very convinced of the "inherently unconscious character of the will", since we can be "mistaken" about our own will.[83] The fact that our will and our actions were "indirectly also followed by feelings" was based on the fact that our actions themselves and their success were "just as good objects of knowledge" as any other process: therefore, it was "quite wrong" to regard the will as the "direct origin of the feelings".[84]

4.1.4 *Raffaele Garofalo (1851–1934)*

Raffaele Garofalo, along with Lombroso and Ferri, was one of three key authors in the positivist movement.[85] It has been said they constituted "an inseparable trinity".[86] There were, nevertheless, differences in their positions:[87] Lombroso focused on anthropology (he was a medical doctor), Ferri tended towards anthropology, and Garofalo was a lawyer.[88] The latter targeted "laws and their application", where Ferri's ideas were designed for "sociologists and philosophers".[89] Working together, they created valuable contributions.[90] However, Garofalo was also a fruitful scholar

---

[80] Schneider (1882), pp. 275–276.

[81] Schneider (1882), p. 278.

[82] Schneider (1882), p. 278: "Auch in neuester Zeit ist die Ansicht, dass der Wille die erste Bedingung zur Entstehung der Erkenntniss und der Gefühle sei, dass die Gefühle nur die Reactionen auf die Bedürfnisse und Triebe des Willens, die Befriedigung (Lustgefühl) oder Nichtbefriedigung (Unlustgefühl) desselben ausdrücken, und dass sie das Mittelglied bilden, vermöge dessen wir von unserm eigenen an sich unbewussten Willen überhaupt etwas erfahren".

[83] Schneider (1882), p. 279.

[84] Schneider (1882), p. 283.

[85] Garofalo (1890b), p. 8: "The founders and main apostles thereof [are]: Lombroso, Ferri and Garofalo".

[86] Garofalo (1890b), p. 11.

[87] Ferri (1895).

[88] Collin (1927), pp.435–452.

[89] Garofalo (1890b), p. 8.

[90] Garofalo et al. (1886). Of the same authors, *cnfr*. Garofalo et al. (1890).

in his own right.[91] Two of his works in particular are worth mention: first the *Criminologia*[92] and, secondly, *Riparazione alle vittime del delitto*.[93] They were both translated into Spanish by Dorado Montero,[94] allowing Spanish jurists to engage with the works of this Italian criminologist. As the translation of the first one was nearing publication, Garofalo personally thanked Dorado Montero:

> I am very happy that the publication of the *Criminologia* is near and I am very grateful for the care which you are taking in translating this book into the beautiful Spanish language.[95]

Dorado Montero defined *Criminologia* as the "most characteristic and peculiar work of Garofalo".[96] It constituted: "the most systematic book that the emerging school had produced at the time (and maybe even until today) [. . .]. It brought the concept of natural crime forward for the first time".[97] What was particularly remarkable in this work was that Garofalo added a new element: the adaptability of the offender to social environment, which meant that "the criminal measure must [should] be determined by the possibility of the adaptation of the offender, [. . .] by examining the conditions of existence in which it may be presumed that he ceases to be fearsome".[98]

That being said, all of this corresponded to the rationale for punishment, since as soon as one focused on "the criterion for indicating [. . .] the most suitable form of social sanction" and "its degree", the conversation entered the "technical-legal part of criminal sociology".[99] In this respect, Garofalo shed some light on his *Di un criterio positivo della penalità*.[100]

Dorado Montero also referred to the *Riparazione* as "if not the most important", certainly "the most personal, exclusive and characteristic work from the author".[101] In his extensive foreword to the translation, he began with a simple contextualisation for the reader: the clash between the old, classical school of Criminal law and the new, positivist (or Italian) school. While the first was "incongruent and illogical" and nothing could "be extracted out of it", the latter was made up of nothing but a set of "nihilists of punitive law" who "became delirious" and tried to "turn every criminal

[91] Garofalo (1880, 1884, 1885, 1886, 1887a, b, 1888a, 1891a, 1914).

[92] Garofalo (1885).

[93] Garofalo (1888b).

[94] Garofalo (1890a, b).

[95] "Carta de Raffaele Garofalo a Pedro Dorado Montero", Letter III, GREDOS: *FPDM. Correspondencia de Pedro Dorado Montero. General.* https://gredos.usal.es/handle/10366/76721 . "Sono molto lieto che la pubblicazione della Criminologia sia prossima e le sono molto grato de la cura che Ella si é data di traduire questo libro nella bella lingua spagnuola", pp. 1–2.

[96] Garofalo (1890b), p. 9.

[97] Garofalo (1890b), p. 11.

[98] Garofalo (1891b), p. 330.

[99] Ferri (1884b), p. 688.

[100] Garofalo (1880).

[101] Garofalo (1890b), p. 15.

into a sick man".[102] It was worth pointing out that both the biographical and bibliographical data that Dorado Montero used in the text were obtained by first-hand correspondence. He wrote to Garofalo several times to inquire about information later used to elaborate the foreword.[103] When Dorado Montero introduced Garofalo ("from 1876, when he was barely 20 years old, he was already publishing articles which were very critical of the dominant theories in Criminal law and, in general, on the problem of punitive justice"),[104] he was essentially copying from a letter received in Italian.[105] This technique was repeated several times. When he stressed out that since the publication of the *Criminology*,[106] "two Italian editions and three French editions have seen the light";[107] when mentioning that Garofalo had been "one of the founders of the new review *La scuola positiva nella giurisprudenza penale*, which has been published in Naples under the direction of Giulio Fioretti since its appearance in 1891 until the present year, and is now published in Rome under the direction of the professor and deputy Enrico Ferri";[108] noting that "Garofalo has continued his career as a magistrate and is a Magistrate of the Regional Court";[109] indicating that "he has been appointed by the Italian Government as a member of the Commission working on the reform of the Criminal Procedure Code and on the elaboration of a new one";[110] and summarising the various congresses which the Italian jurist assisted, namely "Rome (1885, November), [. . .] the second Congress of Criminal Anthropology in Paris (1889),

[102]Garofalo (1890b), p. 6.

[103]"Carta de Raffaele Garofalo a Pedro Dorado Montero", Letter III, GREDOS: FPDM. Correspondencia de Pedro Dorado Montero. General. https://gredos.usal.es/handle/10366/76721. "qui acchuso é il cenno biografico che Ella mi domanda", p. 1.

[104]Garofalo (1890b), p. 10.

[105]"Carta de Raffaele Garofalo a Pedro Dorado Montero", Letter III, GREDOS: FPDM. Correspondencia de Pedro Dorado Montero. General. https://gredos.usal.es/handle/10366/76721. "Fin dal 1876 cominció a pubblicare articoli critici sulla teoria di diritto penale dominante ed in generale sul problema della giustizia penale", p. 4.

[106]Garofalo (1890b), p. 12.

[107]"Carta de Raffaele Garofalo a Pedro Dorado Montero", Letter III, GREDOS: FPDM. Correspondencia de Pedro Dorado Montero. General. https://gredos.usal.es/handle/10366/76721. "[...] ebbe due edizioni italiane e tre edizioni francesi", p. 5.

[108]"Carta de Raffaele Garofalo a Pedro Dorado Montero", Letter III, GREDOS: FPDM. Correspondencia de Pedro Dorado Montero. General. https://gredos.usal.es/handle/10366/76721. "Su quest'ultimo anno fu uno dei fondatori della 'Scuola positiva', rivista pubblicata finora in Napoli dall'avvocato G. Fioretti ed ora in Roma dal Professore Enrico Ferri", p. 6.

[109]"Carta de Raffaele Garofalo a Pedro Dorado Montero", Letter III, GREDOS: FPDM. Correspondencia de Pedro Dorado Montero. General. https://gredos.usal.es/handle/10366/76721. "Il Garofalo ha continuato la sua carriera di magistrato. Egli ha ora l'età di circa 40 anni ed é Consigliere di Corte di Appello", p. 7.

[110]"Carta de Raffaele Garofalo a Pedro Dorado Montero", Letter III, GREDOS: FPDM. Correspondencia de Pedro Dorado Montero. General. https://gredos.usal.es/handle/10366/76721. "Ha avuto dal Ministero italiano l'incarico di lavorare allá preparazione di un nuevo codice di procedura penale", p. 7.

the Congress of Criminal law in Brussels (1889), the Penitentiary Congress in Saint Petersburg (1890) and the Juridical Congress in Florence (1891)".[111]

Dorado Montero's assessment of Garofalo was a very positive one. No wonder, as he considered his writings to "distil in the most organic and complete way [...] the system of criminal contemporary positivism".[112] It is little surprise, too, that when comparing with Lombroso and Ferri, he did not consider them as "reflective, elaborated, systematised, logically interrelated and congruent" as Garofalo.[113] However, Dorado Montero had an objection: in short, Garofalo ought not to limit himself to developing one specific principle in the new Criminal law, but should rather develop the rest of those linked to it. Those 'principles' were stated by the correctionalist school:

> Garofalo, and the others with him, are very close to take the plunge, and they will do so as they get rid of the influence that some of the classical doctrines (which they attack so much) still exert on them.[114]

As regards how to treat criminals, Garofalo honestly believed that there were two kinds of wishes: apparent and real. He focused on the real wishes, and realised that there was a preventive aim (expulsion of the criminals from society) and a repressive aim (compensation for damage). Just after Lombroso's second edition of *L'uomo delinquente* and Ferri's *La teorica dell'imputabilità e la negazione del libero arbitrio*,[115] Garofalo published a very interesting study on this topic.[116]

Numerous statements from Dorado Montero addressing Garofalo and Fioretti show that he disagreed with them on certain aspects of their theories. He thought their determinist postulates were incoherent: "it is very strange that those who, because they are determinists cannot attribute to individual free will the psychic and physical anomalies of a person, but nonetheless want to make him responsible for them, as if it was in his power to make them disappear".[117] That was why Dorado Montero judged the penal rigour in "writers of the 'New Italian School'"—especially Garofalo—as "unjustifiable", and accused them of "cruelty and vengeful spirit

---

[111] Garofalo (1890b), p. 15. "Carta de Raffaele Garofalo a Pedro Dorado Montero", Letter III, GREDOS: FPDM. Correspondencia de Pedro Dorado Montero. General. https://gredos.usal.es/handle/10366/76721. "Le sue principali relazioni sono quelli fatti al congresso di antropologia criminale di Roma (1885) e di Parigi (1889), al congresso di diritto penale di Bruxelles (1889), a quello penitenziario di Pietroburgo (1890) ed a quello giuridico di Firenze (1891)", p. 6.

[112] Garofalo (1890b), p. 25.

[113] Garofalo (1890b), p. 25.

[114] Garofalo (1890b), p. 30: "Garofalo, y los otros con él, están muy cerca de dar este paso, y lo darán cuando se vayan sacudiendo del influjo que, á su pesar, ejercen sobre ellos algunas, no todas, de las doctrinas clásicas, que tanto combaten".

[115] Ferri (1884b), p. 688.

[116] Garofalo (1878).

[117] Dorado Montero (1915), p. 338: "parece bastante extraño que quienes por ser deterministas no pueden atribuir á la voluntad libre del sujeto las anomalías físicas y psíquicas que en él radican, quieran hacerle responsable de las mismas, como si estuviera en su mano el hacerlas desaparecer".

towards criminals".[118] In the emergence of the new Italian school, he saw "wasteful attempts" aimed at knowing the "causes producing crime", without asking what "did the crime consist of".[119] Once they realised this mistake, they tried to fix it:

> Garofalo started to do so with his *Criminologia*, whose first chapter was devoted to the definition of the 'natural crime', i.e. a crime that was always a crime per se regardless of time and place.[120]

Additionally, Garofalo was particularly harsh concerning "non-fool" criminals,[121] frequently seeking the death penalty; a demand which he did not make when the criminal was, indeed, a fool.[122] Ferri was also quite severe: he wanted those criminals to "clean up swamp terrains and those infected with malaria" and to employ their labour in "public works".[123] On the other hand, Dorado Montero carried out a book review of Lombroso's *La superstizione sozialista*.[124] His contributions to the *Revue internationale de sociologie* made him very popular too.[125] Dorado Montero's approach to insane criminals was far kinder than either Garofalo or Ferri.[126]

4.1.5 Enrico Ferri (1856–1929)

Enrico Ferri[127] produced an extensive body of work.[128] Dorado Montero quoted Ferri in his claims that social, anthropological and physical factors were more inextricably interconnected than was thought, and could not be separated from the crime.[129] He also made brief reference to Secchi and his work *L'unità delle forze fisiche*[130] as another author supporting the idea of interconnection.

In 1896, Ferri stated that "no more than 20 years ago, the organic and psychic description of the criminal began with the works of Cesare Lombroso and the Positive Criminal School".[131] Even if traditional Criminal law had been forged

---

[118] Dorado Montero (1915), p. 341.

[119] Dorado Montero (1915), pp. 535–536.

[120] Dorado Montero (1915), pp. 535–536.

[121] Those who are not exempt from responsibility.

[122] Dorado Montero (1915), p. 11.

[123] Dorado Montero (1915), p. 11.

[124] Dorado Montero (1895b), pp. 773–777.

[125] Garofalo (1909).

[126] Dorado Montero (1906a), pp. 141–143.

[127] Ferri (1881); Ferri (1896); Ferri (1883); Ferri (1884a); Ferri (1894).

[128] To see a vast bibliography *vid.* Sbriccoli (1976), pp. 63–81.

[129] Dorado Montero (1889), p. 74.

[130] Secchi (1886).

[131] Ferri (1896), p. 15.

"without searching for its deep nourishing roots" within the "pathological soil of individual and social degeneration",[132] the new trends were progressively coming to bear.

> In fact, Classical Criminal science, from Cesare Beccaria to Francesco Carrara, dealing exclusively with crime, had always left the criminal in the shadows, taking him to be a unique and average type of man like all the others—except for exceptional cases of obviously abnormal circumstances, such as childhood and congenital deaf-mutism or manifest madness or drunkenness.[133]

Courts in the traditional criminal law system attributed "criminal actions" performed to the criminal, not to degeneration,[134] but to their "guiltiness".[135] Nevertheless, the new human science started "rather highlighting the differential characters from delinquent to delinquent" and replaced "the classic type [of criminal], unique and colourless", presenting instead many "different figures of the delinquent man".[136] At the end of the nineteenth century, psychiatry gave "precise and complete descriptions",[137] which only came to improve and to enrich previous positivist theories such as "Morel's great theory of human degeneration".[138]

Unsurprisingly, Ferri's theory evolved from a focus on the biological influences on criminal behaviour, and the social aspects which came to play a predominant role: "it is not just limited to a biological inferiority, such as idiocy, madness, suicide, etc." but it rather arose because of the "pressure of the environment itself" which had "an antisocial aggressive power".[139] Ferri's thought did not "remain stationary"; going beyond the "sterile boundary of sociology", he was able to "free himself from a paralysis of development, reaching the practical and fruitful side of socialism".[140] However, he never stopped believing that biology had an influence, as depicted by Paul Bourget:[141]

> Since race is to an entire people what temperament is to an individual, it is easy to see that the thesis of *Cosmopolis* coincides with the fundamental conclusion of criminal sociology, that

---

[132]Ferri (1896), p. 15.

[133]Ferri (1896), p. 16: "Infatti, scienza classica criminale, da Cesare Beccaria a Francesco Carrara, occupandosi esclusivamente del delitto, aveva sempre lasciato nella penombra il delinquente, attribuendogli un tipo unico e medio di uomo come tutti gli altri -meno casi eccezionalisimi di circostanze evidentemente anormali, come l'infanzia e il sordomutismo congenito o la pazzia manifesta o l'ubriachezza".

[134]De Montyel (1894).

[135]Ferri (1896), p. 22.

[136]Ferri (1896), p. 17.

[137]Ferri (1896), p. 22–23.

[138]Morel (1857); Morel (1864); Morel (1860).

[139]Ferri (1896), p. 18.

[140]Ferri (1896), p. 70.

[141]Bourget (1894).

> crime is a phenomenon determined not only by the conditions of the social environment, but also, and at the same time, by biological conditions.[142]

Perhaps the most influential work of Bourget was *Le disciple*.[143] In it, the main character, Adrien Sixte, was a renowned philosopher. He wrote three books in which one may observe the influence of Darwin, Spencer and Ribot, among others:

> These years of continuous labour in this hermitage at the street Guy-de-la- Brosse had produced, besides the *Anatomy of the Will*, a *Theory of the Passions*, in three volumes, whose publication would have been still more scandalous than that of the *Psychology of God*.[144]

Sixte had a very routine life until he was accused of having incited a young man to commit a crime under the influence of his novels. A very interesting debate on the limits of responsibility followed. The criminal's mother attributed responsibility to Sixte,[145] but the latter rejected this. Bourget's aim was to fight "the consequences of determinism, scienticist, materialist and cynical psychology, which are embodied by the figure of Adrian Sixte".[146]

Ferri's ideas were echoed in the work of Dorado Montero, with particular influence on his doubts about man's free will and, subsequently, the issue of inherent contradictions in criminal responsibility:

> by admitting from the common conscience, misled by the spiritualist illusions of the pretended free will in man, that madness is a disease and a 'misfortune' (as was recognized until the first years of our century) [...], the figure of the insane criminal carried and still carries with it [...] a living contradiction—for, it is said, if he is insane he is not a criminal.[147]

Dorado Montero also agreed with Ferri on the uselessness of prisons. For them, penitentiary institutions were highly counter-productive:

> Prison in short doses, as costly as it is stupid and corrupting, and then the police surveillance, which becomes nothing but a persecution that ruins the less wicked without curbing the more

---

[142]Ferri (1896), p. 125: "E poichè la razza è per un popolo quello che il temperamento è per un individuo, così è facile vedere che la tesi de Cosmopolis coincide colla conclusione fondamentale della sociologia criminale, che il delitto è un fenomeno determinato non soltanto dalle condizioni dell'ambiente sociale, ma altresì, ed insieme, dalle condizioni biologiche".

[143]Bourget (1901).

[144]Bourget (1901), p. 34: "Ces années d'un labeur continu dans cet ermitage de la rue Guy-de-la-Brosse avaient produit, outre cette *Anatomie de la volonté*, une *Théorie des passions*, en trois volumes, dont la publication aurait été plus scandaleuse encore que celle de la *Psychologie de Dieu*".

[145]She produced a booklet produced by her son in prison entitled "Confession of a Young Man of the Period" in order to prove that influence.

[146]Echevarría (2003) Crimen y responsabilidad. El País, 25.01.2003. https://elpais.com/diario/2003/01/25/babelia/1043455154_850215.html.

[147]Ferri (1896), p. 23: "ammettendosi dalla conscienza comune, fuorviata dalle illusioni spiritualistische del preteso libero arbitrio nell'uomo, che la pazzia è una malattia ed una 'sventura' (ciò che del resto si è disconociuto fino ai primi anni del nostro secolo) e il delitto invece è una 'colpa', la figura del delinquente pazzo portava e porta con sè, nel senso comune, una contraddizione vivente -giacchè, si dice, se è pazzo non è delinquente-".

> perverse, end up completing the figure of these 'castaways of society', who then drag their existence in a purulent and chronic sequence of mediocre crimes and irreparable recidivism—much more a product of social degeneration than of individual pathology itself.[148]

Of the four types of criminal,[149] Ferri referred to the occasional criminal as an individual with "organic and psychical abnormalities".[150] Yet, those abnormalities were "much less serious and frequent than in other criminals". The perfectly normal man, stated Ferri, "does not exist either in the physiological or in the psychological organism".[151] Examples of such criminal were quite well-known: the adulterer, the thief, the gambling addict or the violent when provoked, among others. In order to exemplify that this criminal type was so common that almost everyone could identify with it, Ferri came up with the hypothesis of *Tuer le mandarin*,[152] which he incorrectly attributed to Rousseau.[153] In a nutshell, the story depicted the possibility of killing a rich Chinese man and inheriting his fortune by just pressing a button, without anyone ever knowing such a thing had happened. This was a hypothesis designed to show how easily one could find individuals willing to do so, given that the crime would be anonymous, and it would have no legal or social consequences at all.

The born criminal could be seen in Zola's novel, Ferri said. The protagonist, Jacques Lantier, was "a true type of born criminal, epileptic in nature, with accesses of necrophilia or sexual perversion of the corpse".[154] Like many other authors of his time, Ferri could not avoid falling into the errors of primitive positivism, and ventured at establishing dubious rules which would nowadays be called "pseudoscientific":

> Since often people's highly developed feelings of altruism are matched by their limited intelligence, those who lack moral sentiment are often bestowed with an intellect that, despite not being very deep or equilibrated, is notably sharp and lucid.[155]

This improper widening of scientific thought and the consequent "pseudoscience" was mostly due to the proliferation of 'naturalist' and 'psychological novels', which

---

[148]Ferri (1896), p. 24: "Il carcere a brevi dosi, altretanto costose quanto stupide e corrutricci, e poi la sorveglianza della polizia, che diventa il più delle volte una persecuzione che rovina i meno malgavi senza frenare i più perversi, finiscono per completare la figura di questi 'naufraghi della società', che trascinano poi la loro esistenza in una sequela purulenta e cronica di delitti mediocri e di recidive irreparabili-prodotto ben più della degenerazione sociale che non della patologia individuale".

[149]Bonanno (1895), p. 364–383.

[150]Ferri (1896), p. 25.

[151]Ferri (1896), p. 25.

[152]Chateaubriand (1837). The original version was published in 1802.

[153]This mistake came via Balzac, who had wrongly attributed the story to Rousseau on his *Le Père Goriot*. For further information vid. Coimbra (1967).

[154]Ferri (1896), p. 119.

[155]Ferri (1896), p. 20: "Giacchè, come avviene spesso che nelle persone a sentimenti sviluppatissimi di altruismo corrisponda intelligenza limitata, così a chi manca di sentimento morale natura prodiga spesso un ingegno, se non profondo ed equilibrato, pero molto acuto e lucido".

portrayed the "deterministic conditions of environment" and the "states of mind of the individual", respectively.[156] Many authors, including Ferri, were convinced that they could find criminological traits[157] and medically diagnosed diseases within these novels:

> Before Cesare Lombroso, who as we shall see was hardly the genius that Shakespeare was in the portrayal of his characters, or Dostoyevsky in his observation, unfortunately personal, of the convicts in Siberia, or the talent of Eugene Sue in his observation of the Parisian slums could delineate the sociological type of the born criminal; but after the creation of criminal anthropology, this type has already entered contemporary art, especially through the initiative of Émile Zola.[158]

Charcot found that the "physical stigmata" and "characteristic attitudes"[159] of those deformed and demoniacs in art reproduced "[...] the features and poses that the modern scientist detects and studies in those [people] suffering from severe hysteria and hystero-epilepsy".[160] The doctor Edouard Lefort published a monograph illustrated with 109 heads,[161] which had been preceded by Edmondo Mayor's anthropological-criminal study on the iconography of the Caesars.[162] Lefort arranged such work "at the style of Charcot", i.e. trying to find out whether the characteristics matched those represented by the different artists performing the criminals in art.[163] Back then, the faith in science was superlative to the extreme—even using the "objective traits" of criminals described in novels as evidence—hardly scientifically rigorous—rather than resorting to the old-fashioned, aprioristic, neoclassical postulates of Criminal law:

> Art [...] has almost always kept alive, even in the observation of criminals, the presence of human reality and its positive physiological and psychic attitudes, against the more or less platonic aberrations of a metaphysical nebula.[164]

---

[156] Ferri (1896), p. 103.

[157] Tebaldi (1884). Vid. First Part, Chap. 2 (*Tipi di deviazione fisionomica*) and Second Part, Chap. 4 (*Le espressioni in relazione ai disordini psico-fisici*), pp. 28–46 and pp. 112–133, respectively.

[158] Ferri (1896), p. 19: "Appena il genio di Shakespeare, come vedremo or ora, nella figurazione dei suoi personaggi o quello di Dostoïevsky nella osservazioni, purtroppo personale, dei forzati in Siberia o il talento di Eugenio Sue nell'osservazione dei bassi fondi parigini, hanno potuto, prima di Cesare Lombroso, delineare il tipo sociologico del delinquente nato; che però, dopo la creazione dell'antropologia criminale, è già entrato nell'arte contemporanea, specialmente per l'iniziativa di Emilio Zola".

[159] Charcot (1887).

[160] Ferri (1896), p. 28.

[161] Lefort (1892). In his statement of purpose, Lefort aims at addressing "the most important question" he has ever been asked for: "Should we deem every criminal as an insane, as many people admit it? Or if no criminal is insane, where does his responsibility begin?".

[162] Ferri (1896), p. 31.

[163] Lefort (1892), p. 2.

[164] Ferri (1896), p. 29: "L'arte [...] hanno quasi sempre mantenuta viva, anche nell'osservazione del delinquenti, la presenza della realtà umana e dei suoi positivi attegiamenti fisiologici e psichici, contro le aberrazioni più o meno platoniche di una nebulosa metafisica".

Indeed, the criminal type sensed by Cesare Lombroso and scientifically described by the Italian Anthropological School had "a perfect match in the artistic work of many centuries".[165] Ferri thought this particularly true of Dostoyevsky's *Crime and Punishment* or Émile Zola's *La Bête Humaine* because even if they "load the colours of the truth" they did not come to "alter its relationships and proportions".[166] Certain features Ferri deemed "typically criminal" were, among others, a "coarse and obtuse head, an asymmetrical face, small and grizzly eyes, enormous and square jaws, low and receding forehead, protruding eyebrows and cheekbones, pointed or looped ears (reproducing Darwin's lobule), abundant and hard hair and a sparse or missing beard".[167]

For Ferri,[168] any room for manoeuvre due to "personal factors" was minimal. Just as in positive sciences, the difference "between positive science and metaphysics" meant these extra features only affected the manner or intensity of approach.[169] Even though it was quite common, not all the enthusiasts of the new positivist school rejected any religion in their thinking. Indeed, when Ferri referred to the Third International Congress of Criminal Anthropology, held in Brussels in 1892, he aimed at De Baets, "who was a priest". The Pope himself "declared that he does not want to disown [...] the marvellous conquests of contemporary scientific thought".[170]

With his portrayal of Raskolnikoff,[171] Dostoyevsky achieved his goal of reaching "the deep and obscure roots of volitional determination: from the instinctive flashes of a degenerate cerebration to its precise, but impulsive, almost somnambulistic and automatic muscular realisation".[172]

The intuition that had led Dorado Montero to predict the future development of a genetic science shared its roots with Ferri's blueprint. Indeed, it was quite possible he borrowed the idea from him. Ferri stated that before Darwin "only a descriptive anatomy of organs, tissues and organic elements was made".[173] Even though that was necessary, he advocated something deeper: "genetic anatomy".[174] He did,

[165] Ferri (1896), p. 36.

[166] Ferri (1896), p. 104.

[167] Ferri (1896), p. 32.

[168] Ferri (1881).

[169] Ferri (1896), p. 103.

[170] Ferri (1896), pp. 128–129.

[171] Main character of his novel *Crime and Punishment*.

[172] Ferri (1896), p. 131.

[173] Ferri (1896), p. 132.

[174] Even if the closest thing to their mindset at the time would be limited to "various phases of individual life and in the corresponding various species of the zoological scale". Vid. Ferri (1896), p. 132. Another possibility (solely theoretical) was "tracing the most distant dissimilar embryos in the different psychological stratifications, which in each individual accumulated the hereditary transmission of infinite generations". Also, on the matter, vid. Ferri (1896), p. 132.

however, acknowledge the limitations thereof: "this is located at the opposite extreme of moral anatomy, which is much more difficult".[175]

There was both an environmental and a biological basis for human action, with the former subjected to the parameters set by the latter:

> Beliefs and opinions and theories are themselves the effect, the result, more or less perceived, of this same temperament and environment, since one is born idealist or positivist, mystic or materialist, reactionary or radical, atheist or believer, and in the surrounding variety of scientific or religious or political opinions each man appropriates and absorbs that which best responds to the dispositions, embryonically contained and organised in his physiological and psychic personality.[176]

Ferri also stressed the determining role that intention should perform when determining punishment and when trying establish the guilt in a criminal act:

> Every human action is as much worthwhile and moral or immoral as the internal motives that determine it are worthwhile and moral or immoral. A materially beneficial act may in reality be despicable, if moved by the ignoble aim of seduction or blackmail.[177]

However, ideas about freedom and Ferri's consideration were not a dichotomy. There were contradictions, and certain incompatibilities. The 'freedom' in this scheme was not as simple as 'doing what one would like to'. Ferri avoided such a mistake: "For either by this 'freedom' we mean physical freedom alone, which consists in the absence of impediments to the development of one's own tendencies and activity, however much these may be determined by the individual constitution and the external environment, and then we are in full agreement".[178] This would entail a "full physical and moral determinism", since we would be admitting that "all actions" were an "effect of their determining causes". Yet, this would not exclude "any of man's physical freedoms" such as freedom of movement, only the "freedom of the individual".

"By that equivocal 'freedom' is meant a kind of free-will attenuated and stripped of the most evident oppositions to the facts, and then we are in a state of

---

[175]Ferri (1896), p. 132.

[176]Ferri (1896), p. 140: "Che anzi e credenze ed opinioni e teorie sono esse stesse l'effetto, la risultante più o meno avvertita di questo stesso temperamento e ambiente, poichè si nasce idealisti o positivisti, mistici o materialisti, reazionarî o redicali, atei o credenti e nellà varietà circostante delle opinioni scientifiche o religiose o politiche ogni uomo si appropria ed assorbe quella che più risponde alle disposizioni, embrionalmente contenute e organizzate nella sua personalità fisiologica e psichica".

[177]Ferri (1896), p. 147: "Ogni azione umana per tanto vale ed è morale od immorale, per quanto valgono e sono morali od immorali i motivi interni che la determinano. Un atto materialmente benefico può essere in realtà spregevole, se mosso da scopo ignobile di seduzione o di ricatto".

[178]Ferri (1884a), p. 48: "Infatti o per questa « libertà » si intende la sola libertà fisica, che consiste nell'assenza di impedimenti allo sviluppo delle proprie tendenze e della propria attività, per quanto queste siano determinate dalla costituzione individuale e dall'ambiente esterno, ed allora noi siamo perfettamente d'accordo".

misunderstanding and, moreover, without having the advantages of an open and frank determinism, we have all the damages of the ancient physical goal of free-will".[179]

Therefore, the conclusion that Ferri passed on to Dorado Montero was that the only conceivable realities were "absolute free will or absolute determinism".[180] Dorado Montero's disdain towards 'eclectical schools' and especially 'middle ways' was also discussed by Ferri:

> Every middle way is a nonentity and causes difficulties to sprout at every step. If, finally, by this equivocal and generic 'freedom' is meant the internal energy that each individual has to develop in a way that is precisely individual, proper, different from the others, because each has a special physical-psychic temperament, which makes him react in a special way to the various pressures of the environment, then we are also in agreement; but then, again, we are far from a true 'moral freedom', which, on the contrary, is implicitly recognised as a 'moral freedom'. On the contrary, it implicitly recognises the fundamental determinism of organic and psychic constitution for each individual; a determinism that man has in common with every other living being.[181]

Another trait of Doradian criminal legal philosophy came from Ferri. The latter discussed one of the "most frequent misunderstandings" in "denying the old free will" while at the same time maintaining "an indefinite moral freedom" and "reproaching positivist determinism for reducing man to an automaton and the whole of nature, physical and moral, to a mere mechanism".[182] For Ferri, every human action was the "necessary and unavoidable effect of determining causes"; every man had his own "physiognomy", to whose influence he responded differently "from other men" and from "he himself in different conditions of time and space, since the state of his organism is different".[183] Man was not considered by him as an entity alien to laws of determinism, for he was "nothing more, like every living being, than a machine"; he was subject to the "universal law of causality".[184] Due to a combination of "physical, physiological and psychical causes" he could not act any

---

[179]Ferri (1884a), pp. 48–49: "Oppure per quella equivoca « libertà » si intende una specie di libero arbitrio attenuato e sfrondato delle più evidenti opposizioni ai dati di fatto, ed allora si versa nell'equivoco e per giunta, senza avere i vantaggi di un aperto e schietto determinismo, si hanno tutti i danni dell'antico meta fisico libero arbitrio".

[180]Ferri (1884a), pp. 48–49.

[181]Ferri (1884a), pp. 48–49: "Che se, daultimo, per questa equivoca e generica « libertà » si intende la energia interna che ogni individuo ha di svolgersi in modo appunto individuale, proprio, diverso dagli altri, perchè ciascuno ha una speciale tempra fisio -psichica, che gli fa reagire in un modo speciale alle varie pressioni dell'ambiente, allora siamo pure d'accordo; ma allora, di nuovo, siamo ben lontani da una vera « libertà morale », che anzi si riconosce implicitamente il determinismo fondamentale della costituzione organica e psichica per ogni individuo; de terminismo che l'uomo ha in comune con ogni altro essere vivente".

[182]Ferri (1884a), p. 49.

[183]Ferri (1884a), p. 49.

[184]Ferri (1884a), p. 52.

other way.[185] And the logical, traditional criminal law response was immediately attacked by him as follows:

> [Man] is not machine-made, in the sense of an inorganic mechanism, precisely because it is a living organism, which has its own special responsiveness to external causes, determined necessarily, case by case, by the preceding physical and physio-psychological causes.[186]

A last insight into the Ferri-Dorado Montero connection is in his statement that determinism did not mean the end of life as we knew it: his thought as more nuanced, in the same way that Dorado Montero sometimes looks as if he believed in free will:

> That is why those who say that, once free will is denied men become automatons subject to Muslim fatalism, are rather naive. Men are so little automatons that each of them is endowed with his own special way of reacting against the external environment; but this does not exclude, and indeed demands, physical and moral determinism, for otherwise, if man had a freedom, independent to a little or a lot from the determining causes, one would no longer conceive the same personality as a permanent type of individual character.[187]

In *Polemica in difesa della scuola criminale positiva*,[188] Ferri's added further thoughts on this issue, but this is sufficient for our purposes.

Ferri described Dorado Montero as one of the leading intellectuals of his time advocating "the method and fundamental inductions of criminal sociology".[189] He also included Mott (Universidade de São Paulo), Viveiros de Castro (Universidade do Rio de Janeiro), Lucas (Universidade de Coimbra), Vieira De Araujo (Universidade do Recife), Hamon (Université Nouvelle de Bruxelles), Prins (Université Libre de Bruxelles), van Hamel (Universiteit van Amsterdam), Durckheim (Université de Bordeaux), and Vargha (Universität Graz) in this list.

Ferri also noted that at the First Congress of the International Institute of Sociology (1894), Noricow had presented on "Justice and Darwinism" and Dorado Montero on "Sociology and Criminal law".[190] At the Second Congress of the International Institute of Sociology (1895), Ferri highlighted the contribution on "Crime as a social phenomenon" by Tönnies, Garofalo, Tavares, De Medeiros, Puglia and himself. At the Fourth Congress (1897), Dorado Montero and Puglia

---

[185]Ferri (1884a), p. 52.

[186]Ferri (1884a), p. 52: "Ma non è fatto a macchina, nel censo di meccanismo inorganico, appunto perchè esso è un organismo vivente, che ha una propria e speciale ri spondenza alle cause esterne, determinata necesariamente, caso per caso, dalle cause fisiche e fisio -psicologiche precedenti".

[187]Ferri (1884a), pp. 52–53: "Ecco perché sono pure illusioni quelle di chi dice che, negato il libero arbitrio, gli uomini diventano automi soggetti al fatalismo mussulmano. Gli uomini sono così poco automi, che ognuno di essi è dotato di un proprio e speciale modo di reagire contro l'ambiente esterno; ma ciò non esclude ed anzi esige il determinismo fisico e morale, chè altrimenti, se l'uomo avesse una libertà, indipendente per poco o per molto dalle cause determinanti, più non si concepirebbe la stessa personalità, come tipo permanente di carattere individuale".

[188]Ferri, E., *Polemica in difesa della scuola criminale positiva*, Bologna: Nicola Zanichelli, pp. 85–114.

[189]Ferri (1884a), p. 41.

[190]Ferri (1884a), p. 49.

referred to the "Criminal Justice of the Future".[191] Ferri agreed with Dorado Montero's ideas regarding the evolution of crime. Society had always had a "criminal or repressive ministry", but "by gradually stripping itself of the spirit of revenge, penance and retributive justice" this institution was now to be reduced to its "genuine character of a clinic of preservation from the disease of crime".[192] He credited this idea and its development to Dorado Montero.[193]

Even as Ferri exposed what he called "our positivist theory", he quoted Dorado Montero[194] for the rationale behind moral freedom:

> If we now complete the series of the various species of social sanction, in the extra-legal field, in the civil and administrative field and in the truly criminal field [...] it is easy to see that the traditional theory of moral guilt as a condition of punishability is reduced to making punishment [...] a gratuitous exception to the whole series of sanctions, not only natural but also social, by introducing into the criminal form of social sanction alone an element of 'moral culpability' which is completely unknown or neglected in every other kind of sanction. Therefore, our positivist theory, which does not require this element even in the penal sanction, has the great merit [...] of linking—in full agreement with universal determinism (telluric, organic, social)—this penal sanction to the whole series of natural (physical, biological, social) sanctions, thus, subjecting it to the empire of natural laws themselves and giving it a truly positive and much firmer foundation than that much contested and indecipherable 'moral freedom'.[195]

In his *Sociologia Criminale*,[196] Ferri began his criticism started, just as Dorado Montero had, by criticising the defects of the "abstract reasoning" in Classical Criminal law, since when it moved "further and further away from the real world", it ended up losing its "sense of reality" and creating "illusory difficulties where none

[191] Ferri (1884a), p. 49. Especifically, he readdressed to the *Annales de l'Institut Internationale de Sociologie*, Paris, I, 1895; II, 1896; IV, 1898.

[192] Ferri (1884b), pp. 545–546.

[193] Dorado Montero (1899), p. 255.

[194] Dorado Montero (1893b).

[195] Ferri (1884b), p. 570: "Se noi ora completiamo la serie delle varie specie di sanzione sociale, nel campo extra-legale, nel campo civile ed amministrativo e nel campo veramente criminale—chiudendola fra l'estremo infe- riore della semplice sanzione di disistima pubblica e l'estremo superiore della condanna penale per vero e proprio reato—è facile vedere, che la teoria tradizionale della colpa morale come condizione di punibilità si riduce a fare della pena, propriamente detta, una eccezione gratuita a tutta la serie delle sanzioni, non solo naturali, ma anche sociali, coll'introdurre appunto, nella sola forma penale di sanzione sociale, un elemento di morale colpabilità, che è completamente ignoto o trascurato in ogni altra specie di sanzione. E quindi la nostra teoria positiva, che non richiede questo elemento neanche nella sanzione penale, ha il grande pregio, che è anche una riconferma di verità, di rannodare—in pieno accordo col determinismo universale (tellurico, organico, sociale)—codesta sanzione penale a tutta la serie delle sanzioni naturali (fisiche, biologiche, sociali) sottoponendola quindi all' impero delle stesse leggi naturali e dandole così un fondamento veramente positivo e ben più saldo di quella tanto contestata e indecifrabile 'morale libertà'".

[196] In order to avoid confusion, it should be born in mind that Ferri's *I nuovi orizzonti del diritto e della procedura penale* changed its name on its third edition to *Sociologia criminale*.

exist".[197] His priority was to "leave behind the nebulous heights of aprioristic philosophy" and to restore the "clear observation of everyday facts".[198]

> In our century, the need for a positive, experimental, observational philosophy has imposed itself in order to return to the pure and perennial source of the reality of things.[199]

Thus, whereas the "Classical School cancel[led] all moral responsibility, and therefore also social responsibility", the Positivist Schools argued in favour of extending "social responsibility as far as possible".[200] Ferri contemplated the use of a variety of measures: preventive, reparative, repressive, and eliminative. He has often been accused of being a soft positivist (defending just the two first premises) or of being like the rest of the Lombrosian positivists (and thus, only supporting the latter premises). Even if he is thought of as a hard positivist, there are limits to his position. For instance, his belief that repressive measures "should always be temporary but, as a rule, indefinite"[201] is reminiscent of Dorado Montero's opinion on indeterminate sentences.[202] Ferri thought that eliminative measures ought only to be used "against the most criminal and dangerous actions (atavistic criminality) either because of their seriousness (qualified murders, violent rapes, fires, etc.) or because of the character of the individuals committing them (born criminals, or crazy,[203] habitual)".[204] In a nutshell, the response to criminological problems could be found in what he named after 'sociological medicine' where "the great classes of hygienic measures (preventive means) and therapeutic disciplines (reparative and repressive means) and of surgical operations (eliminative means) constitute the armoury with which society can provide for the permanent necessity of its own preservation".[205]

In the Early Middle Ages, a theory prioritising intention over the material commission of wrongdoing predominated in some sectors, among whom Hugue de Payens was particularly notable.[206] He argued that "sin and guilt did not lie in the act itself, but rather in the intention" and so one who "took life away from an enemy" sinned if "the action was grounded on hate", but was free of sin if he acted "with

---

[197] Ferri (1884b), p. 681.

[198] Ferri (1884b), p. 681.

[199] Ferri (1884b), p. 681: "si è imposta nel nostro secolo la necessità della filosofia positiva, sperimentale, di osservazione, per ritornare alla fonte pura e perenne della realtà delle cose".

[200] Ferri (1884b), p. 686.

[201] Ferri (1884b), p. 687.

[202] Dorado Montero (1912), pp. 5–26.

[203] Escuder (1895); Escuder (1882).

[204] Ferri (1884b), p. 687: "contro le azioni più criminose e pericolose (criminalità atavica) sia per la loro gravità (omicidi qualificati, stupri violenti, incendi, ecc.) sia per il carattere degli individui che le commettono (delinquenti nati, o pazzi, abituali)".

[205] Ferri (1884b), p. 687: "anche nella medicina sociologica le grandi classi di provvedimenti igienici (mezzi preventivi) e discipline terapeutiche (mezzi ripararatorii e repressivi) e di operazioni chirurgiche (mezzi eliminativi) costituiscono l'armamentario, onde la società può provvedere alla permanente necessità della propria conservazione".

[206] First Grand Master and founder of the Knights Templar.

purity of intention".[207] Deploying his understanding of both anthropology and criminal psychology, Ferri concluded that offenders presented many "different anthropological varieties of organic and psychic characters", each of them with the potential and effective "power of anti-social activity". He disregarded the "almost algebraic" type of man assumed by "classical science and legislation".[208] Dorado Montero agreed with Ferri in this: that was why the legislator should elaborate norms jointly with sociologists in order to reflect and adapt the "various means of social defence to the various categories of offenders".[209]

A key idea in Dorado Montero's *Indeterminate Sentence*[210] was also found in Ferri's works, where he in turn quoted Garofalo. The latter had concluded that considering elements other than the crime itself in exercising judgment over criminals ultimately meant "punishing a man not for what he has done, but for what he is capable of doing".[211] In a humorous note, Ferri pointed out that this already took place in classical criminal justice, even if it was not acknowledged.[212] He opposed the arguments of Brusa[213] (Carrara's disciple) and of some of his colleagues by contrasting them with Setti's arguments.[214]

4.1.6 Vincenzo Lilla (1837–1905)

The main goal of Vincenzo Lilla was to "resurrect the Ethics of Aristotle by taking it as a source in Legal Philosophy".[215] Dorado Montero analysed his most influential work,[216] noting that it was "not completely finished",[217] since only the first volume was ever published.[218] Even if Lilla belonged to an idealist school, he was critical within that group:

> The abstract ethics of Hegel, Cousin and Gioberti is declining, as is the formal ethics of Kant, and modern thought turns its eyes to the ethics of Aristotle because he does not mutilate

---

[207] Baños (2017), p. 328.

[208] Ferri (1884b), p. 690.

[209] Ferri (1884b), p. 691.

[210] I refer to his general theory, not to any particular work.

[211] Carnevale (1898), p. 130.

[212] Ferri (1884b), p. 691.

[213] Brusa (1887), pp. 57 ff. He devotes his Chap. 38 to the "The whole treaty of the judicial process focuses on the proof of facts which took place, never of simple possibilities", in order to criticise the process under the new positivist postulates.

[214] Setti (1888). Also, Ferri (1884b), p. 693.

[215] Dorado Montero (1891a), p. 106.

[216] Lilla (1880).

[217] Dorado Montero (1891a), p. 107.

[218] Years later, in 1903, a more detailed work was published: Lilla (1903).

> human nature, but asserts and acknowledges it, as it is, with all its needs, without sacrificing pleasures or goods to virtue, but coordinating them according to the rationality of ends.[219]

Dorado Montero's idea of the fallibility of human nature, which we have referred to on many occasions already, was plausibly received from Lilla. Where Dorado considered the imperfection of human nature, Lilla maintained that "the law has never submitted or conformed to life among men" and would never do so in future "because it is far superior to their imperfections"; across history "law has only showed up under more or less imperfect forms", i.e. "the rule of the strongest, the jus private violentiae, the expression of the national will, etc.".[220] Lilla typically maintained a very strong distinction between rational law and historical law. The first studied "the true and individual essence of the law" whereas the latter one focused on the "several forms it has acquired within history".[221] His idea was that law was "an objective order, a real entity, yet lofty and unfathomable". It was never "achievable in life in all its purity".[222] Law for Lilla was "the natural law of the Scholastics, immutable, absolute, equal, inflexible, of all times and countries", i.e. the "eternal principles of justice".[223]

In a nutshell, Lilla thought there were four kinds of law: ideal law, natural law, positive law and rational law. Natural law was based on a set of values inherent in human nature and human reason, ideal law was a theoretical, idealist model of reference (it did not possess a real character as natural law did), positive law sat between ideal law and natural law (since it was real, but it was not yet so real as natural law because it was still in the making), and rational law was the generic concept that encompassed the previous three ones. Dorado Montero adopted Lilla's definition of ideal law in an attempt to reject the possibility of absolute truths, and to develop a highly relativist framework in which the transcendental problem was avoided.

4.1.7 Leo Tolstoy (1828–1910)

Leo Tolstoy was Dorado Montero's guide in anarchism. Dorado Montero professed a deep feeling of admiration towards him, describing him as "a generous soul, full of

[219] Dorado Montero quotes a paragraph within the Foreword from *Filosofia del Diritto*: "La ética abstracta de Hegel, Cousin, Gioberti, toca ya á su ocaso, y la ética formal de Kant declina, y el pensamiento moderno vuelve los ojos hacia la ética Aristóteles, porque no mutila la naturaleza humana, sino que la afirma y reconoce tal como es, con todas sus necesidades, sin sacrificar los placeres los bienes, ni los bienes á la virtud, sino coordinando los bienes según la racionalidad de los fines". Vid. Dorado Montero (1891a), p. 107.

[220] Dorado Montero (1891a), p. 109.

[221] Dorado Montero (1891a), p. 109.

[222] Dorado Montero (1891a), p. 109.

[223] Dorado Montero (1891a), p. 109.

love for one's neighbour, and enemy of all kinds of oppression".[224] However, he was eager to point out Tolstoy's main difficulty. It was not the fact that his positions varied to such an extent that he challenged and even contradicted his own prior statements: that happens constantly with most authors. The main issue for Tolstoy's comprehensiveness was that he never systematised a treaty of legal, religious, or social philosophy. Dorado Montero offered a solution: either one goes through Tolstoy's whole academic career and constructs a description of his personal analysis, or one uses the secondary sources.[225] Dorado Montero summarised the main systematic schemes in the latter, mainly revolving around two authors: Ossip-Lourié and Paul Eltzbacher. In this, the intertwining relationship between Dorado Montero, Tolstoy, and Eltzbacher is clear. Dorado Montero once dedicated a very discreet article in a Spanish popular review to the latter.[226] In it, he qualified Eltzbacher's work as "purely descriptive",[227] but very "clear" and "exact".[228] What is more striking in that review is that there is plenty of evidence Eltzbacher never committed the same mistakes that their future colleagues would make:

> As a matter of fact, the dictatorial siege of the European democracies, as well as the strong public presence of reactionary Spanish positions, made the destiny of such legal reform perfectly foreseeable [. . .] despite the fact that the jurisdictional guarantees foreseen in the *Ley de Vagos y Maleantes* given to the administrative councils designed for Castejón's 'moral police' were not similar at all-, and which soon underwent a remodelling after the right-wing electoral triumph, whose main contribution was the introduction of the analogy.[229]

The main exponents of positivism became fascists as the twentieth century began. The weaknesses of positivism, i.e. their potentially risky statements, became a real danger when its postulates evolved and met new political developments. Indeed, Jorge Barreiro, when elaborating the *Ley de Vagos y Maleantes,* described Asúa's major mistake[230] to be thinking that law "will constitute a very important instrument to be used with political aims, and that will be easily justified on the basis of the defensist groundings of its precepts. The *Ley de Vagos y maleantes*—as Del Rosal

[224]Calvo González (2010), p. 139: "El conde León Tolstoy, alma generosa, saturada de amor al prójimo, enemiga de toda opresión".

[225]Calvo González (2010), p. 141.

[226]Dorado Montero (1900), pp. 192–193.

[227]Eltzbacher sums up the main objective of his work on the front page: "Je ne propose rien, je ne supose rien, j'expose".

[228]Dorado Montero (1900), p. 193.

[229]Martín Martín (2007), p. 578: "*En efecto, el asedio dictatorial a las democracias europeas, y la vigorosa presencia pública de las posiciones reaccionarias españolas, hacían perfectamente predecible el destino de esta reforma legal, rápidamente apadrinada en las filas del defensismo—aunque en nada se pareciesen las garantías jurisdiccionales previstas en la ley de vagos a los consejos administrativos diseñados para «la policía de costumbres» de Castejón—, y sometida a una pronta remodelación tras el triunfo electoral de las derechas, cuya principal aportación consistió en introducir la analogía*".

[230]Bear in mind that the authors of the draft of the *Ley de Vagos y Maleantes* were Jiménez de Asúa and Mariano Ruiz-Funes, both of them penalists. Vid. Jiménez de Asúa (1933), pp. 577–635.

pointed out—was applied with governmental and repressive aims rather than with the criminological aim it dictated".[231]

He wisely pointed out that the State itself was grounded on violence: "Currently, they abhor the State, and everything it entails (laws, authorities, Courts, public force, etc.), since it is a coercive organisation. 'They' are those who abhor violence as a common bond among men. Spirits enjoying a great morality cannot conceive an order in which such common base is an unjust social order. That is the reason why an army of thinkers exists in the world—not small at all—which attacks what one might call the grounds of social life".[232]

This statement was aimed at anarchists, and to some extent the liberals as well. Both Eltzbacher and Dorado Montero's theoretical bedrock were profoundly influenced by Tolstoy—the former devoted an article in a yearbook to him.[233] Eltzbacher's most influential work[234] was, as aforementioned, translated into Spanish by Dorado Montero, although the name of the Spanish version was slightly different.[235] The chapter of that work devoted to Tolstoy's doctrine was also separately published in the *Boletín de la Institución Libre de Enseñanza.*

As well as making use of Eltzbacher's work, Dorado Montero forged his own personal analysis of Tolstoy, focusing on Tolstoy's novel *Resurrection.*[236] Dorado Montero had a particularly marked enthusiasm for the way in which Tolstoy disseminated his criminal doctrine and penal thought. The Russian writer had done so in an indirect, yet efficient fashion: he shared the essential aspects of his doctrine in an enjoyable and entertaining way, reaching a larger number of people.[237] Tolstoy was known for his Christian version of anarchism, wherein he analysed the time in which he lived and concluded that "the current life is irrational, inhuman, unfair, and anti-Christian. That is why it should be replaced with another, out of which the real order will emerge: an order in which Christ's supreme law will reign, i.e. the rule of love".[238] He was also concerned with the limiting the use of violence: "the key to all

[231] Jorge Barreiro (1975), p. 53: "*La Ley citada será un importante instrumento a utilizar con fines políticos y ello podrá justificarse fácilmente en base al fundamento defensista de sus preceptos. La Ley de vagos y maleantes -como señala Del Rosal- se aplicó con fines gubernativos y represivos más que con el propósito criminológico con que se dictó*".

[232] Dorado Montero (1900), p. 193: "En el día de hoy abominan del Estado, en cuanto organización coercitiva, y de lo que tal organización supone (leyes, autoridades, Tribunales, fuerza pública, etc.) todos cuantos aborrecen la violencia como lazo de unión entre los hombres. Los espíritus de gran delicadeza moral no pueden concebir que un orden que en tal base estriba pueda ser un orden social justo. Tal es la causa por la que actualmente existe en el mundo una falange, no pequeña, de pensadores que atacan lo que puede llamarse los «fundamentos» de la vida social".

[233] Eltzbacher (1900a), pp. 266–282.

[234] Eltzbacher (1900b).

[235] Eltzbacher (1901).

[236] Tolstoy (1899).

[237] Calvo González (2010), p. 141.

[238] Calvo González (2010), p. 142.

of Jesus Christ's teaching relies on the precept of never applying violence, not even to resist evil".[239]

Resurrection explored those questions through the perspective of the character Nekhlyudov. After his visit to a prison, he had observed "people of a very simple nature, nor good neither bad, holding the traditional moral notions of the peasant and the Christian, yet they had been detached from them little by little in order to acquire other values which admitted the legitimacy of all sorts of violence".[240] The character was also described as having social concerns relating to many topics, namely: whether free will exists or not; whether the physical measurements of the human skull related to criminality and guilt; the possibility that criminal behaviour was a heritable trait; whether criminality and immorality exist innately; what are exactly concepts like morality, insanity, degeneration, or character mean; what influence climate, ignorance, imitation spirit, or hypnotism have over crime, etc.[241] Whatever the answers to these questions, Nekhlyudov was firmly convinced that penalties were not to be used: "nobody can or should impose penalties on his equals, and when he does so, he is producing real and immeasureable social damage, leaving aside injustices".[242]

Given the sphere of Tolstoy's true concerns, Nekhlyudov never focused on the most far-reaching question: what should be done about criminals? That question would only have been important to him if punishments produced a decrease in crime, and if they corrected criminal behaviour.[243] At this point, one of Tolstoy's central issues arises: "automorphism". This phenomenon consists in the automatic reassertion of a certain lifestyle when a person only engages with social groups which legitimised and support the same, positively reinforcing the behaviour. This effect might occur in either direction: in both lower (poor people and criminals) and upper (wealthy individuals and religious factions) class groups.

> According to common understanding, the thief, the murderer, and the prostitute should be ashamed of their lifestyle. Indeed, they should not. People who, by chance or by their own mistakes, happen to get to a wrong position become so habituated with it that there is nobody to get out of their minds the idea that their profession is good, and to further reassert themselves in such position, they keep themselves inside the circles made up by their equals, where their choices are highly approved.[244]

---

[239] Calvo González (2010), p. 143: "La clave de todas las enseñanzas de Cristo se halla en el precepto que manda no aplicar nunca la violencia, ni siquiera para resistir al mal".

[240] Calvo González (2010), p. 145: "En la prisión había visto Neklindoff naturalezas sencillas, ni buenas ni malas, penetradas de las tradicionales nociones morales del aldeano y del cristiano, que poco a poco se habían despojado de esas nociones para adquirir otras que consistían en admitir la legitimidad de toda violencia".

[241] Calvo González (2010), p. 147.

[242] Calvo González (2010), p. 146: "Nadie puede ni debe, según él, imponer penas a sus semejantes, y el
imponerlas produce, además de injusticias, verdaderos e innumerables daños sociales".

[243] Tolstoy, L., *Resurrección*, tomo III, pp. 156–157.

[244] Tolstoy, L., *Resurrección*, tomo I, p. 182: "Comúnmente se cree que el ladrón, el asesino y la prostituta deben avergonzarse de su género de vida. No es así. Las personas que por azares de la

Conceived as an almost identical reproduction of Tolstoy's thought, Dorado Montero's thinking about crime also involved seeking the primordial causes and going beyond the boundaries of the criminal act itself. For both authors, it was necessary to do so: for Tolstoy, "from those facts that law labels crimes, it is not possible to attribute guilt to those who commit them, but to other causes external to themselves".[245] For the main character of the novel *Resurrection*, Nekhlyudov, these external causes and circumstances were deplorable.

If the novel's main concerns were cruelty and hypocrisy, a significant part was also devoted to the time consuming nature of judicial processes. Criticisms of endless delays in judicial processes are nothing new, and this topic has recurred since the Middle Ages: it was often tackled by Cerdán de Tallada.[246]

Tolstoy's final solution for criminals might seem somewhat utopian: they do not need to be punished, but to be forgiven (up to seventy-seven times).[247] This formed part of his Christian anarchism. In *Resurrection*, Nekhlyudov is told by an old man that God is the only one who knows how to punish and reward: humans do not. In a similar vein, Dorado Montero pointed out that:

> All evil comes from the fact that men have attempted something impossible: while being themselves evil, they want to correct the others.[248]

Dorado Montero was making an indirect appeal: he was asking that his and Tolstoy's theory and ideals be considered, even though it was abstract in approach and presented in fiction. It is not a coincidence that this statement was located at the end of his masterpiece. His petition read as follows:

> that scholars of every kind take heed of the reasoning and warnings from our author, think about them, and do not reject them because they are reckless or utopian. All innovations begin with such a character but, nonetheless, the turn into common sense and become widely accepted truths after some time; just as all the words in a language started as mere barbarisms and neologisms, but ended up constituting a catalogue of pure, traditional terms.[249]

---

suerte o por errores propios llegan a una falsa posición se connaturalizan de tal modo con ella, que no hay quien les quite de la cabeza que su oficio es bueno, y para confirmarse en tal opinión, se mantienen dentro de los círculos que están formados por sus iguales y donde se aprueban altamente sus opciones".

[245] Calvo González (2010), p. 151: "Para Tolstoi, de los hechos que las leyes califican de delitos y como tales castigan no es posible considerar culpables a quienes los cometen, sino a otras causas que residen fuera de ellos".

[246] On this matter see the study carried out by Pérez Marcos (2005), pp. 755–802. On the same author, but shifting the focus towards the Civil law implications, see Obarrio Moreno (2008).

[247] The Holy Bible, Mt. 18, 21–22.

[248] Dorado Montero (1915), pp. 604–605: "Todo el mal proviene de que los hombres han emprendido una cosa imposible: siendo malos ellos mismos, quieren corregir a los demás. Hombres viciosos intentan corregir a hombres viciosos".

[249] Dorado Montero (1915), p. 609: "que los estudiosos de todo género [. . .] se hagan cargo de los razonamientos y advertencias de nuestro autor, se paren ante ellos y los mediten, en lugar de rechazarlos de plano y sin más por descabellados o por utópicos. Todas las innovaciones han empezado por tener este carácter, y, sin embargo, han venido con el tiempo a pasar a la categoría de verdades de sentido común y aceptación general; de la propia suerte que todas las palabras de una

Another aspect of this thinking should be addressed: Eltzbacher, an author Dorado Montero was heavily influenced by, was German. Thus, his analysis of Tolstoy's works was completed using German translations of the original Russian texts. A crucial terminological difference must therefore be stressed:

> Tolstoy does not call his doctrine on law, State, and property 'anarchism'. The anarchism he describes is a theory advocating for a life without government, whose way of achieving it is the use of violence

[250]
.

This is a crucial difference. The former (Tolstoy's "doctrine on law, State, and property") might be labelled 'Christian anarchism'. However, the latter part of the statement is referring to the standard description of anarchism. There is a clear difference between them on the use of violence: where the standard form of anarchism allows violence (especially in revolutions to take power), Tolstoy rejected it in all circumstances. Tolstoy was described as an anarchist, but this difference raises questions about his fit in that category. It was Tolstoy's Christian anarchism which inspired Dorado Montero: an ironic development given that he had rejected the Catholic Church. Tolstoy's relationship with positivism was similarly difficult to describe: he was a positivist and he was not. Tolstoy's thought did not match any of the existing Christian Churches,[251] and instead he drew attention to what he called Christ's pure doctrine.[252]

> Churches have not only remained alien to Christ's doctrine, but they have been enemies to it.[253]

Tolstoy was convinced that the Church had, in adjusting itself to the demands of the modern world, modified the pure doctrine of Christianity. This adapted doctrine was what the world accepted. This was particularly interesting in relation to humility and vows of poverty, where Tolstoy was critical of Church greed. This adaptation made it harder to accepted and implement Christ's real doctrine, rather than the cleverly altered version, and, knowing this, "Churches invent subtleties to show that men live in harmony with the law of Christ, when they actually live against it".[254]

---

lengua han comenzado por ser barbarismos y neologismos, y han acabado por formar el catálogo de las voces puras y castizas".

[250] Eltzbacher, P., *Der Anarchismus*..., p. 197: "Tolstoj nennt seine Lehre über Recht, Staat und Eigentum nicht Anarchismus. Als Anarchismus bezeichnet er die Lehre, welche ein Leben ohne Regierung als Ziel aufstellt und dieses durch Anwendung von Gewalt verwirklicht sehen möchte".

[251] His dissidence went far beyond a strict reliance on the argument that atheism and anticlericalism were the new, ground-breaking trends on his time.

[252] Eltzbacher, P., *Der Anarchismus*..., p. 197.

[253] Ibid.: "die Kirchen sind stets der Lehre Christi nicht blos fremd, sondern ihr gradezu feindlich gewesen".

[254] Eltzbacher, P., *Der Anarchismus*..., p. 198: "Die Kirche erdachte Spitzfindigkeiten, um darzuthun, dass die Menschen, indem sie dem Gesetze Christi entgegen lebten, mit ihm im Einklang lebten".

On the other hand, Tolstoy rejected the idea of leaps of faith; another idea he shared with Dorado Montero, who saw in Tolstoy a rational faith, not trusting a creed or blind faith. In words of Eltzbacher, Tolstoy was especially critical of the latter, giving an example of a Buddhist man:

> If a man has gotten to know Islam, yet he keeps on being a Buddhist, what has happened is that the old blind belief has been replaced by a rational conviction.[255]

Eltzbacher noted that Tolstoy established a precept of non-violent resistance on the basis of the 'supreme rule of love': "Never resisting evil means never using violence on another, i.e. do not ever perpetrate any act contradicting love".[256] Tolstoy himself referred to specific biblical verses reflecting his Christian belief:

> Ye have heard that it hath been said, an eye for an eye, and a tooth for a tooth: but I say unto you, That ye resist not evil: but whosoever shall smite thee on thy right cheek, turn to him the other also.[257]

Eltzbacher was very systematic and carried out a study looking at each major anarchist thinker: Godwin, Proudhon, Stirner, Bakunin, Kropotkin, Tolstoy, and Tucker. He investigated the thoughts of each of these authors on the same three themes: law, state and property.

In the first place, a vision of legal order very much grounded in natural law was held: "he rejects, as a matter of principle, every norm that depends on man's will; every norm whose maintenance is entrusted to man's power, especially to courts; which deviates from the moral law, which is different within the different territories; and which can be arbitrarily changed at any moment".[258] Dorado Montero, however, preferred the ultra-personalised conception of morality in Tolstoy: "The kingdom of God is not outside in the world, but in man's own soul".[259]

Tolstoy's vision of law therefore involved an inherent conflict: law, by its very nature, went against his commitment to non-violent resistance. Since human law implemented coercive, restrictive, and violent measures, Tolstoy concluded that law was always violent.[260] Notwithstanding that, the commitment to non-violence in law has also been held by scholars holding very differing positions

---

[255] Eltzbacher, P., *Der Anarchismus...*, p. 201: "Hat er den Islam kennen gelernt und ist dennoch Buddhist geblieben, so ist an die Stelle des froheren blinden Glaubens an Buddha die vernünftige Oberzeugung getreten".

[256] Tolstoj (1885), p. 17: "Widerstrebe nicht dem Übel bedeutet: widerstrebe niemals dem Bösen, dass heisst: thu nie einem anderen Gewalt an, das heisst: begeh nie eine Handlung» die der Liebe zuwiderläuft".

[257] *The Holy Bible*, Mt. 5, 38–39.

[258] Eltzbacher, P., *Der Anarchismus...*, p. 210: "denn er verwirft grundsätzlich jede Norm, die auf dem Willen von Menschen beruht, durch Menschengewalt, insonderheit durch Gerichte, aufrechterhalten wird, vom Sittengesetz abweichen, in verschiedenen Gebieten verschieden sein und jederzeit will kürlich geändert werden kann".

[259] Tolstoj (1892), p. 50: "Das Reich Gottes ist nicht draussen in der Welt sondern in der Seele des Menschen".

[260] Tolstoj (1885), p. 29.

to anarchism, such as Professor Jesús Ballesteros and his school of thought.[261] Further, Tolstoy pointed out something that studies in criminology and prison reports would expose in the following years: human criminal laws do nothing but increase the number of criminals. Criminality seemed to skyrocket after the passing and implementation of new criminal laws.

> Christ says: you believe that your laws reduce and fight back crime, yet they do nothing other than increase it; there is just one way to prevent evil, and it consists in returning good for evil, and doing good to all.[262]

This way of thinking would also help soften the blows of criticism and complaints from many scholars such as Concepción Arenal (past)[263] and Dorado Montero himself in his *El reformatorio de Elmira* (future).[264]

Tolstoy also analysed the state. As with law, the state was something that went directly against his Christian thought: Christian doctrine denied the validity of any form of government. In later years, Dorado Montero's thought itself on this evolved and the *cuestión social* left room for other more technical books.[265]

4.2 Other Influences

4.2.1 Karl Christian Friedrich Krause (1781–1832)

The early origins of correctionalism in Spain can be traced back to the Spanish Preventive School, which heavily relied upon the ideas of Seneca. This was a specifically Hispanic trend, and it is possible to speak of the Spanish correctionalist school[266] which emerged in the second half of the nineteenth century. For Antón Oneca, correctionalist ideals firmly resisted variation at the beginning, but only because "it was within a particular sector of the Spanish intelligentsia"—Krausism, "whose daughter was the German doctrine of the *Besserungstheorie*". However, as time went on, Spanish doctrine started to develop its own thought: rather than

---

[261] His idea of non-violent resistance was grounded in a very particular view of Christian humanism, of which it is the main representative work: Ballesteros (2006). Other relevant works are quoted: Ballesteros (1989); Ballesteros (1984); Ballesteros (1995). A very detailed description of his prolific writing can be found on his personal website: https://jesusballesteros.es/.

[262] Tolstoj (1885), pp. 45–46: "Ihr glaubt, dass Eure Gesetze das Übel verbessern, sie vergrössern es aber nur; es giebt nur einen Weg, dem Übel zu steuern, er besteht darin, Böses mit Gutem zu vergelten, allen ohne Unterschied Gutes zu thun".

[263] Arenal (1883b), pp. 468–475. From the same author, vid. Arenal (1883a).

[264] Dorado Montero (1898). This work fundamentally aimed to provide a ground-breaking model of preventative Criminal law.

[265] Dorado Montero (1902); Dorado Montero (1903); Dorado Montero (1905); and Dorado Montero (1906b).

[266] Jorge Barreiro (1975), p. 45. In this assertion, Jorge Barreiro quoted a very relevant work on the Spanish correctionalist school: Antón Oneca (1960).

continuing to develop Röder's doctrine, a Spanish tradition considered several purposes for punishment. Where the tradition had started with Seneca, it continued with "the theologians and moralists of the sixteenth and seventeenth centuries", into the "Enlightenment period".[267] Traditional correctionalist doctrine established the correctional purpose as the sole end of punishment.[268] According to Alberto Jorge Barreiro, Spanish Correctionalism (the newer form) changed the idea: correctional should not be the only purpose of punishment.[269] In my opinion, this is what made Dorado Montero's theory unique. His contemporaries were Spanish Correctionalists, but the correctional purpose or the desire to change the criminal seemed to be the only purpose he defended.[270] In this sense, Dorado Montero was in line with traditional correctionalism: "There is no other way possible in restoring law using punishment but to acknowledge correction as the essential end".[271] Dorado Montero did not, therefore, fit the Spanish tradition which held that punishment had several ends.[272] Krause[273] also inherited certain ideas from Johannes Nagler concerning the social purpose of punishment.[274]

4.2.2 Antonio Marro (1835–1913)

Antonio Marro was an Italian psychiatrist and sociologist who also worked at the Asylum of Turin. He was the disciple and successor of Caesare Lombroso, and held that the crime had a biological origin.[275] Marro along with other penalists such as Bianchi, Benedikt or Garofalo, developed his doctrine considering Ferri's work at the Congress of Criminal Anthropology which took place in Rome in 1885.[276]

Dorado Montero first referred to Marro in his *La antropología criminal en Italia*,[277] and often quoted from Marro's most famous work,[278] which he thought

[267] Jorge Barreiro (1975), p. 45.

[268] Silvela (1903), p. 8.

[269] Antón Oneca (1944).

[270] Antón Oneca (1951), p. 85. According to him, one of the greatest "mistakes" of Dorado Montero was vesting the special prevention as the only possible end for the penalty. I find it rather surprising that Antón Oneca judged Dorado in such a harsh manner bearing in mind they belonged to different schools.

[271] Silvela (1903), p. 230: "No queda, pues, más camino para llegar á la restauración del Derecho por la pena que, que reconocer en ésta la enmienda como fin esencial".

[272] "Silvela tries to harmonise the two principles of absolute justice and correction, without forgetting that of the general prevention", vid. Antón Oneca (1960), p. 1018.

[273] Krause (1828); Krause (1874).

[274] Nagler (1918). Nagler (1970), pp. 48–54.

[275] Marro (1887); Marro (1897).

[276] Dorado Montero (1889), p. 67.

[277] Dorado Montero (1889), p. 19.

[278] Marro (1887).

"worthy of mention alongside Lombroso's *Uomo delinquente*" and, even though it was "not so complete as the latter", it was a very "ordered" and "frugal" work which avoided the temptation to "draw bold and premature conclusions".[279]

4.2.3 *Luigi Lucchini (1847–1929)*

Dorado Montero described the Italian jurist and politician Luigi Lucchini as a scholar "rejecting free will". However, he was "quite concerned for some years" to find a legal basis on which to erect the "responsibility of criminals".[280]

> "What other reason but to impose a penalty, instead of a protective or healing treatment, would someone want to find out who is responsible, i.e. who deserves it and who does not? [. . .] Among those penalists, the duality penalty-treatment remains alive".[281]

In the first volume of his work, Dorado Montero identified many of the criticisms which could be raised against Lucchini. How could he justify the application of the penalty as an evil? Which individuals ought to suffer it? How would he ground imputability, a foundation which his theory so urgently needed?[282] Unsurprisingly, this was the moment at which positivist authors elaborated so many "theories on the rationale of criminal imputability independently from free will" establishing a clear distinction between "imputable and non-imputable individuals" and the "acts falling within the first or the second category". This included:[283]

> Tarde (personal identity and social resemblance), Poletti, Liszt and some others (normality of the agent), Impallomeni, Manzini and Alimena (propensity to psychological constraint), Conti, Lucchini, Vida (integrity of intelligence), Ferri and other writers from the anthropological school (the mere fact of living in society and its need for defence).[284]

Ferri agreed with taking this view of Lucchini: he "remained in a true eclecticism" and did not even think it appropriate to "deny any free will", thus remaining in the "circle of old ideas", especially when he attempted to "replace volitional freedom with freedom of the intellect".[285]

---

[279] Dorado Montero (1889), p. 158.

[280] Dorado Montero (1915), p. 10.

[281] Dorado Montero (1915), p. 10: "¿Para qué, sino para imponer pena propiamente dicha, no tratamiento protector ó curativo, se quiere saber quiénes son responsables, es decir, quiénes la merecen, y quiénes no?" [. . .] En estos penalistas continúa viva la dualidad de pena y tratamiento".

[282] Dorado Montero (1915), pp. 432–433.

[283] Dorado Montero (1915), pp. 432–433.

[284] Dorado Montero (1915), pp. 432–433: "Como las de Tarde (identidad personal y semejanza social), Poletti, Liszt y algunos otros (normalidad del agente), Impallomeni, Manzini y Alimena (susceptibilidad de coacción psicológica), Conti, Lucchini, Vida (integridad de la inteligencia), Ferri y otros escritores de la escuela antropológica (el mero hecho de vivir en sociedad y la necesidad de defender a ésta),".

[285] Ferri (1884a), p. 50.

After reading Lucchini's *Elementi di procedura penale*, Dorado Montero found that one of the "major defects" was precisely that "there were no great novelties in the doctrine" and he stood "too close to the traditional theories".[286] However, Lucchini made a "praiseworthy attempt" at reducing the subject of "criminal prosecution" to the "scientific system".[287] Further, changes from one system to the other "were not implemented and should not be implemented in an abrupt manner, but rather gradually" and Lucchini could be of interest given that the process of change needed "people of a truly conservative spirit" who progressively assumed and "incorporated the seed of regeneration".[288] It was a rather poetic way of describing an eclectic individual.

4.2.4 Giulio Fioretti

Giulio Fioretti's most important contribution for our purposes was that he "sustained 'the impossibility of considering the conscious motives of the action as an absolute criterion of imputability'".[289]

Nevertheless, his objections to doing so, even if "correct as a psychological observation", were not valid against the "criterion of determining motives" since he was referring to the "daily habitual actions" people performed without conscious motives, almost automatically.[290] Whilst his approach might be appropriate for many kinds of actions, however, "deliberating and committing a crime" was not an "unmotivated action", since it was done without thinking of the determining reasons.[291] Therefore, a crime could only be committed unconsciously in the case of an insane offender, and that was the only case in which the criterion of motives did not apply.[292]

4.2.5 Ugo Conti (1864–1942)

Dorado Montero frequently quoted Ugo Conti, an Italian politician and professor. In a chapter he contributed to the *Completo Trattato teorico e practico di Diritto penale*

---

[286] Dorado Montero (1895a), p. 399.

[287] Dorado Montero (1895a), p. 399.

[288] Dorado Montero (1895a), p. 400.

[289] Ferri (1884b), p. 693–694: "la impossibilità di considerare i motivi coscienti dell'azione come criterio assoluto della imputabilità".

[290] Ferri (1884b), p. 684–685.

[291] Ferri (1884b), p. 684–685.

[292] Ferri (1884b), p. 684–685.

secondo il Codice unico del regno d'Italia,[293] he focused on a matter which was very important matter to Dorado Montero throughout his life: responsibility. The scope of Conti's study was limited to determining the role of responsibility in each of the ten specific crimes contained in Articles 49–60 of the Italian Criminal Code. Those were: committing a crime whilst obeying an authority, self-defence, necessity, excusable excess, incitement, error in personam, minority of age, deaf-muteness, mitigating circumstances and responsibility of a third party under someone else's supervision.[294] The Italian Criminal Code also contained other circumstances excluding or mitigating responsibility for a crime (including ignorance of the law, voluntariness, mental disorders or drunkenness): although Conti focused on those ten,[295] the development of those other crimes was also relevant to his thinking.

4.2.6 Herbert Spencer (1820–1903)

Herbert Spencer was the main representative of positivism in England. English positivism was enshrined in Carle's monography, appearing as a convenient exchange with Germany and its idealism:

> Thus, [...]English positivism migrated to Germany, where it adopted a more systematic position and almost approached materialism; in turn, German idealism partially penetrated positivist England. Today in England there is a positivist [movement], which clearly tends to idealise itself. However, in Germany, the intellectuals are tired of an idealism which went too far, and react against it, diving into a patient and forbearing examination of the facts. It could also be said that Spencer and Hegel are converging: while Hegel is looking for a solid base for his speculations on the immense number of facts collected by Spencer, the latter, in order to dominate and to unify the facts, resorts to an abstract conception similar to Hegel.[296]

The contribution of Herbert Spencer was decisive for the introduction of positivism into several countries, according to Dorado Montero: "Everything that they [abstract/idealist schools] have been losing in Italy has been gained by positivism [. . .] mostly due to Spencerian evolutionism".[297] Ferri agreed: "In a very short space

[293] Dorado Montero (1891b), pp. 265–267.

[294] Dorado Montero (1892), p. 460.

[295] Dorado Montero (1892), p. 460.

[296] Carle (1880), p. 640: "*Così, per arrestare lo sguardo all'età nostra, il positivismo inglese emigrò oggidi nella Germania, ove assunse un incesso più sistematico, e venne pressochè accostandosi al materialismo; e alla sua volta lo stesso idealismo Germanico riusci in parte a penetrare nella positiva Inghilterra. Di qui la conseguenza, che oggi nell'Inghilterra trovassi un positivismo, che tende palesemente as idealizzarsi: mentre in Germania gli intelletii ormai stanchi di un idealismo, che si era spinto tropp'oltre, cercano di reagire contro di esso approfondendosi in un essame paziente e longanime dei fatti. Quasi si direbbe che Spencer ed Hegel stanno avviandosi l'uno verso dell'altro: mentre Hegel cerca una base alle sue speculazioni nel numero immenso di fatti raccolti dallo Spencer, questi, per dominare e unificare i fatti stessi, ricorre ad una concezione astratta, simile a quella di Hegel*".

[297] Dorado Montero (1889), p. 18.

of years, almost simultaneously, key contributions to positive science were made by Darwin in biology, Spencer in natural philosophy, and by Marx in social science".[298]

In his *Nuovi orizzonti*,[299] Ferri also used Spencer's works in order to provide two examples illustrating the rationale for imputability.[300] Whereas in "inorganic machines" final actions ultimately depended on "external causes", in "organic beings" the action of external causes was only a small part of a process in which "internal" and "physiological" causes prevailed.[301]

4.2.7 Alexander Herzen (1812–1870)

Alexander Herzen was a Russian philosopher and economist. He was referred to in one of Dorado Montero's works[302] as one of the "current representatives of positivism".[303] Ferri also quoted him[304] as an example of a purely positivist approach:

> Indeed, physiology, and more recently psycho-pathology thanks Ribot's work, combined to demonstrate that the individual human will is completely subject to natural influences that are not only moral or psychological, but purely physical, rather than being its more or less absolute ruler.[305]

References

"Carta de Raffaele Garofalo a Pedro Dorado Montero", Letter III, GREDOS: FPDM. Correspondencia de Pedro Dorado Montero. General. https://gredos.usal.es/handle/10366/76721

Antón Oneca J (1944) La prevención general y la prevención especial en la teoría de la pena. Discurso leído en la apertura del Curso académico de 1944–1945. Universidad de Salamanca, Salamanca

Antón Oneca J (1951) La utopía penal de Dorado Montero. Ediciones Universidad, Salamanca

---

[298] Ferri (1896), pp. 102–103: "nello stesso brevissimo giro di anni, quasi contemporaneamente, basi vitali di scienza positiva furono date alla biologia da Darwin, alla filosofia naturale da Spencer e alla scienza sociale de Marx".

[299] Ferri (1884a), p. 50.

[300] Spencer (1871), p. 226. Of the same author, Spencer (1879), p. 272.

[301] Ferri (1884a), p. 50.

[302] Dorado Montero (1889).

[303] Dorado Montero (1889), p. 19.

[304] Herzen (1874).

[305] Ferri (1884a), p. 39: "La fisiologia infatti, e più recentemente, per opera del Ribot la psicopatologia concorrono a dimostrare la volontà umana individuale completamente soggetta alle influenze naturali di ordine non solo morale o psicologico, ma puramente fisico, anzichè esserne la dominatrice, più o meno assoluta".

Antón Oneca J (1960) La teoría de la pena en los correccionalistas españoles. In: Estudios Jurídico-Sociales, Homenaje al Profesor Legaz y Lacambra. Universidad de Santiago de Compostela, Santiago
Arenal C (1883a) Estudios penitenciarios. Imprenta de T. Fortanet, Madrid
Arenal C (1883b) Lettre à M. Le Directeur General de L'Administration Pénitentiaire D'Espagne. Bulletin de la Société Générale des Prisons:468–475
Ballesteros J (1984) Sobre el sentido del derecho: introducción a la filosofía jurídica. Tecnos, Madrid
Ballesteros J (1989) Postmodernidad: decadencia o resistencia. Tecnos, Madrid
Ballesteros J (1995) Ecologismo personalista: cuidar la naturaleza, cuidar al hombre. Tecnos, Madrid
Ballesteros J (2006) Repensar la paz. Ediciones Internacionales Universitarias, Madrid
Baños P (2017) Así se domina el mundo, 1st edn. Editorial Ariel, Barcelona
Bonanno G (1895) La classificazione dei delinquenti e il reo per passione. Archivio di psichiatria 16:364–383
Bourget P (1894) Cosmopolis. Lemerre, Paris
Bourget P (1901) Le disciple. Plon-Nourrit, Paris
Brusa E (1887) Sul nuovo positivismo nella giustizia penale. Unione Tipografico, Torino
Calvo González J (2010) El alma y la ley. Tolstói entre juristas. España (1890–1928), 1st edn. Comunicación Social, Colección "Historia y presente", Sevilla-Zamora
Cantoni C (1870a) Corso elementale di Filosofia, vol II. Francesco Vallardi, Milano
Cantoni C (1870b) Corso elementale di Filosofía, vol I. Francesco Vallardi, Milano
Carle G (1880) La vita del diritto nei suoi rapporti colla vita sociale. Studio comparativo di filosofia giuridica. Fratrelli Bocca, Torino
Carnevale E (1898) L'arbitrio del giudice nell'applicazione della pena. Riv. pen., ag. 98
Carpintero Benítez F (2008) La ley natural: historia de un concepto controvertido. Encuentro, Madrid
Charcot JM (1887) Les démoniaques dans l'art. Delahaye et Lecrosnier, Paris
Chateaubriand F (1837) Génie du christianisme. Beaulé et Jubin, Paris
Coimbra Martins A (1967) O Mandarim assassinado. Ensaios Queirosianos, Lisboa
Collections of Adam Pierson (University of Amsterdam). https://archives.uba.uva.nl/agents/people/1742. Accessed 20 Aug 2019
Collin F (1927) Étude critique du système de Ferri. Revue de droit pénal et de criminologie 4:435–452
De Montyel M (1894) Impulsions homicides consécutives á la lecture d'un roman passionel chez un degénéré. Annales médico-psychologiques
Dorado Montero P (1889) La antropología criminal en Italia. Imprenta de la Revista de Legislación, Madrid
Dorado Montero P (1891a) El positivismo en la ciencia jurídica y social italiana. Imprenta de la Revista de Legislación, Madrid
Dorado Montero P (1891b) Recensión de la obra de Jules Lacointia: 'Code pénal d'Italie. RGLJ 39(78):265–267
Dorado Montero P (1892) Recensión la obra de Ugo Conti: 'Gli articoli 49 á 60 del Codice penale italiano'. RGLJ 40(81):460
Dorado Montero P (1893a) Problemas de Derecho penal. Imprenta de la Revista de Legislación, Madrid
Dorado Montero P (1893b) Problemas jurídicos contemporáneos. La España Moderna, Madrid
Dorado Montero P (1895a) Recensión a la obra de Luigi Lucchini: 'Elementi di procedura penale'. Revista de Derecho y de Sociología 3(1):399–400
Dorado Montero P (1895b) Recensión a la obra de Raffaele Garofalo: 'La superstizione socialista'. Revista de Derecho y de Sociología 6(1):773–777
Dorado Montero P (1898) El Reformatorio de Elmira. La España Moderna, Madrid

Dorado Montero P (1899) Du droit pénal répressif au droit pénal préventif. Annales Institut International de Sociologie, Paris
Dorado Montero P (1900) Der Anarchismus, von Dr. Paul Eltzbacher. La España Moderna 139: 192–193
Dorado Montero P (1902) Bases para un nuevo Derecho penal. José Gallach
Dorado Montero P (1903) Valor social de leyes y autoridades. Sucesores de Manuel Soler
Dorado Montero P (1905) Los peritos médicos y la justicia criminal. Hijos de Reus
Dorado Montero P (1906a) Los peritos médicos y la justicia criminal. Hijos de Reus, Madrid, pp 141–143
Dorado Montero P (1906b) De penología y criminología. Kessinger Publishing
Dorado Montero P (1912) La sentencia indeterminada. Revista general de legislación y jurisprudencia 120:5–26
Dorado Montero P (1915) El Derecho protector de los criminales. Ed. Jiménez Gil, Madrid
Echevarría I (2003) Crimen y responsabilidad. El País, 25.01.2003. https://elpais.com/diario/2003/01/25/babelia/1043455154_850215.html
Eltzbacher P (1900a) Die Rechtsphilosophie Tolstojs. Preußische Jahrbücher 100(2):266–282
Eltzbacher P (1900b) Der Anarchismus: Eine ideengeschichtliche Darstellung seiner klassischen Strömungen. J. Guttentag, Berlin
Eltzbacher P (1901) El Anarquismo según sus más ilustres representantes: Godwin, Proudhon, Stirner, Bakunin, Kropotkin, Tucker, Tolstoy, etc. La España Moderna, Madrid
Escuder JM (1882) El crimen de un loco y un imbécil. RGLJ 61:75
Escuder JM (1895) Locos anómalos. Sucesores de Rivadeneyra, Madrid
Ferri E (1881) I nuovi orizzonti del diritto e della procedura penale. Zanichelli, Bologna
Ferri E (1883) Socialismo e criminalità. Fratelli Bocca, Torino
Ferri E (1884a) I nuovi orizzonti del diritto e della prozedura penale. Nicola Zanichelli, Bologna
Ferri E (1884b) Sociologia criminale. Casa editrice italiana, Roma
Ferri E (1894) Socialismo e scienza positiva (Darwin, Spencer, Marx). Casa editrice italiana, Roma
Ferri E (1895) Discordie positiviste sul socialismo: Ferri contra Garofalo. R. Sandron, Palermo
Ferri E (1896) I delinquent nell'arte. Libreria Editrice Ligure, Genova
Garofalo R (1878) Studi recenti sulla penalità. Tip. Perrotti, Napoli
Garofalo R (1880) Di un criterio positivo della penalità. Dottor Leonardo Vallardi, Napoli
Garofalo R (1884) Alcune osservazioni sul progetto del codice penale con relazione di Zanardelli presentato alla camera dei deputati da Savelli il 26 novembre 1883. Frattelli Bocca, Torino
Garofalo R (1885) Criminologia: studio sul delitto e sulla teoria della repressione. Frattelli Bocca, Torino
Garofalo R (1886) Le Type criminel. F. Alcan, Paris
Garofalo R (1887a) Le délit natural. F. Alcan, Paris
Garofalo R (1887b) L'anomalie du criminel. F. Alcan, Paris
Garofalo R (1888a) Contro la corrente! Pensieri sulla proposta abolizione della pena di morte nel progetto del nuovo codice penale italiano. Ernesto Anfossi, Napoli
Garofalo R (1888b) Riparazione alle vittime del delitto. Frattelli Bocca, Torino
Garofalo R (1890a) Indemnización á las víctimas del delito. La España Moderna, Madrid
Garofalo R (1890b) La criminología: estudio sobre el delito y sobre la teoría de la represión. La España Moderna, Madrid
Garofalo R (1891a) Criminologia: studio sul delitto e sulla teoria della repressione, 2nd edn. Fratelli Bocca, Torino
Garofalo R (1891b) Dei recidivi e della recidiva. L. Vallardi, Milano
Garofalo R (1909) De la solidarité des nations dans la lutte contre la criminalité. Revue internationale de sociologie, Paris
Garofalo R (1914) Commentario del Nuovo codice di procedura penale. F. Vallardi, Milano
Garofalo R, Ferri E, Lombroso C, Fioretti J (1886) Polemica in difesa della scuola criminale positiva. Nicola Zanichelli, Bologna

Garofalo R, Ferri E, Lombroso C, Fioretti J (1890) La escuela criminológica positivista. La España moderna, Madrid
Gentile G (2016) Entstehung und Entwicklung der modernen Philosophie in Italien: Die Platoniker. Schweizerischer Wissenschafts- und Universitätsverlag, Biel/Bienne
Giner de los Ríos F, Calderón A (1907) Zur Vorschule des Rechts. Kurzgefasste grundsätze des Naturrechts in 47 vorlesungen. Dieterichsche Verlagsbuchhandlung, Leipzig
Herzen A (1874) La physiologie de la volonté. Baillière, Paris
Jiménez de Asúa L (1933) Ley de vagos y maleantes. Un ensayo legislativo sobre la peligrosidad sin delito. Revista General de Legislación y Jurisprudencia 82:577–635
Jorge Barreiro A (1975) Las medidas de seguridad en el Derecho español. Civitas, Madrid
Kant E (1867) G. B. Vico Studii Critici E Comparativi. Stabilimento Civelli, Torino
Kant E (1907) La filosofia teorética. Bocca, Milano
Krause KCF (1828) Abriss des Systems der Philosophie des Rechts. Diet- erichsche Buchhandlung
Krause KCF (1874) Das System des Rechtsphilosophie. F. A. Brockhaus
Krause KCF (1892) Vorlesungen Über Naturrecht: Oder Philosophie des Rechtes und des Staates. Otto Schulze, Leipzig
Lefort E (1892) Le type criminel d'après les savants et les artistas. Storck, Lyon
Lilla V (1880) Filosofia del Diritto. Presso Nicola Joven Libraio Editore, Napoli
Lilla V (1903) Manuale di filosofia del diritto. Società Editrice Libraria, Milano
Marey M (2011) ¿Es la exigencia kantiana de universalización un procedimiento suficiente para establecer contenidos morales-éticos? Algunas consideraciones acerca de una respuesta negativa a esta pregunta. ARETÉ Revista de Filosofía 1(23):79–108
Marro A (1887) I caratteri dei delinquenti: studio antropologico-sociologico. Fratelli Bocca, Torino
Marro A (1897) La pubertà studiata nell'uomo e nella donna in rapporto all'antropologia, alla psichiatria, alla pedagogia ed alla sociologia dal dottor Antonio Marro. Fratelli Bocca, Torino
Martín Martín S (2007) Penalística y penalistas españoles a la luz del principio de legalidad (1874-1944). Quaderni fiorentini per la storia del pensiero giuridico moderno 36(1):503–609
Morel BA (1857) Traité des dégénérescences physiques, intellectuelles et morales de l'espèce humaine et des causes qui produissent ces variétés maladives. J. B. Baillère, Paris
Morel BA (1860) Traité des maladies mentales. Librairie Victor Masson, Paris
Morel BA (1864) De la formation du type dans les variétés dégénérées. J.B. Baillière, Paris
Nagler J (1918) Die Strafe: eine juristisch-empirische Untersuchung. Scientia Verlag, Aalen
Nagler J (1970) Die Strafe: eine juristisch-empirische Untersuchung. Scientia Verlag, Aalen
Naucke W (1962) Kant und die psychologische Zwangstheorie Feuerbachs. Hansicher Gildenverlag. Joachim Heitmann
Obarrio Moreno JA (2008) La pretericián en los Commentaria del jurista Cerdán de Tallada. Revista General de Derecho Romano 11:14
Pérez Marcos RM (2005) Tomás Cerdán de Tallada, el primer tratadista de derecho penitenciario. Anuario de Historia de Derecho Español 75:755–802
Quisbert E (2008) Historia del Derecho penal a través de las escuelas penales y sus representantes. Centro de Estudios de Derecho
Röder KDA (1867) Die Herrschenden Grundlehren von Verbrechen und Strafe in Ihren Inneren Widersprüchen: Eine Kritische Vorarbeit zum Neubau des Strafrechts. Julius Riedner, Wiesbaden. Spanish edition: Röder KDA (ed) Las doctrinas fundamentales reinantes sobre el delito y la pena en sus interiores contradicciones: ensayo crítico preparatorio para la renovación del Derecho penal. Librería de Victoruiano Suárez, Madrid
Röder KDA (1876) Las doctrinas fundamentales reinantes sobre el delito y la pena en sus interiores contradicciones: ensayo crítico preparatorio para la renovación del Derecho penal. Librería de Victoriano Suárez, Madrid
Sbriccoli M (1976) Elementi per una bibliografia del socialismo giuridico italiano. Giuffrè Editore, Milano
Schneider GH (1880) Der thierische Wille. Verlag von Ambr. Abel, Leipzig
Schneider GH (1882) Der menschliche Wille. Dümmlers Verlagsbuchhandlung, Berlin

Secchi PA (1886) L'unità delle forze fisiche. Tipografia Forense, Roma
Seeger H (1892) Die Strafrechtstheorien Kants und seiner Nachfolger im Verhältnis zu den allgemeinen Grundsätzen der kritischen Philosophie. Laupp, Tübingen
Setti A (1888) L'azione penale privata e la scuola positiva. Riv Carc 18
Silvela F (1903) El Derecho penal español. Estudiado en los principios y en la legislación vigente en España. Establecimiento tipográfico de Ricardo Fé, Madrid
Spencer H (1871) Les premieres príncipe. Baillière, Paris
Spencer H (1879) Essais. Baillière, Paris
Tebaldi A (1884) Fisionomia ed expressione studiate nelle loro deviazioni. Drucker & Tedeschi, Padova
Testa A (1843) Della Critica della raggione pura di Kant. Veladini e Comp, Lugano
Testa A (1848) Collezione degli opuscoli editi ed inediti. A. Del Majno, Piacenta
The Holy Bible, Mt. 18, 21–22
Tolstoj L (1885) Darlegung des Evangeliums
Tolstoj L (1892) Worin besteht mein Glaube?
Tolstoy L (1899) Воскресение. Niva
Tolstoy L, Resurrección, tomo I

Chapter 5
Dorado Montero's Criminal Doctrine: The Protective Law of the Criminals

Abstract In this chapter, the core of his theory is duly analysed. The most relevant aspect to highlight is his rejection of absolutist theories and of the idea that there was an invariable conception of crime being the same through time and history. The plasticity of the proposal was immensely subjective, as to assert that without changing a bit the real legal order, by solely modifying one's own mental order, individuals could sometimes take for good what other people deem as evil. Furthermore, the five specific elements of the Derecho protector de los criminales is extensively addressed, namely the delinquent, the treatment, the criminal procedure, the punishment and the imputability. At the end, the concept of indeterminate sentence is explained, a new approach to how judgements should be delivered regarding the serving of the sentence to better meet the needs of the criminals. This would constitute the future, most well-known proposal of Jiménez de Asúa.

Dorado Montero developed a very extensive theory of punishment in his *Derecho Protector de los Criminales*. He did not think the "act itself" had "absolutely equal importance" in every single "case or circumstance". Instead, he focused on subjective "evaluation" and "categorisation".[1] He continued to reject absolutist theories and the idea there was an invariable concept of "crime" across history and time. For him, the key thing was how to evaluate and classify crime. This was particularly important in establishing an adequate treatment—not, notably, an adequate punishment. Rather than focus on the criminal act, he focused on the criminal as a person:

> It seems to me that, by not paying enough attention to this, we fall into many errors, and above all, into the fundamental error of believing that there is only one moral and juridical order, absolute and immutable, which is usually the one that its defenders offer us as such, i.e. the one that they subjectively form and to which they afterwards grant objective reality (without realising what they are doing).[2]

---

[1] Dorado Montero (1915), p. 16.

[2] Dorado Montero (1915), p. 18: "Me parece a mí que, por no fijarse en esto lo suficiente, se cae en bastantes errores, y sobre todo, en el fundamental de creer que solo existe un orden moral y jurídico, orden absoluto é inmutable, que suele ser cabalmente el que como tal nos ofrecen sus defensores, es

J. Franco-Chasán, *The Reception of Positivism in Spain*, Studies in the History of Law and Justice 28, https://doi.org/10.1007/978-3-031-46435-5_5

Punishment was so relative that the principle *propter necessitatem illicitum efficitur licitum* could be applied here: without any change to the "real legal order", and by solely "modifying my own mental order", one could sometimes "take for good" what at other times, with a different mental order, was "deem[ed] evil".[3] Excuses involving self-defence could be included within this category given that they partially "diminished" some criminal acts.[4] Two examples were provided: the first concerned the legitimacy of homicide in wartime amongst the Waldensians[5] in the Middle Ages; the second was similar to Tolstoy's literary illustrations.[6] Effectively, "there is [...] no other justice or injustice in the world, but what [men] mentally create for their particular use".[7]

Dorado Montero critically analysed both his own proposal and the new penal law. The latter's effectiveness was ground in acceptance by society. If a particular social trend (like a new approach to criminal law) had wide support from the majority of the population, it would be the most powerful instrument for change. Those new ideas would be adopted as the beliefs of the masses, and in doing so remain both dogmatic and uncontested.[8] Aiming at either intimidation or correction when punishing criminals were the same in this respect: "They are both teleological functions, which look to a future result. They are therefore organised around the achievement of that objective".[9] Big discussions as to the primary purpose of punishment were useless. There were only two possibilities: either to speak of punishment as a teleological reality, or as an abstract idea. Positivists and correctionalists adopted the former stance; the teleological school and the Hegelians (within the Neapolitan school) the latter. The teleological school in particular sought neither to adjust punishment to the seriousness of the crime, nor to adopt gradations of responsibility: punishment should instead be proportionate to what was required to achieve the pursued end, that is, to intimidate and correct criminal behaviour.[10] Absolute theories of crime focused on punishing people for crimes already committed, but teleological theories focused on the future commission of crimes: "Strictly speaking, one cannot talk about criminal responsibility—and its corresponding penalty—except within the so-called absolute criminal theories".[11] At first, Dorado Montero

decir, el que ellos subjetivamente forman y al que luego (sin percatarse de lo que hacen) dan realidad objetiva".

[3]Dorado Montero (1915), p. 20.

[4]Dorado Montero (1915), p. 20.

[5]The Waldensians were Christians (who would later join Protestantism) which preached apostolic poverty as a way to perfection.

[6]Dorado Montero (1915), p. 20.

[7]Dorado Montero (1915), p. 23: "[...] no hay en el mundo, para los hombres, otra justicia ni otra injusticia sino las que ellos mismos crean mentalmente para su uso particular [...]".

[8]Dorado Montero (1915), p. 185.

[9]Dorado Montero (1915), p. 186.

[10]Dorado Montero (1915), p. 187.

[11]Dorado Montero (1915), p. 187.

was very categorical: if the need for reform arose because of a lack of efficacy in the correction of criminals, then all the penalties which did not fulfil this goal ought to be overruled. This idea can be explored by looking at the several elements of crime individually.

5.1 The Delinquent

Dorado Montero's theory was abstract and engaged with various abstracts of legal philosophy. One entire chapter in one of his main works analysed the idea of the "delinquent".[12] This included consideration of voluntariness,[13] intention,[14] dangerousness as a requirement for punishment, atavistic and evolutionary criminality and the great variety of criminals. He mainly focused on challenging topics such as the application of law, its interpretation, legal sources and the non-retroactivity of laws.[15] Criminal dogmatics and legal science in their strict forms were deliberately overlooked, because he sought to change criminal law through legal philosophy, not through dogmatics.[16] This, however, did not mean that he was not good at the latter, as Asúa pointed out.[17] Dorado Montero was led to relativise punishment:

> If it is recognised that there are no criminal offences because such offences are man-made definitions based on prevailing systems of value, then how can one admit the existence of individuals possessing criminal characteristics or tendencies?.[18]

However, a mystery remained: how, then, could he possibly speak of some people as 'morally inferior'?[19] It was difficult to establish a coherent link between his utopian theory and this particular expression (and its consequences), since his view on approaches to morality was that there was 'equal value in them all'.[20] He was against any pre-established conception of truth and held that no moral was good or evil per se.[21] It was, however, possible to fit the idea of 'moral deterioration' or 'degeneration' of criminals within his theory[22]—although this was not a core concern for Dorado Montero. He thought of it as an inferior trait found amongst criminals, and

[12] Dorado Montero (1902), pp. 37–53.

[13] Dorado Montero (1911), pp. 42–77, 95–110.

[14] Dorado Montero (1911), pp. 78–94, 149–216.

[15] Ramos Pascua (1995), p. 506.

[16] Ramos Pascua (1995), p. 506.

[17] Jiménez de Asúa (1971), pp. 1617–1630.

[18] López-Rey (1956), p. 610.

[19] Dorado Montero (1905), pp. 74–83.

[20] Dorado Montero (1902), pp. 25: "Moral conceptions find themselves under the foot of equality. None of them can assume, on solid grounds, the right to become an organ monopolising the truth".

[21] The "trascendental problem" can be observed here as well.

[22] Those terms linked him to the Old Spanish Correctionalist School, but he departed from that school by including positivist elements in his theory.

always linked it to ideas about improvement. Biological determinism therefore found little space in his theory, since that allowed for the possibility of correction.[23] This was a contrast with Lombroso's theory, where it was a central idea. The success (or lack thereof) of Lombroso' approach, which was transplanted from Italy to Germany,[24] and afterwards, from Germany to Spain,[25] was primarily attributable to the social conditions in those countries rather than the merits of the theory itself.[26]

Lombroso had made an "early reference" to Darwin and to biological evolution in his work.[27] Gadebusch Bondio[28] has emphasized Lombroso's "development towards less rigorous penalties".[29]

> At the 5th Congress for Criminal Anthropology in Amsterdam (1901), it became clear that Lombroso' school had taken a turn towards eugenics which, according to Gadebusch Bondio, had been tolerated but not supported by Lombroso and Ferri.[30]

5.2 The Treatment

Despite its undeniable link with positivism, the treatment Dorado Montero foresaw in the Protective Law of the Criminals was not purely about defending society. For him, criminal sanctions were not primarily about protecting society, but protecting the individual. In this respect, he differed from the purest form of positivism:

> Whether we dealt with old or young people, male or female, individuals in these or those circumstances, the sense and procedure in reaction were identical in all cases: retaliation, expiation and retribution for the crime committed, which is what penalties were for. Guardianship and protecting the criminal were things no one thought of, since he [the criminal] was not deemed to need them.[31]

---

[23] Martín Martín (2007).

[24] Gadebusch Bondio (1995).

[25] Maristany (1983), pp. 361–382.

[26] Álvarez-Uría (1983).

[27] Burk (2005), p. 214: "Gadebusch Bondio hat auf einen überzeugenden Beleg einer frühen Bezugnahme Lombrosos auf Darwin hingewiesen".

[28] Professor Mariacarla Gadebusch Bondio is a philosopher and historian of medicine. Since February 2017, she has been the Head of the Institute for Medical Humanities (previously the Institute for the History of Medicine) at the Rheinische Friedrich-Wilhelms-University of Bonn. Link: https://www.medhum.uni-bonn.de/en/team/leitung-en?set_language=en.

[29] Burk (2005), p. 222: "Gadebusch Bondio hebt hervor, Lombroso habe eine Entwicklung zu weniger rigorosen Strafvorstellungen durchgemacht".

[30] Burk (2005), p. 225: "Auf dem 5. Kongreß für Kriminalanthropologie in Amsterdam (1901) zeigt sich, daß sich innerhalb der Schule Lombrosos eine eugenische Richtung herausgebildet hatte, die so Gadebusch Bondio, von Lombroso und Ferri zwar nicht unterstützt, doch toleriert worden sei".

[31] Dorado Montero (1915), p. 220.

The period of time in which Dorado Montero lived was characterised by the discovery and development of experimental medicine[32] and physiology[33] as two vital tools in criminal law and criminology. It was in this period that theories which "contribute[d] to establishing a differentiation between the figure of the mentally ill person and the criminal" developed.[34] The criminal law policy of each country was, ultimately what determined how criminals were treated.[35] In any case, the costs incurred in treating criminals ought not to be defrayed by the convicted nor by his family, but should be met by the whole society (whether that was the municipality, province or the State itself).[36] The rationale for this was very clear: when the "subject is individually exculpated, he is exonerated from the penalty (a punishment) and the whole society is charged, thus, with asserting collective responsibility therefore".[37]

5.3 Criminal Procedure

Dorado's idea of the criminal procedure was a very vague, general one: he never had in mind any "revolutionary methods or processes". He instead thought that changes "could be achieved by a process of social evolution, resulting from the process of the sciences, especially of psychology", which according to him would eventually "absorb sociology and anthropology".[38] However, when addressing the issue, Dorado Montero declared that the existing "scaffold of judicial and procedural institutions... should disappear" and "leave the way open" to other procedures.[39] López-Rey summarised the proposed new procedural system: "The existing criminal procedure would be replaced by a flexible one, adaptable to the circumstances of each case, and having as its sole aim curing the offender or potential offender".[40] Dorado Montero thought existing criminal procedure was highly counterproductive, creating an unnecessary confrontation between the two parties:

> Both become enemies during criminal proceedings in which the judge, as a representative of society, practically only takes into account what can be used against the offender, whilst the latter reacts in an opposite way and refers only to what is in his favour.[41]

---

[32]Bernard (1859).

[33]Béclard (1862); Magaz i Jaime (1871); Quesada i Agius (1880); Prochiantz (1990).

[34]Calvo González (2003), p. 268.

[35]Dorado Montero (1902), pp. 130–132.

[36]Dorado Montero (1893a), p. 35.

[37]Dorado Montero (1893a), p. 35: "al exculpar individualmente al sujeto y librarle de pena, de castigo, se inculpa á toda la sociedad en que aquél se ha producido y se afirma la responsabilidad colectiva de la misma".

[38]López-Rey (1956), p. 609.

[39]Dorado Montero (1902), p. 107.

[40]López-Rey (1956), p. 610.

[41]López-Rey (1956), p. 609.

Everything would change if the procedure were instead to consider the two parties as having the same aims and interests.[42] The features of the process should be based on "individual rights subordinated to the effectiveness of the treatment", "flexible criminal codes" with open, non-binding provisions, no distinction between "juvenile or adult treatments", and no need for attorneys, solicitors or other figures, only "judges specially trained in the relevant disciplines (anthropology, psychology and sociology)" and "provisional diagnosis".[43] In a nutshell:

> The traditional conception that the offender has paid his debt to society as soon as he has completed his sentence has no place in Dorado's protective system.[44]

Dorado Montero's theory was never close to being implemented: a certain degree of social stability and governance would have been required for that to happen. Some scholars have described it as more of a utopian vision.[45] The problem was that all the abstract (formal) requirements were perfectly coherent, but the idea that the material aspects could simply be attained by meeting the theoretical requirements simply did not work.

It is not fair to maintain that, because his theory had aspects which were deterministic and positivistic, Dorado Montero sought the brainwashing of criminals in order to generate a new, unproblematic individual. Positivism sought to modify individuals, but did not care about the individual criminal's personality: positivists instead supported a total or partial replacement of that person's psyche. Dorado Montero drew a hard line against this undesirable and totalitarian approach by establishing that his main objective was to protect the individual. The closest he came to endorsing the aforementioned and ill-timed positivist ideas about reform was when he said was that psychology[46] was "charged with the task of replacing the old soul with a new soul".[47] But the personality of the offender ought to remain intact; it was just their soul (meaning here their predisposition towards their actions) which should be replaced. Having their personality annihilated either by means of educative correction or biologically was to be forbidden (much later, the technique of lobotomy was developed and, in turn, prohibited). This guarantee was so important that became the name of his theory: the *Derecho Protector de los Criminales*. The 'protection' of criminals was the cornerstone which defined and structured their whole treatment. It confirmed Dorado Montero's theory as one of the most brilliant of this time: not an equidistant, eclectic theory, but rather the most rights-based, functional, and predominantly determinist theory of all of nineteenth century Europe.

---

[42] Dorado Montero considered that "judge and defendant behave to each other as two enemies". Vid. Dorado Montero (1902), p. 108.

[43] López-Rey (1956), p. 610.

[44] López-Rey (1956), p. 610.

[45] Antón Oneca (1951), p. 85. For a more scientific perspective on the qualifier 'utopian' vid. Sánchez Granjel (1989), pp. 155–170.

[46] Dorado Montero (1906a), pp. 28–31.

[47] Dorado Montero (1915), p. 22.

When describing the penal sanctions and corresponding techniques to be used, Dorado Montero regularly referred to the "moral correction of offenders". This might lead to confusion, because whilst the term "moral" regularly appeared in Dorado Montero's writings—moral inferiority of the criminal, moral deterioration, morally weak persons, etc.—it was used to mean 'personality' or 'personal attitudes', rather than what guides our actions between good and evil. He called this 'morality' for two reasons: as has already been discussed, religious thinking had influenced his work. For Dorado Montero, religion was one of the components of morality—but by no means the sole element—and his religious education meant that many of the concepts he used were Christian in origin. Many of the other legal constructions he articulated were impregnated with religious etymology, too. This means that when working through his publications, one must be careful with the terms he used, as not all of them were endowed with the legal meaning that one might expect. In some places, reading and understanding Dorado Montero requires a comprehensive reinterpretation, and it is easy to become confused, given the feeling of a permanent conflict within his ideas. Sometimes, he even contradicts himself: religious expressions vie on the one hand with determinist assertions on the other, and neoclassical language contrasts positivistic content.

The second reason for his specific use of the term 'moral' was that he wanted his audience to better understand his futuristic project. He adapted a positivist narrative to the language found in the predominant morality. His contemporaries were not remotely ready for such statements; nor were those of Jiménez de Asúa (soon after Dorado Montero), twentieth century thinkers or even society today. The rejection of Dorado's approach was based in both ignorance and fear. On the one hand, his society was simply not able to understand his advanced insights, which were ahead of his time. On the other hand, there was a reaction and thinking returned to traditional conceptions. Lombroso's developments were completely deprived of humanity. Later came Jiménez de Asúa and the rise of fascism, Nazism, and other totalitarian movements. Nowadays, we are told that the mapping of human genetics could lead to changes in virtually any single human characteristic.[48]

It was not only that Dorado Montero wanted the population in general to understand his ideas: he also wanted the academic elites of his time to accept his theory. Perhaps eclecticism (a school of thought supposed to be closer to positivism) was the only one that developed significant interest in Spain, leaving aside the traditional law and, to a minor extent, *corrreccionalismo*.[49] In a land more suited to eclectical positions, the introduction of positivism was somehow achieved because, at some point, a huge part of the school (the Catholics and supporters of the Neoclassical Schools) insisted on adopting Dorado Montero as part of their own doctrine. Even if his message endured some modifications and was a bit distorted, it was eventually accepted despite mislabelling as a neoclassical theory, or even as eclectic. That valuable 'appropriation' took place quite a long time after he first

[48] Warneck (2021).

[49] Dorado Montero (1907), pp. 401–437.

published his work, and it was not easy for Dorado Montero in the immediate years that followed the disclosure of his theory.[50]

Criminal procedure was more likely to be tackled in positivist writing than in idealist theories. The latter usually focused on the rationale of punishment, or on questions of legal philosophy, seeking to address issues which had an objective answer. That objectivity might come from either 'divine will' or 'human nature', but both cases established a common ground (or set of norms) binding all members of society. Positivism, however, tended to propose a minimum set of norms which also bound everyone, but were based only on science.[51] Positivists were likely to deny the existence of any universal truth, considering the idea of such a mere illusion for the human spirit, i.e., a utopia. Instead of what they argued was a wasted effort in trying to achieve a consensus, they focused on well-grounded rules for norms and legal procedures. In this sense, idealism "rode free" in almost "every branch" (legal philosophy, politics, economy, Roman law, international law), whereas the positivist trend "has invaded first, and with more strength than any other legal branch, criminal law and criminal procedure".[52] The Critical School was a latecomer, so "it has only a certain dominance in legal philosophy, criminal law, and sociology".[53] Antón Oneca considered correctionalism and criticised it—somewhat unfairly:

> The reality of the processes and the prisons is not questioned if all those condemned are corrigible, nor is what should be done about those who, when succumbing to an external stimulus which is difficult to repeat, do not need a second education.[54]

However, the Protective Law of the Criminals required a personalised, individual treatment for every criminal, and the question whether a certain individual was corrigible or not was always raised. In fact, the criminal procedure, shared some traits with the scientific method. Such a method had begun to be applied in social sciences and the humanities:

> As long as the law turns its back against science, the Criminal code will not be fair, nor reasoned, nor complete. Everything that is related to humanity must look for its rationale and for its basis in knowledge of nature and the human organism.[55]

When Dorado Montero wrote his first work studying the Italian Positivist School, he devoted Chap. 10 (Principal Merits of the New School) to pointing out that the main virtue thereof "could be summarised in just one statement": having applied to this branch of the law "the procedure of the experimental sciences, i.e. the positive

[50]This aspect will be further developed in the chapter exploring Dorado Montero's affiliation, even this topic could aim for an entire book of its own.

[51]See here the influence of English empiricism, mainly Lock and Hume.

[52]Dorado Montero (1889), p. 15.

[53]Dorado Montero (1889), p. 15.

[54]"No se pregunta la realidad de los procesos y las prisiones si todos los condenados son corregibles ni qué ha de hacerse con aquellos que, sucumbiendo a un estímulo exterior de difícil repetición, no necesitan segunda educación".

[55]López Bago (1888), p. 99.

method".[56] For some, there was no other option but to start applying that method everywhere in the social sciences: "And so positive philosophy tries to demonstrate that it is not possible to study social phenomena applying any method other than the experimental method". Dorado Montero advocate for this approach in order to prevent extreme positionings into which positive schools often fell, especially the need "not to attach importance to causes which are not important" or "not to exaggerate their place".[57] Dorado Montero identified this in other scholars too. In Vanni's *Programma critico di Sociologia*[58] and *Il problema della filosofia del diritto*,[59] the author agreed with Dorado Montero in the urgent need to "reconstruct... every social discipline according to the modern criterion arising from the new requirements in the sciences".[60] However, for other scholars, this movement had too great a grip[61] and was not an appropriate stance, since it would give rise to hugely disordered, mixed up and inexact assertions.[62]

In *Datanomics*,[63] Llaneza pointed out that the main obstacle in data protection is attempting to solve a technological question as if it was a legal question, and that we should instead fight technological problems with technology. Similarly, Dorado Montero called for a change of approach: within social defence, scholars were seeking to fight criminality as if it were a legal question; but a medical or psychiatric matter must be fought with medicine, not laws. Defining criminality as a scientific matter, rather than a moral one, would allow the law to overcome the main problem positivism faced: the criticism of the application of the scientific method to social sciences.[64] By assuming that criminality was a medical matter, not a legal one, any conflict over methods was avoided. Pseudo sciences had begun their attempts to affect other disciplines, and many works had appeared in that vein. Their titles demonstrated the scientific, utilitarian and positivist influences shaping them,[65] for instance Alfred Fouillée's works, particularly *Tempérament et charactère selon les individus*.[66]

In a conversation between the evolutionary biologist Justin García and the sociologist Georges-Claude Guilbert, the latter said that "in gender studies they

[56] Dorado Montero (1889), p. 151: "*Todos ellos pueden condensarse en uno solo, que es el de haber aplicado á esta rama del derecho el procedimiento de las ciencias experimentales, ó lo que es igual, el método positivo*".

[57] Dorado Montero (1889), p. 25.

[58] Vanni (1888).

[59] Vanni (1890).

[60] Dorado Montero (1893b), p. 428.

[61] Masferrer (2020a), p. 344: "These works emerged in a historical context of fascination for the use of the positivist method in science—in general—and the biological and medical sciences—in particular–".

[62] Masferrer (2009), pp. 115–118.

[63] Llaneza (2019).

[64] Dorado Montero (1906a), pp. 19–22.

[65] Fernández (1995), pp. 75–83.

[66] Fouillée (1895).

mostly assume we are not born biologically determined" and that "everything is exclusively the result of socialisation, and of the progressively permeating influence of education, family and society".[67] García was certainly shocked, not because he thought the opposite, but because of the adverb "exclusively". Biology and sociology are opposed here: biology focuses on empirical data, and sociology on long, complex (often purely theoretical) approaches. Biology focuses on a posteriori conclusions, whereas sociology deals with a priori, man-made statements. Positivism and the Neoclassical Schools were, respectively, reproducing this same pattern.

At the risk of oversimplification, this can be illustrated thus.[68] Sociologists usually reject biological explanations in a very dogmatic way, as did the Neoclassical Schools. Both revolve mainly around ideology, and, unsurprisingly, often include logical contradictions. Most Neoclassical Schools 'betray' this dogmatic aspect when trying to explain particular ideas: namely that criminality does not faithfully follow (or has little connection with) the rules of instruction, education and moral guidance, or that in societies with more permissive attitudes towards criminality there are no more criminals than in more repressive societies. If purely scientific findings showed something contradicting the man-made scaffold of theory, Neoclassicists would not usually accept that finding: their theoretical constructions came first, and any scientific outcomes should fit that theory, not vice versa. In an illustrative footnote, Dorado Montero calmly reflected on the experimental method. According to him, "metaphysic and abstract theories have moved away from reality", thus building penology only "the way Sieyès constructed the constitutions", i.e. in a very artificial, a priori manner. The experimental method in the new school played a significant role, thought the need for it "had already been sensed by the correctionalists themselves".[69] The problem was that they overstepped what was "fair", taking "criminal law out of its own sphere" and "creating a new metaphysics" which was at least as exaggerated as that of the Neoclassical Schools'.[70]

It was, nonetheless unclear whether criminal law should still be considered a human science, or whether it would someday enter the sphere of the empirical sciences. Jiménez de Asúa, the most notable disciple of Dorado Montero, once said: "In a distant future, criminology will end up swallowing criminal law".[71] Were this to happen in the near future, the argument that 'it is not correct to apply the scientific method to moral sciences' would be definitively overruled and the final victory of the scientific, positivist conception would be likely. This

[67] Estupinyà (2013), p. 311.

[68] I am fully aware that sociology was a very prominent branch of the positivist schools, thus, can hardly be suspected of sharing the rigidity characteristic of neoclassical statements. Yet, it may be contrasted with an even more positivist discipline (i.e. biology) to avoid being so Manichaean. That, in turn, allows us to see that the matter was far more complex, and that even within Positivist Schools there were more or less dogmatic models on a diverse spectrum.

[69] Dorado Montero (1889), pp. 173–174.

[70] Dorado Montero (1889), pp. 173–174.

[71] Jiménez de Asúa (1944), p. 13: "En el remoto mañana la Criminología se tragaría al Derecho penal".

controversy had been raging since the early stages of empiricism, but never entirely tackled. It seemed that the final stages of a great and hitherto inconclusive debate were coming.

It now seems true that biological and medical sciences will take over whole legal fields, more silently than in Lombroso's age, but in a much more deterministic manner. In my opinion, this is the main challenge that criminal law will face in the coming decades. Dorado Montero was too generous as regards the period of time for this change;[72] but with modern scientific developments, it seems it will now not be long until he is proven correct. The traditional conception of criminal law needs an urgent argument for resolving this, or time and scientific findings will expose its vulnerabilities. Its defenders find themselves with an urgent need for a new ground-breaking theory which does not simply ground their work on the argument that the hard sciences involve "the incorrect use of a methodology not suited for social science".[73]

5.4 Punishment

The positivists of the new criminal school refuted the concept of crime as a "product of the free will of the agent".[74] They considered the crime as a "very complex knot" which resulted from the interaction of "infinite causes", and so also rejected the "ancient concept of penalty".[75] It might, nonetheless seem that the new school was incoherent, as it continued to use both the terms 'crime' and 'penalty'. However, those concepts had to be emptied of their former meanings. Thus, a 'crime' should not mean that a person by their "free will commits a crime or abandons the righteous path", nor should 'penalty' be understood as a "set of mediaeval concepts of

[72]He estimated that this takeover would take place when socialism emerged, and steps were made towards a bourgeois society—he envisioned this roughly 50 years after his death. However, the rise of fascism and other worldwide political events disrupted any such political developments.

[73]Masferrer (2020b), pp. 3–4: "his dualism (res cogitans–res extensa) paved the way for those who understood that the scientific method needed to be empirical (res extensa), and that even social sciences should adopt this method because otherwise they would be (dis)regarded as a mere opinion, but not as a real science". Of the same author, vid. Masferrer (2020b), p. 2: "There is no doubt that not all immoral behaviour—or sins—should be criminalized: sins and crimes are not the same, as the moral and legal orders differ. It follows that Human law should never attempt to forbid all vices. The relation between criminal law and morality derives from the relation between politics, law and morality, whose provinces are different. Moral laws and civil laws have different limits and practical purposes. The sphere of moral law is much broader than civil law, which means, for example, civil laws should never concern themselves with the criminal thoughts a person may have inasmuch as they do not go beyond that, i.e. any kind of external act. As to practical purposes, civil laws have their own ethical-practical rationality, which affects not only the reasoning process but also the realm to which it applies".

[74]Dorado Montero (1889), p. 126.

[75]Dorado Montero (1889), p. 126.

redemption and retribution".[76] On the basis of several works,[77] Dorado Montero pointed out that "modern positivists of Criminal law [. . .] have failed to refrain from falling into the traditional concern according to which the penalty is a natural consequence of the crime and it is applied because the crime has occurred".[78] Criticisms gained force as positivists such as Garofalo sought the eradication of the criminal as a means of social revenge.[79] Surprisingly, this kind of attitude was found not only in the writings of anthropological positivists, but also amongst social positivists. This particularly outraged Dorado Montero:

> How was it possible that Ferri included within the means of defence against criminals available to society those which are repressive and neutralising, leaving aside the preventive and restorative measures?.[80]

He criticised Marro and Puglia in similar terms. This sort of contradiction may have been due to the fact that all of them continued to think of punishments and penalties as inherently evil. This was not consistent with positivist commitments: the penalty ought not to have such a connotation. According to the main theory Dorado Montero developed towards the end of his life,[81] the penalty should be considered the appropriate treatment of an individual in abnormal circumstances. After pointing out the inexorable march of history,[82] a rhetorical question expressed his indignation:

> How can these two contradictory statements from the positivist penalists be explained: that the effectiveness of punishments in prevent crimes is insignificant, and that the humanitarian tendencies of the classical school concerned with the fate and wellbeing of criminals, especially amongst Beccaria and Howard's henchmen, are to be considered unhealthy and indefensible?.[83]

---

[76] Dorado Montero (1889), p. 127.

[77] Garofalo (1885), p. 67; Ferri (1884), p. 121.

[78] Dorado Montero (1889), p. 127: "los positivistas modernos del Derecho penal [. . .] no han sabido sustraerse á la tradicional preocupación según la cual la pena es una consecuencia natural del delito y se aplica porque el delito ha existido".

[79] Dorado Montero (1889), p. 129.

[80] Dorado Montero (1889), p. 128: "¿Cómo era posible que Ferri incluyera entre los medios de defensa de que la sociedad puede disponer contra los criminales, además de los preventivos y reparadores, los represivos y eliminativos".

[81] Dorado Montero's theory of the Protective Law of the Criminals was best outlined in his work *El Derecho protector de los criminales* (2 vols).

[82] Noting Beccaria's objective of lowering and abolishing many existing penalties, and Howard's improvements of living conditions in prisons.

[83] Dorado Montero (1889), p. 129–130: "¿cómo pueden explicarse estas dos contrarias afirmaciones de los penalistas positivos: que la eficacia de las penas para prevenir los delitos es insignificante, y que las tendencias humanitarias de los penalistas clásicos, especialmente de los secuaces de Beccaria y Howard, que se preocupan mucho de la suerte y bienestar de los delincuentes, sean malsanas é indefendibles?".

The first statement reflected Garofalo's ideas, the second Ferri. Again, both branches of positivism (the anthropological and the social) were said to concur in their contradictions.

Moreover, two clear steps towards the construction of a new concept of punishment were identified. Firstly, the idea of a punishment as a means of repression should be completely abolished; or, if not, it should at least have a preventative rather than repressive character. Secondly, since the causes of crime were multivarious, the means to remove and prevent crime should be too: criminal law should respond to the three classes of factors: anthropological, social and physical.[84] This recognition sometimes places Dorado Montero within ongoing correctionalist or positivist trends, rather than as a figure presenting a unique correctionalism or as a plain and ambiguous eclectic.

Dorado Montero lived in a period in which the most popular approach to criminal doctrine was eclecticism. This ius-philosophical trend was led by the Italian penalist Pellegrino Rossi, whose Spanish counterpart was Joaquín Francisco Pacheco.[85] A brief outline of the history of criminal law suggested four main approaches. Firstly, there were the Mediaeval and early Modern criminal law authorities like Thomas Aquinas. Regrettably, political tensions in that period had led to a great deal of violence, authoritarianism and biased decisions in the *Ancien Régime*. A change came with the enlightened criminal law after the French Revolution (most notably led by Beccaria, Feuerbach and Bentham).[86] Next, a liberal criminal law based on ideas of individuality, the principle of legality, and the systematic indexing of crimes developed. This suited perfectly contemporary Spanish politics, valuing moderation, mixture, cultural dependence on France and conservatism. Spain was departing from Enlightenment thinking and geared towards ideas considering the overlap of law and morality in order to end perceived abuses from the older period. The fourth phase was the development of positivism and social defence in the works of Ferri,

[84] Dorado Montero (1889), p. 130.

[85] At that time, a doctrinal discussion arose around the extent of Pacheco's originality: some authors defended him (Romero Girón, Gutiérrez Fernández, and Calvo Rubio), whereas some others maintained he just copied all or some of Rossi's ideas (Dorado Montero or Antón Oneca, among others). The main way to check this out was to read his work *Estudios de Derecho penal. Lecciones pronunciadas en el Ateneo de Madrid.*

[86] Yet, it was true that in a parallel way in Germany, absolutist theories of the penalty developed thanks to Kant, Binding, and Hegel. However, in order to avoid historical oversimplifications, vid. the nuance analysis on the relation between law and morality in the Enlightenment: Masferrer (2020b), p. 110: "Some may argue that the criminalization of sexual misbehaviours in the eighteenth century was due to the absolutist political system, which was reluctant to undertake the needed reforms to modernize criminal law. In my view, this is not entirely true. A careful examination of the ideas of some of the most remarkable thinkers of the Enlightenment era revealed that the secularization of criminal law did not necessarily imply the decriminalization of those behaviours which according to some scholars, perpetrators needed to have been punished for their sinful character. As will be seen, the ideas of some authors such as Montesquieu, Beccaria, Rousseau, Voltaire, Kant, Bentham, and Blackstone, regarding some of the sexual misbehaviours which were persecuted and punished in the early modern age, do not show a clear break with the supposed 'Christian' or 'moralizing' of criminal law".

Garofalo, and Lombroso. A rough simplification of this scheme of development might label the approaches as retributive, preventative, retributive (with prevention and amendment as additional, but unnecessary, goals), and preventative, respectively. Any attempt to label Dorado Montero as an eclectic, was subject to the context of the time period he worked within, and its politics. The label neglected his legal-doctrinal framework, which should be prioritised over the historical aspect. The doctrinal framework for eclectical work, which was pre-eminently concerned with retribution, was discussed in parliamentary debates:

> They did not strive to hold spiritualist or utilitarian principles; they took what came in handy from each school. They adopted a prudent system; they did not want to create a philosophy, but to draft a practical Code for their fellow-citizens [. . .] If he [the legislator] forgets about the real world, he is seeking to impose his particular restrictions on a people not ready to follow them.[87]

De La Serna's conciliatory tone here was distinct from what Spanish legislators and scholars were accustomed to up until that point. A few lines later, he asserted that "such issues can be solved even better by talented people with a general education who have no worries concerning schools of thought, entrenched habits, and free from such a yoke as that under which we have learned, and which subjugates us".[88] Thus, the multifaceted character of the predominant doctrine could be summarised: "no absolute penal system followed, yet the purpose of punishment corresponded, primarily, to the principle of expiation or retribution".[89]

In short, Dorado Montero could not be considered an eclectic author at all. One of the main exponents of eclecticism, Francisco Pacheco, held that punishment had three purposes. In descending order of relevance, those were expiation (retribution), intimidation, and reforming the criminal.[90] The latter was the core of Dorado Montero's criminal theory, but Pacheco considered it the least important of the three ends: for him, only the first two were truly essential.[91] Thus, as Emilia Iñesta has noted, for the eclectic Pacheco's eclecticism, "amendment/correctionalist purposes" were not part of the character of criminal law, but merely represented a "vague longing for civilisation and culture".[92] They were relevant, but never as important. If Pacheco read Dorado Montero's work,[93] he would surely have rejected the proposal as external to the purposes of criminal law. If the main purpose of punishment in Dorado Montero's theory was the amendment of the criminal, since the main aim of the eclectic movement was still retribution/expiation, the values were incompatible. There were also other aspects of Dorado Montero's work which

---

[87] *Diario de Sesiones de las Cortes*, No. 81 (13.03.1848).

[88] *Diario de Sesiones de las Cortes*, No. 81 (13.03.1848).

[89] *Diario de Sesiones de las Cortes*, No. 81 (13.03.1848).

[90] Pacheco (1848), p. 207.

[91] Pacheco (1848), p. 207.

[92] Iñesta-Pastor (2011), p. 272.

[93] It should be noted that Pacheco was writing much earlier in time than Dorado Montero. When Pacheco passed away in 1865, Dorado Montero was only 4 years old.

alienated him from the electrical school: his views on the determination of the penalty,[94] his steadfast belief in free will[95] and the unwavering reliance on natural law. Once social contract theory had declined in popularity,[96] the predominant nineteenth century doctrine rejected the artificial rationale of positive law and restored traditional conceptions from natural law. Unsurprisingly, Pacheco saw social crime as moral crime, as did other eclectics.

Additionally, they differed on the possibility of variations in the absoluteness of the law. Pacheco agreed with some variations, but always within the much broader framework of a well-defined law: "*evil* is just one, always; yet, *evils* change depending on epochs, peoples, doctrines, and customs. [...] The *duty* is one, yet *duties* are manifold as per ages and nations. *Law* is one, yet the number of *laws* increases, diminishes, changes, and modifies according to the civilisation. The *holy* is one, yet *its idea* is neither conceived nor applied the same way".[97] Dorado Montero, however, plainly accepted variations without any fundamental framework. He did not acknowledge a universal, invariable truth:

> Let us change a man's condition and we will witness how he changes his moral values: let us imagine him rich, instead of poor; Catholic, instead of Muslim; producer, instead of consumer; employer, instead of worker; republican, instead of royalist; French, instead of Spaniard; trader, instead of peasant or philosopher, and we will be astonished how much his morals vary, sometimes with the speed and the ease with which actors change their roles, their clothes and their physiognomy.[98]

This denial of an immutable reality was taken from Ferri, who had earlier presented it in a very similar way: "If, therefore, we take two men or one man at different times, we shall see that their reactions to the same external cause will be very different, not

---

[94] Iñesta-Pastor (2017), pp. 517–528.

[95] "Freedom, innate to human beings, entailed the possibility of the breakdown of natural rules governing oneself. The violation thereof was a moral wrong, which constituted an appalling yet unavoidable consequence of liberty". Pacheco (1881), p. 8: "*La libertad, innata en el hombre, traia como forzosa ilacion el posible quebrantamiento de las reglas naturales que le rigen: el quebrantamiento de esas reglas era moralmente el delito; desgraciada pero inevitable consecuencia de aquella libertad*".

[96] Iñesta-Pastor (2011), p. 269: "Pacheco would thoroughly criticise social contract theory, the defence theory (grounding the penalty on the need to defend society, the main representative thereof was Romagnosi), and Bentham's utilitarian ideas about punishment". Professor Masferrer has explored the rationale for this rejection of the social contract as the only measure to create the law on behalf of Pacheco, vid. Masferrer (2020b), p. 120: "Joaquín Francisco Pacheco, one of the drafters and the main commentator of the 1848 SCC, argued that society has the right to approve criminal laws, but these laws should be in accordance with nature and reason, since society has no right to decide what is just or unjust".

[97] Pacheco (1881), p. 13: "*El mal es uno, uno siempre; pero los males varían, segun las épocas, y los pueblos, y las doctrinas, y las costumbres. El deber es uno; pero los deberes son diversos, con arreglo á las edades y á las naciones. El derecho es uno; pero los derechos se aumentan, se disminuyen, se truecan y modifican segun la civilizacion. Lo santo es uno; pero no en todas partes está concebida ni aplicada su idea de la misma suerte*".

[98] Dorado Montero (1915), p. 22.

because some new element of moral freedom has been born in man, but only because the development of the psychic factors of his action is greater in him".[99]

However, Pacheco's focus on retribution was very different from Kant's rigidity. Both agreed that the rationale for punishment had a "cardinal basis, i.e. innate notions of abstract crime and of punishment in general, whose character does not admit of variation as long as our species shall last".[100] Their positions were, however, enormously different when it came to everything else (especially the determination of the penalty). Pacheco did not think it was possible to build a philosophy of punishment. In order to systematise and structure punishment, "the only origin and principles of penal laws are things like ordinary instinct, sometimes passion, sometimes doctrines arising from a misguided morality—or even some considerations stemming from the political organisation of states".[101] Whilst Kant maintained that the determination of the penalty should remain unchanged, Pacheco[102] was convinced that there was no science of penal law: no theory even deserved that name.[103]

Any attempt to link eclecticism with correctionalism, or to group Dorado Montero with the eclectics, should be rejected. As Antón Oneca noted: "I believe that the term 'expiation' as used by penalists from Écija has a different meaning than 'purifying punishment'—which is what the correctionalists mean by it. It is instead identified with the concept of absolute justice".[104] Dorado Montero's disdain towards Pacheco was also notorious. One of his red lines was Pacheco's *Lecciones*: "though they were written in a very rhetorical and pompous way, they bore not only little substance, but the little they had was almost entirely borrowed; the source was Rossi's *Traité de droit pénal*".[105] Undeniably reflecting Dorado Montero's German influences, he pointed out that even if Pacheco was to be the legal writer of reference for some more years, those aiming towards study and research would increasingly opt for Spanish translations of Röder's works, for Silvela's *Tratado de Derecho penal*, and for articles, pamphlets, and oral lectures being produced in Salmerón,

[99]Ferri (1884), p. 51: "Per cui, se si prendono due uomini od uno stesso uomo in tempi diversi, noi vedremo che saranno sva riatissime le reazioni loro ad una stessa causa esterna, non già perchè nell 'uomo sia nato qualche nuovo elemento di libertà morale, ma solo perchè maggiore è in esso lo sviluppo dei fattori psichici della sua azione".

[100]Pacheco (1881), p. 15: "*bases capitales, nociones ingénitas del crimen abstracto y de la pena en general, cuyo carácter no admite variacion en tanto que dure nuestra especie*".

[101]Pacheco (1881), p. 16: "*El instinto solo de ordinario, que algunas veces la pasion, queotras las extravagantes doctrinas de una desatinada moralidad, que otras, por último, consideraciones deducidas de la organización política de aquellos estados, son los únicos gérmenes y los exclusivos principios de las leyes penales*".

[102]Pacheco was also known as the penalist from Écija, name of his hometown.

[103]Pacheco (1881), p. 16: "*No hay ciencia de este derecho: no hay teoría que merezca tal nombre para él*".

[104]Antón Oneca (1965), p. 481: "*Creo que la palabra expiación empleada por el penalista ecijano no tiene la significación de castigo purificador, como en los correccionalistas, sino que se identifica con la justicia absoluta*".

[105]Dorado Montero (1906b), pp. 136–137.

Giner, Azcárate, and among the rest of the Spanish krausists.[106] Dorado Montero definitively rejected retributionism and, despite being surrounded by an eclectic environment, simply not share their doctrine. It is therefore, tempting to describe him as a positivist, but this is not correct either: insofar as it was possible to do so at the time, he felt that the main goal of punishment should not be plain prevention but real reform of the criminal.

One of the most revealing insights Dorado Montero had was pointing out that the traditional retributive system had not yet been overturned; mostly due to views on morality.[107] A modern example would be 'compliance' systems, which comprise of written documents, functions, processes and controls designed to help an organisation comply with its legal obligations.[108] These systems do not fulfil any function other than identifying guilty individuals, i.e. the person responsible. Normally, this enables the attribution of pecuniary responsibility. Take, for instance, in the recent Covid-19 pandemic, the supply of a set of medical protective masks in Spain. A complaint was raised before the Spanish Ministry of Labour and Social Economy concerning the University Hospital Parc Taulí.[109] The masks doctors were using were not effective,[110] meaning medical personnel were exposed to infection.[111] As a result, healthcare experts decided that those responsible for this situation ought to be accountable. In this case, the purpose of the punishment[112] was a softened form of revenge: someone had to pay. However, this was not the only aim: it was also important to ensure that doctors' professional tasks could be performed with a minimum degree of safety. It is true that human nature might sometimes lead one to overlook certain duties, but the permanent risk of a sanction in most cases helps to encourage the pursuit of excellence. Retribution may not be the central element here, but preserving some penalty and maintaining an unavoidable punishment (per Kant) serves this purpose: it encourages some members of society to consider themselves 'on notice' and to give their best efforts.

An anarchist system in which everything is regulated by the conscience of the populace is presented as highly desirable in both old and modern utopian works, such as Thomas More's.[113] This system goes hand in hand with Dorado Montero's proposal, and he thought that as society progressed it would be towards anarchism. However, almost 200 years have elapsed since his work, and none of this is in force.

---

[106] Dorado Montero (1906b), p. 137.

[107] Dorado Montero (1903), pp. 129–148.

[108] Definition taken from https://www.compli.com/compliance-solutions/compliance-topic-centers/compliance-management-system/.

[109] The main hospital of the city of Sabadell, Barcelona (Catalonia, Spain).

[110] Filed on 15.04.2020; seen 18.04.2020.

[111] The FFP2 masks provided did not have sufficient filtering capacity for the Covid-19 virus. The pore size, whilst theoretically able to filter particles down to one micron in size, was significantly bigger, allowing the virus to pass through.

[112] Dorado Montero discussed this in Dorado Montero (1905), pp. 7–58.

[113] More (Apolo) (1937).

Modern society still requires a level of formality in punishments, as well as in many other responsibility-related activities: the construction of a house, prevention of medical negligence or simply acting 'right'. A different design could work for small communities. However, in bigger communities or mass societies, one can more easily 'hide' one's own mistakes and avoid accountability: a system based on trust is not viable. This is also why, punishment nowadays is not concerned with retribution, but with 'standard fulfilment'—this is to say, providing a 'minimum framework' to avoid poor fulfilment of duties. In the same way that education systems still require examinations and grades, the penal system also retains this basic, restrictive character. The debate on when mankind will reach the kind of society Dorado Montero envisioned, or what the necessary conditions for doing so are, is purely anthropological, and exceeds the scope of this work. It belongs to another science of knowledge, notwithstanding that it was one of the milestones in Dorado Montero's work.

5.5 Imputability

The environment in nineteenth century Spain was heavily influenced by a theory of imputability grounded almost exclusively on free will.[114] Spanish thinking on the subject continued to centre on absolute theories, but some innovations introduced mitigating and aggravating circumstances and quietly disrupted traditional criminal law principles.[115] The Supreme Court started to accept modifying circumstances and a wider, less rigid notion of imputability.[116] What had been a very simple, unequivocal concept became a number of theories of responsibility. The "classical theory" which consisted in a "moral and social responsibility, based upon the notions of obligation, free will, and personality", evolved into "modern theories".[117] The latter were divided into three broad approaches: a "mere social responsibility" based on the "notion of defending the social organism"; a "social and moral responsibility without the suppression of free will"; and a "social and moral responsibility reduced to a simple noumenon".[118] Eclecticism, both political and legal, was on the rise. Even if the positivist conception of imputability was far from being implemented, certain advances were being made and ideas like the possibility of a 'dangerous state' were being considered.

[114] González González (1994).

[115] Builla Alegre (1885). Also, vid. Masferrer (2012), pp. 353–354.

[116] González del Alba (1897).

[117] Vid. the schematic display of such classification in Bernaldo de Quirós (1898), p. 143.

[118] Bernaldo de Quirós (1898), p. 143. A noumenon is a concept used within philosophy in order to refer to an object that cannot be perceived by the senses, but rather by an intellectual or abstract understanding.

After some years, in 1931, Jiménez de Asúa rejected the idea of the 'dangerous state' because the concept of criminal capacity was essential for criminal law. However, in 1945, he changed his mind by finding a place for the idea within the concept of criminal capacity. This was an intelligent step, as it helped to overcome the old "free will vs determinism" debate. Asúa divided responsibility into two categories: subjective and objective. He focused on the dangers of the criminal's lifestyle as a risk to society and asserted the need to consider criminal capacity as distinct from free will.[119] This was a major development, because he approached criminal capacity from a psychological perspective—an approach which now prevails. At the time, the sole meaning of "criminal capacity" was concerned with "the capacity to know one's own duty", although Salillas had drawn attention to the 'crazy criminal'.[120] Progressively, the schools of legal thought started to realise that an inevitable clash on the grounds of imputability was imminent: it was, without doubt, the aspect on which the two schools differed most.[121]

The theoretical grounds for this discussion dated back to Stoicism. The Stoics had a similar approach to the Lombrosian determinists: if everything "obeys the laws of nature, how can we tell mankind to abide those laws, bearing in mind that humans cannot avoid this in any case?".[122] Lombrosian determinists had to grapple with the same problem: if the criminal was born this way, and could not help his tendencies and criminal acts, how could somebody like Lombroso treat him with such hatred and contempt?[123] Criminals were not masters of their own destiny. They were not responsible; they were not accountable for their own acts. Why were Lombroso and other positivists so insensitive to the individual? Stoics responded: man was a rational being, and so entitled to make his own decisions. Their determinism was not absolute: "the outcome is that, strictly speaking, no action is by itself good or bad because within determinism there is no place for voluntary action nor for moral responsibility".[124] However, this was not determinism—it had been qualified so much that it was not determinism anymore and embraced the concept of free will. This was precisely what Dorado Montero criticised. Since purely deterministic systems had to make room for these exceptions, their whole system failed. Despite their name, this conception was not determinist at all. Unsurprisingly, he condemned this poor positioning,[125] which struggled to reconcile free will and determinism. For Dorado Montero, the new penal law should be determinist as to the ultimate consequences:

---

[119] Roldán Cañizares (2018), p. 186.

[120] Salillas (1899), pp. 117–142.

[121] González del Alba (1896), T. XXCVIII and XXCIX; Romero de Tejada (1886), pp. 741 and ff.

[122] Copleston (1946), p. 348.

[123] Spanish supporters of Lombroso nonetheless differed from him. Vid. Campos and Huertas (2013), pp. 309–323.

[124] Copleston (1946), p. 348.

[125] Named after 'eclécticos' in Spain.

> The predicament arises precisely when one wants, at the same time, to punish more or less a set of individuals when compared to those understood to be normal, i.e. the referral/baseline individuals. They are to be punished more, with a preventive or preserving penalty or with a security measure against their dangerous tendencies; yet they are to be punished less, with a penalty basing its roots on their personal merit, thus entailing a penalty that assumes capacity and responsibility.[126]

Since these tendencies could not be reconciled, Dorado Montero noted that the most frequent solution was to "give up on the grounds of pure reason before life's demands and attend the needs of 'practical reason'".[127] Both the 'determinists' and the 'free willers' agreed this was the 'way out' of the paradox.[128]

Copleston disagreed: "no determinist system can be coherent in practice" and it should not "catch us by surprise" given that "freedom is one reality we are conscious about" and "although it can be theoretically excluded, it is newly re-introduced again where we least expect it".[129] Criminal theorists of the new school denied "man's free will" as the "main foundation of all their doctrine"; and they were aware that without this premise the "whole building would crumble".[130] Enrico Ferri himself pinpointed criminal imputability as key.[131] His point of view evolved: "whereas at first he grounded imputability [*imputabilidad*] on the denial of free will's, he now denies [...] that the criterion for criminal capacity is intelligence, but rather social defence". In Ferri's *I nuevi orizzonti del diritto e della prozedura penale*,[132] the first chapter was devoted to denying free will and criminal responsibility. The starting point was traditional criminal law and classical legal philosophy:

> Man is endowed with free will, with moral freedom: he may want good or evil. Therefore, if he chooses to do evil, he is imputable and must be punished. And depending on whether or not he is free, or whether he is more or less free in this choice of evil, he is also imputable or not, or more or less imputable and punishable.[133]

He pointed out that positivist physio-psychology had "completely annihilated any belief in 'free will' and 'moral freedom'", two concepts which were a "mere illusion of subjective psychological observation".[134] The free will of "wanting a certain thing instead of another" was described as a "pure illusion" which stemmed from "lack of

---

[126] Dorado Montero (1915), p. 147.

[127] Dorado Montero (1915), p. 152.

[128] Dorado Montero (1915), p. 152.

[129] Copleston (1946), p. 348.

[130] Dorado Montero (1889), p. 26.

[131] Vid. Ferri (1878).

[132] Ferri (1884), pp. 33–71.

[133] Ferri (1884), p. 33: "L'uomo è dotato di libero arbitrio, di libertà morale: può volere il bene od il male; e quindi, se sceglie di fare il male, esso ne è imputabile e deve esserne punito. E secondo che esso è o non è libero, oppure è più o meno libero in questa scelta del male, è anche imputabile o no, oppure più o meno imputabile e punibile.".

[134] Ferri (1884), p. 33: "la fisio – psicologia positiva ha completamente annientata questa credenza nel libero arbitrio, nella libertà morale, che si dimostra una pura illusione della osservazione psicologica soggettiva".

knowledge of the physiological precedents".[135] Thus, it was not surprising that "external phenomena, whose precedents we ignore" were incidental; whereas internal phenomena "are free".[136] Even if we ignored their causes, it did not mean they did not exist. Many physiological or social reasons for taking decisions remained unknown; "less evidence does not mean less existence", and so one should acknowledge "will's subordination to those causes".[137] As science evolved, they were revealed but then they could no longer be attributed to free will. This process of the amplification of knowledge was highlighted while referring to the latest findings from Buckle and Wagner:[138] "statistics reveal the submission of individual wills [...] to external influences from the physical and social environment".[139] But even where there were purely environmental or biological factors within human control, "each of us has experienced" how "our free will and even our own feelings can be modified".[140] He was thinking of examples such as 'climate', a 'nervous breakdown' due to stress at work or a 'deep digestive process'.[141]

Dorado Montero was heavily influenced by Ferri's denial of free will. Ferri was known as having begun as a radical denier and, later, turning to more moderate positions. This was a major issue for Dorado Montero, who received many ideas from Italian positivist authors. The minimum expression of the idea was that "no philosopher" ever maintained that "memory or intelligence" were "independent from their determining causes".[142] This was the softest position he held, whereas the general rule was more radical:

> If we get rid of the old conception of the will as a spiritual faculty in its own right, from which the fiat of every deliberation ought to flow and give a positive conception of what is called the will, the inconceivability of a real free will becomes even more evident.[143]

Before the abstract, a priori conceptions of good and evil, if we asked "positive psychology for a less fantastic idea of the spiritual faculties" its answer would be that those spiritual ideas were "nothing but abstractions of our mind".[144] Ferri's rationale for the rejection free will could be summarised:

---

[135] Ferri (1884), p. 34.

[136] Ferri (1884), p. 34.

[137] Ferri (1884), p. 41: "Ma minore evidenza non significa minore esistenza [...] riconoscere codesta soggezione della volontà alle cause".

[138] Buckle (1865); Wagner (1864).

[139] Ferri (1884), p. 40.

[140] Ferri (1884), p. 40.

[141] Ferri (1884), p. 40.

[142] Ferri (1884), p. 42: "nessuno dei filosofi ha sostenuto mai che la memoria o l'intelligenza siano indipendenti dalle loro cause determinanti".

[143] Ferri (1884), p. 42: "spogliandoci del vecchio concetto di una volontà, presa come facoltà spirituale per sè stante, onde dovrebbe scaturire il fiat per ogni singola deliberazione, e facendoci invece un concetto positivo di ciò che chiamasi volontà, riesce anche più evidente l'inconcepibilità di un vero e proprio libero arbitrio".

[144] Ferri (1884), p. 43.

> There is no memory, but individual acts of memory, just as there is no intelligence, but individual thoughts, and so on. Similarly, the will is nothing but the synthetic abstraction of all the individual volitional acts we perform, and there is no will as an entity in its own right that issues volitional commands from time to time.[145]

Thus, there was no pre-established system of free morals; there were only acts or decisions taken on grounds we do not know well. So, the psycho-physiological work of "deliberating" brought us to a "state of consciousness", the so-called volition, and led individuals to perform (or not) "certain movements". After confirming this process, Dorado Montero came to the conclusion that there was "no will per se", but only individual acts of volition, and the latter were nothing but "the consciousness of the physical-psychological process that is [were] about to take place". This was what made it impossible for Ferri to "conceive moral freedom or free will".[146] He surrendered, admitting that the "influences of the environment" and their "variations" inflicted a deadly blow to "moral freedom"[147] and made "all psychological and social science impossible and absurd".[148] Even statistics revealed the "subjection of individual wills", taken collectively, to the "external influences" of the physical and social environment.[149] Ferri referred to many other writers who agreed in this, as well as other issues.[150]

Ferri was led to a dep questioning of the feasibility of moral freedom as the basis of "the whole edifice of human responsibility", given that moral freedom was "so strongly contested even by orthodox thinkers" and received "such serious and daily denials from the most incontestable factual observations". No wonder he asked himself how the criminal theorist could claim that a conception of criminal law had the "dignity and force of a true science".[151] Dorado talked about the transition from one school to another, because even if "conclusions of positive psychology concerning the free will issue are not completely admitted" certain "concessions" were made which were assuredly both "a transition to the complete recognition of the new ideas" as well as "a sure indication of their final triumph".[152] He was averse to the idea of a mild school or mitigated version of the idea:

[145] Ferri (1884), p. 43–44: "non esiste una memoria, ma singoli atti di memoria, come non esiste un'intelligenza, ma singoli pensieri e via dicendo. Allo stesso modo, la volontà altro non è che l'astrazione sintetica di tutti i singoli atti volitivi da noi compiuti e non esiste quindi una volontà, come ente per sè stante, che emetta di tanto in tanto dei comandi volitivi".

[146] Ferri (1884), p. 44.

[147] Ferri (1884), p. 40.

[148] Ferri (1884), p. 45.

[149] Ferri (1884), p. 40: "la statistica rivela la sottommissione delle volontà indivuali, colletivamente prese, alle influenze esterne dell' ambiente fisico e sociale".

[150] Schopenhauer (1887); Maudsley (1879); Ribot (1883); Scolari (1881), pp. 174 ff.; Rossi (1856), p. 141; Mancini (1875), p. 171.; Lucchini (1878); Lucchini (1879); Buccellati (1874), p. 43; Buccellati (1882), paragraph 185.

[151] Ferri (1884), p. 46.

[152] Ferri (1884), p. 47.

> Psychologists, who stand between the old and the new, deny the existence of true free will, but support a certain ill-defined 'freedom', which serves, as always, to please the majority, who now like to show themselves as progressive while remaining attached to traditions; but it does not serve science.[153]

A concluding example was provided involving two dogs who did not react the same way to a scenario. As Ferri indicated, in the field of "inorganic machines" the ultimate reaction depended "solely upon external causes", but in the field of "organic beings" the rules were different: the action of "external causes" was supplemented by that of "internal, physiological causes".[154]

In conclusion, Dorado Montero distinguished between subjective and objective responsibility:

> The same scientific progress that serves as the basis for change from individual to collective responsibility demands an additional transformation: that of subjective responsibility into objective responsibility.[155]

If the penalty was to be regarded as an evil, the criterion to measure it ought to be "exclusively subjective". The determinist theory was entirely illogical in this: asking for the "imposition of a punishment" on someone who did not deserve it (since he was not free) was both a "contradiction" and a "cruelty".[156] Nevertheless, if punishment was "considered as a good", the criterion for its imposition should be "exclusively objective", thus, one subject to criminal treatment would not 'deserve it' but 'need it'.[157] In turn, this required a concept of so-called "diffuse responsibility".[158] Both "wrongly named" penal responsibility and civil responsibility should be "diffuse".[159]

5.6 Indeterminate Sentences

The conditional sentence was born in Boston, invented for underage criminals and minors, and it was only some time later that it was extended to adult criminals.[160] In essence, it allowed "the tribunals to order, in certain cases, the suspended execution

[153]Ferri (1884), p. 47: "I psicologi, che stanno fra il vecchio ed il nuovo, negano la esistenza del vero e proprio libero arbitrio, ma sostengono una certa 'libertà' mal definita, che serve, come sempre, ad accontentare le maggioranze, che ora amano di mostrarsi progressive pur restando attaccate alle tradizioni; ma non serve pero allá scienza".

[154]Ferri (1884), p. 50.

[155]Dorado Montero (1893a), p. 27: "El mismo progreso científico que sirve de base al cambio de la reponsabilidad individual en colectiva exige así bien otra transformación, á saber: la de la responsabilidad de subjetiva en objetiva".

[156]Dorado Montero (1893a), p. 27.

[157]Dorado Montero (1893a), pp. 29–30.

[158]Dorado Montero (1893a), p. 27.

[159]Dorado Montero (1893a), p. 31.

[160]Dorado Montero (1900), pp. 1–2.

of criminal sentences under their jurisdiction".[161] This approach was disruptive compared to the neoclassical conception of criminal sentences, where "the aim is to pre-determine the time of punishment in accordance with the law, with the legal objective of the penalty, *quasi re bene gesta*, completely disregarding whether serving such a punishment made them worse and more harmful than before (even though everybody is convinced of this)".[162]

This new approach also made its way to Spain. In 1899, the Minister of Justice, the Count of Torreanaz, presented a bill to Parliament,[163] which contained "the first conditional sentence, and the only one we have had".[164] Dorado Montero was worried that the public would consider the Minister's proposal a "temporary revolution" and, in 1900, he published an article giving an "account of the countries which had already adopted it" or were "about to do so".[165] This concerned the following countries:

> England, the first European nation where the conditional sentence was transplanted from North America (by the Probation of First Offenders Act of 8 August 1887); Belgium, the first nation of the continent where the institution of reference was introduced (by the law of 31 May 1888); France (law Bérenger of 26 March 1891); canton of Neuchâtel (art. 339 of the Criminal code of 29 May 1891); Duchy of Luxemburg (law of 23 May 1892); canton of Geneva (law of 29 October 1892); Portugal (law of 6 July 1893); Norway (law of 2 May 1894); Saxony (order of the Ministry of Justice of the Kingdom of Saxony of 25 March 1895); Prussia (Royal Order of the King of Prussia of 23 October 1895); Wurttemberg (rescript of 24 February 1896); Bavaria (ministerial order of 24 March 1891); Hamburg (resolution of the Senate of 30 April 1896); canton of Vaud (law of 13 May 1897).[166]

---

[161] Dorado Montero (1900), pp. 1–2.

[162] Röder (1867), p. 34: "*Ebendarum Sperrt man die Sträflinge noch oft genug ein nicht nur ohne alle Rücksicht auf die Wahrseinlichtkeit oder auch nur Moglichkeit der Erreichung oder Förderung des gemeinen sowohl als des eignen Besten fondern man lässt die auch, nach Ablauf der doch vorgeblich dem Recht und Rechtszweck der Strafe entsprechend vorausbestimmten Strafzeit, quasi re bene gesta wieder los, ohne nur danach zu fragen, ob Sie nicht gerade durch die Strafe weit schlechter und gefärlicher geworden find als sie es vorher waren, ja trotzdem, das mann hiervon überzeugt ist*".

[163] Dating 08.01.1900, published in the Official Gazette on 10.01.1900.

[164] Acknowledging that the Code Montilla in 1902 may have attempted to introduce similar reforms. Vid, Dorado Montero (1915), p. 152, footnote 1: "by virtue of which the Courts were entitled to suspend, in certain cases and under certain conditions, penalties depriving freedom for 6 months (Book I, Title III, Chap. IV, Article 84—the only one in the chapter-)".

[165] Dorado Montero (1915), p. 152.

[166] Dorado Montero (1900), p. 2: "Inglaterra, primera nación europea, donde la condena condicional fué trasplantada de Norte América (por the probation of first offenders act de 8 Agosto de 1887); Bélgica, primera nación del continente, donde se introdujo la institución de referencia (por la ley de 31 Mayo 1888); Francia (ley Bérenger de 26 Marzo de 1991); cantón de Neuchatel (art. 339, Código penal de 29 Mayo de 1891); ducado de Luxemburgo (ley de 23 Mayo 1892); cantón de Ginebra (ley de 29 Octubre 1892); Portugal (ley de 6 Julio 1893); Noruega (ley de 2 Mayo 1894); Sajonia (orden del Ministerio de Justicia del reino de Sajonia de 25 Marzo 1895); Prusia (Real orden del Rey de Prusia de 23 Octubre 1895); Wurtemberg (rescripto de 24 Febrero 1896); Baviera (orden ministerial de 24 Marzo de 1891); Hamburgo (resolución del Senado de 30 de Abril 1896); cantón de Vaud (ley de 13 Mayo 1897). Además, hay proyectos de leyes especiales sobre el particular en otros sitios

There were also legal drafts and projects for special laws in other places: in Italy; in the Swiss canton of Ticino; more recent projects of Criminal Code in France; the Federal Swiss Code, the Austrian Code, the Hungarian Code. All of them utilised conditional sentences. In Germany, and in some other places, there were several attempts to introduce them (discussed in both the Reichstag and the territorial 'diets').[167] Conditional sentences were broadly known about long before Torreanaz's bill: "it has existed for nothing less than 30 years in the United States" and it had been 13 years since their introduction in Europe. Dorado Montero complained of the delay in adopting them in Spain: "we play exactly the same role as regards the capitals of third and fourth role".[168] It could be argued that the origins of the proposal were French, because for "a very long time" when Spain tried to legislate on some matters, France was "the sole country we know how to turn our eyes to, in order to take it as a model".[169] This idea was criticised by some scholars, however, as an inaccurate stereotype.[170] The real origin of the idea was Belgium: Torreanaz had referred to "the French law on attenuation and aggravation of the penalties (also known as Law Bérenger)", but "Bérenger was not the author of the conditional sentence" having taken it "from other places", specifically Belgium—despite the fact that had had presented a project in France in 1884.

> If we have a look all over Europe and consider the necessity of penitentiary progress, we realise that the races bathed by the North Sea are those that perform better. The first place belongs to the Scandinavian countries, the Netherlands and Belgium; afterwards, England, Germany, and France; later on, Switzerland, Italy, Austria-Hungary and Russia; finally, Portugal, Spain, Romania and the states at the south of the Danube; thus, with few exceptions, progress in this matter shrinks as we move away from the septentrional sea.[171]

If this idea was not that ground-breaking, why did Dorado Montero consider it to be a transcendental tool? It was because it introduced a new model, alleging the need to implement changes, but never intending to foster a change of model. Dorado Montero, who did advocate for a change of model, knew that with indeterminate sentences in the old model, the clash between the two would be so irreconcilable that it would inevitable mean the development of a new model:[172]

> The conditional sentence does not harmonise with the capital ideas that constitute and sustain the regular criminal law, which is a criminal law from the past; brutal, vindictive,

---

(como en Italia y en el cantón del Tesino); los proyectos de Código penal más recientes, como el francés, el federal suizo, el austríaco, el húngaro, etc., admiten la condena condicional; en Alemania y en otros lugares se han hecho tentativas para introducirla, habiéndose llegado á discutir ya en el Reichstag sobre el asunto, del propio modo que también en las dietas territoriales".

[167] Dorado Montero (1900), p. 3.

[168] Dorado Montero (1900), p. 1.

[169] Dorado Montero (1900), p. 1.

[170] Masferrer (2014, 2017, 2020c).

[171] Rivière, A., *Révue Pénitentiaire*, December 1897, p. 1.253.

[172] Dorado Montero (1898), p. 119.

repressive, retributive. It only harmonises with a new criminal law, utilitarian, of social prevention and foreseeable, of social hygiene, of preventive police [. . .].[173]

Naturally, Dorado Montero's approach to indeterminate sentences[174] took some elements from Ferri's preventive police:

> According to Ellero's thinking, these preventative or social hygiene means can be divided into two main categories. The measures of direct policing close to the crime, which are the least useful and effective, because they aim only to prevent crime when the causes have already developed (and therefore have a repressive or compressive character). However, there are those that, for the reason aforementioned, have until now been thought and used almost exclusively in science, and especially in legislation. Secondly, the measures of indirect and remote policing, which tend to remove or make less evil the causes of crime, and as such, as far as they extend their effectiveness, are true and proper penal substitutes, as I called them, because 'once the crime is removed, the punishment is removed at the same time'.[175]

The logic behind this was overwhelming. For example, imagine a Civilisation A which settled on the shores of the River A. In turn, Civilisation B settled on the shores of the River B. Civilisation A evolved: it generated culture, architecture, and universities; it developed agriculture, industry, manufacturing; and created a complex society with politics, education, and health care, etc. So did Civilisation B. Suddenly, River A dried up, triggering enormous changes in Civilisation A in order to survive. These changes affected all parts of society radically: technology, ecology, consumption, economy, etc. However, the River B maintained its flow and Civilisation B did not experience any significant changes. Perhaps they started constructing skyscrapers because they were running out of space for housing as the population grew, but no major changes were implemented. What happened then? In Civilisation B, reforms and changes were superficial, with limited importance. However, changes to core elements like the existence of River A are not isolated changes, and their impact is transformative. This precipitates a change of model—as in Civilisation A. This was precisely what Dorado Montero tried to do. Even if he was sometimes mistaken for an eclectic, he was seeking a radical change of model, but in a very calm, discreet manner.

---

173 Dorado Montero (1900), p. 1: "La condena condicional no se armoniza con las ideas capitales que informan y sostienen el derecho penal corriente, que es derecho penal del pasado, brutal, vengativo, represivo, retributivo; no se armoniza sino con un derecho penal nuevo, utilitario, de previsión y prevención social, de higiene social, de policía preventiva".

174 Dorado Montero (1912), pp. 5–26.

175 Ferri (1884), p. 684–685: "Questi mezzi preventivi o di igiene sociale si distinguono alla lor volta, secondo il concetto dell'Ellero, in due grandi categorie. I provvedimenti di polizia diretta e prossima al delitto, che sono i meno utili ed efficaci, perchè mirano soltanto ad impedire il reato, quando già le cause ne sono sviluppate (e perciò hanno indole repressiva o compressiva), e sono tuttavia quelli a cui, per la ra- gione ora accennata, quasi esclusivamente si è pensato ed avuto ricorso finora nella scienza e sopratutto nella legislazione. I provvedimenti, in secondo luogo, di polizia indiretta e remota, che tendono a togliere od a rendere meno malefiche le cause stesse del reato, e come tali, sin dove estendono la loro efficacia, sono veri e proprii sostitutivi penali, coni'io li chiamai, perchè 'tolto il delitto è tolta al tempo stesso la pena'".

> Isn't it true that in this way, by vesting the judges of a certain faculty of granting pardon, the penal system receives a death blow, a system in which we have nursed (the retributive penal system)?.[176]

He aimed for a change from the abstract model of criminal law to a more utilitarian one: "before the demands of abstract justice and abstract logics there are the impositions of reality, or in other terms, the real truth, the utilitarian justice".[177] He had assumed that Luis María de la Torre y de la Hoz (commonly known as the Count of Torreanaz) knew "very well all of this" and that he knew "what his project of 8 January was bringing him towards". For him, the system which Torreanaz was starting to introduce could be described as follows:

> It distinguishes itself from the expiatory, retributive, restorative sense of the penal function, and it enrols de facto in the promotion and defence of the utilitarian and preventive penal system; the latter takes as the criterion to punish not the crime committed (in order to punish in proportion to its seriousness and redeem the offender), but the degree of dangerousness of that criminal (to try to avoid it, if possible); the one that asks for the penalty to be applied, not when abstract justice so requires, and in as much quantity as it demands, but solely when -and as far as- social need, utility and social convenience requires, and as a means to prevent the commission of future crimes.[178]

For him, the best model was the latter, since "more useful, more human, more fair work is done, even if one deviates from the rules of so-called absolute justice [. . .] leaving the criminals without penalty rather than imposing it".[179] He took his main argument for such a view from the Howard Association in London, given that "making a child or a youngster into a prisoner" normally entailed that they were "lost forever".[180] However, not all great personalities agreed that the prisoner was lost in prison. Ernst Bertrand, for instance, was sceptical.[181]

---

[176] Dorado Montero (1900), p. 5: "¿No es verdad que de esta manera, al propio tiempo que se otorga á los juzgadores una cierta facultad de conceder indultos, se da un golpe de muerte al sistema penal, en medio del que nos hemos amamantado, al sistema penal retributivo, al fundado".

[177] Dorado Montero (1900), p. 5: "frente á las reclamaciones de la Justicia y de la lógica abstractas, se hallan las imposiciones de la realidad, ó lo que es lo mismo, la verdad real, la justicia utilitaria.".

[178] Dorado Montero (1900), p. 5: "se aparta del sentido expiatorio, retributivo, reparador, represivo, en suma, de la función penal, y que se alista de hecho entre los promovedores y defensores del sistema penal utilitario y preventivo, del que toma como materia y criterio de punibilidad, no el delito realizado (para castigarlo en proporción á su gravedad, para hacérselo expiar á su autor en proporción al merecimiento de éste), sino el grado de peligro que el delincuente ofrezca (para procurar conjurarlo, si lo hay); del que pide que se aplique la pena, no puando la justicia (abstracta) lo quiera, y en tanta cuantía como ella lo exige, sino solamente cuando y hasta donde lo reclame la necesidad social, la utilidad y la conveniencia social, y como medio de impedir la perpetración de futuros delitos".

[179] Dorado Montero (1900).

[180] "The minors shall never be recluded in prisons".

[181] The question was initially set out regarding the opposition of solitary confinement vs. communal confinement. Vid. Félix Sevilla, F., "Mi viaje por Francia y Bélgica. Un magistrado penitenciario", *Vida penitenciaria*, Madrid, No. 55, Año II, 1933, pp. 12–14, p. 13: "el sistema celular de larga duración con la creencia errónea que el delincuente pierde en la celda su sentido social y se deshumaniza. [. . .] han reconstituido completamente su vida, no llegando la reincidencia más que al 12 por 100 de los liberados".

Dorado Montero did have some criticisms of the proposal. Firstly, why did the project try to "limit the power of the tribunals" to use conditional sentences to just "three specific penalties"[182] out of approximately twenty contained in the general list (Art. 26 Criminal Code)"? Even for those two, why did they not extend the conditional sentence to "the fullest degree, limiting it to the minimum"? Secondly, why could conditional sentences not be applied to "those condemned for misdemeanours"? Dorado Montero did not understand why conditional sentences were reserved to those committing crimes only. Thirdly, many perpetrators[183] were excluded from the conditional sentencing powers: "Won't their stay in prison be as harmful as for the rest?".[184] Finally, why were conditional sentences, which would later be developed by his pupil Jiménez de Asúa,[185] always used for young criminals, "disregarding which crime as well as the circumstances"?[186]

Dorado Montero's thinking on indeterminate sentences was particularly influenced[187] by the notes on conditional sentences from various congresses: the International Penitentiary Congresses of Saint Petersburg and Paris of 1890 and 1895, respectively; those held in the Brussels meeting of the International Union of Penal Law in 1889; the 21° Congress of the German jurists held in Cologne in 1891; and those of Hungarian Legal Congress held in Budapest in 1896".[188] He also read the work of Rivière and M. Tallack, the Secretary of the Howard Association (mentioned above), especially his book *Penological and preventive principles*.[189] He also took note of the International Penitentiary Congress of Paris (1885)—specifically the report of the commissioners from the USA—and issue XXI of the *Révue Pénitentiaire*[190] in

[182]Namely, the Spanish 'arresto mayor', 'presidio' and the 'prisión correccional'.

[183]"External security of the State, crimes against humanity, crimes against the Parliament or the Ministerial Council, violent theft in an uninhabited place, larceny or scam worthy of more than 100 pesetas, havocs and anarchists, smuggling and fraud, those which can only be pursued at the request of a party, and those which the Tribunal deems adequate". Vid. Dorado Montero (1900).

[184]Dorado Montero (1900), pp. 1–2.

[185]Jiménez de Asúa (1913).

[186]Dorado Montero (1900), pp. 1–2.

[187]Dorado Montero (1911), pp. 313–322.

[188]Dorado Montero (1900), pp. 1–2.

[189]Tallack (1889).

[190]The Official Gazette of the Société Générale des Prisons (*Butlletin de la Société Générale des Prisons*) was created in 1877. After 25 years, in 1892, it turned into the *Revue pénitentiaire et de droit penal.* Among its members and founders, Marc Ancel, René Bérenger or Gabriel Tarde are notable. The *Comité des travaux historiques et scientifiques* also highlights BENOIST Charles (1861–1936)—membre fondateur, BERARD Auguste (1802–1846)—membre, BERGERON Jules (1817–1900)—membre, BOULEY Henri (1814–1885)—membre, CHABRIÈRES Maurice (1829–1897)—membre, CHEYSSON Émile (1836–1910)—membre, DAGUIN Fernand (1848–1922)—membre, DUFAURE Jules (1798–1881)—membre fondateur, GLASSON Ernest Désiré (1839–1907)—membre, JOLY Henri (1839–1925)—président, LEFÉBURE Léon (1838–1911)—membre fondateur, LEREDU Georges (1860–1943)—membre, 1885-; secrétaire; trésorier; président, 1924, LYON-CAEN Charles (1843–1935)—membre, PICOT Georges

1897.[191] References inside Spain, included Concepción Arenal, Salillas, Cadalso, Guillén y López Cancio, Ramón Albó y Martí, Lastres and Romero Girón. La Sagra was briefly considered before being set aside for "being a little distant".[192]

No analysis on this issue would be complete without the work of Dorado Montero's contemporary Fernando Cadalso Manzano.[193] Dorado Montero had noted the prominence[194] of two of his works: *Estudios penitenciarios*[195] and *Diccionario de legislación de prisiones.*[196] Cadalso Manzano came into contact with Dorado Montero at the International Penitentiary Congress of Paris of 1895. Dorado Montero wrote the *Reformatory of Elmira,*[197] which Cadalso read and whose model he tried to copy. In that book, Dorado Montero explored the main aspects of criminal law and criminology, but Fernando Cadalso had been present at the aforementioned facility and decided to analyse Dorado's work in the *Revista de Prisiones y de Policía.*[198] Though Cadalso was not the only one reviewing it,[199] he was very astute. He warned the reader: even if the work was very interesting from the "legal point of view", it was far more interesting from the "penitentiary point of view".[200]

Cadalso opened the analysis by criticising the system used in Pennsylvanian prisons (particularly in Philadelphia) and their implementation of the Auburn system.[201] After exploring ideas such as those of the Medical Association of New York and its President (Mr Flint), he concluded that the criminal system in force was no longer valid. The growth of criminality and recidivism rates was worrying,

(1838–1909)—membre, ROGER Henri (1809–1891)—membre, TARDE Gabriel de (1843–1904)—membre, VOISIN Félix (1832–1915)—président, and WURTZ Adolphe (1817–1883)—membre, 1877–1883.

[191] Dorado Montero (1900), pp. 1–2.

[192] Dorado Montero (1900), pp. 1–2.

[193] He was born just 2 years before Dorado Montero (1859–1939).

[194] Dorado Montero (1900).

[195] Cadalso y Manzano (1983).

[196] Cadalso y Manzano (1907).

[197] Dorado Montero (1898).

[198] The National Library of Spain (Biblioteca Nacional de España) reports that the *Revista de Prisiones y de Policía* was the continuation of the *Revista de las Prisiones*, which began to be published in 1893 in Madrid, and Fernando Cadalso carried on directing it. The new review had a new section devoted to the police (since the judicial police body was created in 1896). After some years, it recovered its original name *Revista de las Prisiones* (1899–1903). Link: http://bdh.bne.es/bnesearch/biblioteca/Revista%20de%20prisiones%20y%20de%20polic%C3%ADa/qls/0003768531;jsessionid=0E37023FF5B7FE4CF14337AF62DD25B7.

[199] Benito (1898), p. 191.

[200] Cadalso y Manzano (1898), p. 445.

[201] Also known as the "rule of silence", this system forbade prisoners to talk when they met at a workschool, school or during other communitarian occupations. For an accurate distinction between the Pennsylvania/Philadelphia system (separate system) and the Auburn system (silent system), vid. Ramos Vázquez (2013), pp. 110–111; pp. 112–116.

"especially among the young and habitual criminals, reaching in some cases the 40%".[202] The most visible elements of the new system developing were "the societies of patronage, the schools of reform, the prison colonies, etc., which exist in France, Switzerland, Belgium, Germany, England, Sweden, the aforementioned reformatory, and the ones which were planned for North America".[203] After exposing the two possible systems (punitive—looking back to the committed crime—and preventative—looking forward to prevent crimes from taking place), and stressing that the Reformatory of Elmira clearly took the latter approach, he focused on its objective. Cadalso, quoting Dorado Montero, was critical of the goal to "reform of the criminal", where the "word reform should not be understood as a "substantial reform of the individual, as the pure correctionalists aimed at with their concept of 'correction' (which was highly ambiguous and yielded impractical results)".[204] The word 'reform' actually meant the "reasonable possibility that the convicted, once he is free, acts in a way that does not violate laws".[205] The main objective was that the criminal became "less predisposed to committing crime" than a "non-criminal belonging to his same [social] class".[206] The reciprocal feedback between Dorado Montero and Cadalso was noteworthy. The idea of the indeterminate sentence also came from Cadalso: "when the delinquent is reformed, the penalty does not have raison d'être any longer and it is over. Due to this, the sentences imposed on the inmates at the reformatory are indeterminate, and that is also why parole or conditional freedom is granted".[207] Such a system provided that the released criminal would have a 6-month period "out of the reformatory" without any special guardianship in order to weigh whether "complete freedom" could be awarded or not.[208]

In the following issue of the review,[209] Cadalso further analysed Dorado Montero's proposal. This second part was more focused on the physical description of the penitentiary establishment, but there was some consideration of the spirit of the new system: "the Reformatory is not guided by inflexible legal precepts nor by casuistical regulations set beforehand".[210] Thus, its function was closer to judicial discretion, though in this case, it did not depended on the judge but on the maximum power within the penitentiary: on both the "Board of Managers" and the "General Superintendent".[211] The reformatory, however, was graver than it might look: it was

[202] Cadalso Manzano (1898), p. 446.

[203] Cadalso Manzano (1898), p. 446.

[204] Cadalso Manzano (1898), p. 447.

[205] Cadalso Manzano (1898), p. 447.

[206] Cadalso Manzano (1898), p. 447.

[207] Cadalso Manzano (1898), p. 447: "cuando el delincuente se halla reformado, la pena no tiene razón de ser y acaba. Por esto las sentencias impuestas á los reclusos en el Reformatorio son indeterminadas, y por esto también se otorga la libertad ó liberación condicional".

[208] Cadalso Manzano (1898), p. 448.

[209] Cadalso Manzano (1898) pp. 453–455.

[210] Cadalso Manzano (1898), p. 453.

[211] Cadalso Manzano (1898), p. 454.

different to the renowned Schools of Reform,[212] in which young criminals[213] were accepted, but only those having committed misdemeanours.[214] Finally, some statistics were highlighted, as Cadalso referenced a paragraph of Dorado Montero concerning the characteristics of criminals within the institution:

> Of them, 68% are completely illiterate; 75% lack a regular and remunerative profession; 92% have lived without the benefits of a good domestic environment; 75% are under the average well-being levels corresponding to their social class.[215]

The third part of the analysis addressed the classification of inmates.[216] There were three possibilities: the "testing" group, the "neutral" group, and the "conviction" group. Dorado Montero described this classification in detail.[217] The modus operandi was very simple: everyone entered the neutral group and, if after 6 months their behaviour was rated as good or bad, they would move to the first or to the second group, respectively. Once within the "testing" group, if another 6 months elapsed with positive results, they got parole; if, after another additional 6 months, good results continued, they would receive "complete freedom".[218] The institution had two further categories: "incorrigibles" and "those who are deemed reformed, but there are still reasons to keep them inside".[219] Those in the first group were rebellious against "all the means the Reformatory has", and were, therefore, "expelled" and "relocated" in a regular prison. The latter were employed within the institution.[220] After naming the several "prices" the inmates could aim at, he concluded with a remark that "moral and religious influences are used in order to increase and to favour the ethical power of the inmates".[221]

Nonetheless, Dorado Montero was not a penitentiarist. Notwithstanding what Oliver Olmo said,[222] where Concepción Arenal and Cadalso Manzano were petentiarists, Dorado Montero was a penalist. Either way, the truth was that, despite all the efforts made by many experts in both fields,[223] prison remained almost the same: "such 'invariability' was not even altered by the progressive experience of the Second Republic, which did not modify the punitive-award character of the

212 "Escuelas de Reforma".

213 Between 16 and 30 years old.

214 Cadalso Manzano (1898), p. 454.

215 Cadalso Manzano (1898), p. 455.

216 Cadalso Manzano (1898), pp. 461–463.

217 Dorado Montero (1898), pp. 43–44.

218 Cadalso Manzano (1898), p. 461.

219 Cadalso Manzano (1898), p. 462.

220 Cadalso Manzano (1898), p. 448. 462.

221 Cadalso Manzano (1898), p. 463: "se hace uso de las influencias morales y religiosas para aumentar y favorecer el poder ético de loa reclusos".

222 As quoted by Oliver Olmo (2007), p 90.

223 As for the penitentiary reform efforts in Spain at the beginning of the twentieth century and their specific instruments (the Regulation of 5 May 1913, Dueso's penitentiary colony, advances in Primo de Rivera's time or Victoria Kent's reforms), vid. Ramos Vázquez (2013), pp. 395–450.

progressive system, since it kept on assessing the submission and obedience of the convicted as a means for obtaining freedom".[224]

Núñez asserted that the "relationship of Pedro Dorado Montero with Italian positivist criminology" was a topic that historiography has tackled most. Some considered him a "critic of positivism" acting as a very "powerful curb" to the ideas of Lombroso; some that he was a "disciple and friend of Ferri"; others that he was an adherent of "eclecticism" or a "positivist correctionalist".[225]

The work of Núñez shed some light on the relationship between Dorado Montero and Cadalso. In one of Cadalso's attempts at wining a professorship in 1910,[226] Dorado Montero was a member of the Tribunal in charge of examining his application.[227] When the sixth International Penitentiary Congress took place in Brussels,[228] both Cadalso and Dorado Montero were appointed on behalf of Spain. Cadalso was designated Vice President of the Fourth Section (Minors), and Dorado Montero was a substitute for another participant (José Álvarez Mariño).[229] They also had long conversations in Brussels, as Dorado Montero had recently published *The Reformatory of Elmira*.[230]

Núñez recalled Saldaña's comments on Cadalso and his trip to the USA. He contacted American reformatories, unlike other Spaniards like Ventura de Arquellada, Marcial Antonio López or Dorado Montero who "had written their books without moving out of their homeland and with data comfortably extracted from other works: books born out of books".[231] This claim may be qualified, as Dorado Montero was one of our most internationalised authors, speaking several languages, and attending international congresses. Regrettably, due to his health, he did not carry research abroad as often as he could have (bearing in mind he also planned to conduct research in France, but had to cancel the trip).

References

Álvarez-Uría F (1983) Miserables y locos. Medicina mental y Orden social en la España del siglo XIX. Tusquets, Barcelona

Antón Oneca J (1951) La utopía penal de Dorado Montero. Ediciones Universidad, Salamanca

[224]Núñez (2014), p. 75: "Invariabilidad ni siquiera alterada por la experiencia progresista de la Segunda República que no modificó el carácter punitivo-premial del sistema progresivo al continuar valorando la sumisión y obediencia de los penados como medio para obtener su libertad".

[225]Núñez (2014), p. 96.

[226]Criminal Law at the University of Oviedo.

[227]Núñez (2014), p. 118.

[228]Núñez (2014), p. 210.

[229]Núñez (2014), p. 210.

[230]Núñez (2014), p. 210.

[231]Núñez (2014), p. 333. Also, in the same sense Saldaña (1925), pp. 241–42.

Antón Oneca J (1965) El Código penal de 1848 y D. Joaquín Francisco Pacheco. Anuario de derecho penal y ciencias penales 18:473
Béclard J (1862) Traité élémentaire de physiologie humaine, 4th edn. Labé, Paris
Benito L (1898) Noticias bibliográficas. El reformatorio de Elmira (Estudio de Derecho Penal preventivo). Revista General de Legislación y Jurisprudencia 98:191–191
Bernaldo de Quirós C (1898) Las nuevas teorías de la criminalidad. Imp. Revista de Legislación, Madrid
Bernard C (1859) Introduction à l'étude de la médecine experimental. Collège de France, Paris
Buccellati A (1874) La razionalità del diritto penale. Hoepli, Milano
Buccellati A (1882) Il nihilismo e la ragione del diritto penale. Hoepli, Milano
Buckle HT (1865) Histoire de la civilisation en Anglaterre. Librairie Internationale, Paris
Builla Alegre A (1885) Teoría de las circunstancias atenuantes y eximentes de responsabilidad criminal según el Código español: ¿Cabe alguna modificación en vista de los nuevos estudios frenopáticos? RGLJ 67:470
Burk T (2005) Geschichte der Degenerationstheorien. Thomas J. Burk (personal blog)
Cadalso y Manzano F (1898) El Reformatorio de Elmira. Revista de Prisiones y de Policía 46:445–448
Cadalso y Manzano F (1907) Diccionario de legislación penal, procesal y de prisiones. Imprenta de J. Góngora y Álvarez, Madrid
Cadalso y Manzano F (1983) Estudios penitenciarios: presidios españoles, escuelas clásica y positiva y colonias penales, con un breve compendio de la legislación, costumbres jurídicas y prácticas penitenciarias que rigen en los establecimientos. Centro editorial de F. Góngora, Madrid
Calvo González J (2003) Naturalismo y direcciones criminológicas a finales del siglo XIX en España. Revista de derecho penal y criminología 12:255–270
Campos R, Huertas R (2013) Lombroso but not Lombrosians? Criminal anthropology in Spain. In: Knepper P, Ystehede PJ (eds) The Caesare Lombroso Handbook. Routledge, Abingdon, pp 309–323
Copleston F (1946) A history of philosophy. A&C Black
Diario de Sesiones de las Cortes, No. 81 (13.03.1848)
Dorado Montero P (1889) La antropología criminal en Italia. Imprenta de la Revista de Legislación, Madrid
Dorado Montero P (1893a) Problemas jurídicos contemporáneos. La España Moderna, Madrid
Dorado Montero P (1893b) Reseña al libro de Anziolotti: 'La Filosofia del Diritto e la Sociologia. RGLJ 41(82):427–429
Dorado Montero P (1900) Sobre la facultad de indultar las penas, concedida á los Tribunales. Revista Política y Parlamentaria 7:1–2
Dorado Montero P (1902) Bases para un nuevo Derecho penal. Manuel Soler, Barcelona
Dorado Montero P (1903) Valor social de leyes y autoridades. Sucesores de Manuel Soler, Barcelona
Dorado Montero P (1905) Nuevos derroteros penales. Henrich & Compañía, Barcelona
Dorado Montero P (1906a) De Criminología y penología. Viuda de Rodríguez Serra, Madrid
Dorado Montero P (1906b) Los peritos médicos y la justicia criminal. Hijos de Reus, Madrid
Dorado Montero P (1907) El correccionalismo penal y sus bases doctrinales. Revista general de legislación y jurisprudencia 55(11):401–437
Dorado Montero P (1911) La psicología criminal en nuestro Derecho legislado. Hijos de Reus, Madrid
Dorado Montero P (1912) La sentencia indeterminada. Revista General de Legislación y Jurisprudencia 120:5–26
Dorado Montero P (1915) El Derecho protector de los criminales. Ed. Jiménez Gil, Madrid
Estupinyà P (2013) S=EX^2. La ciencia del sexo. Debate

Fernández P (1995) La novela médico-social: entre fisiología y sociología. Eduardo López Bago y el naturalismo radical. La novela y el mercado literario en el siglo XIX. Rodopi B.V., Ámsterdam
Ferri E (1878) La teorica dell' imputabilità e la negazione del libero arbitrio. Barberá, Florencia
Ferri E (1884) I nuovi orizzonti del diritto e della prozedura penale. Nicola Zanichelli, Bologna
Fouillée A (1895) Tempérament et caractère selon les individus, les sexes et les races. Félix Alcan, Paris
Gadebusch Bondio M (1995) Die Rezeption der kriminalanthropologischen Theorien von Cesare Lombroso in Deutschland von 1880–1914. Diss. phil. Abhandlungen zur Geschichte der Medizin und der Naturwissenschaften, p 70
Garofalo R (1885) Criminologia: studio sul delitto e sulla teoria della repressione. Frattelli Bocca, Torino
González del Alba P (1896) La imputabilidad ante las escuelas antropológicas. RGLJ 88:212
González del Alba P (1897) Locura o imbecilidad incompletas. Doctrina del Tribunal Supremo. RGLJ 90:261
González González J (1994) La imputabilidad en el Derecho penal español. Imputabilidad y locura en la España del siglo XIX. Comares, Granada
Iñesta-Pastor E (2011) El Código penal español de 1848. Tirant lo Blanch, Valencia
Iñesta-Pastor E (2017) Tradición e influencias extranjeras en la clasificación de las penas en los códigos españoles decimonónicos. In: Masferrer A (ed) La Codificación penal española. Tradición e influencias extranjeras: su contribución al proceso codificador (Parte General). Thompson Reuters Aranzadi, Pamplona
Jiménez de Asúa L (1913) La sentencia indeterminada. El sistema de penas determinadas 'a posteriori', Reus, Madrid
Jiménez de Asúa L (1944) El derecho penal del futuro. In: Mora Guarnido J (ed) El mundo de la posguerra. Mundo atlántico, Buenos Aires
Jiménez de Asúa L (1971) Recordando a D. Pedro Dorado Montero. Revista de Estudios Penitenciarios 195:1617–1630
Llaneza P (2019) Datanomics: Todos los datos personales que das sin darte cuenta y todo lo que las empresas hacen con ellos. Deusto
López Bago E (1888) El preso. La Inquisición moderna, Estudios de la vida humana en cárceles y presidios. Novela médico-social. Imprenta de José Góngora, Madrid
López-Rey M (1956) X. Pedro Dorado Montero (1861-1919). In: Mannheim H (ed) Pioneers in criminology. Stevens and Sons, London, pp 605–612
Lucchini L (1878) Rivista critica del Progetto Vigliani. Rivista penale
Lucchini L (1879) Corso di diritto penale. Siena
Magaz i Jaime J (1871) Tratado elemental de fisiología humana. Est. Tip. de Narciso Ramírez, Barcelona
Mancini PS (1875) Lettere a Mamiani sul diritto di punire. Livorno
Maristany L (1983) Lombroso y España: nuevas consideraciones. Anales de literatura española 2: 361–382
Martín Martín S (2007) Penalística y penalistas españoles a la luz del principio de legalidad (1874-1944). Quaderni fiorentini per la storia del pensiero giuridico moderno 36(1):503
Masferrer A (2009) Codification of Spanish criminal law in the nineteenth century: a comparative legal history approach. JCL 4(1):115–118
Masferrer A (2012) Spanish legal traditions. Dykinson, Madrid
Masferrer A (2014) La Codificación española. Una aproximación doctrinal e historiográfica a sus influencias extranjeras y a la francesa en particular. Thomson Reuters Aranzadi, Cizur Menor
Masferrer A (2017) La Codificación penal española. Tradición e influencias extranjeras: su contribución al proceso codificador (Parte General). Thomson Reuters Aranzadi, Cizur Menor
Masferrer A (2020a) The reception of the positivist school in the Spanish criminal doctrine (1885-1899). GLOSSAE Eur J Leg Hist 17:303–352

Masferrer A (2020b) The role of nature in the secularization of criminal law in Europe (17th–19th centuries). The criminal law of the enlightenment revisited. In: Masferrer A (ed) Criminal law and morality in the age of consent. Springer, Cham, pp 97–144
Masferrer A (2020c) La Codificación penal española. Tradición e influencias extranjeras: su contribución al proceso codificador (Parte Especial). Thomson Reuters Aranzadi, Cizur Menor
Maudsley H (1879) La physiologie de l'esprit. Germer Baillière, Paris
More T (1937) Utopía: el estado perfecto. Apolo, Barcelona
Núñez JA (2014) Fernando Cadalso y Manzano: medio siglo de reforma penitenciaria en España (1859–1939). Universidad de Valladolid, Valladolid
Oliver Olmo P (2007) Historia y reinvención del utilitarismo punitivo. In: Gastón Aguas JM, Mendiola F (coords) Los trabajos forzados en la dictadura franquista. Instituto Gerónimo de Uztáriz, Pamplona
Pacheco JF (1848) Estudios de Derecho penal. Lecciones pronunciadas en el Ateneo de Madrid. Imprenta y fundación de Manuel Tello, Madrid
Pacheco FJ (1881) El Código penal concordado y comentado. Imprenta y fundición de Manuel Tello, Madrid
Prochiantz A (1990) Claude Bernard, La révolution physicologique. PUF, Paris
Quesada i Agius B (1880) Tratado elemental de fisiología general. Est. Tip. de Eduardo Cuesta, Madrid
Ramos Pascua I (1995) El positivismo jurídico en España: D. Pedro Dorado Montero. Anuario de Filosofía del Derecho 12:503–546
Ramos Vázquez I (2013) La reforma penitenciaria en la historia contemporánea española. Dykinson, Madrid
Ribot TA (1883) Les maladies de la volonté. Germer Baillière, Paris
Röder KDA (1867) Die Herrschenden Grundlehren von Verbrechen und Strafe in Ihren Inneren Widersprüchen: Eine Kritische Vorarbeit zum Neubau des Strafrechts. Julius Riedner, Wiesbaden
Roldán Cañizares E (2018) Luis Jiménez de Asúa: un jurista en el exilio. Universidad de Sevilla, Sevilla
Romero de Tejada JG (1886) La imputabilidad ante las escuelas criminológicas. Revista de los Tribunales 30:741–763
Rossi P (1856) Trattato di diritto penale. Società Editrice, Torino
Saldaña Q (1925) La reforma de los jóvenes delincuentes en España. Progreso penitenciario. Revista de disciplina penal 540:241–242
Salillas R (1899) Los locos delincuentes en España. RGLJ 64:117–142
Sánchez Granjel L (1989) Medicina y Antropología en la génesis de la utopía penal de Dorado Montero. Eguzkilore. Cuaderno del Instituto Vasco de Criminología 3:155–170
Schopenhauer A (1887) Essai sur le libre arbitre. F. Alcan, Paris
Scolari S (1881) Istituzioni di scienza política. Tip. Citi, Pisa
Tallack W (1889) Penological and Preventive Principles. Wertheimer, Lea & Co., London
Vanni I (1888) Prime linee di un programma critico di Sociologia. Tipografia di V. Santucci, Perugia
Vanni I (1890) Il problema della filosofia del diritto. Donato Tedeschi e Figlio, Verona
Wagner A (1864) Die Gesetzmässigkeit in den scheinbar willkührlichen menschlichen handlungen. Boyes & Geisler, Hamburg
Warneck L (2021) The Promises of CRISPR Genome Editing in Biomedicine. Labiotech. https://www.labiotech.eu/interview/crispr-therapeutics-genome-editing/. Accessed 3 Mar 2021

Chapter 6
Locating Dorado Montero in Spanish Doctrine

Abstract Dorado Montero has often been misunderstood and some scholars have attributed to him certain meanings or whole ideas which he never expressed. According to my understanding, the classification of Dorado Montero followed three 'waves'. In the first wave, Dorado Montero was simply included within the positivists. He was lumped together with Lombroso, Ferri and Garofalo. Sometime after, the second wave tried to bring Dorado Montero back to the neoclassical postulates (López-Rey easily fits in this wave). Finally, a current third wave tried to draw him back to positivism. Whether this was due to the rise of neuroscience, biological sciences and new disciples as 'neurolaw', I cannot possibly conform to fully discredit and underestimate this third wave. Dorado Montero was very much confident when he deliberately denied freewill. Besides, the influence he had in other authors and posterior schools is mentioned (Bernaldo de Quirós is particularly relevant).

Nevertheless, it can be asserted that Dorado Montero has been simplistically ascribed within Italian positivism. That is why it is more adequate to label his thought as simply Doradian, since the number of nuances prevent him from being included within one group.

Dorado Montero did not articulate a practical model. The theory he maintained did not become a real system, other than perhaps the main ideas behind the indeterminate sentence. His thought amounted to a profoundly theoretical approach, yet very ambitious, almost utopian. The several proposals he attempted to provide were not applicable neither to the historical and political reality of his time nor nowadays. After a scrutiny of his works, the reader might have the impression that he is still owed a clear proposal. Besides, the systems he drafted, were so abstract that the longed solution to the unfair system of Criminal law back on his time could not be found.

J. Franco-Chasán, *The Reception of Positivism in Spain*, Studies in the History of Law and Justice 28, https://doi.org/10.1007/978-3-031-46435-5_6

6.1 Labelling the Unclassifiable

Humans need classifications. They never work completely, but it is central element for our limited capacities that we have tools to enable us to better understand reality. Classifications help us to overcome oversimplified categories and appreciate nuance. A foundation is needed.

As regards Dorado Montero's doctrinal affiliations, one quotation captures the essence of this section:

> They have attributed to him [to Dorado Montero] ideas which he never expressed or have identified him with some of the theories held by certain penal schools of his time.[1]

López-Rey was warning here that Dorado Montero was not an Italian positivist, nor was he a determinist. He was right in that Dorado Montero has been simplistically ascribed to the Italian Positivist School. However, some legal historians and legal philosophers took advantage of this statement to instead place Dorado Montero in the traditional system of criminal law and the Neoclassical Schools. Within the those disposed to do so, there were three factions. The first consisted of scholars aiming to camouflage their neoclassical affiliation by arguing he created a 'middle term proposal'. These were the same scholars who labelled him an 'eclectic'. The second faction consisted of authors who, acknowledging Dorado Montero's religious disaffection, asserted that his Christian influences led to a mixture of new positivist ideas within acceptable Christian limits. The third faction comprised a group which believed that, by virtue of a mistranslation (namely 'correctionalism' being used instead of 'positivism' or 'social defence'), he had created a third way. For them, correction was not the same as correctionalism: the term was so unique that one should respect the original language expression 'correccionalismo'. All three groups held that Dorado Montero did not deny free will, which placed him within the Neoclassical Schools. Free will was therefore a key concept in determining his line of thought.

During what I have loosely labelled the 'first wave', Dorado Montero was simply grouped with the positivists, lumped together with Lombroso, Ferri and Garofalo. Some time after, the 'second wave' tried to bring him back within the neoclassical postulates (especially López-Rey). Finally, a current 'third wave' has tried to claim him once again for positivism. Whether this has been due to the rise of neuroscience, biological sciences and new disciplines such as 'neurolaw' is speculative,[2] but it is not possible to fully discredit this third wave, nor should it be underestimated. However, Dorado Montero confidently and deliberately denied the existence of free will.

It may be inferred from the above that the quotation from López-Rey is not entirely accurate. Regardless of one's personal beliefs, a close study of Dorado Montero does not permit the assertion that he was "mistakenly categorised as a

[1] López-Rey (1956), p. 605.

[2] Picozza (2011).

determinist". It remains true that (1) he had a religious crisis, (2) he abnegated from Catholicism and (3) he remained a sceptic his whole life. It was this eternal doubt which made Dorado Montero the way he was, and made his Protective Law of the Criminals one of the most critical theories in all of nineteenth century Europe.

Once his view on free will has been clarified, his other positions should be similarly analysed. Another speculation has been that Dorado Montero's theory combined correctionalism and positivism: "Dorado's theory tries to reconcile two very different things: Comte's positivist ideas with some of the old Spanish School of thought aiming at the moral 'enmienda' (moral correction of the offender)".[3] A group of scholars eager to claim him for the Neoclassical Schools held he was not a positivist, and that he was trying to fight positivism by mixing it with a genuinely Spanish neoclassical theory ('enmienda').[4] This is too simplistic: "His life was a twofold struggle: he first fought against traditional criminological ideas and systems, and secondly, against his physical handicap".[5] He clearly referred to the fact he saw himself as fighting the neoclassical conception of criminal law, because he was powerfully innovative and fought the traditional ideas of his time. These paragraphs do, however, demonstrate how easily one can place Dorado Montero on one side or the other, depending on the desired outcome.

López-Rey was, however, correct when he highlighted that Dorado Montero was sometimes considered radical. Given his critical, bitter theorising against the administration and judiciary, some authors thought he was advocating the dissolution of the state. Others, particularly Kropotkin and Silonief, adopted the more specific but equally oversimplified view that Dorado Montero was an abolitionist. According to them, he held that penal law as such should disappear. This is not correct, either: Gumplowicz's influence was to emphasise to Dorado Montero that the state had an enormous role to play. Thus, he said "there is no possible law existing without the State itself, and citizens have no rights other than those granted by the State".[6] Not only did he always regard peaceful political evolution as far more desirable than political revolution, but he was fully aware that his system was so ahead of its time that it could not be implemented except far in the future. He was aware of the many inadequacies of spirit in his own time. He challenged society's capacity to develop and adopt his proposed model. Dorado Montero's project could only take place after necessary transformations had taken place:

> The political and criminal foresight of Asúa and Ruiz Funes follows the correctionalist path of Dorado, and deems the existence of a democratic State of law an indispensable requirement for its implementation, not in the current form but according to the parameters of liberal statalism, i.e. as a representative institution of the national will and as a guarantor of the rights by means of an auto-limitation of its sovereignty. Asúa's opinion also includes the

---

[3]López-Rey (1956), pp. 607–608.

[4]Ramos Vázquez (2013), pp. 217 ff.

[5]López-Rey (1956), pp. 606.

[6]Gumplowicz (1915), pp. 85–86: "No hay Derecho sino en el Estado, y los ciudadanos no tienen otros derechos que los que el Estado le adjudica".

condition of the emergence of socialism, thought he did not reject advances made by liberal democracy.[7]

This was especially ironic since Dorado Montero's most well-known pupil, Luis Jiménez de Asúa, experienced the same difficulties when re-defining the future of criminal law dogmatics. Asúa thought criminal law was divided into three stages, namely: bourgeois criminal law (neoclassical), transitionary criminal law (in his time) and the *Derecho Protector de los Criminales* (following Dorado Montero's model).

In the transitionary period, Jiménez de Asúa used the expression 'immediate future' out of which stemmed a real belief in the rapid arrival of socialism. This idea was probably influenced by the settlement of the Soviet regime which he talked about at the end of the 20th century. He set his hopes on the Soviet Union's law following the way set out in his criminal evolution: to reach a criminal law based on socialist principles being, in turn, a future example for Europe and America.[8]

The combination of Dorado Montero and Jiménez de Asúa offered many advantages in understanding a common reality in their different approaches. They both knew that society had not yet reached the necessary stage of evolution. Whereas Dorado Montero blamed this on the excessively dominant position of traditionalism, Jiménez de Asúa cited the risk of such theories turning into totalitarianism. For Dorado Montero, his society was still far too immersed in the principles of neoclassical criminal law and could not embrace the new ideas and perspectives established by positivism and correctionalism. Society had simply stagnated in regards to criminal law. For Jiménez de Asúa, though, the inadequacy of social standards originated in totalitarianism. The rise of positivism degenerated into totalitarian political systems harming the reputation of the new criminal system. Indeed, racism was starting to be a problem in Lombroso's time as most of his postulates were misinterpreted by Nazi theories (even if that was not his original aim): "Bulferetti's interpretation—that enthusiasm for ethical values such as charity, individual freedom and freedom of thought saved Lombroso from slipping into racism—must be put into perspective".[9] That was why, at the end of his academic career, he decided to abandon the new conception of criminal law: "he was conscious that, in his time, it

[7]Martín Martín (2007), p. 577: "*La prospectiva político-criminal de Asúa y Ruiz Funes prosigue la senda correccionalista de Dorado, y sólo estima requisito indispensable para su gradual implantación la existencia de un Estado democrático de derecho, concebido no al modo actual, sino según los parámetros del estatalismo liberal, esto es: como institución representativa de la voluntad nacional y garantizadora de los derechos a través de la autolimitación de su soberanía. La opinión de Asúa incluye además la condición del advenimiento del socialismo, pero no desdeña los avances conquistados al amparo de la democracia liberal*".

[8]Roldán Cañizares (2018), p. 82.

[9]Burk (2005), p. 233: "Bulferettis Deutung, der Enthusiasmus für ethische Werte wie Wohltätigkeit, individuelle Freiheit und Freiheit des Denkens etc. habe Lombroso vor einem Abgleiten in den Rassismus bewahrt, muß relativiert werden".

was necessary to maintain the classical guarantees of law; but he did not reject them [...] he just postponed them for a future society".[10]

As has been discussed, Dorado Montero's relationship with natural law was a complicated one. Its origin could be traced back to Gumplowicz's rejection of natural law: "None of the authors on natural law, nor any of the philosophers who are always talking about such rights, have been able to prove [the existence of natural law]".[11] Dorado Montero acknowledged that such a position was very common among positivist authors, but his own denial of natural law was far from oversimplified. He was aware that, even though human relations were endowed with guarantees only when defended by the state, they had existed before it, in something he called a "poorly-defined state" (equivalent to Ardigò's "potential law", Cogliolo's and Pulia's "moral nebula", and Gumplowicz's "simple morality stage").[12] They admitted that the main problem was determining the origin of rights, so an inevitable question arose: does the state grant rights, or just recognise a pre-existing reality? Gumplowicz had struggled with the same problem ("the origin does not lay in natural law, and they are not innate but are elaborate within society, as real needs demand").[13] However, Dorado Montero soon set himself apart from Gumplowicz: Dorado Montero understood that the origin of rights was not to be found in the state because when social opinion became too strong for the public power to ignore it, one might somehow start to identify "rights" (similar to Grotius' conception of "perfect rights").[14]

Dorado Montero had undoubtedly developed a legal philosophy whose central point of view rested on understanding normativities in a broad sense:

> The opposing side did not want to see in man rights other than those really acknowledged and guaranteed to him, i.e. those rights which he can effectively assert, and has wrongly believed (in our view) that man cannot assert any other rights than those legally recognised and provided with a legal action.[15]

Contemplating the old Roman question "leges vs. iura", Dorado Montero's approach to the production of normativity sought to extend the traditional conception of rules by adopting the concept of 'multinormativity':

> The term 'multinormativity' is aimed at a number of phenomena, which are also discussed under the title of 'legal pluralism'. This is particularly true with regards to what usually

[10]Roldán Cañizares (2018), p. 84.

[11]Gumplowicz (1877), p. 13: "Was immer die Naturrechtslehrer und Philosophen von einem folchen Rechte sprechen, keiner von ihnenkann uns ein folches ausserhalb der Verbindung mit dem Staate zeigen".

[12]Gumplowicz (1915), p. 86.

[13]*Ibid.*

[14]Salam (2014), p. 19.

[15]Dorado Montero (1893), p. 15: "La dirección opuesta no ha querido ver en el hombre otros derechos que los que realmente le son reconocidos y garantizados, es decir, los derechos que puede hacer valer, y ha creído, equivocadamente a nuestro juicio, que no puede hacer valer más que los legalmente reconocidos y provistos de una acción".

> appears as the conceptual core of 'legal pluralism', i.e. the coexistence of different modes of normativity in the same social space and the related questions of classification, legitimation and collision. 'Multinormativity' is also directed at different forms of normativity and not only to those that are traditionally counted among the sources of law.[16]

The need for a method for this enterprise has led to the suggestion of an historicist approach to global legal history. From this historical perspective, law and other modes of normativity are seen as forming one part of the totality of propositions that members of a culture consider true, and are relevant in producing approved behaviour. This suggestion is not new, and encompasses normative knowledge the Western tradition labels as social, religious, indigenous norms, state law and, especially, natural law,[17] customs,[18] and common sense.[19] Practical knowledge, implicit understandings and all other norms and rules with significance for the production of normative knowledge are an object of global legal history—and they are also, obviously, the results of that process. The object of global legal history is normative knowledge in this wide sense.

Internationally, a famous assertion attributed to Jiménez de Asúa claimed that "criminal law will be engulfed by criminology".[20] Some sciences did absorb others: anthropology and sociology were subsumed by psychology (especially correctional psychology).[21] Yet, Dorado Montero, under the influence of Anzilotti, suspected that it was improbable that sociology could absorb "every social science" (including legal philosophy), because the latter would "retain its autonomy" and enrich itself using "the data from sociology".[22] Nevertheless, Ferri seized on the opportunity in a paper by Dorado Montero (*Du droit pénal répressif au droit pénal préventif*) to refer to Vicente Lanza: "one can see how correctly some eclectics have been able to claim the apostles of the new verb (the positive criminal school) do not concern themselves with the search for the rational genesis of the right to punish after all".[23] Ferri thus distinguished Dorado Montero from the eclectics, placing him alongside the positivists.

---

[16]Duve (2017), pp. 90–91: "Der Begriff ›Multinormativität‹ auf eine Reihe von Phänomenen, die auch unter dem Titel des ›Rechtspluralismus‹ diskutiert werden. Das gilt vor allem im Blick auf das, was üblicherweise als Begriffskern des ›Rechtspluralismus‹ erscheint, die Koexistenz verschiedener modi von Normativität in demselben sozialen Raum und die damit verbundenen Fragen von Klassifikation, Legitimation und Kollision. Auch ›Multinormativität‹ richtet sich auf verschiedene Formen von Normativität, und zwar nicht allein auf solche, die traditionell zum Kreis der Rechtsquellen gezählt werden".

[17]Long before Codification, the Kingdom of Valencia (currently Spain) included natural law as a source of legal authority, alongside privileges, fueros or royal legislation.

[18]Masferrer (2012), p. 196: "Usatges de Barcelona".

[19]Masferrer (2012), p. 196: "Common law [including both Roman and Canon law], equity and common sense".

[20]*Annales de la Faculté de Droit et des Sciences Politiques de Strasbourg*, "Les orientations nouvelles des sciences criminelles et penitentiaires", Paris: Dallaoiz, 1954.

[21]López-Rey (1956), p. 609.

[22]Dorado Montero (1893), p. 428.

[23]Lanza (1899), p. 4.

Another statement of López-Rey poses questions about Dorado Montero's affiliations:

> In combining free will and determinism, i.e. in admitting both of them, Dorado goes further than the old Spanish penologists, to whom free will was the basic element of any penal treatment. On the other hand, in admitting a determinism mitigated by free will, he did not go as far as the supporters of the Italian Positive School.[24]

This assertion is problematic, as it seeks to place Dorado Montero in a position somehow original and equidistant from the two opposing doctrines, inviting countless contradictions. Efforts to justify such an eclectic position conspicuously failed. Copleston had already identified the problem in dealing with free will and determinist theories:

> Since the Stoics defended that everything obeyed the laws of nature, the following objection should be made to them: 'Why is man being told to keep to the rules of nature if he cannot avoid submitting to them in any case?' Stoics would respond that man is rational and, thus, even if he always has to act according to natural laws, he has the privilege of knowing and consciously accepting them. So, it follows that the moral exhortation has an end: man is free to change his inner attitude. This entails, of course, a modification of the determinist thesis, if not something else... There cannot and will not be any determinists who can be complete consequentialists, and Stoics do not constitute an exception from this rule.[25]

Actually, there were determinist postulates which were consequentialist, if we assume that determinist theses were completely incompatible with free will, and they were irreconcilable and antithetical. Criticisms of Copleston were based on this assumption, as his critics aimed at those determinists who admitted to some free will as being incoherent. However, a similar criticism could be levelled against the supporters of free will. And so, Copleston's last assertion required a nuance: Stoics were not inconsistent because they were determinists, but because supporters of free will envisioned a universal god whose natural rules no one could escape from.[26]

In his otherwise brilliant analysis of the Stoics, Copleston acknowledged that Stoic determinism soon experimented with a great modification in practice. For example, Cleantes' perspective on virtue,[27] and discussions of the fact that humans necessarily followed the path drawn by destiny. Seneca held that "fate leads the willing and drags the unwilling",[28] but the Stoics considered men "free to change his inner attitude and to adopt another [attitude] of submission and resignation rather

[24]López-Rey (1956), p. 611.

[25]Copleston (1946), p. 348. In relation to Copleston's analysis, vid., Hicks (1919), pp. 88–89. "Instead of renouncing the task of attaining an impossible wisdom, the school introduced the conception of progress toward virtue. [...] Cleanthes says in a striking passage: 'Man walks in wickedness all his life or, at any rate, for the greater part of it. If he ever attains virtue, it is late and at the very sunset of his days'". As to the last quotation, he referred to Pearson (1891), p. 281.

[26]Some neoclassical scholars would respond that God allows for a parcel of free will, which is a difficult proposition: the free will element is reintroduced inside a determinist scheme. This is in interminable debate.

[27]Cappelleti (1994), pp. 33–50.

[28]"Ducunt volentem fata, nolentem trahunt".

than that of rebellion".[29] Stoics ended by "admitting a scale of values".[30] In short, if men's actions were entirely determined, there would be no reason to bother in attempting to behave correctly or in improving themselves. They decided to encourage people to do their best, and in doing so, had to introduce free will again:

> This rigorous moral idealism is characteristic of 'early Stoicism'; late Stoics insisted much more on the notion of progress, wary of encouraging man to follow the paths of virtue and to persevere on them.[31]

In practice, this meant that the free will element was introduced unintentionally. It was particularly significant that free will was sometimes a key aspect which man consciously sought to explain, and at other times an undesirable element that appeared in supposedly deterministic systems:

> No determinist system can ever be consistent in practice. This should not surprise us, since freedom is a reality of which we are conscious, and even if it is theoretically excluded, it is again introduced where least expected.[32]

Dorado Montero partially agreed with this, but he disagreed with the core proposition: it overlooked the many criticisms of the Neoclassical School. In short, both the determinist and free will schools could be coherent—provided they did not admit contradictory elements of free will and determinism into their respective schemes. Dorado Montero fiercely disagreed with those who defended determinism in their analysis, but nonetheless accepted that modicum of free will as well. This was not consistent, and he could never agree with such an incoherent argument:

> It is not possible to admit grades within [free will]. Either one is free, or one is not. And if one is free, all men are so equally, all men act so because they want to, and any force is imposed on his conduct leading him to the action. Those who speak of 'relative free will', i.e. freedom which is in part free and in part not, in part indifferent and neutral and in part undetermined, fails to realise that this idea has no defence; given the obstacles when the will is imposed upon (motives for acting, physiological impulsions, nervous exaltation, passions, etc.) have the power to drag it in a determined direction [...] such will is resultingly enslaved; and loses all spontaneity [...] On the contrary, if the will overcomes all the snares [...] remaining absolute owner of itself, in puris naturalibus, [...] we come to the location of true absolute freewill. No third exit seems possible: a will that obeys natural causality to a certain extent and, to some extent as well, flies away from its control and only depends on itself [...].[33]

---

[29] Copleston (1946), p. 348.

[30] Copleston (1946), p. 348.

[31] Copleston (1946), p. 349: "Este riguroso idealismo moral es característico del primer estoicismo; los estoicos posteriores insistieron mucho más en la noción de progreso, cuidándose de animar al hombre a que entrase por las sendas de la virtud y perseverase en ellas".

[32] Copleston (1946), p. 348.

[33] Dorado Montero (1906), p. 18: "No es posible admitir grados en ella; ó se es libre, ó no; y de serlo, todos los hombres lo son de igual manera, todos obran porque quieren y como quieren, sin que en su conducta se interponga fuerza alguna que les lleve forzosamente á la acción. Los que hablan del libre albedrío relativo, es decir, de una libertad en parte libre y en parte no, en parte indiferente y neutra y en parte determinada, no se hacen cargo de que tal concepción no tiene defensa; pues si las trabas que á la voluntad se ponen (motivos del obrar, impulsiones fisiológicas, exaltación nerviosa, pasiones, etc.) tienen poder bastante para arrastrarla en una dirección

He firmly criticised the supporters of the Eclectic School for accepting a glimpse of determinism within a free will theory, causing the whole theory to crumble. Dorado Montero's hatred of inconsistency was not new, or only directed at this school: it reminded him of Spinoza's 'Empire within another Empire'.[34] The latter claimed that, within a Judaeo-Christian background, one might assert that God ruled everything and, thus, nothing escaped his control, but that humans were endowed with a small parcel of free will or capacity to decide. Spinoza allowed that we could ignore our deterministic consciences and, consequently, think oneself endowed with free will. Dorado Montero was opposed to this possibility: man's nature cannot be as a state within a state.[35] This idea has been revied by many legal philosophers,[36] in Catholic doctrine and in liberal criminal law systems.[37] In any case, Spinoza clearly thought that both 'virtues' and 'vices' formed part of human nature. Humans are guided by appetites, but neglect their causes:

> They mistakenly confuse effect with cause. And so, everything that appears to be the fruit of a free will determination is actually submitted to a strict and necessary causal determination. The human soul is not exempted from this causal link of the divine expression of necessary substance. There is no 'absolute' or 'free' will man can find in human soul, but rather the soul is determined to want this thing or that due to a cause, which is also determined by another cause, which in turn is determined by another, and so on to infinity.[38]

An illustrative example from Polo Blanco assists in shedding some light on the matter: "If a rock falling down would suddenly acquire conscience, it would also think that it was falling due to its very free determination. It would think that it was doing so, whilst completely ignoring the inexorable law which determined it".[39] The reason was to be found in Spinoza's *Tractatus Theologicus*:

> Such statement can only hold if we depart from a metaphysics of the human soul which does not conceive it as produced by natural causes but rather 'immediately created by God', and which is so independent from the rest that it possesses an absolute power to determine and righteously use reason. Notwithstanding that, this did not even happen to the first man, who could not avoid his fall. Besides, should we admit that this first man 'had the power of righteously using his own reason', how could he possibly have been deceived? Precisely because of this, Spinoza would clearly reject such an interpretation: experience has

---

determinada [...] dicha voluntad queda esclavizada, perdiendo toda espontaneidad [...] Por el contrario, si la voluntad vence todas las asechanzas que se le tiendan [...] quedando en absoluto dueña de si misma, in puris naturalibus, [...] venimos á parar al verdadero libre albedrío absoluto. No parece posible otra tercera salida: una voluntad que obedezca hasta cierto punto á la causalidad natural, y hasta cierto punto también se sustraiga á ella y no dependa sino de su antojo [...]".

[34] Field (2012), p. 29.

[35] Depending on the language version, the expression might be expressed in terms of states and empires, but the umbrella concept is the same, capturing a notion of independent but interrelated content arranged as a matryoshka.

[36] Fichte was most notable in this respect.

[37] Campos Marín (2007), pp. 85–105.

[38] Polo Blanco (2008), p. 66.

[39] Polo Blanco (2008), p. 66.

> repeatedly shown that [. . .] if it was in our power to live according to reason, instead of by desire, we would always opt to act in accordance with the guidance of reason.[40]

And so, in Jiménez Sánchez analysis, Spinoza highlighted the unavoidable character of our passions:

> Everybody is drawn by his own pleasure. Likewise, the first man experienced this, given that he did not have the power to correctly use his reason, but instead was like us: subjected to his passions.[41]

In Spinoza's eagerness to restructure religion, he presented a radically different concept of natural law. Traditionally, Christian natural law consisted of a civil/ constitutional law controlled by natural law, but Spinoza had a civil law which would try to limit and manage natural law, since the latter was based on our bold, ever-increasing capacities (even passions).

If the Catholic conception defended limitations of our natural characteristics, Spinoza's natural law simply referred to our power in the state of nature (which he was in favour of). Ultimately, it was nature itself struggling to expand, to grow uncontrollably, and to exploit all possibilities of reaching human potential.[42] Where the voluntarist conception found its equivalent constitutional order in Bentham's legal positivism, and the essentialists had Locke's ius-naturalism, the multitudes' conception enshrined in Spinoza's theory presented an alternative doctrine equidistant from Hobbesian individualism and scholastic natural law. Though it is easy to mistake him as a representative of a sub-branch of contractualism, Spinoza's idea of how to govern the 'multitude' was far from the *Leviathan*.[43] His proposal was not 'revolutionary' in the sense of seeking the abolition of the state—had this in common with Dorado Montero. A legal, institutional framework was still required in order for his theory to work. If human relations were a conflict between needs and wishes (*vid.* Spinoza's *conatus* vs. passions[44]), an organic legal structure was necessary. "If all of them were effectively guided by reason, states would not be needed any longer, and instead a society of wise men based upon agreement would be established".[45] Since this was not the case as concerned human nature, the dichotomy of a state and constitution was required. In this sense, both Spinoza and Dorado Montero ended up surrendering to the requirements of practical reason. Society[46] could not be constituted by a mere transference of individual rights for the benefit of a third person/institution placed above them. This would entail that they surrendered their own power (*potentia*). Though contractualism did accept that some

[40] Jiménez Sánchez (2012), p. 216.

[41] Jiménez Sánchez (2012), p. 217.

[42] It was also possible to find notable parallells between some of Nietzsche's (1844–1900) claims and of Dorado Montero (1861–1919).

[43] Hobbes (1943).

[44] Fallas Vargas (2004), p. 27.

[45] Spinoza (1984), E4P37S.

[46] Here 'society' should be understood as 'constitution'; another part of the mental exercise we must do to reinterpret these terms in accordance with how these authors framed them.

rights were inalienable, its *rationale* was different: "Hobbes' argument is not grounded on material impossibility of such waiver, but in the logical impossibility of giving up one's own conservation. Whereas, for Spinoza it is ontologically impossible to separate the individual's own right-power".[47] Spinoza's scheme helped to avoid any radical break that might arise from the transition between two legal philosophies with different constitutional models, namely legal naturalism and legal positivism. Before the constitutional diatribe of 'compilation vs. codification' and 'history vs. reason', he advocated a bridged transition among the two models. Spinoza's philosophical position was, after all, not so distant from Dorado Montero.

Returning to López-Rey's assertion, it appears rather surprising, given that in Dorado Montero's main work he was not enthusiastic about conciliating fusions between determinism and free will. There is some sense in which López-Rey is correct: Dorado Montero did relent in the free will and determinism debate and, at one point, he said that men at the end of their punishment should settle themselves to the needs of practical reason.[48] Dorado Montero also mentioned this eclectic perspective in his writing. Correctionalists held that the cause of crime was the criminal's act of will, but they did not consider that this will was spontaneous, in contrast to the determinists, who maintained that crime was just a product of causality. Dorado Montero thought that the two points of view would 1 day converge, but only when humanity had a deeper understanding of human nature and the mechanisms guiding human action: "Chemistry, histology and physiology have here a wide horizon in which they can perform".[49] In claiming this, he was emphasising that when scientific knowledge grew, it would reveal which of the two possibilities was correct. One of the two theories would be proved right; but a mixture of the two of them could never be truly consistent. Even in the present day, it is difficult to define and limit the role of mitigating or aggravating circumstances in assessing criminal responsibility, or to agree on the particular way in which they are to be applied.

Finally on López-Rey's statement,[50] the fact that Dorado Montero was not so inhumane as certain Lombrosian theories, and did not adopt Garofalo's attitude towards criminals does mean in itself that he did not accept determinism.[51] He accepted a great part of it, and labelling him an eclectic because of this is a poor solution, misleading and unclear. The humanist elements in his thinking mean we cannot call Dorado Montero a determinist and stay loyal to the truth: he was as determinist as the Italian positivists.

In one sense, Dorado Montero's determinist hypothesis matched what Stephen Hawking would say many years later. The latter thought there might be some sort of universal law according to which all our actions were predetermined, and that no

[47] Peña Echevarría (2012), pp. 48–49.

[48] Dorado Montero (1915), pp. 139–140.

[49] Dorado Montero (1915), p. 65.

[50] 'He did not go as far as the supporters of the Italian Positive School'. Vid. p. 229 of this book.

[51] Campos and Huertas (2013), pp. 309–323.

single aspect of our lives was left to free will. Dorado Montero had said, similarly: "We assume that no part or element from nature stops exerting its influence, more or less immediately, on the performing of such effects; it is just that at present we are not able to identify all the steps of the corresponding process".[52] Claiming to know how human nature works, i.e. being sure of the degree of accountability that exists in human nature, in order to justify the punishments we have established, is inaccurate. Dorado Montero favoured transcendental doubt over the arrogance of making claims based on unreliable knowledge. Precisely because determinists acknowledged that there were many things escaping our 'purported' free will, it was (1) a safer option, and one which facilitated the abolition of the death penalty (a goal the eclectics shared), (2) a far humbler approach than that of the supporters of free will and (3) a better fit for Dorado Montero's open perspective. He was clear: "doing is a result of wanting, and wanting, in turn, is a result of countless physiological, physical and chemical actions determining it. But all of them remain largely ignored by the individual inside whom they take place".[53]

Dorado Montero found it hard to credit eclecticism as a viable and coherent system. Like the eclectics, he was against the death penalty, but it was because of his doubt. Within the judicial process, there could be human mistakes, whether administrative or procedural. Secondly, there was always the possibility of an unknown disease impairing a human's criminal capacity, and thus impacting on their accountability. Some determinism, however little, was implicit in the latter scenario, but once admitted, there could be no degrees:

> Will draws from his own [human] nature, from his own [human] way of being, from his own [human] sort which has not been freely chosen but received *a fortiori*.[54]

It is less common, but the idea continues to recur that Dorado Montero should be placed within a Catholic scheme of doctrine. His faith that education and culture could overcome society's problems with the traditional conception of free will, and his notion of responsibility suggest this. Although he formally rejected Catholicism, his de facto ideas suggest otherwise. However, it is important not to over-emphasise the influence of Catholicism on his approach. It was educators and formative systems which he thought should consider new scientific developments in order to change human conduct:

> I am inclined to think that by means of modifying our chemical composition subsequently our organic structure (macro or micro), our inner psyche will be modified too, and so will our personality, our will and our actions. I cannot speak about this right now: not as to proportion nor to extent, but I am sure this will be modified. I guess that psychologists and educators will find in a deep talisman to this respect in bromatology, chemistry (especially biological chemistry) and in their coadjutant factors such as hygiene, surgery and orthopaedics. What is all of this but use and performing of the correctionalist system?.[55]

---

[52] Dorado Montero (1915), p. 204.

[53] Dorado Montero (1915), pp. 210–211.

[54] Dorado Montero (1915), p. 207.

[55] Dorado Montero (1915), p. 229.

Thinking that education alone could modify someone's actions suggested an authoritarian, superficial approach for him. This would be to force human nature to formally change, without altering what was actually driving the individuals' decisions. Influences affecting the individual's will could only be impacted through the organic structure.[56] Education was nothing but a model of pressure and oppression.[57] So, it should be mostly an organic, physical transformation, even if repetition was a conditio sine qua non to generate new, desirable habits.[58]

The old penal system was based on a widespread idea that the will of criminals was as healthy and complete as the will of law abiding persons. The only appropriate response was the imposition of painful punishments, given that crime was considered a completely voluntary and conscious decision.[59] Although Dorado Montero did not live in the authoritarian period at the start of the twentieth century, he was already aware of the risks of abandoning the traditional, neoclassical criminal law and all the guarantees developed after the French Revolution. He did not need to see the great wars and rise of totalitarianism and fascism to foresee the problem that an extremely open conception of criminal law could generate. He understood that society was not yet ready, as well as Jimenez de Asúa did later: "society had not yet evolved to the extent of being able to abandon the criminal guarantees of the bourgeois law, so that the maintenance of liberal system's chinks was still essential".[60] This is not to make personal or reckless assumptions about Dorado Montero's positivism, although López-Rey noted:

> In spite of his positivism and determinism, Dorado is here, as in other important aspects of his theory, under the evident influence of the old Spanish School of Penology.[61]

It would still be incorrect to argue that Dorado Montero simply mixed old penalism and determinism. Christian influences (from the old Spanish Penalist School) were introduced through his use of religious expressions and analogies, but the content itself was not based on the old Penalism or Christian thinking: resemblances were mostly a matter of form. Sometimes, the influence of those ideas on the substance of his theory is visible, but their impact was not profound. López-Rey claimed that when Dorado Montero spoke about 'spiritualisation of the penalty/Criminal law' he had in mind the importance of psychological factors.[62] In sum, though the terms he used were particularly religious ('only when the old soul has been replaced by the new one we can say that the individual has been cured'), that did not make his theory

---

[56]That was why a range of scholars categorised him as a 'biological determinist' or 'biological positivist'.

[57]Reminiscient of Hermann Hesse's work *Demian* and the coercive German education depicted therein.

[58]Dorado Montero (1915), p. 218.

[59]Dorado Montero (1915), p. 220.

[60]Roldán Cañizares (2018), p. 83.

[61]López-Rey (1956), p. 611.

[62]López-Rey (1956), p. 611.

a religious one, nor did it suddenly make his thought neoclassical; or show that he thought penal neoclassicism had the same weight as determinism.

Finally, López-Rey wrongly held that Dorado fundamentally represented a continuation of the 'correccionalista' Spanish Penological School of thought whose origin could be traced back to Seneca.[63] The authors making up the aforementioned school of thought believed in free will. Dorado engaged with several Spanish thinkers throughout his works (particularly Cerdán de Tallada, Juan Eusebio, Lardizábal y Uribe, Marcos Gutiérrez, and Mr Ramón Salas),[64] but their very rationale was completely different: his legal philosophy, again, led to a strong determinism. Indeed, determinism had a direct impact in his day-to-day relationships. Even if, in Salamanca, Dorado's students accepted him and the teaching body deferred to him, he was not an uncontroversial figure. Many of his students were astonished by his new arguments (and his enthusiasm for determinism) and raised complaints with the university administrators.[65] He also had several intellectual clashes on this subject with important personalities, particularly the confrontation in Valencia with Father Cámara:

> He faced Tomás Cámara, Father Cámara as he was commonly referred to, who cursed him from the pulpit. He was very close to excommunication and exile. [...] The Bishop presented himself as a fundamentalist and as a defender of high classes, against whom Dorado wanted to seize the control they exercised over the poorest by means of criminal law.[66]

After some consideration, we could observe that his 'transcendental doubt' and the difficulty of classifying him according to one school or another came together: "Perhaps this is the best legacy Dorado Montero received from the krausoinstitutionalism (whose legacy has been so discussed): his wide, tolerant, flexible way of facing several questions, having a look at problems from different perspectives, bearing in mind countless aspects and taking into account the opinion of diverse schools. His trip to Italy, where he studied Law, Philosophy and Anthropology, opened his thought to all scientific and ideological currents of the university world at the time, mainly composed of several intertwined trends".[67] It is not unusual to reject his supposed affiliation with eclecticism, or with correctionalism:

> Since the very moment in which Dorado Montero based his Protective Law of the Criminals on the determinist hypothesis, thus placing the child and the adult on the same level, and the sane and the insane, he had to renounce the idea of responsibility, and thus, move away considerably from Röder and other correctionalists, who conceived the criminal as a free man to lead his will to do good, just as he had led it before in evil.[68]

[63] López-Rey (1956), p. 612.

[64] Dorado Montero (1915), p. 487.

[65] Vid. Chap. 1 for biographical information.

[66] Juanes Díaz (2019). https://www.lagacetadesalamanca.es/opinion/dorado-montero-YX624818.

[67] Antón Oneca (1960), p. 1024.

[68] Antón Oneca (1960), p. 1024: "Desde el momento en que basó Dorado Montero su Derecho protector de los criminales en la hipótesis determinista, colocando en el mismo plano al niño y al

The idea that he moved "considerably away from Röder" was something that Dorado Montero himself pointed out when criticising the school:

> It had necessarily to suffer from those defects which the aprioristic doctrines usually have - above all the lack of data. That is why his points of view were very exclusive and narrow, focusing his attention mainly on the improvement of the criminal, judging that the only cause for his objectionable actions were weaknesses or the perversion of his will. Thus, he neglected the study and reform of other organic and social causes that make up the determining environment of such will.[69]

It is as surprising to refer to Dorado Montero as a correctionalist as an eclectic. He stressed the aforementioned problem with free will within the correctionalist school, too:

> Besides, this school was affected by an essential vice: admitting and setting as the basis of the penalty the free will of the agent, which is incompatible with the inner sense of the whole correctional system.[70]

Towards the end of his academic career, Dorado accepted the "sense" of correctionalism, without adopting it as a whole:

> The leading conclusion of the lessons of criminal anthropology and sociology cannot be other than [...] the acceptance of the criminal sense of correctionalism.[71]

Indeed, his self-awareness of the need not to engage in a simple eclecticism was made clear in the his very first work: "Without being eclectics, simply by loving the truth, one must wait and wish for the mutual correction, rectification and rapport of both tendencies; such will bring another more complete and less exclusive approach. Therefore, the independence of criminal law must be ensured; it ought not to be enfeoffed to criminal anthropology nor to sociology, etc., but it is necessary to consider the assistance of such sciences".[72]

---

adulto, al sano de mente y al loco, hubo de renunciar a la idea de responsabilidad, alejándose considerablemente de Röder y de los demás correccionalistas, quienes concebían al delincuente como hombre libre para dirigir su voluntad hacia el bien, así como la había dirigido anteriormente en el sentido del mal".

[69] Dorado Montero (1893), p. 12: "tuvo necesariamente que adolecer de aquellos defectos de que adolecen las doctrinas aprioristas, de la falta de datos sobre todo; y por eso sus puntos de vista fueron harto exclusivos y estrechos, concentrando principalmente su atención en la mejora del delincuente, juzgando que la única causa de su obrar reprensible era la debilidad o perversión de su voluntad, y descuidando el estudio y reforma de otras causas orgánicas y sociales que forman el ambiente determinador de aquella voluntad".

[70] Dorado Montero (1893), p. 12: "Además, esta escuela estaba afecta de un vicio esencial, el de admitir y colocar como base de la penalidad la libertad del agente, la cual es incompatible con el sentido interno de todo el sistema correccional".

[71] Dorado Montero (1915), p. 341: "El resultado á que llevan las enseñanzas de la antropología y de la sociología criminales no puede ser otro, en el fondo, a mi juicio, que la aceptación del sentido penal del correccionalismo".

[72] Dorado Montero (1889), pp. 173–174: "*Sin ser eclécticos, más amando la verdad, debe esperarse y desearse la mutua corrección, rectificación y compenetración de ambas tendencias; lo cual dará por resultado otra más completa y menos exclusiva. Hay, pues, que recabar, sí, la independencia*

One reasons to be reluctant in using the term "eclectical" with Dorado Montero was that he himself was very strict when categorising schools. In analysing the several criminal law projects of the nineteenth century, Antón Oneca pointed out that Dorado Montero did not consider Luis Silvela as a full correctionalist, but rather a "halfway correctionalist", and did so because Silvela and other scholars[73] "admitted 'retribution' as means for correction".[74] He even used a term ("semicorrectionalist") that helped to illustrate the complexity of classifying such a doctrine and its different gradations. Dorado Montero had thus, from his first publications,[75] refused to class the Terza Scuola as "eclectical". He attempted to critically use the old neoclassical grounds with new scientific adaptations:

> There are those who, still sticking to the old ideas, seek to maintain them along with the new ones, uniting them in an impossible connubium, which we do not even dare to call eclecticism, as we cannot betray the etymology of the word.[76]

This is without even mentioning the "many positivists" who were firmly "determined to correct positivism" and who could be described as "fledgling positivists (the so-called critical positivists)".[77] Dorado Montero identified mainly Puglia, Cogliolo, and Vanni in this group, but also mentioned three other authors accepting the conception of the contractual organism of Fouillée, namely Gustavo Bonelli (with "certain differences"), Colajanni ("vindicating its priority with regards to De Greef"), and Icilio Vanni ("but with certain reservations in the *Programma critico di Sociologia*").[78] Finally, there were those who were not able to get used to the new conditions and, thus were left to "sway in uncertainty" and choose sides "depending on the circumstances".[79] He included "Pessina, Gabba, Del Giudice, Filomusi-Guelfi, Miraglia and even, to a certain extent, Carle himself".[80] These writers continued "paying a tribute to idealism" especially to Hegelian models, whilst at the same time acknowledging the need for Legal Philosophy to "have in mind... the

del Derecho penal, no infeudarlo á la antropología criminal, á la sociología, etc., pero hay que tener en cuenta también los auxilios de estas ciencias".

[73]Dorado Montero (1906).

[74]Antón Oneca (1972), p. 259.

[75]Dorado Montero (1891), p. 249: "no es ecléctica, sino crítica y conciliadora, y que tiene, por consiguiente, un entero valor científico que no tienen las teorías eclécticas; que abraza y funde en un solo término los dos que eran antitéticos, tomando como base las doctrinas naturalistas y levantándose sobre ellas á la concepción del ideal".

[76]Dorado Montero (1891), p. 249: "aquellos que, apegados todavía á las ideas antiguas, pretenden mantenerlas al lado de las nuevas, uniéndolas en imposible connubio, que ni eclecticismo nos atrevemos á llamar, siquiera por no hacer traición á la etimología de la palabra".

[77]Dorado Montero (1891), p. 249: "Sin hablar de muchos positivistas que, como hemos mostrado, se proponen corregir el positivismo y que muy bien podrían incluirse en el grupo de los positivistas de nuevo cuño, esto es de los positivistas críticos".

[78]Dorado Montero (1891), p. 249.

[79]Dorado Montero (1891), p. 249.

[80]Dorado Montero (1891), p. 249.

gains" made by the "so-called experimental sciences".[81] He concluded that: "actually, they neither belong to the critical direction which we are examining [...], nor can they be exactly included within the purely idealist direction".[82] Dorado Montero's theories suggested a more positivistic flavour, not the neutral (often meaningless) classification of 'eclectic'. Some authors who came after him identified his special place in doctrine, as when Antón Oneca described him as a: "respectful son of the correctionalist school" in whom, nevertheless, the "positivist influence" first acquired "during his stay in Bologna as a scholar of the *Colegio de San Clemente*" remained.[83]

However, there are certain nuances in which a more eclectic positioning can be glimpsed. When Dorado Montero described the first stages of the development of positivism, he identified three: from 1865 to 1870 under the influence of Gabelli, Villari, and Angiulli; from 1870–1880, in which the influence of positivism grew exponentially; and from 1880-onwards, when positivism ruled and dominated "in almost all spheres of thought with no contradiction".[84] The latter comment showed that Dorado Montero appreciated the existence of some incoherence in positivist postulates. Later, he would argue that while the representatives of the positivist and the neoclassical schools fiercely fought for dominance, a third school developed which was "more rational" precisely "for being less exaggerated", and he thought that latter would prevail.[85] Dorado Montero attributed a general idea to Carle—although there is no evidence of where this came from[86]—that "the Italian people are very fond of middle terms, and very willing, by nature, character, customs and history to equally move away from German idealism and English positivism".[87] He ended up using the term 'eclecticism'. When referring to this sort of 'Terza Scuola' he concluded:

> Many people will unfairly call [this new philosophical trend] 'eclectic', which, strictly speaking, is the only one which exists in Italy, but there are infinite nuances which can exist between the two opposed colours.[88]

Thus, something close to a doctrinal eclecticism can be found in Dorado Montero's work. When analysing divorce, he concluded that:

---

[81] Dorado Montero (1891), p. 249.

[82] Dorado Montero (1891), p. 249.

[83] Antón Oneca (1960), p. 1024: "*Hijo respetuoso de la escuela correccional, en quien, sin embargo, prevaleció la influencia positivista, recibida durante su estancia en Bolonia como escolar del Colegio de San Clemente*".

[84] Dorado Montero (1889), p. 13.

[85] Dorado Montero (1889), p. 13.

[86] It probably belongs to Carle's single work quoted in La antropología criminal en Italia: Carle (1880).

[87] Dorado Montero (1889), p. 13.

[88] Dorado Montero (1889), p. 14: "dirección que muchos llamarán injustamente ecléctica; que en puridad es la única existente en Italia, aunque con los infinitos matices que pueden existir entre dos colores opuestos".

> The legislator should not only take into account the opinion of the majority, but he should also take into account the opinion of the minority and pay attention to it. If there is any majority to be heard, it is that of the wise men and people of relevance in the country; not [the opinion] of all the inhabitants without distinction, because, in this case, the over-excitement of the passions may conquer a great number of followers in favour of a rule which is neither the best nor the fairest. Truth, just as virtue, is usually in the hands of a few.[89]

Jorge Barreiro noted that Dorado Montero was well known because of his "doctrinal eclecticism" and because he conceived of punishment as "a protection or tutelage of the criminal" whilst grounding that thesis in the "determinist hypothesis": an equidistant positioning between correctionalism and positivism.[90] Others did not use the term "eclectic" but nonetheless resorted to synonyms thereof. Jiménez de Asúa used the term "Spanish critical positivism".[91] However, Dorado Montero had acknowledged the excesses of positivism: "positivism has sometimes gone too far in its assertions, because the position required it: it was completely contrary to idealism. In order to offset exaggeration and imbalance, another similar or greater strength was called for. Against the absolute and sole dominion of the abstract school in Italy (especially in law), they had to profess the absolute and sole dominion of the positivist and experimental school".[92] This third school began in Italy, was named after the *Terza Scuola*, and its main exponents were Bernardino and Alimena.[93]

In the early stage of his academic career, Dorado Montero made a definitive statement on his eclectic positioning when affirming that positivism, "far from being the doctrine of the future, will end up creating room for a third way [...] the doctrine of critical positivism, a product of the fusion and correction of idealism and positivism". A description of this "third school" was provided: "to reach the Kantian solution with presence of new elements which Kant could not know, even if he wondered about them".[94] His definition merged a doctrine based on Kant's philosophy with new scientific and positivistic ideas. He adopted a reconciliatory tone, asserting that new theories were "nothing but an unavoidable consequence" of the

[89] Dorado Montero (1892), p. 198: "El legislador no debe tener en cuenta tan solo la opinión de la mayoría, sino que también debe hacerse cargo de la minoría, y atenderla. Si á alguna mayoría debe atender es á la de los sabios y á las de las personas de cierta representación en el país, no á la de todos los habitantes sin distinción, porque, en este caso, la sobreexcitación de las pasiones puede conquistar un gran número de adeptos en favor de una regla que no es la mejor ni la más justa. La verdad, como la virtud, suelen ser patrimonio de pocos".

[90] Jorge Barreiro (1975), p. 46.

[91] Jiménez de Asúa (1949–1963), p. 139.

[92] Dorado Montero (1889), p. 19: "el positivismo ha ido á veces demasiado lejos en sus afirmaciones, porque así lo requería su misma posición, de todo en todo contraria al idealismo; en cuanto para contrabalancear una exageración, un desequilibrio, se necesita otra exageración y desequilibrio, de la misma, y á veces mayor fuerza que los primeros. Contra el absoluto y único dominio de la escuela abstracta en Italia, sobre todo en el derecho, ha debido forzosamente venir el absoluto y único dominio de la escuela experimental y positiva".

[93] Vinci (2020).

[94] Dorado Montero (1889), p. 20.

old ones.[95] He assumed that the former were a necessary step in humanity's development, and that going only part of the way was not the same as going the wrong way.[96] This was another piece of evidence that Dorado Montero was not particularly radical: he did not support the idea of a positivist movement which broke with the past, but rather perceived an evolution from the original Classical School. He did not approve of the arrogant, bittersweet attitude of the Anthropological School, which thought themselves superior and original compared to the leading Classical School:

> It is, after all, rather strange that precisely those who rest the most on the principle *natura non facit saltum*, i.e. the principle of the gradual evolution of every organism, are the ones claiming that their science came into the world all of a sudden.[97]

Denial of free will was both "explicit and implicit among thinkers from all times" and an "exigence of contemporary society". Many thinkers argued for the "possibility of renouncing this premise [free will] as the grounds for imputability and criminal liability".[98] Something similar happened to laws and codes when, for the purposes of criminal responsibility, they "attended more to material and moral damage" rather than the "voluntary element of the action". This was not surprising, since the idea (alongside recognising mitigating and aggravating circumstances) already existed within the Classical School: Beccaria and Filangieri had considered it, as well as within the new school. Dorado Montero recognised that the correcctionalist school also engaged with these issues.[99]

Dorado Montero's main criticism of the Positivist School was that they took one principle out of all possible positivist premises, namely: determining punishment according to the personal circumstances of the criminal, rather than focusing on the seriousness of the crime. For the new science to work properly, it actually needed to accept all the principles of positivism, as they "require and complement each other".[100] Otherwise, there was nothing but "contradiction and inconsistency".[101] In reviewing Jules Lacointa's work, Dorado Montero highlighted that the author fell into many contradictions, for instance in allowing the death penalty but criticising the Italian penal code for having abolished it.[102] Tensions in relation to the death penalty were natural, according to Bernaldo de Quirós:

> At this stage, the old question concerning only the death penalty pervades all penalties, and those advocating the abolition of the former join hands with those who wish to abolish penal

[95] Garofalo (1890), p. 18.

[96] Gaarder (2002), p. 65.

[97] Garofalo (1890), p. 18: "No deja de ser extraño que, precisamente aquellos que más se sirven del principio natura non facit saltum, esto es, del principio de la evolución gradual de todo organismo, sean los que pretenden que su ciencia haya venido al mundo completamente de golpe".

[98] Garofalo (1890), p. 19.

[99] Garofalo (1890), p. 20.

[100] Garofalo (1890), p. 26.

[101] Garofalo (1890), p. 26.

[102] Dorado Montero (1891), pp. 265–267.

> servitude as a whole. From Beccaria to Röder, and from him to Vargha, Dorado, Poletti, and Solovieff, over a century, this process has gone on and still continues, completed on the positivist side by the elaboration of that penal substitute which is destined to better fulfil its function in civilized countries, namely, the system of tutelage which is being organized in penitentiary science.[103]

Within the Italian Criminal Code, even though Lacointia agreed that the death penalty was legitimate, he praised the abolition of many punishments which entailed "refusal of certain personal rights". He was thinking of "defamatory punishments",[104] "seizure of goods", "forced labour" and "corporal punishments", among others.[105] Punishments ought to be "reforming", as shown by "solitary confinement" (pp. 38–39) and "conditional freedom" (pp. 40–41); yet, at the same time, be "afflictive and exemplary", as the "death penalty" and "life imprisonment" (pp. 35–37) were.[106] That was probably why Dorado Montero, when setting out his own classification, maintained that Lacointa "did not belong to the new anthropological school, nor to the old 'expiation' schools, or the pure correctionalist school" but should be "included within the eclectic school".[107] Nevertheless, there were certain elements which Dorado Montero agreed with, such as "judicial discretion in determining the penalty", "compensation for those wrongfully accused" and acknowledging "modifying circumstances of responsibility".[108] For Dorado Montero, the whole system should be adopted. Utilising some principles from the classical school, others from correctionalism and two or three of the positivists was the wrong approach: 'partial' models would crumble. Even if a positivist feature like accepting personal circumstances was accepted in place of the classical approach (which considered only the seriousness of the crime), leaving aside the rest of the positivist principles was an incorrect stance. Punishment as a special education that the criminal required due to his situation of inferiority was not accepted; the idea that punishment was not a harm, but was actually a good was not acknowledged; the notion of punishment as retribution was not even considered; and the penalty's imposition *quia peccatum est* instead of *ne peccetur* was not contemplated.[109] Consequently, "the separation of those assertions, so intertwined" could only "mutilate the system" and "lead it to a mistake".[110] And so, most of "insoluble contradictions" resulted from positivists trying to combine "principles that mutually reject each other" and "belonging to incompatible systems

---

[103] Bernaldo de Quirós (1898), pp. 236–237.

[104] In Spanish, "penas infamantes". For a detailed historical study vid. Masferrer (2001). On the same issue vid. Cañizares Navarro (2020).

[105] Dorado Montero (1891), p. 266.

[106] Dorado Montero (1891), p. 267.

[107] Dorado Montero (1891), p. 266.

[108] Dorado Montero (1891), p. 267.

[109] Garofalo (1890), pp. 26–27.

[110] Garofalo (1890), p. 27.

themselves".[111] Ultimately, that was the problem for Garofalo when he argued in favour of certain characteristics which were difficult to reconcile with his positivist position: he demanded the application of the penalty *quia peccatum est*; he complained that punishments progressively acquired a 'disciplinary correctional' character; he asked for an increase in severity of repression; he frequently asked for the death penalty—including for intimidation; and he opposed mitigations.[112] Some of his claims reminded Dorado Montero far too much of the classical postulates he particularly abhorred: "the idea of the penalty as revenge, as a punishment, as a retribution of the harm inflicted".[113] Therefore, positivist credibility was undermined: if they defended a *quia peccatum est* conception (instead of a *ne peccetur* one, as they should), trying to understand the circumstances of the criminal and letting it affect the penalty was pointless. This was one of the many contradictions within the positivist school.[114]

Dorado Montero, "who was a disciple of Ferri",[115] was not amenable to a clear doctrinal categorisation. He advocated for a "detachment" and "openly rejected the naturalist-criminological canon" because he deemed the "belief in the 'born criminal' and the repressive social defence" ultimately incompatible with a "progressive (correctionalist) and preventative conception".[116] Even if we think of Dorado Montero as more of a positivist than an eclectic, there remains the question of whether he was more of a correctionalist than a positivist, too. This was not a concern for him: "both of them have met the same essential purpose, i.e. even if both have been born on their own without caring one for each other, they are daughters of the same social cause: the need to reform criminal law".[117] He talked about a process of the 'correctionalisation' of the positivist school. Essentially, the correctionalist school had paved the way for the positivists. The latter "received from correctionalism its most wholesome and acceptable part". The "decisive step" which the positivist school had to take was "denying any repressive character" in the penalty, in order to acknowledge that the only end was preventative.[118] Ultimately, the schools and their doctrines needed to merge, and labels were not important.

---

[111] Garofalo (1890), p. 27.

[112] Garofalo (1890), p. 28.

[113] Garofalo (1890), p. 28.

[114] Garofalo (1890), p. 29: "The new school is riddled with those inevitable contradictions".

[115] Calvo González (2003), p. 263.

[116] Calvo González (2003), p. 263.

[117] Garofalo (1890), p. 22: "Ambas han respondido al propósito esencial, esto es, que ambas, aunque han nacido de por sí y sin preocuparse la una de la otra, son hijas de la misma causa social: la necesidad de reformar la penalidad".

[118] Garofalo (1890), p. 22.

6.2 The 'Doradian' Contribution

Dorado Montero had great insights in criminal science and its role. He asserted that penal science found itself "in very critical moment", which all sciences experienced when they discovered "the experimental method", i.e. their so-called "analytical moment".[119] This period was characterised by a key feature: researchers were so focused "on determining the basis of such sciences" that they forgot that "general induction" which is, essentially, the result of "the coordination of a well-known body of data, and the co-penetration and systematisation of all subordinate inductions belonging to different fields of exploration".[120] Unsurprisingly, that now seems to true of wider society, in which the use of "big data" has encouraged numerous disciplines and their respective knowledge bases to combine, generating interdisciplinary wisdom.

Concerned researchers did what Descartes said must be done in philosophy: "as the new house is erected, one must make use of the old one; as the new general criminal conceptions are elaborated [. . .], one must keep on using the old conceptions".[121] It was precisely the "cause for inevitable contradiction", the trap into which all who were "trying to reconstruct on new basis the edifice of Criminal law" fell, which was also responsible for "leaving the foundations standing".[122] They claimed "a set of reforms", whose spirit "could not be other than that of the criminal function as a completely preventive one".[123] Dorado Montero's project should not be summarised as the mixture of the neoclassical school and positivism, but a mixture between correctionalism and positivism, i.e. "the union of the correctionalist school and of the positivist one, the infusion of spirit of the first one into the messy cluster of data of the second one; the widening of the metaphysical, closed framework of the former one with the young, lively infusion arising from experimental observation which the latter brings".[124]

Seeking to describe Dorado Montero's particular impact raises its own concerns because two visions of him have collided. The first view was a post-Dorado Montero one. His influence, modernity or degree of success were assessed compared to later standards. The second view perceived him in his own time, to ask to what extent his arguments were accepted or contested. It is important to take into account the latter, since it determined the degree of acceptance of his philosophy at the time it was developed. Nowadays, the bias is too big, and it would be blatantly incorrect to assert

[119]Dorado Montero (1893), p. 9.

[120]Dorado Montero (1893), p. 9.

[121]Dorado Montero (1893), p. 10–11.

[122]Dorado Montero (1893), p. 10–11.

[123]Dorado Montero (1893), p. 10–11.

[124]Dorado Montero (1893), p. 14: "la unión de la escuela correccionalista y de la positiva, la infusión del espíritu de la primera en el cúmulo no muy ordenado de datos de la segunda, el ensanchamiento del molde metafísico y cerrado de aquélla con la sangre joven y viva, procedente de la observación experimental, que trae ésta".

he had particular importance in Spain during the period in which positivism was dominant. The issue was perhaps not the concern we might have in hindsight, that his theory was susceptible to being co-opted by totalitarianism, fascism and Nazism—it was simply too different from neoclassical thought. Pointing out that he was very ahead of his time also tends to distort any analysis of the reception of doctrinal positivism in Spain. It may even be that neo-classical thinkers attempted to exaggerate the extent to which Dorado Montero's theories were not accepted. Positivists, on the other hand, have tried to magnify his relevance in an attempt to show the accuracy of their own statements, given that Dorado Montero's thinking was undeniably closer to positivism.

It has been widely accepted that Jiménez de Asúa was the main figure in the development of the legal dogmatics of criminal law. It was Dorado Montero who planted the seed of the early development of that discipline in Spain, and he was the precursor for criminal science. His sharp personality and the fresh approach he brought to penal law were praised by Valentí i Camp:

> Dorado Montero, who was one of our few, real wise men, brought to penology a very wide revisionist principle [. . .] Martínez Ruiz (Azorín) depicted the figure of Dorado Montero in a very adequate sentence when he said: 'He is a man that embraces reality and thinks'.[125]

Unlike some, Dorado Montero did not focus on publications and overlook his teaching obligations. He was both a prolific writer with cutting-edge academic publications, and a devoted and outstanding teacher: "Not just his contribution to penology, but his contribution to teaching and pedagogy will not remain unnoticed".[126] The *Révue internationale de sociologie* consecrated one section to the Castilian author in one volume:

> We have learned of the death of several sociologists whose memory must be remembered. [. . .] Mr Pedro Dorado Montero was born in Navacarros on May 19th 1861. He became professor of Criminal law at the University of Salamanca. He developed a great interest in criminal sociology and anthropology. He translated into Spanish many of the writings of R. Garofalo. He was the author of several works in Spanish such as: *Criminal Anthropology in Italy*, *Positivism in the Italian Social and Legal Science*, *Criminal Law Problems*, *The Reformatory of Elmira*, *Studies of Preventive Criminal Law*, *Criminal Law in Spain*, *Grounds for a New Criminal Law*, *New Criminal Horizons*, *Medical Exigencies and Criminal Justice*, *About Criminology and Penology*, *Criminal Psychology in Our Legislation*, *The Protective Law of the Criminals*, *Social Value of Laws and Authorities*, and *Law and Its Priests*. Dorado Montero welcomed the foundation of our review and since its very origin appeared on the lists of its main collaborators. In the next year, he contributed a long article on responsibility in crime and its extension, published in our edition issued in September 1894. Furthermore, Mr Dorado was one of the first scholars who entered the International Institute of Sociology after its foundation. He became a member on 15th August 1913. In the third congress, held in Paris in July 1897, he sent a very important

[125] Valentí i Camp (1922), p. 105: "Dorado Montero, que era uno de nuestros pocos sabios de verdad, llevó a la Penología un criterio ampliamente revisionista [. . .]. Martínez Ruiz (Azorín) trazó en una frase acertadísima la silueta de Dorado Montero cuando dijo: 'Es un hombre que se abraza a la realidad y piensa".

[126] Maldonado de Guevara y Fernández Ocampo (1919), p. 38.

> study: *The Role of Criminal Justice in the Future*. It started a great discussion in which several personalities took part, such as Ferdinando Puglia, Jacques Novicow, René Worms, Casimir de Kelles-Krauz, Paul de Llilienfeld, Oscar d'Araujo, Alfred Espinas (of whom only two remain alive). This publication could not fail to remember this collaboration. It did so by electing Mr Pedro Dorado Montero among its vice-presidents for the year 1918. This deserving Spanish criminologist very much appreciated the distinction spontaneously granted on behalf of his colleagues. It was one of the last one he received. After being struck by disease, he decided to retreat to Salamanca on 16th January 1919.[127]

René Worms referred to him as a 'criminologist'. Many others referred to him as a 'sociologist'—but actually Dorado Montero was a 'penalist'.[128] The boundaries between those sciences were not clear, for instance criminal anthropology was rebaptised as 'criminology' some years later. Positivism was the general scheme under which those disciplines were included, and many of Dorado Montero's ideas had more in common with sociology than with criminology (so to speak, the "sociological theses" which were defended by "Gabriel Tarde, Durkheim or even Ferri").[129] Dorado Montero was named one of the persons responsible for the reception of positivism in Spain: "Rafael Salillas, Pedro Dorado Montero (1861–1919) and Constancio Bernaldo de Quirós (1873–1959) were directly responsible or induced a new awareness and interest leading to the reception".[130]

Dorado Montero had an important impact on many authors—whether national, European, or international. In a letter dated 25th February 1910, Alfonso S. Carranza asked Dorado Montero to read his book *Régimen carcelario argentino* and give some feedback on it.[131] He looked for his "informed opinion" and enclosed a copy. Apparently, he "had read Dorado Montero's valuable works on criminal law" and "took some paragraphs which absolutely matched the ideas" he held.[132] Carranza was not the only one. Others such as Edmund Mezger, Luis Jiménez de Asúa, Hanz Welzel,[133] José Álvarez-Buylla Godino, Constancio Bernaldo de Quirós and José Antón Oneca were influenced by Dorado Montero. The latter three are discussed further below.

Franz von Liszt (1851–1919) and Pedro Dorado Montero (1860–1919) lived in approximately the same period of time. In the following generation, Luis Jiménez de Asúa (1889–1970) and José Antón Oneca (1897–1981) also lived in nearly the same period of time. There were large interconnections between the four jurists. José

---

[127] Worms (1920), pp. 328–329.

[128] Though he touched on many other related sciences, his main field was Penal law.

[129] Masferrer (2020), pp. 303–352.

[130] Calvo González (2003), p. 263: "Inductores o directos responsables en la nueva sensibilidad e interés que conduce a esa recepción habrían sido el mencionado Rafael Salillas, así como Pedro Dorado Montero (1861–1919) y Constancio Bernaldo de Quirós (1873–1959)."

[131] Carranza (1909).

[132] "Carta de Alfonso S. Carranza a Pedro Dorado Montero", *FPDM. Correspondencia de Pedro Dorado Montero con intelectuales hispanoamericanos*, https://gredos.usal.es/handle/10366/76721.

[133] His contribution and influence revolved mainly around "finalism" as opposed to "causalism". Vid. Roldán Cañizares (2018), pp. 307–309, 311–318.

Antón Oneca attended von Liszt's seminars on criminal law; [134] Von Liszt was the greatest influence on Jiménez de Asúa, who was the most outstanding pupil of Dorado Montero. Jiménez de Asúa, alongside Mariano Ruiz-Funes, was on the examining tribunal when Antón Oneca applied for the Chair of Criminal law at the University of Salamanca.[135] He came to direct the review *Anuario de Derecho Penal y Ciencias Penales* and in his writing he especially focused on:

> criminal codification processes in Spain, as well as criminal reformism in Enlightenment philosophy (Marquis of Beccaria, Manuel de Lardizábal y Uribe, Jeremy Bentham; with respect to theories of the special prevention of penalties, although with a prevalence of retribution and some vanguardist statements on general prevention), and criminal correctionalism and its doctrinal basis in Spain (Félix de Aramburu y Zuloaga and Pedro Dorado Montero; the correctionalist-positivist trend on the rehabilitation or resocialisation of the inmate).[136]

Lardizábal, a key Spanish penologist,[137] related to other enlightened scholars such as Jovellanos and Martínez Marina. His own influence was, nevertheless, independent from those authors, since his work was known in Latin America, and spread the ideas of Beccaria (the author who shaped the majority of his thought) there. However, the originality of Lardizábal's work has often been stressed.[138] He was known as the Spanish Beccaria,[139] thanks to the importance of his ideas on criminal reform.

Lardizábal's thought was, indeed, complex. As Dorado Montero himself explained, it was difficult to label:

> The basis of his thinking is the Christian rationalism of the Second Spanish Scholastics, without any contact with the classical school, much less with the liberal rationalist and laicist of his days, with which, nevertheless, he shared the same concern for the reform of societies and institutions.[140]

---

[134] *Diccionario biográfico español (Real Academia de la Historia).* Link: http://dbe.rah.es/biografias/11648/manuel-mariano-de-lardizabal-y-uribe.

[135] He finally obtained the Chair in 1923.

[136] *Diccionario biográfico español (Real Academia de la Historia).* Link: http://dbe.rah.es/biografias/11648/manuel-mariano-de-lardizabal-y-uribe: "los procesos de codificación penal en España, así como del reformismo penal en la filosofía de la Ilustración (marqués de Beccaria, Manuel de Lardizábal y Uribe, Jeremy Bentham; respecto de las teorías de la prevención especial de las penas, aunque aún con predominio de la teoría de la retribución, y precursores planteamientos de la prevención general), y correccionalismo penal y sus bases doctrinales en España (Félix de Aramburu y Zuloaga y Pedro Dorado Montero; dirección correccionalista-positiva sobre rehabilitación o resocialización del preso)".

[137] Lardizábal y Uribe (1782).

[138] Quintero Olivares (2016), p. 67: "Lardizábal, in many of his stances, initiates by displaying Beccaria's opinion, and then he develops his own opinion, whether he agrees or disagrees with Becaria".

[139] In words of Quintiliano Saldaña.

[140] Soria Sesé, L., "Manuel Mariano de Lardizábal y Uribe", *Diccionario biográfico español (Real Academia de la Historia).* Link: http://dbe.rah.es/biografias/11648/manuel-mariano-de-lardizabal-y-uribe: "La base de su pensamiento es el racionalismo cristiano de la segunda escolástica española, sin ningún contacto con el de la escuela clásica y menos aún con el racionalista liberal y laico de sus

Part of this complexity was his varied background: he frequently quoted "thinkers belonging to the naturalist rationalism of the seventeenth century (like Grotius or Puffendorf)" as well as "contemporaries who did not agree with his thought (like the jurist and politician Brissot de Warville or Rousseau)".[141] Antón Oneca explained that he differentiated himself from the enlightened foreign penalists in listing among the particular ends of the penalty, in the first place, reform. Throughout this work it has been emphasised that Jiménez de Asúa is seen as the father of legal dogmatics, and it was not surprising that his pupil, Antón Oneca, was remarkable for the "dogmatic construction of the crime of assault-delito de lesiones".[142] Finally, on a descending line of influence, one of Antón Oneca's most well-known pupils was Marino Barbero Santos,[143] an outstanding scholar who, in turn, directed the doctoral thesis of Luis Alberto Arroyo Zapatero.[144]

Another key author was José Álvarez-Buylla Godino. A letter he wrote to Dorado Montero,[145] points to several key ideas. One is that he considered himself both an "admirer" and a "disciple" of Dorado Montero. The second was that he had decided to write to him because his "beloved professor" and "friend of Dorado Montero", Mr Adolfo Posada,[146] had instructed him to do so after he asked for "a book in legal anthropology, other than those of Ferri and Lombroso". The third was that those books were "not very extensive" and that were "translated into French or Spanish". Unfortunately, we do not know whether Dorado Montero answered the letter, or what reading he would have recommended if he did.

The writer Constancio Bernaldo de Quirós also professed to being influenced by Dorado Montero in his work *Las nuevas teorías de la criminalidad*.[147] He said that Spain had "two other works of the same character" whose "worth" was enormous, namely: Dorado Montero's *Criminal Anthropology in Italy* and Aramburu's *Modern*

---

días, con el que, no obstante, compartió una misma preocupación por la reforma de la sociedad y de las instituciones".

[141] Soria Sesé, L., "Manuel Mariano de Lardizábal y Uribe", *Diccionario biográfico español (Real Academia de la Historia)*. Link: http://dbe.rah.es/biografias/11648/manuel-mariano-de-lardizabal-y-uribe.

[142] Calvo González, J., "José Antón Oneca", *Diccionario biográfico español (Real Academia de la Historia)*. Link: http://dbe.rah.es/biografias/11648/manuel-mariano-de-lardizabal-y-uribe.

[143] Barbero Santos (1980).

[144] In 2019, he held a Conference on the 100-year death anniversary of Pedro Dorado Montero. Vid. Arroyo Zapatero, L. A., "Centenario de la muerte de Don Pedro Dorado Montero: 100 años de ciencia penal en España", *Instituto de Derecho Penal Europeo e Internacional (Universidad de Castilla-La Mancha), Ciudad Real, 08.10.2019. Laura Pascual Matellán, whose work I quoted before, also took part in the aforementioned tribute.*

[145] "Carta de José Buylla Godino a Pedro Dorado Montero", *Gredos: FPDM. Correspondencia de Pedro Dorado Montero*. Link: https://gredos.usal.es/handle/10366/100228.

[146] His full name was Adolfo González-Posada y Biesca. He was full Professor of Political Law at the University of Oviedo, Senator on behalf of Oviedo (1921–1922) and, above all, a very prolific writer.

[147] Bernaldo de Quirós (1898). I use the English version: Bernaldo de Quirós (1912).

Penal Science.[148] However, both of these works addressed only the "anthropological aspect" of the topic. Even if they constructed novel accounts with "extraordinary apparatus unknown to jurists" they were "limited... to Italy".[149] That was why, 10 years after their publication, Bernaldo de Quirós decided to "complete and continue them" to the best of his ability.[150] The only thing that did not convince him was "Dorado's personal equation", i.e. his "his tendency to muddle up matters".[151] This was a rather odd remark, given that he also labelled Dorado Montero a 'radical', alongside Vargha, Tolstoy and Solovyov.[152] They repudiated "the double entry penology of the reformers and developed only its preventative side", but this ideology was "already in the decline".[153] The positivism which "took form in Italy under the influence of Ardigò and Siciliani", and the "organic correctionalism" which developed in Spain under the influence of Giner were "happily combined by Dorado"—a "fusion perhaps never realised until now".[154] This 'radical branch' culminated in " Tolstoy, who, according to Goldenweiser, has illustrated in his *Resurrection* the paradox of considering 'punishment as a crime and crime as a punishment'".[155] Bernaldo de Quirós also considered the role of the indeterminate sentence:

> We can easily understand how the principle of indeterminate sentencing, or rather, the principle of sentencing without previous determination, is applicable to the general problem of fixed penalties. Posed this way, it relates to corrective doctrine. It is difficult to understand how a writer like Garofalo criticises it; on one hand, he declares the object of punishment is the correction of the delinquent, but on the other, he establishes a fixed term for each crime, that is, a certain number of days, months, or years in a state institution. Garofalo's Spanish translator, Dorado Montero, has felt it his duty to rectify this statement, citing a Spanish correctionalist against it,[156] who in several of his works argued against fixed penalties, even before Kraepelin and Willert asked for their abolition.[157]

Willert claimed that "to establish a fixed term for each crime" would be like a physician prescribing "a treatment for a patient determining which day he was to leave the hospital, whether cured or not".[158]

---

[148] Masferrer (2020), pp. 327–335.

[149] Bernaldo de Quirós (1898), p. 20.

[150] Bernaldo de Quirós (1898), p. 20.

[151] Bernaldo de Quirós (1898), p. 102.

[152] Bernaldo de Quirós (1898), p. 135.

[153] Bernaldo de Quirós (1898), p. 135.

[154] Bernaldo de Quirós (1898), p. 136–137.

[155] Bernaldo de Quirós (1898), p. 138.

[156] Bernaldo de Quirós was referring to Francisco Giner de los Ríos. Vid. Giner de los Ríos (1873), p. 170: "Among the many historical negations of the right understanding of punishment must be mentioned [...] the serious error of determining a priori and in an absolute way the duration of the penalty announced in the sentence, as if it could be anything but the one thing necessary to accomplish the end in view, and which, at the time the term is served, is still extremely uncertain".

[157] Bernaldo de Quirós (1898), pp. 174–175.

[158] Bernaldo de Quirós (1898), pp. 174–175.

To conclude, it should also be stressed that Bernaldo de Quirós translated Enrico Ferri's works[159] into Spanish.[160] The translation had a pointed impact in Spain and became the version used most frequently there.

6.3 Final Thoughts

It was hypothesised at the outset of this work that Dorado Montero did not articulate a complex system nor a systematic arrangement in his writing. His theory was profoundly theoretical, and very ambitious, almost utopian. His proposals were not designed for the historical and political reality of his own time, nor the present day. Even a careful scrutiny of his works may leave the reader with the impression that a clear proposal is lacking. Dorado Montero drafted the outline of systems which were so abstract that the solution he longed for, which would seek to address unfairness in criminal law, could not be implemented. In order to carry out his project, mixing those "ingenious intuitions of the great poets of abstract philosophical speculation" (a priori, theoretical discussions) with the "certitude arising from the observance of facts, comparison and inductions deriving therefrom", a multitude of other changes in society would have to occur first. As a result, both Dorado Montero and his theory have been described as 'utopian'.[161] However, it was a remarkably realistic utopia if so:

> In pursuit of this work, the cooperation of many scholars and the assistance of many generations is needed, given its nature. Thus, the claim that just one or few can carry it out, even if they were geniuses, turns out to be reckless, absurd, and ridiculous.[162]

Dorado Montero's theory was pure abstraction, but a lack of concrete reality was not an uncommon feature of scholarly writing in his time period: "Dorado appears as a committed intellectual inasmuch as he believes he has solutions, but they are general and abstract, as if this character of generality was almost a general rule for his time".[163] We are human beings living in a mundane world: we need a practical system to live with, even if imperfect to a greater or lesser extent, and a system with defects is preferable to no system at all. Paradoxically, Dorado Montero had an extremely abstract theory, but also acknowledged the necessity of theory meeting the needs of 'practical reason'. Before the contradiction of determinism versus freewill, he observed that the most common solution was to "abandon, before the demands of

---

[159] Ferri (1896).

[160] Ferri (1899).

[161] Antón Oneca (1951); Sánchez Granjel (1989).

[162] Dorado Montero (1893), p. 15: "Para una obra semejante, se necesita, dada su misma índole, la cooperación de muchos estudiosos y el concurso de muchas generaciones, por eso, la pretensión de que uno solo, ó pocos, aunque sean genios, han de poder llevarla á cabo, es una pretensión temeraria, absurda y hasta ridícula".

[163] Blanco Rodríguez (1982), p. 9.

life, the *fueros* of 'pure reason' (or theoretical reason) in order to attend to the demands of 'practical reason'".[164] This was a way out amongst both supporters of determinism and the new system, for free will advocates and the defenders of traditional ideas.

On the other hand, Dorado Montero predicted a future for the newly developing sciences which are do indeed shape the modern current world. It is true that certain disciplines and sectors of science openly make 'scientific' claims for positions which are irrational.[165] Nevertheless, the growth of the biological sciences and 'genetics' was both predicted by him and necessary according to his rationale.[166] Modern work combines criminal law, genetics, neurology, psychology and sociology: we are living in a second Lombrosian period.[167] If criminal anthropology[168] was the ground-breaking discipline in Dorado Montero's time, the modern equivalent is the development of neurolaw.[169] This new field is hard to delimit, and even encompasses some mathematical concepts, for instance making use of 'partial differential equations'.[170] This scientific concept[171] forms part of abstract theories allowing analysis of evolutionary parentage. It is used in a huge variety of subjects including medicine (for instance, in detecting and tracing the evolution of a tumour); economics (for example in stock market behavioural predictions); industrial sectors (in predicting the rate of deterioration of industrial or technological devices); and ecology (to anticipate the rate of extinction of species). What it is interesting here is the extent to which extent partial differential equations can be used to predict and follow the evolution of criminality rates. They are being currently used in judgements and in courtrooms.[172] This technique is not free of criticism, however.[173] This is another tool used to explore the problem of free will, and its implications for social and moral responsibility just as Dorado Montero and others did long ago.[174] Even psychology had adopted some ideas from biology into its discipline.[175]

---

[164]Dorado Montero (1915), p. 152.

[165]Morse (2011), pp. 837–859; Morse (2015), pp. 38–72; Morse (2004); Morse (2006). Also, in a parallel way: Greene and Cohen (2004), pp. 1775–1785; Bechtel and Hamilton (2007).

[166]Blair et al. (2005); Romeo (2012); Sacco (2007); Seung (2012); Zeki (2004); Andorno (2013); Aronson (2010), pp. 93–108; Casonato (2009); and Gabbard (2007).

[167]*Conference Was Lombroso Right? The historical legacy of Neurosciences*, Seminar of the GERN (Groupement Européen de Recherches sur les Normativités), 2010–2013.

[168]The old-fashioned term to refer to Criminology.

[169]Goodenough (2010), pp. 61–92; Lehrer (2008); Lynch (2009).

[170]PDE as to its acronym in English.

[171]Farlow (1982). It was reprinted in an edition from Dover in 1993, and newly reprinted in a 2003 edition. The concept, though with new implications as regards philosophical and legal areas, is not new at all.

[172]Uttal (2009); Canepa (1987).

[173]Opocher (1948); Holmes (1897), pp. 457–478.

[174]Morse (2007), pp. 203–220.

[175]De Jong (2002), pp. 441–462.

Finally, an eclectic concern ought to be addressed, regardless of Dorado Montero's dislike for the school. Nothing ever stays the same, no matter how well-grounded the moral, political, or philosophical system we adopt is. Neoclassicals faced a change of paradigm and, when debates between neoclassical and positivist approaches resulted, the outcome was not the victory of one particular paradigm. Positivist exaggerations were dismantled, whilst neoclassical ideas concerning penalties and responsibility were forever altered by the conflict. Dorado Montero changed the foundational conditions for both schools, leaving them the same base arguments but depriving them of the possibility of maintaining absolute theories: they would never hold the same meaning as they had in the sixteenth, seventeenth and eighteenth centuries.[176]

As a tribute to Dorado Montero, let us not seek simple, eclectic theories. We ought neither to swim against the momentum of history, nor be carelessly drawn along by its flow.

References

Antón Oneca J (1951) La utopía penal de Dorado Montero. Ediciones Universidad, Salamanca

Antón Oneca J (1960) La teoría de la pena en los correccionalistas españoles. In: Estudios Jurídico-Sociales, Homenaje al Profesor Legaz y Lacambra. Universidad de Santiago de Compostela, Santiago

Antón Oneca J (1972) Los proyectos decimonónicos para la reforma del Código penal español. Anuario de Derecho Penal y Ciencias Penales 25(2):259–273

Barbero Santos M (1980) Marginación social y Derecho represivo. Bosch, Barcelona

Bechtel W, Hamilton A (2007) Reductionism, integration and the unity of the sciences. In: Kuipers T (ed) Philosophy of science: focal issues. Elsevier, New York

Bernaldo de Quirós C (1898) Las nuevas teorías de la criminalidad. Imprenta Revista de Legislación, Madrid

Bernaldo de Quirós C (1912) Modern theories of criminality. Little, Brown and Company, Boston

Blair J et al (2005) The psychopath: emotion and the brain. Blackwell, Malden

Blanco Rodríguez JA (1982) El pensamiento sociopolítico de Dorado Montero. Centro de Estudios Salmantinos, Salamanca

Burk T (2005) Geschichte der Degenerationstheorien. Thomas J. Burk (personal blog)

Calvo González J (2003) Naturalismo y direcciones criminológicas a finales del siglo XIX en España. Revista de derecho penal y criminología 12:255–270

Campos R, Huertas R (2013) Lombroso but not Lombrosians? Criminal anthropology in Spain. In: Knepper P, Ystehede PJ (eds) The Caesare Lombroso handbook. Routledge, Abingdon, pp 309–323

Campos Marín R (2007) Crimen y locura. La patologización del crimen en la España de la Restauración. Norba Revista de Historia 20:85–105

Canepa G (1987) L'esame psicodiagnostico nei giudizi medico legali di accertamento e revisione della pericolosità sociale. In: Traveso GB (ed) Criminologia e psichiatria forense. Giuffrè, Milano

Cappelleti AJ (1994) La ética de Cleantes. Revista venezolana de Filosofía 30:33–50

[176] I have discussed this elsewhere: Franco-Chasán (2020), p. 354.

Carle G (1880) La vita del diritto nei suoi rapporti colla vita sociale. Studio comparativo di filosofia giuridica. Fratelli Bocca, Torino
Carranza A (1909) Régimen carcelario argentino. Talleres Gráficos la Victoria, Buenos Aires
Copleston F (1946) A history of philosophy. Paulist Press
De Jong LH (2002) Levels of explanation in biological psychology. Philos Psychol 4:441–462
Dorado Montero P (1889) La antropología criminal en Italia. Imprenta de la Revista de Legislación, Madrid
Dorado Montero P (1891) El positivismo en la ciencia jurídica y social italiana. Imprenta de la Revista de Legislación, Madrid
Dorado Montero P (1892) Recensión de la obra de L. Olivi 'El congreso jurídico de Florencia y la cuestión del divorcio'. Revista General de Legislación y Jurisprudencia 82(41):196–198
Dorado Montero P (1893) Problemas jurídicos contemporáneos. La España Moderna, Madrid
Dorado Montero P (1906) De Criminología y Penología. Viuda de Rodríguez Serra, Madrid
Dorado Montero P (1915) El Derecho protector de los criminales. Editorial Jiménez Gil, Madrid
Duve T (2017) Was ist ‹Multinormativität›? – Einführende Bemerkungen. Rechtsgeschichte Leg Hist 25:81–101
Fallas Vargas F (2004) El conatus como categoría radical en la teoría política de Spinoza. Revista de Filosofía, Universidad de Costa Rica XLII:27
Farlow SJ (1982) Partial differential equations for scientists and engineers. John Wiley & Sons, New York
Ferri E (1896) I delinquenti nell'arte. Libreria Editrice Ligure, Genova
Ferri E (1899) Los delincuentes en el arte. Librería de Vitoriano Suárez, Madrid
Field S (2012) Democracy and the Multitude: Spinoza against Negri. Theoria 59(131):21–40
Franco-Chasán J (2020) Pedro Dorado Montero: a transitioning figure. GLOSSAE. Eur J Leg Hist 17:353–395
Gaarder J (2002) Sophie's world. Berkley Books, New York
Gabbard GO (2007) Psychodynamic psychiatry. Raffaelo Cortina, Milan
Garofalo R (1890) Indemnización á las víctimas del delito. La España Moderna, Madrid
Giner de los Ríos F (1873) Principios de Derecho penal, Madrid
Goodenough OR (2010) Law and cognitive neuroscience. Annu Rev Law Soc Sci 6:61–92
Greene J, Cohen J (2004) For the law, neuroscience changes nothing and everything. Philos Trans R Soc Biol Sci 359:1775–1785
Gumplowicz L (1877) Philosophisches Staatsrecht. Manz, Wien
Gumplowicz L (1915) Derecho político filosófico. La España Moderna, Madrid
Hicks RD (1919) Stoic and Epicurean. C. Scribner, New York
Hobbes T (1943) Leviathan. J. M. Dent & Sons, London
Holmes O (1897) The path of the Law. Harv Law Rev 8:457–478
Jiménez de Asúa L (1949-1963) Tratado de Derecho penal, vol II. Losada, Buenos Aires
Jiménez Sánchez JJ (2012) Los fundamentos del Estado político en Spinoza. Anales de la Cátedra Francisco Sánchez 46:230
Jorge Barreiro A (1975) Las medidas de seguridad en el Derecho español. Civitas, Madrid
Juanes Díaz S (2019) Dorado Montero. La Gaceta de Salamanca, Salamanca. https://www.lagacetadesalamanca.es/opinion/dorado-montero-YX624818
Lanza P (1899) Fondamento razionale e fini della pena
Lardizábal y Uribe M (1782) Discurso sobre las penas, contrahido á las leyes criminales de España, para facilitar su reforma. J. Ibarra, Madrid
Lehrer J (2008) Proust was a neuroscientist. Mariner Books, San Diego
López-Rey M (1956) X. Pedro Dorado Montero (1861-1919). In: Mannheim H (ed) Pioneers in criminology. Stevens and Sons, London, pp 605–612
Lynch Z (2009) The neuro revolution. In: How brain science is changing our world. St. Martin's Press, New York

Maldonado de Guevara y Fernandez Ocampo L (1919) Elogio de Dorado Montero y otros catedráticos de Salamanca. Discurso pronunciado en la Universidad de Salamanca en la apertura del curso 1919 a 1920. Impr. Núñez, Salamanca

Martín Martín S (2007) Penalística y penalistas españoles a la luz del principio de legalidad (1874-1944). Quaderni fiorentini per la storia del pensiero giuridico moderno 36(1):503–609

Masferrer A (2001) La pena de infamia en el Derecho histórico español. Contribución al estudio de la tradición penal europea en el marco del ius commune. Dykinson, Madrid

Masferrer A (2012) Spanish legal traditions, 2nd edn. Dykinson, Madrid

Masferrer A (2020) The reception of the positivist school in the Spanish criminal doctrine (1885-1899). GLOSSAE. Eur J Legal Hist 17:303–352

Morse SJ (2004) New neuroscience, old problems. In: Garland B (ed) Neuroscience and the Law. Dana Press, Washington DC

Morse SJ (2006) Moral and legal responsibility and the new neuroscience. In: Illes J (ed) Neuroethics: defining the issues in theory, practice and policy. Oxford University Press, New York

Morse SJ (2007) The non-problem of freewill in forensic psychiatry and psychology. Behav Sci Law 25:203–220

Morse SJ (2011) Avoiding irrational neurolaw exuberance: a plea for neuromodesty. Mercer Law Rev 62:837–859

Morse SJ (2015) Criminal law and common sense: an essay on the perils of a promise of neuroscience. Public Law Leg Theory Res Paper Ser 99:38–72

Opocher E (1948) Il problema della giustizia nel materialismo storico. Bocca, Milano

Pearson AC (1891) The Fragments of Zeno and Cleantes, London

Peña Echevarría J (2012) Cómo se ordena la potencia de la multitud. Instituciones y derecho de la ciudad en la teoría política de Spinoza. Revista Laguna, Universidad de Valladolid 31:48–49

Picozza E (2011) Neurolaw. An introduction. Springer, New York

Polo Blanco J (2008) Notas en torno a la Ética de Spinoza. Bajo palabra Revista de Filosofía 3:61

Quintero Olivares G (2016) Beccaria y el Iluminismo jurídico italiano en la cultura jurídica hispánica. In: Arroyo Zapatero L, Estrada Michel R, Nieto Martín A (eds) Metáfora de la crueldad. La pena capital del tiempo de Cesare Beccaria al tiempo actual. Ediciones de la Universidad de Castilla-La Mancha, Cuenca

Ramos Vázquez I (2013) La reforma penitenciaria en la historia contemporánea española. Dykinson, Madrid

Roldán Cañizares E (2018) Luis Jiménez de Asúa: un jurista en el exilio. Universidad de Sevilla, Sevilla

Romeo F (2012) Antropologia giuridica: un percorso evoluzionista verso l'origine della relazione giuridica. Giappicheli Editore, Torino

Sacco R (2007) Antropologia giuridica. Il Mulino, Bologna

Salam A (2014) Perfect and imperfect rights, duties and obligations: from Hugo Grotius to Immanuel Kant. Merton College

Sánchez Granjel L (1989) Medicina y Antropología en la génesis de la utopía penal de Dorado Montero. Eguzkilore. Cuaderno del Instituto Vasco de Criminología 3:155–170

Seung S (2012) Connectome: how the brain's wiring makes us who we are. Houghton Mifflin Harcourt, Boston-New York

Spinoza B (1984) Ética demostrada según el orden geométrico, 4th edn. Editorial Nacional, Madrid. E4P37S

Uttal W (2009) Neuroscience in the courtroom. Lawyers & Judges Publishing Company Inc

Valentí i Camp S (1922) Ideólogos, videntes y teorizantes. Minerva, Barcelona

Vinci S (2020) Bernardino Alimena and Emanuele Carnevale: the third school of criminal law searching for a compromise. GLOSSAE Eur J Leg Hist 17:48

Worms R (1920) Chronique. Rev Int Sociol 28:328–329

Zeki S (2004) Law and the brain. Oxford University Press, Oxford

Chapter 7
Conclusions

Abstract Dorado Montero was not an eclectic of any sort. Even if labelling him as a 'correctionalist' is definitely more accurate than considering him as a plain eclectic author, it is still incorrect. His ius-philosophical and criminal thought lays undeniably closer to positivism than to neoclassical postulates. However, his thought is not an orthodox positivist one, but rather a very personal positivist thought: a Doradian positivism. The strength behind his reasoning was the consistency: he pursued coherence to its last consequences, and no contradictions can be appreciated on his legal philosophy. His independent thought led him to be very critical with the great schools of his time: he exposed all the incoherences found in the neoclassical thought, those even greater inconsistencies in the eclectics and the exaggerations and recurring mistakes of positivists themselves.

Regarding the recognition this author is still owed nowadays, it can be maintained that he was partially responsible for the introduction of positivism in Spain, but since the triumph of positivism as such did not take place, the figure of Dorado Montero has been traditionally underestimated. Undeniably, his Protective Law of the Criminals was describing the criminal law of the future: yet nor the future of Dorado Montero's society, neither the one of his disciple Jiménez de Asúa, but the criminal law of the future of our society. The future of both criminal law and criminology is currently taking the path described by him.

This book has set out a number of conclusions in relation to the work and thought of Pedro Dorado Montero. The first is that, contrary to the existing historiography, Dorado Montero was not an eclectic of any sort. It is more accurate to call him a 'correctionalist', but still incorrect. His ius-philosophical and criminal thought is best placed closer to positivism than to neoclassical postulates.

However, despite being a positivist, many elements of his work described above, including the predominance of the aura, if not the substance, of natural law aura in Spain, the common philosophical background of his society, and his particularly strict Christian education, shaped his thought in a unique way. He was not an orthodox positivist: he instead developed a very personal positivist approach we might call Doradian positivism.

J. Franco-Chasán, *The Reception of Positivism in Spain*, Studies in the History of Law and Justice 28, https://doi.org/10.1007/978-3-031-46435-5_7

Whilst supporters of neoclassical law and positivists have criticised Dorado Montero's theory, he was nothing if not consistent in his intellectual approach. He pursued a coherence of thought and followed his premises through to their logical conclusions.

Two legacies of Dorado Montero's work must be distinguished. He was a key figure - alongside some other writers, philosophers, medical doctors and psychologists - in the introduction of positivism in Spain, and in its success as a theoretical approach. He produced numerous translations which allowed Spanish jurists to engage with new trends in criminal law and ius-philosophical writing. In addition, the rich notations on texts in other languages he produced before any translation often filled dozens of pages, and his countless book reviews also had a major impact. The culmination of Dorado Montero's prolific biography was that he consistently exposed the incoherencies in neoclassical and eclectic thought, and the exaggerations and mistakes of the positivists. The latter often resorted to the older penal conceptions of crime, an effort which diluted the essence of their theories, or even transformed their claims into a kind of undefined and contradictory eclecticism. Dorado Montero was even more sceptical of these untidy attempts than of pure positivism itself—the latter, at least, was internally consistent.

Dorado Montero was not popular in his own time (or, indeed, today) in that he rejected the concept of free will. He was immersed in a world of abstract ideas, combining a Kantian rationality with advances in criminal anthropology (criminology) and sociology, to describe a reality in which every moral value or legal representation was nothing more than a product of mankind's imagination. It was in the human mind that morality, law, and culture were created and developed, and as a consequence there were as many possible moral and legal orders as there were individuals on the planet. This conflicts with the idea of a shared morality but, strangely - and confusingly for the novice reader - it reflects a number of anarchist ideals, especially Tolstoy's Christian anarchism. This entails further confusion: if the main criticism was that abstract rationalism (Hegel) lost contact with reality and developed a 'transcendental problem', the easy solution was to conclude it was a common mistake among positivists (a very common one given extreme nominalism and the rejection of a shared common philosophical culture). Nevertheless, Dorado Montero reconciles the religious aspect within a Christian anarchism, making Doradian positivism more difficult to understand.

Dorado Montero accepted positivist postulates as to the rationale for the penalty, and in relation to determining that penalty. In contrast, mainstream Spanish thought accepted the latter but not the former. Whilst interest in Dorado Montero's work has increased in the last few decades, his poor fit with the dominant approach in his own time explains the relative neglect of his work. Having helped introduce positivism in Spain, its failure to fully triumph as the pre-eminent legal theory meant that Dorado Montero did not offer the right field of research for exploring interesting topics and reaching sound conclusions. His limited popularity was a product of timing, not substance. Eventually, analysis of Doradian positivism did assist in construing twentieth century penal law and in developing the criminal law of the future.

Dorado Montero's Protective Law of the Criminals described one such criminal law for the future: it was not the law of his own society, nor that of the next generation. More recent developments suggest that the future of both criminal law and criminology may yet take the path described by the penalist from Navacarros.

This proposed future is taking shape as new findings are produced in neurology, medicine, psychology and genetics, and old debates are re-opened. We may speak once again of free will and determinism; or in a more detailed way of the shaping of criminal law and freedom, and how law is to face biological determinism and its moral and legal implications for individual rights and freedoms in western civilisation. This leads us to an even more concerning question: is the existence of those individual rights sustainable in the context of new developments in genetics and biology? Dorado Montero acknowledged the momentum of history, which cannot be stopped. He once referred to neoclassical thought as an ancient tree with many branches, sterile and incapable of producing fruit; whereas the young tree of positivist was lighter, more flexible, and more likely to take over. The result neoclassical-positivist debate produced a new reality which did not eclectically mix their ideas but progressed both theories along their own lines of development. Even nineteenth century neoclassical law had changed its general approach and accepted some ideas closer to a positivist rationale under the sway of historical momentum. Modern day debates between positivism (softened by eclectic approaches) and biological determinism and newly developed genetic sciences may send that same historical momentum in a new direction, where those soft positivists might adopt more determinism whilst the genetic and biological determinists remain the same. But even if we thought nothing had changed, even the debate between the two positions and their doctrinal disagreement entails an invisible step forward. The point is not to avoid such steps: resisting the march of history is foolish and ineffective, but to work on new arguments in soft positivism, in order to develop a better, more ethically and morally sound theory and face that invisible step head on.

Sources and Bibliography

Primary Sources

Dorado Montero P (1889a) La antropología criminal en Italia. Imprenta de la Revista de Legislación, Madrid
Dorado Montero P (1889b) La ciencia penal en la Italia contemporánea. RGLJ 37(74):258
Dorado Montero P (1889c) La ciencia penal en la Italia contemporánea. (II). RGLJ 37(75):132–132
Dorado Montero P (1890) Fundamentos racionales de la libertad de enseñanza. BILE XIV:33–36; 55–59; 65–70
Dorado Montero P (1891a) El positivismo en la ciencia jurídica y social italiana. Imprenta de la Revista de Legislación, Madrid
Dorado Montero P (1891b) Comentario a la obra de A. Naquet: 'Socialisme collectiviste et socialisme libéral'. RGLJ 79
Dorado Montero P (1891c) Reseña a la obra de A. Lepetit: 'Del socialismo'. RGLJ
Dorado Montero P (1891d) Opiniones recientes sobre el delincuente y el delito. (I). RGLJ 39(78): 23–38
Dorado Montero P (1891e) Opiniones recientes sobre el delincuente y el delito. (II). RGLJ 39(79): 300–307
Dorado Montero P (1891f) Recensión de 'Estadística de la Administración de justicia en lo criminal durante el año 1890 en la Península é islas adyacentes'. RGLJ 39(79):421–432
Dorado Montero P (1891g) El Positivismo en la ciencia jurídica y social italiana. RGLJ 39(78): 178–178
Dorado Montero P (1891h) Recensión de la obra de Jules Lacointia: 'Code pénal d'Italie'. RGLJ 39(78):265–267
Dorado Montero P (1891i) El Derecho Civil. RGLJ 39(78):316–353
Dorado Montero P (1891j) Recensión de la obra de Henri Marcy: 'L´accusé devant la loi pénale de France'. RGLJ 39(78):503–506
Dorado Montero P (1892a) Concepción Arenal: estudio biográfico. La España Moderna, Madrid
Dorado Montero P (1892b) Problemas de sociología política. RGLJ 40(81):346–372
Dorado Montero P (1892c) Miseria y criminalidad. Periódico La Democracia
Dorado Montero P (1892d) El absolutismo y la democracia. Periódico La Democracia
Dorado Montero P (1892e) Recensión a la obra de Enrique Gil y Robles: 'El absolutismo y la democracia'. RGLJ 40(81):219–224

J. Franco-Chasán, *The Reception of Positivism in Spain*, Studies in the History of Law and Justice 28, https://doi.org/10.1007/978-3-031-46435-5

Dorado Montero P (1892f) Recensión la obra de Ugo Conti: 'Gli articoli 49 á 60 del Codice penale italiano'. RGLJ 40(81):460–460
Dorado Montero P (1892g) Recensión de la obra de Eduardo Cimbali: 'Il non intervento'. RGLJ 40(80):641–645
Dorado Montero P (1893a) Reseña al libro de Anziolotti: 'La Filosofia del Diritto e la Sociologia'. RGLJ 41(82):427–429
Dorado Montero P (1893b) Reseña a la obra de Della Volta: 'La riduzione delle ore di lavoro e suoi effetti economici'. RGLJ 82
Dorado Montero P (1893c) Comentario al libro de Angel Vaccaro: 'Le basi del diritto e dello Stato'. RGLJ 41:82
Dorado Montero P (1893d) Comentario al trabajo de Antonio Menger: 'El Derecho civil y los pobres'. RGLJ 92
Dorado Montero P (1893e) Sobre algunos estudios modernos acerca del Derecho civil. BILE XVII:56–64
Dorado Montero P (1893f) Algunos elementos para la reforma de nuestra enseñanza. BILE XVII:133–138
Dorado Montero P (1893g) Estudio crítico sobre la doctrina de Garofalo y de la nueva escuela criminalista. BILE XVII:172
Dorado Montero P (1893h) Recensión de la obra de Herbert Spencer: 'Dalla libertà alla schiavitù'. Revista de Derecho y de Sociología 1(1):138–138
Dorado Montero P (1893i) Problemas de Derecho penal. RGLJ 41(83):5
Dorado Montero P (1893j) Recensión de la obra de Carlo D'Addosio: 'Il duello dei camorristi'. RGLJ 41(83):159–160
Dorado Montero P (1893k) Recensión de la obra de Eugenio Florian: 'La teoría psicológica della diffamazione'. RGLJ 41(83):421–423
Dorado Montero P (1893l) Recensión de la obra de L. Olivi: 'El Congreso jurídico de Florencia y la cuestión del divorcio'. RGLJ 41(82):196–198
Dorado Montero P (1893m) Recensión de la obra de Riccardo Dalla Volta: 'La riduzione delle ore di lavore e i suoi effetti economici'. RGLJ 41(82):222–223
Dorado Montero P (1893n) Recensión de la obra 'La scienza del Diritto privato. RGLJ 41(82): 437–437
Dorado Montero P (1893o) Problemas de Derecho Penal: Sobre el valor de la ley, como única fuente de derecho en materia penal. (I). RGLJ 41(82):449–464
Dorado Montero P (1893p) El derecho penal de la Iglesia y el del Estado (I). RGLJ 63(126): 193–215
Dorado Montero P (1893q) Recensión de la obra de G. Tarde: 'Les transformations du Droit'. RGLJ 41(82):631–633
Dorado Montero P (1893s) Problemas de Derecho penal. Imprenta de la Revista de Legislación, Madrid
Dorado Montero P (1893t) Problemas jurídicos contemporáneos. La España Moderna, Madrid
Dorado Montero P (1894a) A propósito de la causa de Varela. La España Moderna 65
Dorado Montero P (1894b) Sobre el valor de la ley como única fuente de derecho en materia penal. BILE 18:410
Dorado Montero P (1894c) Libros recientes sobre la cuestión social. BILE XVIII:87–96
Dorado Montero P (1894d) Recensión de la obra de Angelo Majorana: 'Teoría sociológica della costituzione politica'. RGLJ 42(85):170–172
Dorado Montero P (1894e) Recensión de la obra de Tullio Martello: 'L´economia política antimalthusiana e il socialismo'. RGLJ 42(85):389–390
Dorado Montero P (1894f) Recensión de la obra de Vadalá: 'L´ordinamento della legge positiva nella societá'. RGLJ 42(84):209–210
Dorado Montero P (1894g) Recensión de la obra de Umberto de Bonis: 'Il diritto penale italiano nelle due scuole predominanti'. RGLJ 42(84):423–423
Dorado Montero P (1894h) Recensión de 'Archivio giuridico'. RGLJ 42(84):604–605

Dorado Montero P (1895a) Recensión a la obra de Carmelo Grassi: 'Sulla punibilitá dell´adulterio'. RGLJ 43(87):454–455
Dorado Montero P (1895b) Recensión a la obra de Luigi Lucchini: 'Elementi di procedura penale'. Revista de Derecho y de Sociología 1(3):399–400
Dorado Montero P (1895c) Recensión a la obra de Raffaele Garofalo: 'La superstizione socialista'. Revista de Derecho y de Sociología 1(6):773–777
Dorado Montero P (1895d) Revista de revistas. Revista de Derecho y de Sociología 1(5):578–592
Dorado Montero P (1895e) Recensión a la obra de G. Vadala-Papale: 'Dati psicologici nella dottrina giuridica e sociale di G.B. Vico'. Revista de Derecho y de Sociología 1(5):648–650
Dorado Montero P (1895f) Revista de revistas. Revista de Derecho y de Sociología 1(4):429–444
Dorado Montero P (1895g) Recensión a la obra de Valentín Letelier: 'La ciencia del Derecho administrativo'. Revista de Derecho y de Sociología 1(4):515–516
Dorado Montero P (1895h) Revista de revistas. Revista de Derecho y de Sociología 1(3):329–350
Dorado Montero P (1895i) Recensión a la obra de Georges Vidal: 'Cours rèsumé de Droit penal'. Revista de Derecho y de Sociología 1(3):397–399
Dorado Montero P (1895j) Recensión a la obra de A. Hamon: 'Psychologie du militaire professionnel'. Revista de Derecho y de Sociología 1(2):256–260
Dorado Montero P (1895k) Recensión a la obra de Carlo Augias: 'Società, socialismo, anarchia'. Revista de Derecho y de Sociología 1(2):260–261
Dorado Montero P (1895l) Revista de revistas. Revista de Derecho y de Sociología 1(1):76–89
Dorado Montero P (1895m) Recensión de la obra de G. Vadalá-Papale: 'Le leggi nella dottrina di S. Agostino e S. Tommaso'. Revista de Derecho y de Sociología 1(1):129–133
Dorado Montero P (1895n) Recensión a la obra de Arturo J. Johannis: 'Sui rapporti tra capitale e lavoro'. RGLJ 43(87):220–221
Dorado Montero P (1895o) La sociología y el derecho penal. RGLJ 43(86):22–40
Dorado Montero P (1895p) Recensión a la obra de J. K. Ingram: 'Storia della Economía política'. RGLJ 86:217–218
Dorado Montero P (1895q) Recensión a la obra de Ricardo Dolz y Arango: 'La seguridad social y la libertad individual'. RGLJ 43(86):626–626
Dorado Montero P (1895r) La Educación de la Magistratura. La Administración. Revista Internacional de Administración, Hacienda y Política II
Dorado Montero P (1895s) Reseña a la obra de M. Poscand: 'Sobre el sistema democrático'. Revista Política Iberoamericana
Dorado Montero P (1896a) Organización judicial. La Administración III
Dorado Montero P (1896b) Reseña a la obra de A. Hamon: 'Psychologie de l'anarchiste socialiste'. La España Moderna 86
Dorado Montero P (1896c) Reseña a la obra de Juan Grave: 'La sociedad futura'. La España Moderna 90
Dorado Montero P (1896d) Reseña al trabajo de Vicente Santamaría de Paredes: 'El concepto de organismo social'. La España Moderna 93
Dorado Montero P (1896e) Comentario a las obras de Sidney Webb: 'Women on the factory acts', 'The difficulties of individualism' and 'Rapport sur la politique fabienne'. La España Moderna 96
Dorado Montero P (1896f) Función de las leyes y la autoridad en la evolución social. Revista Política Iberoamericana
Dorado Montero P (1896g) Del derecho penal represivo al preventivo. (I). RGLJ 44(89):256–262
Dorado Montero P (1896h) Recensión a la obra de Lorenzo Benito: 'Ensayo de una introducción al estudio del Derecho mercantil'. RGLJ 44(89):585
Dorado Montero P (1896i) Recensión a la obra de Pedro Ellero: 'De la certidumbre en los juicios criminales'. RGLJ 44(88):404–404
Dorado Montero P (1897a) Reseña a la obra de Pedro Estasen: 'Los orígenes de la vida económica'. p 103
Dorado Montero P (1897b) Sobre el socialismo. El País

Dorado Montero P (1897c) Del derecho penal represivo al preventivo (II). RGLJ 45(90):5
Dorado Montero P (1897d) Del derecho penal represivo al preventivo. (III). RGLJ 45(91):252–252
Dorado Montero P (1897e) Recensión a la obra de G. Fiamingo: 'El protezionismo sociale contemporaneo'. RGLJ 45(90):381–382
Dorado Montero P (1898a) Algunas indicaciones sobre el concepto de las faltas. Revista general de legislación y jurisprudencia 46(92):330–339
Dorado Montero P (1898b) Reseña al trabajo de Alessandro Chiappelli: 'Il socialismo e il pensiero moderno'. La España Moderna 115
Dorado Montero P (1898c) Reseña al trabajo de Severio Merline: 'Pro e contro il socialismo'. p 109
Dorado Montero P (1898d) Del loco delincuente en el derecho penal (II). RGLJ 46(93):5–27
Dorado Montero P (1898e) Recensión a la obra de Constancio Bernaldo de Quirós: 'Las nuevas teorías de la criminalidad'. RGLJ 46(93):377–378
Dorado Montero P (1898f) Sobre el último libro de Salillas y la teoría criminológica de este autor. (I). RGLJ 46(93):483–499
Dorado Montero P (1898g) Del derecho penal represivo al preventivo. RGLJ 46(92):60–69
Dorado Montero P (1898h) Algunas indicaciones sobre el concepto de las faltas y sobre el tratamiento penal de quienes las ejecutan. RGLJ 46(92):330–339
Dorado Montero P (1898i) Recensión a la obra de Giuseppe Tammeo: 'La Statistica'. RGLJ 46(92): 385–387
Dorado Montero P (1898j) Del loco delincuente en el derecho penal. (I). RGLJ 46(92):420–432
Dorado Montero P (1898k) Recensión de Antonio Menger: 'El derecho civil y los pobres'. RGLJ 46(92):550–553
Dorado Montero P (1898l) El Reformatorio de Elmira. La España Moderna, Madrid
Dorado Montero P (1898m) La Patria. Ciencia Social 8:225–233
Dorado Montero P (1898n) Errores judiciales: Locos condenados por los Tribunales. REIS: Revista Española de Investigaciones Sociológicas 47:263–282
Dorado Montero P (1899a) ¿Quién vigila a los vigilantes? La Revista Blanca 30:141–144
Dorado Montero P (1899b) Du droit pénal répressif au droit pénal préventif. Ann Inst Int Sociol V
Dorado Montero P (1899c) Patria. La Revista Blanca I(17):471–474
Dorado Montero P (1899d) Fórmulas. La Revista Blanca 17(I):471–474
Dorado Montero P (1899e) Contra la caridad. Vida Nueva 82
Dorado Montero P (1899f) ¿Cuestión moral o cuestión de estómago? La Lucha de Clases VI:238
Dorado Montero P (1899g) Comentario a la obra de Macías Picavea: 'El problema nacional'. RGLJ
Dorado Montero P (1899h) Comentario a la obra de Vadala-Papale: 'Il contratto di lavoro. La España Moderna 124
Dorado Montero P (1899i) Reseña a la obra de Napoleone Colajanni: 'Il socialismo'. La España Moderna 25
Dorado Montero P (1899j) Reseña sobre el trabajo de Tullio Martello: 'Economía política antimalthusiana en el socialismo'. RGLJ 85
Dorado Montero P (1899k) Cuestión social o cuestión de estómago'. La Lucha de Clases
Dorado Montero P (1899l) Las faltas en el derecho legislado español. RGLJ 47(95):5–25
Dorado Montero P (1899m) Recensión a la obra de Hipólito González Rebollar: 'Algunas observaciones acerca de los problemas fundamentales de la ley hipotecaria'. RGLJ 47(95): 417–418
Dorado Montero P (1899n) Recensión a la obra de Francis Galton: 'Fingerprint Directories'. RGLJ 47(95):633–633
Dorado Montero P (1899o) Sobre el último libro de Salillas y la teoría criminológica de este autor. (II). RGLJ 47(94):46–78
Dorado Montero P (1899p) Recensión a la obra de Ricardo Macías Picavea: 'El problema nacional. RGLJ 47(94):400–403
Dorado Montero P (1899q) Recensión a la obra de Lino Ferriani: 'Delinquenti che scrivono'. RGLJ 47(94):569–570
Dorado Montero P (1900a) Sobre el materialismo histórico. La Lucha de Clases VII:290

Dorado Montero P (1900b) Sobre la facultad de indultar las penas, concedida á los Tribunales. Revista Política y Parlamentaria 7:1–2
Dorado Montero P (1900c) Book review of Mambelli, Alberto. Enciclopedia Jurídica 7:220–221
Dorado Montero P (1900d) Concepciones penales y sociales de Tolstoi, según su última novela 'Resurrección'. La España Moderna 144
Dorado Montero P (1900e) Por los pobres. La Lucha de Clases VII:301
Dorado Montero P (1900f) Por los pobres II. La Lucha de Clases VII:319
Dorado Montero P (1900g) Profesiones liberales y profesiones serviles. El Socialista XV:738
Dorado Montero P (1900h) Reseña al trabajo de Juan Uña Sarthou: 'Las asociaciones obreras en España'. La España Moderna 138
Dorado Montero P (1900i) Reseña a la obra de Paul Eltzbacher: 'Der Anarchismus'. La España Moderna 139
Dorado Montero P (1900j) Comentario a la obra de F. Virgili: 'Cooperazione nella sociologia e nella legislazione. La España Moderna 144
Dorado Montero P (1900k) La pena propiamente dicha ¿es compatible con los datos de la Antropología y la Sociología criminales? BILE 22
Dorado Montero P (1900l) La asociación en el campo'. El Combate
Dorado Montero P (1900m) La Revolución Francesa. ES
Dorado Montero P (1900n) La pena propiamente dicha. BILE XXIV:377–381
Dorado Montero P (1900o) Recensión a la obra de M. Binos: 'La femme au barreau'. RGLJ 48(97): 564–565
Dorado Montero P (1900p) Recension a la obra de Iclio Vanni: 'Il diritto nella totalitá dei suoi rapporti e la ricerca oggetiva'. RGLJ 48(96):441–442
Dorado Montero P (1900q) Ideas de algunos antiguos escritores españoles sobre la prevención de los delitos. RGLJ 48(96):574–594
Dorado Montero P (1901a) Del problema obrero
Dorado Montero P (1901b) Estudios de Derecho penal preventivo. Victoriano Suárez, Madrid
Dorado Montero P (1901c) La Iglesia y el socialismo. La Lucha de Clases VIII:343
Dorado Montero P (1901d) Contribución al estudio de la historia primitiva de España: el Derecho penal en Iberia. Imprenta de la Revista de Legislación, Madrid
Dorado Montero P (1901e) Comentario a la obra de A. Asturano: 'La sociologia morale'. La España Moderna 145
Dorado Montero P (1901f) Alrededor de 70.000 duros. La Lucha de Clases
Dorado Montero P (1901g) Balance penal de España en el siglo XIX. BILE XXV
Dorado Montero P (1901h) Recensión a la obra de Eugenio Florian: 'Del reati e delle pene in generale'. RGLJ 49(99):421–422
Dorado Montero P (1901i) Recensión a la obra de Antonio de Monasterio Galí: 'Biología de los derechos en la normalidad y de su representación'. RGLJ 49(99):617–618
Dorado Montero P (1901j) El derecho penal en la España primitiva. RGLJ 49(98):24–66
Dorado Montero P (1901k) Recensión a la obra de Augusto Pierantoni: 'Gli avvocati di Roma antica'. RGLJ 49(98):635–636
Dorado Montero P (1902a) Bases para un nuevo Derecho penal. Manuel Soler, Barcelona
Dorado Montero P (1902b) Reseña a la obra de M. Chassaian: 'La responsabilité pénale et l'extrême misère'. La España Moderna 158
Dorado Montero P (1902c) Reseña a la obra de G. Zoppola: 'Socialismo contro socialismo'. La España Moderna 158
Dorado Montero P (1902d) Comentario a la obra de N. Pinsero: 'L'individualismo economico e il socialismo contemporaneo. La España Moderna 197
Dorado Montero P (1902e) Reseña a la obra de G.: 'Il socialismo la sua tattica'. La España Moderna 164
Dorado Montero P (1902f) ¿Es igual la ley para todos? La Lucha de Clases
Dorado Montero P (1903a) La Iglesia y la cuestión social. La España Moderna 171

Dorado Montero P (1903b) Valor social de leyes y autoridades. Sucesores de Manuel Soler, Barcelona
Dorado Montero P (1903c) El trabajo función social II. Proceso de emancipación. La Revista Socialista I:17
Dorado Montero P (1903d) ¡Y luego dicen! El Socialista I:17
Dorado Montero P (1903e) El advenimiento del socialismo. La Revista Socialista I:9
Dorado Montero P (1903f) Cómo hay que luchar. La Revista Blanca
Dorado Montero P (1903g) De los abogados y su obra. RS
Dorado Montero P (1903h) Un cualquiera. La Lucha de Clases
Dorado Montero P (1903i) Por una revolución. ES
Dorado Montero P (1903j) El derecho racional y el histórico. RGLJ 103:87–87
Dorado Montero P (1903k) Recensión a la obra de Alessandro Levi: 'Delitto e pena nel pensiero del greci'. RGLJ 51(103):407–408
Dorado Montero P (1903l) Acerca de la base de la función penal. RGLJ 51(102):22–53
Dorado Montero P (1903m) Recensión a la obra de Eugenio Florian: 'Del delitti contro la sicurezza dello Stato'. RGLJ 51(102):425–425
Dorado Montero P (1904a) Sobre la libertad jurídica. La lectura 3
Dorado Montero P (1904b) Justicia liberal y justicia socialista. RS
Dorado Montero P (1904c) Buena morada. La Ilustración Obrera
Dorado Montero P (1904d) ¡Vengan Reyes! La Lucha de Clases
Dorado Montero P (1904e) Recensión a la obra de Giuseppe Gregoraci: 'Della riparazione del danno nella funzioni punitiva'. RGLJ 52(104):180–181
Dorado Montero P (1904f) Recensión a la obra de A. Pozzolini: 'Trattato di diritto penale'. RGLJ 52(104):279–280
Dorado Montero P (1905a) Nuevos derroteros penales. Henrich & Compañía, Barcelona
Dorado Montero P (1905b) La inquisición política. La España Moderna 235
Dorado Montero P (1905c) Antinomias. Labor Nueva 1
Dorado Montero P (1905d) A nuestra imagen. La Revista Socialista 67
Dorado Montero P (1905e) Comentario a la obra de Ernesto Quesada: 'La sociología. Carácter científico de su enseñanza. La España Moderna 202
Dorado Montero P (1905f) ¿Libertad o servidumbre? La España Moderna 204
Dorado Montero P (1905g) La educación correccional. BILE 29
Dorado Montero P (1905h) Educación correccional. BILE XXIX:257–264
Dorado Montero P (1905i) La concepción social retribucionista. La Lectura:489
Dorado Montero P (1905j) El socialismo español y los intelectuales. El Socialista
Dorado Montero P (1905k) Recensión a la obra de Eugenio Florian: 'Trattato di diritto penale'. RGLJ 53(107):310–311
Dorado Montero P (1905l) Recensión a la obra de Alessandro Levi: 'Per un programma di Filosofia del diritto'. RGLJ 53(107):629–630
Dorado Montero P (1906a) Los peritos médicos y la justicia criminal. Hijos de Reus, Madrid
Dorado Montero P (1906b) De Criminología y Penología. Viuda de Rodríguez Serra, Madrid
Dorado Montero P (1906c) Los delitos políticos y los delitos contra la patria. Revista de los Tribunales 40:3
Dorado Montero P (1906d) Sobre el espíritu de rebeldía y el de conservación. La España Moderna:212
Dorado Montero P (1906e) El partido socialista. El Socialista XXI:1051
Dorado Montero P (1906f) A propósito de la boda. Revista Socialista
Dorado Montero P (1906g) El Partido Socialista. El Socialista
Dorado Montero P (1906h) Por la teoría del contrato social. RGLJ 54(109):238–259
Dorado Montero P (1906i) Recensión a la obra de Fernado Ortiz: 'Hampa afro-cubana: Los negros brujos'. RGLJ 54(109):523–525
Dorado Montero P (1906j) Recensión a la obra de Ugo Conti: 'La pena e il sistema del Codice italiano'. RGLJ 54(108):102–103

Dorado Montero P (1906k) Recensión a la obra de Ambrogio Negri: 'La pena nel sceolo presente ed il problema penitenziario'. RGLJ 54(108):349–349
Dorado Montero P (1906l) Hacia un nuevo Derecho Civil. RGLJ 54(108):497–522
Dorado Montero P (1907a) El correccionalismo penal y sus bases doctrinales. RGLJ 55(111): 401–437
Dorado Montero P (1907b) Impotencia humana. La Lectura 80
Dorado Montero P (1907c) Las elecciones y el Partido Socialista. ES
Dorado Montero P (1907d) Sobre los peritos médicos. (II). RGLJ 55(111):24–43
Dorado Montero P (1907f) Recensión a la obra de Marcello Finzi: 'I reati di falso'. RGLJ 55(111): 560–561
Dorado Montero P (1907g) De Re Criminali. RGLJ 55(110):51–66
Dorado Montero P (1907h) Recensión a la obra de Ugo Conti: 'La pena e il sistema penale del Codice italiano'. RGLJ 55(110):246–246
Dorado Montero P (1907i) Recensión a la obra de Guarnieri Ventimigli: 'La delinquenza e la correzione dei minorenni'. RGLJ 55(110):499–500
Dorado Montero P (1907j) Recensión a la obra de Francesco Contuzzi: 'Diritto costituzionale'. RGLJ 55(110):807–808
Dorado Montero P (1908a) ¿Viva el pecado? La Lectura 84
Dorado Montero P (1908b) Liberalismo y antiterrorismo. La Lectura 8:92
Dorado Montero P (1908c) Comentario a la obra de Hermansey: 'El problema social y la enseñanza del derecho. La España Moderna 206
Dorado Montero P (1908d) Valor y función del Estado. RGLJ 56(113):5–35
Dorado Montero P (1908e) De Psicología criminal con especial aplicación a nuestro derecho legislado. (I). RGLJ 56(113):321–354
Dorado Montero P (1908f) La nueva ley de condena condicional. Significación y trascendencia. RGLJ 56(112):209–209
Dorado Montero P (1909a) El Derecho y sus sacerdotes. Revista de legislación, Madrid, pp 1909–1911
Dorado Montero P (1909b) El socialismo español y los intelectuales. El Socialista XXIV:1208
Dorado Montero P (1909c) Más allá. La España Moderna 250
Dorado Montero P (1909d) De algunas antinomias que rodean nuestra vida. La España Moderna 251
Dorado Montero P (1909e) La obra de Lombroso. La Lectura
Dorado Montero P (1909f) De psicología criminal con especial aplicación a nuestro derecho legislado. (II). RGLJ 57(114):29–29
Dorado Montero P (1909g) De psicología criminal con especial aplicación a nuestro derecho legislado (III). RGLJ 57(115):5–5
Dorado Montero P (1909h) Recensión de G. Impallomeni: 'Istituzioni di diritto penale'. RGLJ 57(115):159–160
Dorado Montero P (1909i) Recensión a la obra de Ugo Conti: 'La pena e il sistema penale del codice italiano'. RGLJ 58(117):638–639
Dorado Montero P (1910a) Sobre la intolerancia y sus bases especulativas. La Lectura 3
Dorado Montero P (1910b) La Psicología criminal con especial aplicación a nuestro derecho legislado. (IV). RGLJ 58(117):304–329
Dorado Montero P (1911a) La psicología criminal en nuestro Derecho legislado. Hijos de Reus, Madrid
Dorado Montero P (1911b) Algo sobre lógica y dominación mental. La Lectura 131, 132
Dorado Montero P (1911c) ¡Agarrotados! El Socialista XXVI:1311
Dorado Montero P (1911d) Prólogo a la obra de Valentí y Camp: 'Vicisitudes y anhelos del pueblo español'. Soler, Barcelona
Dorado Montero P (1911e) De psicología criminal con especial aplicación a nuestro derecho legislado (V). RGLJ 59(119):5

Dorado Montero P (1911f) Recensión a la obra de Silvio Longhi: 'Repressione e prevenzione nel diritto penale attuale'. RGLJ 59(119):605–608
Dorado Montero P (1911g) Recensión a la obra de Alfredo Tosti: 'Delle contravvenzioni'. RGLJ 59(118):341–341
Dorado Montero P (1912a) La sentencia indeterminada. RGLJ 60(120):5–26
Dorado Montero P (1912b) El derecho protector de los criminales (I). RGLJ 60(121):227–227
Dorado Montero P (1912c) Perfección y consumación de contratos y de delitos. RGLJ 60(120): 206–218
Dorado Montero P (1913a) Del orden jurídico. RGLJ 61(123):385–398
Dorado Montero P (1913b) ¿Es igual la ley para todos? La Lucha de Clases XXVIII:1438
Dorado Montero P (1913c) Del orden jurídico. RGLJ 123
Dorado Montero P (1913d) El derecho protector de los criminales (II). RGLJ 61(122):217–217
Dorado Montero P (1913e) El derecho protector de los criminales (III). RGLJ 61(123):5–24
Dorado Montero P (1913f) Recensión a la obra de Von Ullmann: 'Trattato di diritto internazionale pubblico'. RGLJ 61(123):565–566
Dorado Montero P (1913g) Recensión a la obra de Vincenzo Manzini: 'Istituzioni di diritto penale italiano'. RGLJ 61(122):381–382
Dorado Montero P (1913h) Recensión a la obra de Alfredo Tosti: 'Delle contravvenzioni'. RGLJ 61(122):549–550
Dorado Montero P (1914a) La guerra y el derecho. Revista de los Tribunales y de Legislación Universal 48:39
Dorado Montero P (1914b) El pleito ese de la accidentalidad. La Revista Socialista XXIX:1803
Dorado Montero P (1914c) En el pleito ese de la occidentalidad. ES
Dorado Montero P (1914d) Recensión a la obra de Eduardo Massari: 'La norma penale'. RGLJ 62(125):161–162
Dorado Montero P (1914e) ¿Pena ó medida? (I). RGLJ 62(124):209–209
Dorado Montero P (1914f) ¿Pena ó medida? (II). RGLJ 62(125):212–238
Dorado Montero P (1914g) Recensión a la obra de Arturo Rocco 'L'oggeto del reato e della tutela giuridica penale'. RGLJ 62(124):197–199
Dorado Montero P (1914h) Recensión a la obra de Giovanni Brunetti: 'Norme e regole finali nel diritto'. RGLJ 62(124):406–407
Dorado Montero P (1915a) El Derecho protector de los criminales, vol 1. Ed. Jiménez Gil, Madrid
Dorado Montero P (1915b) La nueva era del derecho (I). RGLJ 63(127):401–419
Dorado Montero P (1915c) El derecho penal de la Iglesia y el del Estado (I). RGLJ 63(126): 193–215
Dorado Montero P (1915d) El derecho penal de la Iglesia y el del Estado (II). RGLJ 63(127):5–37
Dorado Montero P (1915e) Recensión a la obra de Giacomo Bryce: 'La Reppublica americana'. RGLJ 63(127):177–178
Dorado Montero P (1915f) Recensión a la obra de Giulio Battaglini: 'Il diritto di querela'. RGLJ 63(127):400–400
Dorado Montero P (1916a) El Derecho protector de los criminales. Ed. Jiménez Gil, Madrid, p 2
Dorado Montero P (1916b) Socialismo y justicia socialista. Boletín de la Institución Libre de Enseñanza 680
Dorado Montero P (1916c) La nueva era del derecho. RGLJ 128
Dorado Montero P (1916d) La nueva era del derecho (II). RGLJ 64(128):5
Dorado Montero P (1916e) Socialismo y justicia social. BILE 40
Dorado Montero P (1916f) Sobre la proporción penal. RGLJ 64(129):5
Dorado Montero P (1917a) Correspondència de Pedro Dorado adreçada a Antonio Lecha-Marco
Dorado Montero P (1917b) La natura i la història. Lliçons professades als cursos monogràfics d'alts estudis i d'intercanvi. In: Biblioteca filosòfica: filosofia, psicologia, història de la filosofia. Institut d'Estudis Catalans, Barcelona

Dorado Montero P (1917c) Recensión a la obra de Ugo Conti: 'Diritto penale e suoi limiti naturali'. RGLJ 65(130):413–415
Dorado Montero P (1918) Recensión a la obra de V. Manzini: 'Trattato di diritto penale italiano'. RGLJ 66(133):303–304
Dorado Montero P (1927) Naturaleza y función del Derecho. Reus [posthumous work], Madrid

Legal Literature

Alimena B (1894–1899) I limiti e i modificatori dell'imputabilità. Torino, Fratelli Bocca
Alimena B (1906) Studi di procedura penale. Fratelli Bocca, Torino
Alimena B (1913) Notas filosóficas de un criminalista. Hijos de Reus, Madrid
Alimena B (1915) Principios de derecho penal. Libr. General de Victoriano Suárez, Madrid
Alimena B (1975) Delitos contra la persona. Temis, Santa Fe de Bogotá
Alimena B (1990) El delito en el arte. Temis, Santa Fe de Bogotá
Alonso y Alonso JM (1946) De la vigencia y aplicación del Código Penal de 1822. Revista de la Escuela de Estudios Penitenciarios
Andrade BM (1896) La antropología criminal y la novela naturalista. Sucesores de Rivadeneyra, Madrid
Andrade BM (1899) Estudio de antropología criminal espiritualista. Sucesores de Rivadeneyra, Madrid
Andrade BM (1907) Estudios penales, Madrid: Sucesores de Rivadeneyra, 1897; La moral universal. Victoriano Suárez, Madrid
Andrade BM (1911) Maura und die Konservative Partei in Spanien. Aktien-Gesellschaft Pressverein Konstanz, Konstanz
Andrade BM (1916) Maura y el partido conservador, Madrid: Imprenta de Ramona Velasco. Viuda de P. Pérez
Antón Oneca J (1944) La prevención general y la prevención especial en la teoría de la pena. In: Discurso leído en la apertura del Curso académico de 1944-1945. Salamanca
Antón Oneca J (1951) La utopía penal de Dorado Montero. Ediciones Universidad, Salamanca
Antón Oneca J (1960) La teoría de la pena en los correccionalistas españoles. Estudios Jurídico-Sociales, Homenaje al Profesor Legaz y Lacambra II
Antón Oneca J (1965) El Código penal de 1848 y D. Joaquín Francisco Pacheco. Anuario de derecho penal y ciencias penales 18(3)
Antón Oneca J (1972) Los proyectos decimonónicos para la reforma del Código penal español. Anuario de derecho penal y ciencias penales 25(2)
Balcazar y Sabariegos J (1935) Memorias de un estudiante de Salamanca. Librería de Enrique Prieto, Madrid
Beccaria C (1762) Sobre el desorden monetario y su remedio en los estados milaneses
Beccaria C (1770) Investigación sobre la naturaleza del estilo
Beccaria C (1804) Elementos de economía pública (posthumous)
Beccaria C (1987) Atti di Governo, 1st edn. Mediobanca, Milano
Beccaria C (2014) De los delitos y las penas, 3rd edn. Alianza, Madrid
Béclard J (1862) Traité élémentaire de physiologie humaine, 4th edn. Paris
Beling E (1894) Die geschichtliche Entwickelung der Retorsion und Kompensation von Beleidigungen und Körperverletzungen. Schletter'sche Buchhandlung, Breslau
Beling E (1906) Die Lehre vom Verbrechen. Mohr, Tübingen
Beling E (1928) Deutsches Reichsstrafprozessrecht mit Einschluss des Strafgerichtsverfassungssungsrecht. Walter de Gruyter, Berlin, Berlin
Beling E (1943) Derecho procesal penal. Barcelona, Barcelona

Beling E (1968) Die Beweisverbote als Grenzen der Wahrheitserforschung im Strafprozess. Wissenschaftliche Buchgesellschaft, zweite Ausgabe, Darmstadt
Beling E (1971) Unschuld, Schuld und Schuldstufen: im Vorentwurf zu einem deutschen Strafgesetzbuch. Scientia, Aalen
Beling E (2002) Esquema del Derecho penal: la doctrina del delito-tipo. El Foro, Buenos Aires
Benito L (1898) Noticias bibliográficas. El reformatorio de Elmira (Estudio de Derecho Penal preventivo). In: Revista General de Legislación y Jurisprudencia, vol 98. Madrid, Imprenta de la Revista de Legislación, AñoCuadragésimosexto
Bentham J. An introduction to the principles of morals and legislation, 1780.
Bentham J. Of laws in general, 1782.
Bentham J. Defense of usury, 1787.
Bentham J (1830) The rationale of punishment. R. Heward, London
Berdugo Gómez de la Torre I, Hernández Montes B (1894) Enfrentamiento del Padre Cámara con Dorado Montero. Diputación Provincial, Salamanca, p 46
Bernaldo de Quirós C (1898) Las nuevas teorías de la criminalidad. Imp. Revista de Legislación, Madrid
Bernaldo de Quirós C (1904) Alrededor del delito y de la pena. Viuda de Rodríguez Serra, Madrid
Bernaldo de Quirós C (1919) Dorado Montero y sus libros. Revista de Derecho Privado
Bernaldo de Quirós C (1931) Derecho Penal. Instituto Reus, Madrid
Bernaldo de Quirós C (1940) Cursillo de criminología y Derecho penal. Montalvo, Santo Domingo
Bernaldo de Quirós C (1944) Lecciones de legislación penal comparada. Montalvo, Santo Domingo
Bernaldo de Quirós C (1959) El bandolerismo en España y en México. Jurídica Mexicana, México
Bexon S (1802) Développement de la Théorie des Lois Criminelles par la comparaison de plusieurs législations anciennes et modernes, notamment de Rome, de l'Anglaterre et de la France; suivi de l'application de cette théorie, dans un Projet de Code Criminel, Correctionnel et de Police. Garnery, Paris
Bexon S (1807) Application de la théorie de la législation pénale, ou Code de la sureté publique et particulière, fondé sur les règles de la morale universelle, sur le droit des gens ou primitive des sociétés et sur leur droit particulier, dans l'état actuel de la civilisation; rédigé en projet pour les états de sa majesté le Roi de Bavière; dédié à sa Majesté et imprimé avec son autorisation. Courcier, Paris
Bonanno (1895) La classificazione dei delinquenti e il reo per passione. Archivio di psichiatria XVI:364–383
Bosch García C (1947) Preliminares politicos al primer tratado de comercio entre México y España. El trimestre económico 13(4):712–754
Bourget P (1894) Cosmopolis. Lemerre, Paris
Bourget P (1901) Le disciple. Plon-Nourrit, Paris
Brusa E (1887) Sul nuovo positivismo nella giustizia penale. Unione Tipografico, Torino, p 57 ff
Buccellati A (1874) La razionalità del diritto penale. Milano
Buccellati A (1882) Il nihilismo e la ragione del diritto penale. Milano
Buckle HT (1865) Histoire de la civilisation en Anglaterre, vol 2. Librairie Internationale, Paris
Builla Alegre A (1885) Teoría de las circunstancias atenuantes y eximentes de responsabilidad criminal según el Código español: ¿Cabe alguna modificación en vista de los nuevos estudios frenopáticos? RGLJ LXVII
Cadalso Manzano F (1898a) El Reformatorio de Elmira. Revista de Prisiones y de Policía VI(46): 445–448
Cadalso Manzano F (1898b) El Reformatorio de Elmira II. Revista de Prisiones y de Policía VI(47): 453–455
Cadalso Manzano F (1898c) El Reformatorio de Elmira. Clasificación de los reclusos. Revista de Prisiones y de Policía VI(48):461–463
Cadalso Manzano F (1907) Diccionario de legislación penal, procesal y de prisiones. Imprenta de J. Góngora y Alvarez, Madrid

Cadalso Manzano F (1983) Estudios Penitenciarios: Presidios españoles, y colonias penales, con un breve compendio de la legislación, costumbres jurídicas y prácticas penitenciarias que rigen en los establecimientos. Centro editorial de F. Góngora, Madrid
Cánovas del Castillo A (1800) Problemas contemporáneos. Tello, Madrid
Cánovas del Castillo A (1892) Historia general de España. El Progreso Editorial, Madrid
Cánovas del Castillo A (1910) Historia de la decadencia de España desde el advenimiento de Felipe III al Trono hasta la muerte de Carlos III, 2nd edn. Gutenberg, Madrid
Cantoni CGB (1867) Vico Studii Critici E Comparativi. Stabilimento Civelli, Torino
Cantoni C (1870a) Corso elementale di Filosofia, vol I. Francesco Vallardi, Milano
Cantoni C (1870b) Corso elementale di Filosofia, vol II. Francesco Vallardi, Milano
Cantoni C (1907) Emanuele Kant: la filosofia teoretica. Bocca, Milano
Carle G (1880) La vita del diritto nei suoi rapporti colla vita sociale. Studio comparativo di filosofia giuridica. Fatrelli Bocca, Torino
Carmignani G. Dissertazione critica sulle tragedie di Vittorio Alfieri da Asti, 1806.
Carmignani G. Teoria delle leggi della sicurezza sociale, 1831a.
Carmignani G (1831b) Teoria delle leggi della sicurezza sociale. Annali universali di statistica economia pubblica, storia, viaggi e commercio 30:89–90
Carmignani G (1832) Teoria delle leggi della sicurezza sociale. Biblioteca Italiana ossia Giornale di letteratura scienze ed arti 67
Carmignani G. Elementa juris criminalis, 1833.
Carmignani G (1837) Legislazione - Una lezione accademica sulla pena di morte. Biblioteca Italiana ossia Giornale di letteratura scienze ed arti 86
Carmignani G. Storia delle origini e de' progressi della filosofia del diritto, 1851.
Carnevale E (1930) L'arbitrio del giudice nell'applicazione della pena. Riv Pen 98:130
Carnevale E (1932) Diritto criminale. Società Editrice del Foro Italiano, Roma
Carranza A (1909) Régimen carcelario argentino. Talleres Gráficos la Victoria, Buenos Aires
Carrara F (1886) Programma del corso di diritto criminale: parte generale, 6th edn. Tip. Giachetti Figlio, Prato
Carrara F (1898–1899) Opúscoli di diritto criminale, 5th edn. Fratelli Cammelli, Firenze
Carrara F (1926) Teoría de la tentativa y de la complicidad o del grado en la fuerza física del delito, 2nd edn. Góngora, Madrid
Carrara F (1978–1989) Programa de derecho criminal, 3rd edn. Temis, Bogotá
Carrara F (1992) Cuestiones sobre la tentativa. Temis, Bogotá
Castejón F (1933) El proyecto Pinies de profilaxis social (maleantes) de 1922 y la ley relativa a vagos y maleantes de 4 de agosto de 1933. Revista General de Legislación y Jurisprudencia 163
Charcot JM (1887) Les démoniaques dans l'art. Paris
Chateaubriand F (1837) Génie du christianisme. Beaulé et Jubin, Paris
Colajanni N (1884) Il Socialismo. Filippo Tropea Editore, Catania
Colajanni N (1885) La delinquenza della Sicilia e le sue cause. Tipografia del Giornale di Sicilia, Palermo
Colajanni N (1899) La Sociologia criminale. Filippo Tropea Editore, Catania
Collin F (1927) Étude critique du système de Ferri. Revue de droit pénal et de criminologie 4:435–452
Copleston, F., A history of philosophy, 1946.
Costa, J., Oligarquía y caciquismo como la forma actual de gobierno en España: urgencia y modo de cambiarla, Madrid: Imprenta de los hijos de M.G. Hernández, 1902, 65 ff.
Costa J (1914) Crisis política de España: doble llave al sepulcro del Cid, 3rd edn. Biblioteca Costa, Madrid
De Aramburu y Zuloaga F (1887) La nueva ciencia penal. Exposición y crítica. Librería de Fernando Fé, Madrid
De Montyel M (1894) Impulsions homicides consécutives á la lecture d'un roman passionel chez un degénéré. Annales médico-psychologiques
De Rotterdam E (2011) El Ciceroniano o Del mejor estilo de oratoria. Cátedra, Madrid

Decianus T (1593) Tractatus Criminalis, vol 1 and 2. eredi Niccolò Bevilacqua, Torino
Donoso Cortés J (1851) Ensayo sobre el catolicismo, el liberalismo y el socialismo, considerados en sus principios fundamentales. Rivadeneyra, Barcelona
Donoso Cortés J (1912) The Brothers Karamazov. Heinemann, London
Donoso Cortés J (1956) Crime and punishment. Random House, New York
Donoso Cortés J (1984) Lecciones de Derecho Político. Dostoyevsky, Madrid, p 8 ff
Eltzbacher P (1900a) Die Rechtsphilosophie Tolstojs. Preußische Jahrbücher 100(2):266–282
Eltzbacher P (1900b) Der Anarchismus: Eine ideengeschichtliche Darstellung seiner klassischen Strömungen. J. Guttentag, Berlin
Eltzbacher P (1901) El Anarquismo según sus más ilustres representantes: Godwin, Proudhon, Stirner, Bakunin, Kropotkin, Tucker, Tolstoy, etc. La España Moderna, Madrid
Eltzbacher P (1941) Epistolario a Clarín. Editora Nacional, Madrid, pp 82–83
Escuder JM (1882) El crimen de un loco y un imbécil. RGLJ 61
Escuder JM (1884) Locos lúcidos. RGLJ 63
Escuder JM (1895) Locos anómalos. Sucesores de Rivadeneyra, Madrid
Ferri E (1878) La teorica dell' imputabilità e la negazione del libero arbitrio. Barberá, Florencia
Ferri E (1881a) I nuovi orizzonti del diritto e della procedura penale. Zanichelli, Bologna
Ferri E. Studi dalla criminalità in Francia dal 1826 al 1878, 1881b.
Ferri E (1883) Socialismo e criminalità. Fratelli Bocca, Torino
Ferri E (1884a) Sociologia criminale. Casa editrice italiana, Roma
Ferri E (1884b) I nuovi orizzonti del diritto e della prozedura penale, 2nd edn. Nicola Zanichelli, Bologna
Ferri E (1886) Relazione sui discorsi inaugurali dei rappresentanti il pubblico ministero negli anni 1884 e 1885. Fratelli Bencini, Roma
Ferri E (1887) Los nuevos horizontes del derecho y del procedimiento penal, 2nd edn. Centro Editorial de Góngora, Madrid
Ferri E (1892) Estudios de antropología criminal. La España Moderna, Madrid
Ferri E (1893) Nuevos estudios de antropología criminal. La España Moderna, Madrid
Ferri E (1894) Socialismo e scienza positiva (Darwin, Spencer, Marx). Casa editrice italiana, Roma
Ferri E (1895) Discordie positiviste sul socialismo: Ferri contra Garofalo. R. Sandron, Palermo
Ferri E (1896) I delinquent nell'arte. Libreria Editrice Ligure, Genova
Ferri E (1899) Los Delincuentes en el arte. Librería de Victoriano Suárez, Madrid
Ferri E (1900a) Ciencia positiva. Atlante, Barcelona
Ferri E (1900b) Los hombres y las cárceles. Centro Editorial Presa, Barcelona
Ferri E (1900c) La justicia penal: su evolución, sus defectos, su porvenir. B. Rodríguez Serra, Madrid
Ferri E (1902) Il metodo rivoluzionario. Tipografia cooperativa sociale, Roma
Ferri E (1907) Sociología criminal. Centro Editorial de Góngora, Madrid
Ferri E (1923) I socialisti nazionali e il Governo fascista. La Gironda, Roma
Ferri E (1925) Proyecto preliminar de código penal para Italia. Centro Editorial de Góngora, Madrid
Ferri E (1928a) Principii di diritto criminale: delinquente e delitto. Unione Tipografico- Editrice Torinese, Torino
Ferri E (1928b) Il Fascismo in Italia e l'opera di Benito Mussolini. Paladino, Mantova
Ferri E (1934) Homicidio-suicidio. Reus, Madrid
Ferri E (1982) Il magistrato: dal reclutamento alla formazione professionale: esperienze in Italia e nel mondo. Arti Grafiche Jasillo, Roma
Ferri E (1991) Defensas penales, 6th edn. Temis, Santa de Fe de Bogotá
Feuerbach L (1841) Das Wesen des Christentums. Otto Wigand, Leipzig
Filangieri G (1780) La scienza della legislazione. Milano
Florián E (1925) Il metodo positivo nella scienza del diritto penale. L'Università degli Studi, Modena
Florián E (1927) La teoria psicologica della diffamazione: studio sociologico-giuridico, 2nd edn. Fratelli Bocca, Torino

Florián E (1934a) Parte generale del diritto penale, 4th edn. Francesco Vallardi, Milano
Florián E (1934b) Elementos de derecho procesal penal. Librería Bosch, Barcelona
Florián E (1936) Delitti contro il sentimento religioso e la pietà dei defundi: titolo IV e titolo XII del libro II del codice penale, 4th edn. Francesco Vallardi, Milano
Florián E (1943) Dizionario di criminologia. Francesco Vallardi, Milano
Florián E (1995) De las pruebas penales. Temis, Santa Fe de Bogotá
Fouillée A (1895) Tempérament et caractère selon les individus, les sexes et les races, 6th edn. Félix Alcan, Paris
Garofalo R (1880) Di un criterio positivo della penalità. Vallardi, Napoli
Garofalo R (1884) Alcune osservazioni sul progetto del codice penale con relazione di Zanardelli presentato alla camera dei deputati da Savelli il 26 novembre 1883. Frattelli Bocca, Torino
Garofalo R (1885a) Criminologia: studio sul delitto e sulla teoria della repressione. Frattelli Bocca, Torino
Garofalo R (1885b) La Forza irresistibile, Torino
Garofalo R (1885d) Criminologia: studio sul delitto, sulle sue cause e sui mezzi di repressione. Biblioteca antropologico-giuridica, Torino
Garofalo R (1886a) Le Type criminel, Paris
Garofalo R (1886b) Polemica in difesa della scuola criminale positiva. Nicola Zanichelli, Bologna
Garofalo R (1887a) Le délit naturel, Paris
Garofalo R (1887b) L'anomalie du criminel, Paris
Garofalo R (1888) Contro la corrente! Pensieri sulla proposta abolizione della pena di morte nel progetto del nuovo codice penale italiano. Ernesto Anfossi, Napoli
Garofalo R (1889a) Riforma della procedura penale in Italia. Fratelli Bocca, Progetto di un nuovo codice, Torino
Garofalo R., Dell'Amministrazione della giustizia nel circondario di Napoli, 1889b.
Garofalo R (1890a) La escuela criminológica positivista. La España moderna, Madrid
Garofalo R (1890b) Indemnización á las víctimas del delito. La España Moderna, Madrid
Garofalo R (1891a) Dei recidivi e della recidiva. L. Vallardi, Milano
Garofalo R (1891b) Criminologia: studio sul delitto e sulla teoria della repressione, 2nd edn. Fratelli Bocca, Torino
Garofalo R (1895) La superstizione socialista. Roux Frassati e Co., Torino
Garofalo R (1896) L'educazione popolare in rapporto alla criminalità in Italia. Fratelli Bocca at the Collegio Romano, Torino
Garofalo R (1897) L'individuo e l'organismo sociale. Torino, Bocca, at the Collegio romano, on 21.01.1897
Garofalo R (1900) Justicia y civilizaciốn. La España Moderna, Madrid
Garofalo R (1903a) Le nullità nei giudizii penali e l'istituto della cassazione. E. Marghieri, Napoli
Garofalo R. (1903b) La vendetta e il perdono in Dante, Napoli: Tipografia Angelo Trani, at the Circolo Filologico in Napoli, on 01.06.1903
Garofalo R (1904) La nuova filosofia del diritto criminale. Ermanno Loescher e C, Roma
Garofalo R (1905) El delito como fenómeno social. La España moderna, Madrid
Garofalo R (1907a) I congressi giuridici in Italia. Tip. della R. Università, Napoli
Garofalo R (1907b) Idee sociologiche e politiche di Dante, Nietzsche e Tolstoi: studi seguiti dalla conferenza Ignoranza e criminalità al governo di Parigi nel 1871. Reber, Palermo
Garofalo R (1909) De la solidarité des nations dans la lutte contre la criminalité, Paris
Garofalo R (1914a) Commentario del Nuovo codice di procedura penale. F. Vallardi, Milano
Garofalo R (1914b) Le aggressioni alla forza pubblica e i delinquenti abituali. Tipografia del Senato, Roma
Garofalo R (1916) La guerra e il progresso sociale. Prem. Stab. tip. Federico Sangiovanni & Figlio, Napoli, at R. Accademia di scienze morali e politiche della Società Reale di Napoli
Giner de los Ríos F. Principios de Derecho Penal, Madrid, 1873.
Giner de los Ríos F (1907) Zur Vorschule des Rechts. Kurzgefasste grundsätze des Naturrechts in 47 vorlesungen (Übersetzung). Dieterichsche Verlagsbuchhandlung, Leipzig

Giner de los Ríos F (1916) Principios de Derecho natural. Espasa-Calpe, Madrid, p XIII
Giner de los Ríos F (1933) Educación y enseñanza. Espasa-Calpe, Madrid
Giner de los Ríos F (1969) El reformismo español. Ariel, Barcelona
Gómez de la Serna P (1845) Prolegómenos del derecho. Imp. de Vicente de Lalama, Madrid
Gómez de la Serna P (1853) Tratado académico-forense de los procedimientos, 2nd edn. Librería de Sánchez, Madrid
Gómez de la Serna P (1859) Código de comercio concordado y anotado, precedido de una introducción histórico- comparada, y seguido de la ley de Enjuiciamiento sobre los negocios y causas de comercio...repertorio alfabético de la legislación y del procedimiento mercantil, 3rd edn. Revista de Legislación, Madrid
Gómez de la Serna P (1869) Curso histórico-exegético del derecho romano, comparado con el español, 4th edn. Librería de Sánchez, Madrid
Gómez de la Serna P (1870) Elementos del derecho civil y penal de España, precedidos de una reseña histórica de la legislación española, 9th edn. Librería de Sánchez, Madrid
Gómez de la Serna P (1875) Código de comercio arreglado a la reforma decretada en 6 de Diciembre de 1868 anotado y concordado, leyes y disposiciones posteriores, leyes especiales de enjuiciamiento y repertorio de la legislación mercantil, 6th edn. Revista de Legislación, Madrid
González T (1829) Censo de Población de las provincias y partidos de la Corona de Castilla en el siglo XVI. Imprenta Real, Madrid, p 100
González del Alba P (1896) La imputabilidad ante las escuelas antropológicas. RGLJ XXCVIII, XXCIX
González del Alba P (1897) Locura o imbecilidad incompletas. Doctrina del Tribunal Supremo. RGLJ XC
Grispigni F (1928) Introduzione alla sociologia criminale: oggetto e natura della sociologia criminale il metodo, il concetto sociologico della criminalità. Unione Tipografico- Editrice Torinese, Torino
Grispigni F (1945) Diritto processuale penale, con l'indicazio di tutte le modificazioni legislative posteriori all 8-9-1943 fino al 28-2-1945. Edizioni Italiane, Roma
Grispigni F (1952) Diritto penale italiano. Dott. A. Giuffrè, Milano
Groizard A (1870) El Código penal de 1870, concordado y comentado. Esteban hermanos impresores, Burgos
Grolman KLW (1810) Ausführliches Handbuch über den Code Napoleon: zum Gebrauche wissenschaftlich gebildeter deutschen Geschäftsmänner entworfen. G.F. Heyer, Darmstadt
Grolman KLW (1825) Grundsätze der criminalrechts-wissenschaft. G.F. Heyer, Giessen
Grolman KLW (1826) Theorie des gerichtlichen Verfahrens in bürgerlichen Rechtsstreitigkeiten. Georg Friedrich Heyer, Giessen
Gumplowicz L (1877) Philosophisches Staatsrecht. Mainz, Wien
Gumplowicz L (1892) Derecho político filosófico. La España Moderna, Madrid, p 84
Hegel GWF (1807) Phänomenologie des Geistes, Bamberg
Hegel GWF (1817) Enzyklopaedie der philosophischen Wissenschaften. Heidelberg
Hegel, G.W.F., Grundlinien der Philosophie des Rechts, 1821.
Hegel GWF (1827) Erste Ausgabe. Zweite Ausgabe
Hegel, G.W.F., Dritte Ausgabe, 1830
Hegel GWF (1968) Ciencia de la lógica, 2nd edn. Solar/Hachette, Buenos Aires
Herzen A (1874) La physiologie de la volonté. Paris
Hicks RD (1910) Stoic and Epicurean. C. Scribner, New York
Hobbes T (1943) Leviathan. J. M. Dent & Sons, London
Holmes O (1897) The path of the law. Harv Law Rev 10(8):457–478
Jiménez de Asúa L (1913) La sentencia indeterminada. El sistema de penas determinadas "a posteriori". Reus, Madrid
Jiménez de Asúa L (1915a) La pena previamente indeterminada y las penas retenidas. Actas del Segundo Congreso penitenciario español. Garcybarra, A Coruña

Jiménez de Asúa L (1915b) La recompensa como prevención general. El derecho premial. Reus, Madrid
Jiménez de Asúa L (1917) El anteproyecto de Código penal sueco de 1916: estudio crítico seguido del texto íntegro de la parte general del anteproyecto, traducido íntegramente del sueco. Hijos de Reus, Madrid
Jiménez de Asúa L (1920) El estado peligroso del delincuente y sus consecuencias ante el derecho penal moderno. Reus, Madrid
Jiménez de Asúa L (1921) Los delitos sociales y la reforma del Código penal: conferencia pronunciada en la Real Academia de Jurisprudencia y Legislación en la sesión del día 21 de abril de 1921. Reus, Madrid
Jiménez de Asúa L (1922) Estudio crítico del proyecto de código penal italiano de 1921. Victoriano Suárez, Madrid
Jiménez de Asúa L (1925a) Generalización del principio de la sentencia indeterminada. Revista de Criminología, Psiquiatria y Medicina Legal XII(70)
Jiménez de Asúa L (1925b) Rapport sur le principe de la sentence indéterminée. Troisième question. Première section. Congrès Pènitentiaire international de Londres 1925. Buenos Aires, Talleres gráficos de la Penitenciaría Nacional
Jiménez de Asúa L (1926) El derecho penal en la República del Perú. Tall. Tip. Cuesta, Valladolid
Jiménez de Asúa L (1927a) Endocrinología y derecho penal. Eutanasia y homicidio por compasión: dos conferencias pronunciadas en la Facultad de Derecho de la Universidad de Montevideo en junio de 1925. Imp. Nacional, Montevideo
Jiménez de Asúa L (1927b) Evolución política y derecho penal. Carta al maestro Enrique Ferri, La Prensa
Jiménez de Asúa L (1928) El código penal argentino y los recientes proyectos complementarios ante las modernas direcciones del Derecho penal. Reus, Madrid
Jiménez de Asúa L (1929–1930) Derecho penal: conforme al Código de 1928. Reus, Madrid
Jiménez de Asúa L (1929a) Casos de derecho penal para uso de los estudiantes, 2nd edn. Librería General de Victoriano Suárez, Madrid
Jiménez de Asúa L (1929b) Crónica del crimen. Historia Nueva, Madrid
Jiménez de Asúa L (1929c) Il delitto di contagio venereo: studi e proposte. Fratelli Bocca, Torino
Jiménez de Asúa L (1930) Al servicio del derecho penal: diatriba del Código gubernativo. Javier Morata, Madrid
Jiménez de Asúa L (1933) Ley de vagos y maleantes. Un ensayo legislativo sobre la peligrosidad sin delito. Revista General de Legislación y Jurisprudencia 82(163):577–635
Jiménez de Asúa L (1934) Código penal reformado de 27 de Octubre de 1932 y disposiciones penales de la República, 1st edn. Reus, Madrid
Jiménez de Asúa L (1947a) Derecho penal soviético. Tipografica editora argentina, Buenos Aires
Jiménez de Asúa L (1947b) La sentencia indeterminada, 2nd edn. Tea, Buenos Aires
Jiménez de Asúa L (1955–1964) El criminalista: 2ª Serie. Víctor P. de Zavalia, Buenos Aires
Jiménez de Asúa L (1959) Algunas consideraciones sobre los delitos preterintencionales. Revista jurídica de Buenos Aires, Buenos Aires
Jiménez de Asúa L (1961) Estudios de derecho penal y criminología, vol I. Omeba, Buenos Aires
Jiménez de Asúa L (1962) Comentarios al proyecto de Código penal argentino. Bibliográfica Omeba, Buenos Aires
Jiménez de Asúa L (1963a) Tratado de Derecho penal, vol II. Losada, Buenos Aires
Jiménez de Asúa L (1963b) Estudios de derecho penal y criminología, vol II. Omeba, Buenos Aires
Jiménez de Asúa L (1971) Recordando a D. Pedro Dorado Montero. Revista de Estudios Penitenciarios 195:1617–1630
Jiménez de Asúa L., El derecho penal del futuro. Guarnido JM (dir.) El mundo de la posguerra
Kant I., Prolegómenos a toda metafísica futura que pueda presentarse como ciencia, 1783.
Kant I., Respuesta a la pregunta: ¿qué es ilustración?, 1784a.
Kant I., Idea para una historia universal en sentido cosmopolita, 1784b.
Kant I (1787) Crítica de la razón pura, 1781, 2nd edn

Kant I (1798) Der Streit der Fakultäten. Friedrich Nicolovius, Königsberg
Kant I (1989) Metafísica de las costumbres. Tecnos, Madrid
Kant I (1990) Antropología Práctica (manuscrito inédito de 1785). Tecnos, Madrid
Kant I (1994) Fundamentación de la metafísica de las costumbres. Espasa-Calpe, Madrid
Kant I (2003) El conflicto de las Facultades. Alianza, Madrid
Krause KCF (1803) Grundlage des Naturrechtes. Göpfert, Leipzig
Krause KCF (1820) Die drei ältesten Kunsturkurden der Freimaurer-brüderschaft, Zweite Ausgabe. Arnoldischer Buchhandlung, Erster Band, Dresden
Krause, K.C.F., Abriss des Systems der Philosophie des Rechts, 1828.
Krause KCF (1871) Ideal de la humanidad, 2nd edn. Imprenta de F. Martínez García, Madrid
Krause, K.C.F., Das System des Rechtsphilosophie, 1874.
Krause KCF (1892) Vorlesungen Über Naturrecht: Oder Philosophie des Rechtes und des Staates. Otto Schulze, Leipzig
Krause KCF (2007) Ausgewählte Schriften. Frommann-Holzboog, Stuttgart
La AB (1887) premeditazione: in rapporto alla psicologia, al diritto, alla legislazione comparata. Fratelli Bocca, Roma
Lanza, P., Fondamento razionale e fini della pena, 1899.
Lanza V (1906) L'Umanesimo nel Diritto penale. La Scuola penale umanista, Catania
Lanza V (1924) Instituzioni di diritto penale, Catania
Lardizábal y Uribe M (1782) Discurso sobre las penas, contrahido á las leyes criminales de España, para facilitar su reforma. J. Ibarra, Madrid
Ledesma Á (1919) El maestro Dorado Montero. BILE 43
Lefort E (1892) Le type criminel d'après les savants et les artistes. Storck, Lyon
Lilla V (1880) Filosofia del Diritto. Presso Nicola Joven Libraio Editore, Napoli
Lilla V (1903) Manuale di filosofia del diritto. Società Editrice Libraria, Milano
Liszt F (1896) La legislación penal comparada. Revista de Medicina y Cirugía Prácticas, Madrid
Liszt F (1898) Die Deliktsobligationen im System des Bürgerlichen Gesetzbuch. Kristische und dogmatische Randbemerkungen. J. Guttentag, Berlin
Liszt F (1906) Strafrechtsfaelle zum akademischen Gebrauch, 8th edn. Gustav Fischer, Jena
Liszt F (1927) Le droit international: exposé systématique. Pedone, Paris
Liszt F (1970) Strafrechtliche Aufsätze und Vorträge. Walter de Gruyter & Co., Berlin
Liszt F (1984) La idea de fin en el derecho penal. Edeval, Valparaíso
Lombroso C (1884) L'uomo delinquente, 3rd edn. Fratelli Bocca, Torino
Lombroso C (1890) Medicina legal. La España Moderna, Madrid
Lombroso C (1894) Los anarquistas. Estab. Tip. Sucesores de Rivadeneyra, Madrid
Lombroso C (1895) Los últimos progresos de la antropología criminal. La España Moderna, Madrid
Lombroso C (1902) El delito: sus causas y remedios. Librería General de Victoriano Suárez, Madrid
Lombroso C (1911) Los criminales. Atlante, Barcelona
Lombroso C (1927) La donna delinquente: la prostituta e la donna normale, 5th edn. Fratelli Bocca, Torino
López Bago E (1888) El preso. La Inquisición moderna, Estudios de la vida humana en cárceles y presidios. Novela médico-social. Imprenta de José Góngora, Madrid
Lucchini L (1878) Rivista critica del Progetto Vigliani. Rivista penale
Lucchini L (1879) Corso di diritto penale, Siena
Magaz i Jaime J (1871) Tratado elemental de fisiología humana. Est. Tip. de Narciso Ramírez, Barcelona
Maldonado de Guevara y Fernandez Ocampo L (1919) Elogio de Dorado Montero y otros catedráticos de Salamanca. Discurso pronunciado en la Universidad de Salamanca en la apertura del curso 1919 a 1920. Impr. Núñez, Salamanca
Mancini PS (1875) Lettere a Mamiani sul diritto di punire. Livorno
Marat JP (1773) A philosophical essay on man. J. Ridley, London
Marat JP, Les chaînes de l'esclavage, 1774.
Marat JP (1780) Plan de législation criminelle. Neuchâtel

Marcos Gutiérrez J (1826) Práctica criminal de España. D. Fermín Villalpando, Madrid
Marro A (1887) I caratteri dei delinquenti: studio antropologico-sociologico. Fratelli Bocca, Turin
Marro A (1897) La pubertà studiata nell'uomo e nella donna in rapporto all'antropologia, alla psichiatria, alla pedagogia ed alla sociologia dal dottor Antonio Marro. Fratelli Bocca, Turin
Mill JS (1775) Three essays on religion, 1874. Mirabeau, H. R., Essai sur le despotisme
Mill JS, Essay on bentham, 1838.
Mill JS, Thoughts on parliamentary reform, 1859.
Mill JS, Utilitarianism, 1863.
Mill JS, Auguste and positivism, 1865.
Mill JS, Speech in favor of capital punishment, 1868.
Mill JS, Nature, the utility of religion, and theism, 1874.
Montesquieu (1750) L'esprit des loix. Barrillot & Fils, Genève
More T (1937) Utopía: el estado perfecto. Apolo, Barcelona
Morel BA (1857) Traité des dégénérescences physiques, intellectuelles et morales de l'espèce humaine et des causes qui produissent ces variétés maladives. J. B. Baillère, Paris
Morel BA (1860) Traité des maladies mentales. Librairie Victor Masson, Paris
Morel BA (1864) De la formation du type dans les variétés dégénérées. J.B. Baillière, Paris
Muyart de Vouglans JP, Institutes au droit criminel, 1757.
Muyart de Vouglans JP, Institutions criminelles selon les lois et ordonnances du royaume, 1762.
Muyart de Vouglans JP (1780) Les loix criminelles du Royaume: dans leur ordre naturel. Mérigot
Nagler J (1918) Die Strafe: eine juristisch-empirische Untersuchung. Scientia Verlag, Aalen
Opocher E (1948) Il problema della giustizia nel materilismo storico. Bocca, Milano
Ortega y Gasset J., La educación política española, 1909.
Pacheco JF (1841) Historia de la Regencia de la reina Cristina. Imprenta de Fernando Suárez, Madrid
Pacheco JF (1843) Estudios de legislación y de jurisprudencia. Imprenta de la viuda de Jordán e hijos, Madrid
Pacheco JF (1845) Lecciones de derecho político constitucional. Imp. y Librería de Ignacio Boix, Madrid
Pacheco JF (1847) Comentario a las leyes de desvinculación, 3rd edn. Ramón Rodríguez de Rivera, Madrid
Pacheco JF (1854) Estudios de derecho penal: lecciones pronunciadas en el Ateneo de Madrid en 1839 y 1840, 4th edn. Imp. y Fundición de Manuel Tello, Madrid
Pacheco JF (1881) El Código penal concordado y comentado, 5th edn. Imprenta y fundición de Manuel Tello, Madrid
Prins A (1875) De l'appel dans l'organisation judiciaire répressive. Étude historique et critique
Prins A, Le jury moderne et l'organisation judiciaire, 1877.
Prins A, La philosophie du droit et l'école historique, 1882.
Prins A (1886) Criminalité et répression. Essai de science pénale
Prins A, La loi sur la libération conditionnelle et les condamnations conditionnelles, 1888.
Prins A, Science pénal et droit positif, 1899.
Prins A, La défense sociale et les transformations du droit pénal, 1910.
Proal L (1890a) L'anthropologie criminelle. Le Correspondant 158:431–455
Proal L (1892) Le crime et la peine, vol XV. F. Alcan, Paris, p 544
Proal L (1900) Le crime et le suicide passionnels, vol VI. F. Alcan, Paris, p 683
Proal L (1890b) Les médecins positivistes et les théories modernes de la criminalité, Extrait du Correspondant. Impr. de Soye et fils, Paris, p 52
Proal L (1912) L'expertise médico-légale et la question de la responsabilité. Arch Anthropol Crim XXVII
Puglia F (1883) Prolegomini allo Studio del Diritto repressivo, Napoli
Puglia F, Tratatto di Diritto Penale., Napoli, 1902.
Pulido Fernández Á (1880) La frenopatía y el Código penal. RGLJ LVIII

Pulido Fernández Á (1883) Locos delincuentes. Discursos pronunciados en la Sección de Ciencias Naturales del Ateneo científico y literario de Madrid sobre el tema 'Estado actual de la ciencia frenopática y sus relaciones con el Derecho penal'. Imprenta de la Revista de Legislación, Madrid
Ribot TA (1883) Les maladies de la volonté, Paris
Ríos Urruti F (1919) Don Pedro Dorado Montero, Filósofo del Derecho. Boletín de la Institución Libre de Enseñanza 43
Rivière, A., Révue Pénitentiaire, 1897.
Rocco A (1932) Opere giuridiche. Foro Italiano, Roma
Rocco A (2009) El Problema y el método de la ciencia del derecho penal, 3rd edn. Temis, Bogotá
Rocco A (2001) El objeto del delito y de la tutela jurídica penal: contribución a las teorías generales del delito y de la pena. B de F, Buenos Aires
Röder KDA (1867) Die Herrschenden Grundlehren von Verbrechen und Strafe in Ihren Inneren Widersprüchen: Eine Kritische Vorarbeit zum Neubau des Strafrechts. Julius Riedner, Wiesbaden
Röder KDA (1875) Estudios sobre Derecho penal y sistemas penitenciarios: fundamento jurídico de la pena correccional. Imprenta de T. Fortanet, Madrid
Röder KDA (1876) Las doctrinas fundamentales reinantes sobre el delito y la pena en sus interiores contradicciones: ensayo crítico preparatorio para la renovación del Derecho penal, 3rd edn. Librería de Victoruiano Suárez, Madrid
Romagnosi, G. D., La genesi del diritto penale, 1791.
Romero de Tejada JG (1886) La imputabilidad ante las escuelas criminológicas. Revista de los Tribunales XXX:741 ff
Rossi P (1843) Cours d'économie politique, 2nd edn. Joubert: G. Thorel, Paris
Rossi P (1856) Trattato di diritto penale, Torino
Salillas R (1899) Los locos delincuentes en España. RGLJ LXIV:117–142
Sánchez Rojas J (1919) Pedro Dorado Montero. Boletín de la Institución Libre de Enseñanza XLIII
Schneider GH (1882) Der menschliche Wille. Dümmlers Verlagsbuchhandlung, Berlin
Schneider GH (1880) Der thierische Wille. Verlag von Ambr. Abel., Leipzig
Schopenhauer A (1877) Essai sur le libre arbitre, Paris
Scolari S (1881) Istituzioni di scienza politica, Pisa
Secchi PA (1864) L'unità delle forze fisiche. Tipografia Forense, Roma
Seeger H (1892) Die Strafrechtstheorien Kants und seiner Nachfolger im Verhältnis zu den allgemeinen Grundsätzen der kritischen Philosophie. Laupp, Tübingen, p 81
Sidgwick H (1884) The methods of ethics, 3rd edn. Macmillan, London
Sidgwick H (1887) The principles of political economy, 2nd edn. MacMillan Company, New York
Sidgwick H (1967) Outlines of the history of ethics for English readers. MacMillan, London
Sidgwick H (1981) The methods of ethics, 7th edn. Hackett Publishing Company, Indianapolis
Sidgwick H (2000) Essays on ethics and method. Clarendon Press, Oxford
Silvela F (1839) Colección de proyectos, dictámenes y leyes orgánicas, o estudios prácticos de administración. Imprenta Nacional, Madrid
Silvela F (1874) El Derecho penal estudiado en sus principios y en la legislación vigente en España, vol I. Madrid. and II, Madrid, 1879
Silvela F (1886) El Código penal y el sentido común, Madrid
Silvela F (1898) El Derecho Penal y los sistemas fatalistas y deterministas de la Antropología Criminal. La España Moderna 111:117–148
Silvela L (1903) El Derecho penal español. Estudiado en los principios y en la legislación vigente en España, vol I. Establecimiento tipográfico de Ricardo Fé, Madrid
Spinoza B (1984) Ética demostrada según el orden geométrico, 4th edn. Editorial Nacional, Madrid, p E4P37S
Stirner M (1893) Der Einzige und sein Eigentum. Reclams Universalbibliothek
Stooss C (1892) Die grundzüge des schweizerischen strafrechts im auftrage des Bundesrathes vergleichend. Verlag von H. Georg, Ester Band, Basel – Genf

Tallack W (1889) Penological and preventive principles. Wertheimer, Lea & Co, London
Tebaldi A (1884) Fisionomia ed expressione studiate nelle loro deviazioni. Drucker & Tedeschi, Padova
Testa A (1843) Della Critica della raggione pura di Kant. Veladini e Comp, Lugano
Tolstoj L (1892) Darlegung des Evangeliums. Reclam, Leipzig
Tolstoj L., Das Reich Gottes ist in Euch, 1894.
Tolstoj L., Worin mein Glaube besteht?, 1883.
Tolstoj L (1899) Auferstehung. Eugen Diederichs, Leipzig
Tolstoj L (1891) L'utilità nel Diritto penale classico. Trani, V. Vecchi
Tolstoj L (1903) Saggi critici di sociologia e di criminologia. Fratelli Bocca, Torino
Tolstoj L (1908) Genesi e funzione delle leggi penali. Fratelli Bocca, Torino
Tolstoj L (1898) Les bases sociologiques du droit et de l'état. Giard & E. Brière, Paris
Valentí i Camp S (1922) Ideólogos, videntes y teorizantes. Minerva, Barcelona
Vanni I (1890) Il problema della filosofia del diritto. Donato Tedeschi e Figlio, Verona
Vanni I (1888) Prime linee di un programma critico di Sociologia. Perugia, Tipografia di V. Santucci
Vega Armentero R (1890) ¿Loco o delincuente? Novela social contemporánea. El Porvenir, Madrid
Wagner A (1864) Die Gesetzmässigkeit in den scheinbar willkührlichen menschlichen handlungen. Boyes & Geisler, Hamburg
Worms R (1920) Chronique. Rev Int Sociol 28:328–329
Zola É (1893) La bête humaine. Bibliothèque-Charpentier, Paris

Non-Legal Literature

Andorno R (2013) Principles of international biolaw. Seeking common ground at the intersection of bioethics and human rights. In: Droit bioéthique et société, vol 7. Brussels, Bruylant
Aronson JD (2010) The law's use of brain evidence. Annu Rev Law Soc Sci 6:93–108
Bechtel W, Hamilton A (2007) Reductionism, integration and the unity of the sciences. In: Kuipers T (ed) Philosophy of science: focal issues. Elsevier, New York
Bennett MR, Hacker PMS (2003) Philosophical foundation of neuroscience. Wiley-Blackwell, London
Bernard C (1859) Introduction à l´étude de la médecine experimental. Collège de France, Paris
Bertolino M (2009) Il breve camino del vizio di mente. Un retorno al paradigma organizistico? In: Santosuosso A (ed) Le neuroscienze e il diritto. Ibis, Pavia
Bianchi A (2009) Manuale di neuroscienze forensi. Giuffrè, Milano
Blair JR, Mitchell D, Blair K (2005) The psychopath: emotion and the brain. Blackwell, Malden
Bottalico B (2011) Cognitive neuroscience, decision making and the law. Eur J Risk Regul 2(3): 427–432
Burk T (2020) Geschichte der Degenerationstheorien. Thomas J. Burk (personal blog). https://tjburk.de/de/categories/view/3
Casonato C (2009) Introduzione al biodiritto. Giappichelli, Torino
Churchland PS (1986) Neurophilosophy, towards a unified understanding of the mind-brain. The MIT Press, Cambridge
Churchland PS (2002) Brain-wise: studies in neurophilosophy. The MIT Press, Cambridge
Colorio A (2010) Diritto e cervello: verso le nuove frontiere del neurodiritto. i-lex Scienze Giuridiche, Scienze Cognitive e Intelligenza artificiale (Rivista on-line: www.i-lex.it) 10:371–415
Conference Was Lombroso Right? The historical legacy of Neurosciences. Seminar of the GERN (Groupement Européen de Recherches sur les Normativités), 2010–2013.
De Jong LH (2002) Levels of explanation in biological psychology. Philos Psychol 15(4):441–462

Di Giovine O (2009) Un diritto penale empatico? Diritto penale, bioetica e neuroetica. Giappichelli, Torino
Di Giovine O (2014) Neuroscienze (diritto penale). Enciclopedia del Diritto VII:721–734
Farisco M (2012) Filosofia delle neuroscienze. Edizioni Messagero, Padova
Farlow SJ (1982) Partial differential equations for scientists and engineers. John Wiley & Sons, New York
Gabbard GO (2007) Psychodynamic psychiatry, 4th edn. Raffaello Cortina, Milan
Gadebusch Bondio M (1995) Die Rezeption der kriminalanthropologischen Theorien von Cesare Lombroso in Deutschland von 1880-1914. Diss. phil. (Abhandlungen zur Geschichte der Medizin und der Naturwissenschaften, Heft 70), Husum, 297 Seiten
Gazzaniga MS (2015) Neuroprediction, violence, and the law: setting the stage. Neuroethics 3:67–99
Goodenough OR (2004) A neuroscientific approach to normative judgement in law and justice. Philos Trans R Soc B Biol Sci 359:1709–1726
Goodenough OR, Tucker M (2010) Law and cognitive neuroscience. Annu Rev Law Soc Sci 6:61–92
Greely HT (2014) Will neuroscience radically transform the legal system? In: Slate, 2012: MaRBLe Research Papers Neurolaw, vol V. Maastricht University
Greene J, Cohen J (2004) For the law, neuroscience changes nothing and everything. Philos Trans R Soc B Biol Sci 359:1775–1785
Lehrer J (2008) Proust was a neuroscientist. Mariner Books, San Diego
Leps MC (1992) Apprehending the criminal: the production of deviance in nineteenth century discourse. Duke University Press, Durham
Little B (2019) What type of criminal are you? 19th-century doctors claimed to know by your face. History
Lynch Z, Laursen B (2009) The neuro revolution. How brain science is changing our world. St. Martin's Press, New York
Maudsley H (1879) La physiologie de l'esprit, Paris
McCauley RN (2007) Reduction: models of cross-scientific relations and their implications for the psychology-neuroscience interface. In: Thagard P (ed) Handbook of the philosophy of science: philosophy of psychology and cognitive science. Elsevier, Amsterdam
Morse SJ (2004) New Neuroscience, old problems. In: Garland B (ed) Neuroscience and the Law. Dana Press, Washington DC
Morse SJ (2006) Moral and legal responsibility and the new neuroscience. In: Illes J (ed) Neuroethics: defining the issues in theory, practice and policy. Oxford University Press, New York
Morse SJ (2007) The non-problem of free will in forensic psychiatry and psychology. Behav Sci Law 25:203–220
Morse SJ (2011) Avoiding irrational neurolaw exuberance: a plea for neuromodesty. Mercer Law Rev 62:837–859
Morse SJ (2015) Criminal law and common sense: an essay on the perils of and promise of neuroscience. Public Law Leg Theory Res Pap Ser 99:38–72
Nichols S (2008) How can psychology contribute to the free will debate? In: Baer J, Kaufman J, Baumeister R (eds) Are we free? Oxford University Press, Oxford-New York
Patterson D, Pardo MS (2009) Philosophical foundations of law and neuroscience. University of Alabama Public Law Research Paper
Piccinini G, Craver C (2011) Integrating psychology and neuroscience: functional analyses as mechanism sketches. Synthese 183:283–311
Picozza E (2011) Neurolaw. An introduction. Springer, New York
Quesada i Agius B (1880) Tratado elemental de fisiología general. Est. Tip. de Eduardo Cuesta, Madrid
Roskies AL (2012) How does the neuroscience of decision-making bear on our understanding of moral responsibility and free will? Curr Opin Neurobiol 22:1022–1026

Santosuosso A (2009) Le neuroscienze e il diritto. Ibis, Como-Pavia
Searle JR (2007) Freedom and neurobiology. Reflections of free will, language, and political power. Columbia University Press
Seung S (2012) Connectome: how the brain's wiring makes us who we are. Houghton Mifflin Harcourt, Boston – New York
Sirgiovanni E, Corbellini C, Caporale C (2016) A recap on Italian neurolaw: epistemological and ethical issues. Mind Soc 16. https://doi.org/10.1007/s11299-016-0188-1
Spranger TD (ed) (2012) International neurolaw: a comparative analysis. Springer, Bonn
Uttal W (2009) Neuroscience in the courtroom. Lawyers & Judges Publishing Company Inc
Warneck L (2021) The promises of CRISPR genome editing in biomedicine. Labiotech. https://www.labiotech.eu/interview/crispr-therapeutics-genome-editing/. Accessed 3 Mar 2021
Zeki S, Goodenough O (eds) (2004) Law and the brain. Oxford University Press, London

Bibliography

Álvarez Junco J (1986) La Comisión de Reformas Sociales: intentos y realizaciones. In: De la beneficencia al bienestar social: cuatro siglos de acción social, pp 147–154
Álvarez-Uría F (1983) Miserables y locos. Medicina mental y Orden social en la España del siglo XIX. Tusquets, Barcelona
Andrés-Gallego J (1971) Regeneracionismo y política confesional en España, 1889-1899. Diputación Provincial de Sevilla, Sevilla
Anes y Álvarez de Castrillón R (2009) La economía española de 1868 a 1898. In: Girón Garrote J (ed) Un cambio de siglo 1898: España, Cuba, Puerto Rico, Filipinas y Estados Unidos Anes y Álvarez de Castrillón. Universidad de Oviedo, Oviedo
Aróstegui Sánchez J (ed) (2011) Historia de España. Vicens Vives, Barcelona
Arroyo Zapatero LA (2019) Centenario de la muerte de Don Pedro Dorado Montero: 100 años de ciencia penal en España. In: Instituto de Derecho Penal Europeo e Internacional (Universidad de Castilla-La Mancha), Ciudad Real
Austin J (1951) Sobre la utilidad del estudio de la jurisprudencia. Instituto de Estudios Políticos, Madrid
Austin J (1995) The province of jurisprudence determined. Cambridge University Press, Cambridge
Austin J (1996) Lectures on jurisprudence. Thoemmes Press, Bristol
Austin J (2003) El objeto de la jurisprudencia. Centro de Estudios Políticos y Constitucionales, Madrid
Ballesteros J (1984) Sobre el sentido del derecho: introducción a la filosofía jurídica. Tecnos, Madrid
Ballesteros J (1989) Postmodernidad: decadencia o resistencia. Tecnos, Madrid
Ballesteros J (1995) Ecologismo personalista: cuidar la naturaleza, cuidar al hombre. Tecnos
Ballesteros J (2006) Repensar la paz. Ediciones Internacionales Universitarias, Madrid
Baños P (2017) Así se domina el mundo, 1st edn. Editorial Ariel, Barcelona
Barbero Santos M (1969) Silvio Ranieri y la Escuela Positiva. Anuario de derecho penal y ciencias penales 22(1):5–14
Barbero Santos M (1970) Remembranzas del profesor salmantino Pedro García Dorado Montero en el 50 aniversario de su muerte. In: VV.AA.; Problemas actuales de las ciencias penales y de la Filosofía del Derecho Homenaje al profesor Luis Jiménez de Asúa. Ediciones Pannedille, Buenos Aires
Barbero Santos M (1977) Política y derecho penal en España. Tucar Ediciones, Madrid
Barbero Santos M (1980) Marginación social y derecho represivo. Bosch, Barcelona

Barbero Santos M (1986) La Défense sociale trente ans après. Cahiers de défense sociale: bulletin de la Societé International de Défense Sociale pour une Politique Criminelle Humaniste 13:27–36

Barbero Santos M (1990-1991) El sistema punitivo español. Cahiers de défense sociale: bulletin de la Societé International de Défense Sociale pour une Politique Criminelle Humaniste 17-18: 131–140

Barbero Santos M (1994) Concepto de la pena en el primer Fichte. Boletín de la Real Academia de Extremadura de las Letras y las Artes 5(2):205–215

Barbero Santos M (1996) Pedro Dorado Montero, aportación a su biografía. Revista de Estudios Penitenciarios 22:257–317

Barbero Santos M (2000) Estado constitucional de derecho y sistema penal. Revista de derecho y ciencias penales: Ciencias Sociales y Políticas No. 2

Bernecker WL (2010a) Die Unabhängigkeit Lateinamerikas: europäische Interessen und ambivalente Reaktionen, 1st edn. Ibero-Amerikanisches Institut Preußischer Kulturbesitz, Berlin

Bernecker WL (2010b) Geschichte Spaniens im 20. Jahrhundert. C. H. Beck, München

Beser S (1972) Leopoldo Alas: Teoría y crítica de la novela española. Laila, Barcelona

Blanco Rodríguez JA (1979) El pensamiento político-social de Dorado Montero en el marco de las ideologías sociales de su época (1880-1917). Facultad de Geografía e Historia de la Universidad de Salamanca, Salamanca. (inédita)

Blanco Rodríguez JA (1982) El pensamiento sociopolítico de Dorado Montero. Centro de Estudios Salmantinos, Salamanca

Blanco Rodríguez JA (1984) El socialismo reformista de Dorado Montero. Revista de Estudios 11-12:235–242

Blanco Rodríguez JA (1994) Evolución de un intelectual crítico. Revista de Estudios 33-34:141–168

Bodero Cali ER (2020) Pedro Dorado Montero, el desmitificador de Salamanca. Revista Jurídica Online:21–42

Bomartí Sánchez V (2006) Humanistas europeos (siglos XIV y XVI), 1st edn. Editorial Complutense, Madrid

Buisson I et al (eds) (1984) Problemas de la formación del Estado y de la Nación en Hispanoamérica. Böhlau, Köln

Calvo GJ (2003) Naturalismo y direcciones criminológicas a finales del siglo XIX en España. Revista de derecho penal y criminología 12:255–270

Calvo González J (2010) El alma y la ley. Tolstói entre juristas. España (1890-1928), 1st edn. Comunicación Social, Colección “Historia y presente”, Sevilla-Zamora

Calvo Rubio JA (1966) Pacheco, penalista. Revista de Derecho Judicial. Separata, Madrid

Campos R, Huertas R (2013) Lombroso but not Lombrosians? Criminal Anthropology in Spain. In: Knepper P, Ystehede PJ (eds) The Caesare Lombroso handbook. Routledge, Abingdon, pp 309–323

Campos Marín R (2007) Crimen y locura. La patologización del crimen en la España de la Restauración. Norba. Revista de Historia 20:85–105

Candil Jiménez F (1975) Observaciones sobre la intervención de don Joaquín Francisco Pacheco en la elaboración del Código penal de 1848. Dialnet, Sevilla

Canepa G (1987) L'esame psicodiagnostico nei giudizi medico legali di accertamento e revisione della pericolosità sociale. In: Traveso GB (ed) Criminologia e psichiatria forense. Giuffrè, Milano

Cañizares Navarro JB (2013) El Código penal de 1822: sus fuentes inspiradoras. Balance historiográfico (desde el s. XX). Glossae Eur J Leg Hist 10:109–136

Cañizares Navarro JB (2020) Las penas infamantes en la Codificación penal francesa. Dykinson, Madrid, p 332

Cappelleti AJ (1994) La ética de Cleantes. Revista venezolana de Filosofía 30:33–50

Carpintero Benítez F (2008) La ley natural: historia de un concepto controvertido. Encuentro, Madrid

Cartuyvels Y (2015) La biologisation du crime à la fin du XIXe siècle: quelques enjeux et limites. Jurisprudence. Revue critique I(numéro spécial)

Cartuyvels Y (2020) An introduction to the birth of criminal positivism in Europe and Latin America at the end of the 19th century: rise and resistance. Glossae Eur J Leg Hist 17:1–21

Casabó Ruiz JR (1968) El Código penal de 1822. Universitat de València, València

Coimbra Martins A (1967) O Mandarim assassinado. Ensaios Queirosianos, Lisboa

De la Granja JL, Beramendi J, Anguera P (2001) La España de los nacionalismos y las autonomías. Síntesis, Madrid

De la Rasilla I (2020) International Criminal Justice as Universal Social Defence – Quintiliano Saldaña (1878-1938). In: Megret F, Tallgren I (eds) The dawn of a discipline – international criminal justice and its early exponents. Cambridge University Press

Del Rosal J (1960) Derecho Penal español (Lecciones), II, 1st edn. S. Aguirre Torre Impresor, Madrid

Dierksmeier C (1999) KarlChristian Friedrich Krause und das ‘gute’ Recht. In: Archiv für Rechts- und Sozialphilosophie (ARSP), vol 85. Deutscher Idealismus, Sonderheft, pp 75–94

Dierksmeier C (2002) Die Geschichtlichkeit des Rechts in der Methodologie der Rechtsphilosophie K.C.F. Krauses. Forum historiae iuris

Dolin K (1999) Fiction and the Law. Legal discourse in Victorian and Modernist Literature. Cambridge University Press, Cambridge

Duve T (2017) Was ist ‹Multinormativität›? – Einführende Bemerkungen. Rechtsgeschichte Legal History 25:81–101

Duve T (2020) What is global legal history? Comp Leg Hist 8(2):73–115. https://doi.org/10.1080/2049677X.2020.1830488

Escudero Antonio JA (1985) Curso de Historia del Derecho. Fuentes e instituciones político-administrativas. J. A. Escudero, Madrid

Estupinyà P (2013) S=EX^2. La ciencia del sexo. Debate, p 311

Fallas Vargas F (2004) El conatus como categoría radical en la teoría política de Spinoza. Revista de Filosofía, Universidad de Costa Rica XLII:27

Félix Sevilla F (1933) Mi viaje por Francia y Bélgica. Un magistrado penitenciario, vol 55(II). Vida penitenciaria, Madrid, pp 12–14

Fernández P (1995) La novela médico-social: entre fisiología y sociología. In: Eduardo López Bago y el naturalismo radical. La novela y el mercado literario en el siglo XIX. Rodopi B. V, Ámsterdam- Atlanta, pp 75–83

Fernández P (2021) Remigio Vega Armentero. Diccionario Bibliográfico Electrónico. Real Academia de la Historia. Seen on 7 Jan 2021

Fernández Ruiz-Gálvez E (1992) Ciencia del Derecho, Ciencias Jurídicas, Sociología del Derecho, Filosofía del Derecho. In: Javier de Lucas Martín F (ed) Introducción a la teoría del derecho. Tirant lo Blanch, València, pp 407–427

Field S (2012) Democracy and the Multitude: Spinoza against Negri. Theoria J Soc Polit Theory 59(131):21–40

Fontana i Lázaro J (2007) La época del liberalismo. In: Fontana i Lázaro J, Villares R (eds) Historia de España, 1st edn. Planeta, Barcelona

Fraginals M (1995) Cuba/España. España/Cuba, 1st edn. Crítica, Barcelona, p 296

Franco-Chasán J (2020) Pedro Dorado Montero: a transitioning figure. Glossae Eur J Leg Hist 17: 353–395

Fundación Pablo Iglesias, “Pedro Dorado Montero”. https://www.fpabloiglesias.es/archivo-y-biblioteca/diccionario-biografico/biografias/4883_dorado-montero-pedro

Gaarder J (2002) Sophie’s world. Berkley Books, New York

Galera A (1991) Ciencia y delincuencia. El determinismo antropológico en la España del siglo XIX. CSIC, Sevilla

Gentile G (2016) Entstehung und Entwicklung der modernen Philosophie in Italien: Die Platoniker. Schweizerischer Wissenschafts- und Universitätsverlag, Biel/Bienne
Germann U (2020) Toward new horizons: penal positivism and Swiss Criminal Law reform in the late 19th and early 20th centuries. Glossae Eur J Leg Hist 17:259–276
Godwin W (1946) Enquiry concerning political justice and its influence on morals and happiness, 3rd edn. University of Toronto Press, Toronto
Godwin W (1964) Of population: an enquiry concerning the power of increase in the numbers of mankind being an answer to Mr. Malthus's essays on that subject. Augustus M. Kelley, New York
González González J (1994) La imputabilidad en el Derecho penal español. Imputabilidad y locura en la España del siglo XIX. Comares, Granada
GREDOS, Online repository of the University of Salamanca. https://gredos.usal.es/
Griffin CC (1937) The United States and the Disruption of the Spanish Empire 1810-1822. A study of the Relations of the United States with Spain and the Rebel Spanish Colonies. Columbia University Press, New York
Härter K (2020) Zweckgedanke, social defence and transnational criminal law: Franz von Liszt and the network of positivist criminology (1871-1918). Glossae Eur J Leg Hist 17:150–175
Hernández Díaz JM (1983) Pedro Dorado Montero y la educación. Historia de la educación: Revista interuniversitaria 2:217–228
Hernández Díaz JM (2002) Del Decreto Pidal al primer Rectorado de Unamuno. In: Rodríguez-San Pedro Bezares LE (ed) Historia de la Universidad de Salamanca, vol I, 1st edn. Universidad de Salamanca, Salamanca, pp 239–262
Hobsbawn EJ (1971) Las revoluciones burguesas, 2nd edn. Guadarrama, Madrid
Ibarra Becerra V (2016) La condena de la venganza privada tras la justicia punitiva. Contraste y continuidad entre. La Orestíada de Esquilo. Ideas y valores 65(162)
Iñesta Pastor E (2003) La proyección Hispanoamericana del Código penal español de 1848. In: Actas y Estudios, XIII Congreso del Instituto Internacional de Historia del Derecho Indiano, vol II. Library of Congress, San Juan de Puerto Rico, pp 493–521
Iñesta Pastor E (2010) Història del Dret de l'Ibèria primitiva, la Hispània romana i visigoda. Universitat d'Alacant, Alicante
Iñesta Pastor E (2011) El Código Penal Español de 1848. Tirant Lo Blanch, València
Iñesta Pastor E (2013) La Comisión General de Codificación (1843-1997): De la codificación moderna a la descodificación contemporánea. Anuario de Historia del Derecho español 83:65–103
Iñesta Pastor E (2016) La interpretación del eclecticismo en la doctrina y en la legislación de la España penal del siglo XIX. Ivs Fvgit
Iñesta Pastor E (2017) Tradición e influencias extranjeras en la clasificación de las penas en los códigos españoles decimonónicos. In: Masferrer A (ed) La Codificación penal española. Tradición e influencias extranjeras: su contribución al proceso codificador (Parte General). Thompson Reuters Aranzadi, Pamplona, pp 517–528
Jiménez Sánchez JJ (2012) Los fundamentos del Estado político en Spinoza. Anales de la Cátedra Francisco Sánchez 46
Jorge Barreiro A (1975) Las medidas de seguridad en el Derecho español. Civitas, Madrid
Juanes Díaz S (2019) Dorado Montero. La Gaceta de Salamanca, Salamanca. https://www.lagacetadesalamanca.es/opinion/dorado-montero-YX624818. Accessed 3 Dec 2019
Kayman MA (1992) From Bow Street to Baker Street: mystery, detection and narrative. Macmillan, Basingstoke
Kine M, Carruthers P (2012) Moral responsibility and consciousness. J Moral Philos 9:220–228
Lima Torrado J (1976) La Filosofía Jurídica de Pedro Dorado Montero. Tesis doctoral (inédita), Madrid
Lima Torrado J (2008a) Las claves de la recepción del pensamiento anarquista en la filosofía política de Pedro Dorado Montero. In: Elósegui Itxaso M, Galindo Ayuda F (eds) El

Pensamiento jurídico: pasado, presente y perspectiva. Libro homenaje al prof. Juan José Gil Cremades. El Justicia de Aragón, Zaragoza, pp 417–443

Lima Torrado J (2008b) Las claves de la recepción del pensamiento socialista en la filosofía política de Pedro Dorado Montero. In: AA.VV., Estudios en homenaje al profesor Gregorio Peces-Barba, vol 4. Dykinson, Madrid, pp 537–550

Llaneza P (2019) Datanomics: Todos los datos personales que das sin darte cuenta y todo lo que las empresas hacen con ellos. Deusto

López-Rey M (1960) X. Pedro Dorado Montero (1861-1919). In: Mannheim H (ed) Pioneers in criminology. Stevens and Sons, London. (I use López-Rey, M., Pioneers in Criminology. X. Pedro Dorado Montero (1861-1919). The Journal of Criminal Law, Criminology, and Police Science, Vol. 46, No. 5, Northwestern University Pritzker School of Law, Jan–Feb, 1956, pp. 605-612.)

Málaga Guerrero J (2018) La vida cotidiana en la Salamanca del siglo XX: 1898-1923. Fundación Salamanca Ciudad de Cultura y Saberes, Salamanca

Maluquer de Motes i Bernet J (1999) España en la crisis de 1898: de la gran depresión a la modernización económica del siglo XX. Península, Barcelona

Marey M (2011) ¿Es la exigencia kantiana de universalización un procedimiento suficiente para establecer contenidos morales-éticos? Algunas consideraciones acerca de una respuesta negativa a esta pregunta. ARETÉ Revista de Filosofía XXIII(1)

Mario S (1976) Elementi per una bibliografia del socialismo giuridico italiano. Per la storia del pensiero giuridico moderno. Giuffrè Editore, Milano, pp 1–165

Maristany L (1973) El Gabinete del Doctor Lombroso. Delincuencia y fin de siglo en España. Cuadernos Anagrama, Barcelona

Maristany L (1983) Lombroso y España: nuevas consideraciones. Anales de literatura española 2: 361–382

Martín Martín S (2007) Penalística y penalistas españoles a la luz del principio de legalidad (1874-1944). Quaderni fiorentini per la storia del pensiero giuridico moderno 36(1):503–609

Martín Martín S (2017) Estado punitivo y derechos constitucionales: pasado y presente. Ayer Revista de Historia Contemporánea 105:259–273

Martinson R (1974) What works? Questions and answers about prisons reform. In: The Public Interest, vol 35. Spring, New York

Masferrer A (2001) La pena de infamia en el Derecho histórico español. Contribución al estudio de la tradición penal europea en el marco del ius commune. Dykinson, Madrid, p 429

Masferrer A (2003) Tradición y reformismo en la Codificación penal española. Hacia el ocaso de un mito. Materiales, apuntes y reflexiones para un nuevo enfoque metodológico e historiográfico del movimiento codificador penal europeo. Prólogo de J. Sainz Guerra, Universidad de Jaén:241

Masferrer A (2009) Codification of Spanish criminal law in the nineteenth century: a comparative legal history approach. JCL 4(1):115–118

Masferrer A (2012) Spanish legal traditions. Dykinson, Madrid

Masferrer A (ed) (2014) La Codificación española. Una aproximación doctrinal e historiográfica a sus influencias extranjeras, y a la francesa en particular. Thomson Reuters Aranzadi, Cizur Menor (Navarra)

Masferrer A (ed) (2017a) La Codificación penal española. Tradición e influencias extranjeras: su contribución al proceso codificador. Parte General. Thomson Reuters Aranzadi, Cizur Menor (Navarra)

Masferrer A (2017b) La distinción entre delito y pecado en la tradición penal bajomedieval y moderna. Una propuesta revisionista de la historiografía española, europea y anglosajona. Anuario de Historia del Derecho Español 87:693–756

Masferrer A (2017c) The Lawyers' reality: wrongdoing in Spain in the era of codification. In: Llano S, Sinclair A (eds) Writing wrongdoing: Spain 1800-1936. Tamesis, London, pp 19–33

Masferrer A (2019) Der Beitrag der Theologie und der kanonistischen Wissenschaft zum modernen europäischen Strafrecht. Zeitschrift für die gesamte Strafrechtswissenschaft 131(1):219–238. https://doi.org/10.1515/zstw-2019-0008

Masferrer A (2020a) Criminal law and morality revisited: interdisciplinary perspectives. In: Masferrer A (ed) Criminal law and morality in the age of consent. Springer, Cham

Masferrer A (2020b) The role of nature in the secularization of criminal law in Europe (17th–19th Centuries). The criminal law of the enlightenment revisited. In: Masferrer A (ed) Criminal law and morality in the age of consent. Springer, Cham

Masferrer A (ed) (2020c) La Codificación penal española. Tradición e influencias extranjeras: su contribución al proceso codificador. Parte Especial. Thomson Reuters Aranzadi, Cizur Menor (Navarra)

Masferrer A (2020d) De la honestidad a la integridad sexual. La formación del Derecho penal sexual español en el marco de la cultura occidental, 1st edn. Thomson Reuters Aranzadi, Cizur Menor

Masferrer A (2020e) The reception of the positivist school in the Spanish criminal doctrine (1885-1899). Glossae Eur J Leg Hist 17:303–352

May L (2019) Crime and Lex Talionis. Ancient legal thought: equity, justice, and humaneness from Hammurabi and the Pharaohs to Justinian and the Talmud. Cambridge University Press, Cambridge, pp 150–168

Miller DA (1988) The novel and the police. University of California Press, Berkeley

Moreu ÁC (2006) La recepción de las doctrinas correccionalistas en España. Políticas educativas y metodologías psicopedagógicas. Revista de Educación 340:755–785

Musumeci E (2012) Cesare Lombroso e le neuroscienze: un parricidio mancato. Franco Angeli, Milano

Naucke W (1962) Kant und die psychologische Zwangstheorie Feuerbachs. In: Kieler Rechtwissenschaftliche Abhandlungen, vol 3. Joachim Heitmann, Hansicher Gildenverlag

Núñez JA (2013) Fernando Cadalso y Manzano: Medio siglo de reforma penitenciaria en España (1859-1939). Universidad de Valladolid, Valladolid

Obarrio Moreno JA (2008) La preterición en los Commentaria del jurista Cerdán de Tallada. Revista General de Derecho Romano 11

Oliver Olmo P (2007) Historia y reinvención del utilitarismo punitivo. In: Gastón Aguas JM, Mendiola F (eds) Los trabajos forzados en la dictadura franquista. Instituto Gerónimo de Uztáriz, Pamplona, p 90

Pascual Matellán L (2018) Pedro Dorado Montero. Un pensador heterodoxo, vol 20. Azafea. Revista de Filosofía, Salamanca, pp 111–128

Pascual Matellán L (2021) Pedro Dorado Montero y el correccionalismo español. El difícil desafío de humanizar el Derecho Penal, 1st edn. Tirant Lo Blanch, València, p 522

Peña Echevarría J (2012) Cómo se ordena la potencia de la multitud. Instituciones y derecho de la ciudad en la teoría política de Spinoza. Revista Laguna, Universidad de Valladolid 31:48–49

Pérez Ledesma M (1986) La Comisión de Reformas Sociales y la cuestión social durante la Restauración. De la beneficencia al bienestar social: cuatro siglos de acción social:155–166

Pérez Marcos RM (2005) Tomás Cerdán de Tallada, el primer tratadista de derecho penitenciario. Anuario de Historia de Derecho Español LXXV:755–802

Peset JL, Peset M (1965) «Estudio preliminar», Lombroso y la Escuela positivista italiana. CSIC, Madrid

Pifferi M (2009) Exporting criminology: the individualization of punishment in Europe and America. In: Beck Varela L, Gutiérrez Vega P, Spinosa A (eds) Crossing legal cultures. Martin Meidenbauer, München, pp 441–459

Pifferi M (2011) A proposito di Storia del diritto penale e della giustizia. Scritti editi e inediti (1972-2007), di Mario Sbriccoli. Rivista di storia del diritto italiano 84:480–487

Polo Blanco J (2008) Notas en torno a la Ética de Spinoza. Bajo palabra. Revista de Filosofía 3

Quintero Olivares G (2016) Beccaria y el Iluminismo italiano en la cultura jurídica hispana. In: Arroyo Zapatero L, Estrada Michel R, Nieto Martín A (eds) Metáfora de la crueldad. La pena capital del tiempo de Cesare Beccaria al tiempo actual. Ediciones de la Universidad de Castilla-La Mancha, Cuenca, pp 53–78

Quisbert E (2008) Historia del Derecho penal a través de las escuelas penales y sus representantes. Centro de Estudios de Derecho
Ramos Pascua JA (1995) El positivismo jurídico en España: D. Pedro Dorado Montero. Anuario de Filosofía del Derecho XII:503–546
Ramos Vázquez I (2020) Los delitos de asociación ilícita, coalición o coligación en Francia y España a lo largo del siglo XIX. In: Masferrer A (ed) Tradición e influencias extranjeras en la codificación penal española: parte especial, pp 393–439
Ramos Vázquez I, Ramos Vázquez I (2013) La reforma penitenciaria en la historia contemporánea española. Dykinson, Madrid
Regina María Pérez M (2005) Tomás Cerdán de Tallada, el primer tratadista de derecho penitenciario. In: Anuario de Historia de Derecho Español, vol LXXV, pp 755–802
Rivacoba y Rivacoba M (1962) El centenario del nacimiento de Dorado Montero. Universidad del Litoral, Santa Fé
Rivacoba y Rivacoba M (1963) Recordación de Dorado Montero, vol 152. Cenit, Toulouse
Rivacoba y Rivacoba M (1970) Evocación y vigencia de Dorado Montero. Revista de Ciencias Penales 29(1):15–28
Rivacoba y Rivacoba M (1971) Viejas Remembranzas de Dorado Montero. Revista de Estudios Penitenciarios. Homenaje a Dorado Montero 195(1):1631–1643
Rodríguez Hernández V (1993) La insumisión en Dorado Montero. El tema iusnaturalista en la encrucijada ideológica de la Restauración. Hespérides, Salamanca
Rodríguez Manzanera L (1981) Criminología, 2nd edn. Porrúa, Ciudad de México
Roldán Cañizares E (2017-2018) Luis Jiménez de Asúa: un jurista en el exilio. Universidad de Sevilla, Sevilla
Romeo F (2012) Antropologia giuridica: un percorso evoluzionista verso l'origine della relazione giuridica. Giappicheli Editore, Torino
Sacco R (2007) Antropologia giuridica. Il Mulino, Bologna
Sainz Guerra J (2004) La evolución del Derecho penal en España. Universidad de Jaén, Jaén, p 867
Salam A (2014) Perfect and imperfect rights, duties and obligations: from Hugo Grotius to Immanuel Kant. Merton College
Salmon W (1984) Scientific explanation and the casual structure of the world. Princeton University Press, Princeton
Sánchez González MD (2004) La Codificación penal en España. Los Códigos de 1848 y 1850. Centro de Estudios Políticos y Constitucionales, Madrid, p 484
Sánchez Granjel L (1989) Medicina y Antropología en la génesis de la utopía penal de Dorado Montero. Eguzkilore. Cuaderno del Instituto Vasco de Criminología 3:155–170
Sierra López MV (1997) Las medidas de seguridad en el nuevo Código penal. Tirant Lo Blanch, València
Soria Sesé L., Manuel Mariano de Lardizábal y Uribe. Diccionario biográfico español (Real Academia de la Historia). http://dbe.rah.es/biografias/11648/manuel-mariano-de-lardizabal-y-uribe
Tejada Bergado C (2007) La Banca extranjera en España, 1898-1921. Su incidencia en la consolidación de la banca actual española. Universidad Complutense de Madrid, Madrid
Tiana Ferrer A (1996) The Workers' Movement and Popular Education in Contemporary Spain (1868-1939). Paedagogica Historica 32(3):647–684
Tomás y Valiente F (1969) El Derecho penal de la monarquía absoluta. Siglos XVI, XVII y XVIII. Tecnos, Madrid, p 570
Ureña EM (1990) Orígenes del Krausofröbelismo y masonería. In: Historia de la educación: Revista interuniversitaria, vol 9. Universidad de Comillas, Madrid, pp 43–62
Valls FJ (1971) La filosofía del Derecho de Dorado Montero. Universidad de Salamanca, Salamanca
Van Den Haag E (1992) Commentary: the lex talionis before and after criminal law. Crim Justice Ethics 11(1):2–62. https://doi.org/10.1080/0731129X.1992.9991905

Varela Suanzes J (1997) El debate sobre el sistema británico de gobierno en España durante el primer tercio del Siglo XIX. In: Alvarado J (ed) Poder, Economía y Clientelismo. Marcial Pons, Madrid, pp 97–124

Vervaele JAE (2020) Gerhardus Antonius van Hamel (1842-1917) and the new horizons of criminal justice under penal positivism. Glossae Eur J Leg Hist 17:211–232

Vinci S (2020) Bernardino alimena and emanuele carnevale: the third school of criminal law searching for a compromise. Glossae Eur J Leg Hist 17